FROMMER'S
EasyGuide
TO
Amsterdam, Brussels & Bruges

By
Sasha Heseltine

Easy Guides are ✦ **Quick To Read** ✦ **Light To Carry**
✦ **For Expert Advice** ✦ **In All Price Ranges**

FrommerMedia LLC

Published by
FROMMER MEDIA LLC

ISBN 978-1-62887-118-0 (paper), 978-1-62887-119-7 (e-book)

Editorial Director: Pauline Frommer
Editor: Billy Fox
Production Editor: Heather Wilcox
Cartographer: Elizabeth Puhl
Cover Design: Howard Grossman
Map data for The Hague & Scheveningen and Antwerp © OpenStreetMap contributors
(www.openstreetmap.org).

For information on our other products or services, see www.frommers.com.

Frommer Media LLC also publishes its books in a variety of electronic formats. Some content that
appears in print may not be available in electronic formats.

Manufactured in the United States of America

5   4   3   2   1

AN IMPORTANT NOTE

The world is a dynamic place. Hotels change ownership, restaurants hike their prices, museums
alter their opening hours, and busses and trains change their routings. And all of this can occur
in the several months after our authors have visited, inspected, and written about, these hotels,
restaurants, museums and transportation services. Though we have made valiant efforts to keep
all our information fresh and up-to-date, some few changes can inevitably occur in the periods
before a revised edition of this guidebook is published. So please bear with us if a tiny number
of the details in this book have changed. Please also note that we have no responsibility or liabil-
ity for any inaccuracy or errors or omissions, or for inconvenience, loss, damage, or expenses suffered by anyone as a result of assertions in this guide.

CONTENTS

ABOUT THE AUTHOR

Sasha Heseltine has circled the globe, feeding orphaned wallabies on South Australia's Kangaroo Island, getting lost off-roading in the Sierra Nevada, diving with manta rays in the Maldives, and hot-air ballooning in eastern Poland. Back home in the UK, she reviews hotels and restaurants for local media and writes about her travels for international print and online publications.

ABOUT THE FROMMER TRAVEL GUIDES

For most of the past 50 years, Frommer's has been the leading series of travel guides in North America, accounting for as many as 24% of all guidebooks sold. I think I know why.

Though we hope our books are entertaining, we nevertheless deal with travel in a serious fashion. Our guidebooks have never looked on such journeys as a mere recreation, but as a far more important human function, a time of learning and introspection, an essential part of a civilized life. We stress the culture, lifestyle, history and beliefs of the destinations we cover, and urge our readers to seek out people and new ideas as the chief rewards of travel.

We have never shied from controversy. We have, from the beginning, encouraged our authors to be intensely judgmental, critical—both pro and con—in their comments, and wholly independent. Our only clients are our readers, and we have triggered the ire of countless prominent sorts, from a tourist newspaper we called "practically worthless" (it unsuccessfully sued us) to the many rip-offs we've condemned.

And because we believe that travel should be available to everyone regardless of their incomes, we have always been cost-conscious at every level of expenditure. Though we have broadened our recommendations beyond the budget category, we insist that every lodging we include is sensibly priced. We use every form of media to assist our readers, and are particularly proud of our feisty daily website, the award-winning Frommers.com.

I have high hopes for the future of Frommer's. May these guidebooks, in all the years ahead, continue to reflect the joy of travel and the freedom that travel represents. May they always pursue a cost-conscious path, so that people of all incomes can enjoy the rewards of travel. And may they create, for both the traveler and the persons among whom we travel, a community of friends, where all human beings live in harmony and peace.

Arthur Frommer

THE BEST OF AMSTERDAM, BRUSSELS & BRUGES

Although they're miniscule countries, and neighbors at that, Belgium and The Netherlands are light years away from each other in culture, language, and tradition. Belgium is fractured along an historical divide, expressed in the constant regional and political bickering between Dutch- and Flemish-speaking Flanders in the north and French-speaking Wallonia in the south. The Netherlands is also ruptured, but only geographically, between three great rivers: the Maas, the Waal, and the Rhine.

Diversity is the greatest asset of The Netherlands and Belgium, a state of affairs reflected in the three great cities of Amsterdam, Brussels, and Bruges. Amsterdam is tolerant, open-minded and accepting of its multiracial heritage. Brussels is fast catching up, with the presence of the E.U. headquarters turning parts of the city into a polyglot almost as cosmopolitan as London. And delightful little Bruges sits back and looks beautiful, its multilingual natives graciously welcoming of the onslaught of mass tourism that each summer brings.

It's an easy journey of under 3 hours by road from Amsterdam to Brussels or Bruges, and the route between is interspersed with a number of entrancing destinations. The Hague is the seat of Dutch parliament, Rotterdam the Dutch sea power, and on the Belgian side of the border (not that you'll notice it when you pass it, thanks to the E.U.'s removing all border controls), there's gritty Ghent and sophisticated Antwerp to discover. And that's not forgetting the former battlefields of Flanders, which resonate with the tragedy of Europe tearing itself apart just 100 years ago.

For ease of reading, I have divided this chapter into three sections: Amsterdam and destinations around; Brussels and its neighbors Ghent and Antwerp; and finally Bruges.

Although **Amsterdam** is not the political capital of The Netherlands—that honor goes to Den Haag ("The Hague"; see p. 129)—it is by far the biggest city, the first port of call for 95 percent of visitors, and its cultural influence looms large over the rest of the country. **Brussels** is the capital city of Belgium, and a virtually trilingual city. All the street signs are given in French and German, and nearly everybody speaks English, even if it is sometimes grudgingly. **Bruges** sits beguilingly in the north of Belgium, acting like a magnet for tourists from all over the world. It is confusingly multilingual, and you will hear Flemish spoken everywhere, but most natives speak English.

best AMSTERDAM EXPERIENCES

o **Chilling in a Brown Cafe:** Spend a leisurely evening in a brown cafe, the traditional Amsterdam watering hole. After an evening of imbibing ice-cold beer in one of these, you'll understand the meaning of the Dutch term *gezelligheid*. You'll also probably find you've made lots of new friends, too. See p. 72

o **Cruising Amsterdam's 17th-Century Canals:** Get your bearings with an hourlong canal tour of Amsterdam; you'll see all the major waterways, many famous sights, the expanding architectural landscape north of the IJ river, the workings of the port, and many beautiful canal houses. See p. 83.

o **Discovering the Jordaan:** Once a working-class district and now thoroughly gentrified, Amsterdam's most photogenic *quartier* is chokka with narrow, tree-lined canals and cobbled streets. It has cafes and bars aplenty to discover as well as galleries and independent stores by the dozen. There are also a number of small hotels that are a treat to stay in. See p. 56.

o **Following the Tulip Trail:** Come spring, the place to see the celebrated Dutch tulips in their full glory is Keukenhof Gardens at Lisse, about 45 minutes out of Amsterdam. Here millions of tulips and other flowers create dazzling swathes of color in the spring. Combine your visit with a trip through the bulb fields between Leiden and Haarlem. See p. 123.

o **Seeing Great Paintings:** Everything you've heard about Amsterdam's art museums is true. They are amazing; the three heavyweights are the Rijksmuseum for Dutch Old Masters, the Stedelijk for its world-beating collection of contemporary work, and the Van Gogh for...well, Van Gogh. See p. 92 and 93.

o **Skating on the Canals:** When the thermometer drops low enough for long enough, the canals freeze over, creating picturesque highways of ice through the cities and countryside. At such times, the Dutch take to their skates. Joining them in winter could be the highlight of your trip. If it's not cold enough to freeze, the artificial ice rink in Amsterdam's Museumplein is a good substitute. See p. 101.

best DUTCH FAMILY-FRIENDLY EXPERIENCES

o **Checking out the Windmills at Zaanse Schans:** In flat Holland, wind is ever present, so it's not surprising that the Dutch used windmills to assist with anything from draining polders to sawing wood. At one time, the Zaan district, northwest of Amsterdam, had more than 1,000 windmills. Of the 13 that survive, five have been reconstructed at Zaanse Schans, together with other historical buildings reminiscent of Holland's past. See p. 121.

o **Eating Pancakes:** The Dutch have a famously sweet tooth and pancakes are one of their national staples. Kids love them too, so take a tour aboard the *Pannenkoekenboot* services in Rotterdam (p. 140) and Amsterdam (p. 100) or fill up with pancakes in local bakeries (p. 78).

The Netherlands & Belgium

National Capital

Provincial Capital

Greenest Hotels in The Netherlands

Two of the best among the new breed of hotels awarded Green Key certificates and run along 100-percent sustainable grounds are the **Conscious Hotel Vondelpark** (p. 68) in Amsterdam and the **Court Garden Den Haag** (p. 136).

Both extract their electricity from green sources, serve food that is almost entirely organic, and both are carefully designed in stylish minimalism with upcycled furniture, green bathroom goodies, and rainwater showers.

- **Exploring Rotterdam's Gigantic Harbor:** Kids will love the chance to get out on the River Maas to discover the inner mechanics of the third-largest natural harbor in the world. The company Spido provides frequent daily multilingual tours on modern, well-equipped boats. See p. 140.
- **Seeing The Netherlands in Miniature at Madurodam:** This mini-theme park has three themed zones containing detailed models of Holland's cities and landmark buildings, all scaled down to 1.25 percent. It's your chance to see all of The Netherlands in 1 day. See p. 135.
- **Spending a Day in Scheveningen:** The Hague's charming beach resort is a 15-minute ride on tram No. 9 from the city center and light years away in carefree vibe. The beach is safe for swimming and there are several kiddie-happy attractions close by, including Madurodam (see above), the Omniversum 3D movie theater (p. 134), and Sea Life Scheveningen. See p. 135.
- **Taking the Highest Tea Ever in The Hague Tower:** Whisk the kids up to the 40th floor of The Hague's tallest building for a delicious high tea in the Penthouse Restaurant and Sky Bar. On a clear day views will stretch across the city to the North Sea. Book in advance. See p. 134.
- **Visiting Amsterdam's Child-Oriented Museums:** Surprisingly, considering its rather obvious drawbacks, Amsterdam is a superb destination for family holidays. It's easy to negotiate, there are plenty of green spaces, an excellent zoo at **Artis** (p. 94), and child-friendly museums, including the **Tropenmuseum** (p. 97), **Science Center NEMO** (p. 96), and the **Het Scheepvaartmuseum** (National Maritime Museum; see p. 95).

best DUTCH HOTELS

- **Hotel des Indes, The Hague:** The hotel of choice for diplomats visiting the Peace Palace (p. 134), this former palace has been a hotel since 1881 and is so plush you could sink into it. The rooms are awash with swags, flourishes, and four posters; the service is second to none. See p. 136.
- **Hotel New York, Rotterdam:** Once the HQ of the Holland-America Line, this hotel is now sandwiched between skyscrapers on the River Maas waterside; it's an historic building offering huge, airy bedrooms and fabulous river views. See p. 141.
- **Mauro Mansion, Amsterdam:** A cool, mini design hotel with just a few rooms and a style that's millions of miles away from faceless international chains. It's located in a 16th-century townhouse overlooking a canal in Amsterdam's Old Center and requires booking way in advance. See p. 61.

- **Seven Bridges, Amsterdam:** At some hotels, the owners aren't just running a business—they're doing what they love. The Seven Bridges is that kind of place. Pierre Keulers and Günter Glaner have found both their profession and their passion in this fine hotel. All the furniture, fixtures, and fittings have been selected with loving care and guests receive the same conscientious attention. See p. 65.
- **Steigenberger Kurhaus Hotel, Scheveningen:** This elegant, old-fashioned monolith is poised over the seafront and staying here is like being wrapped in a comfort blanket. Every imagined amenity is available from lavish guestrooms to afternoon tea and fine dining. See p. 136.

best DUTCH EATERIES

- **Brasss Haarlem de Brasserie, Haarlem:** High-end brasserie menus in surroundings that have more glamor than the finest Parisian restaurant. Go for the oysters and lobster. See p. 116.
- **Cafe 't Smalle, Amsterdam:** For the ultimate local Amsterdam experience, this cozy, crowded brown cafe on the Jordaan's Egelantiersgracht is usually thrumming with lively conversation. Escape the crush on the splendid canal-side terrace, a safe haven from which to watch cyclists rushing past. See p. 72.
- **De Blauw, Amsterdam:** With branches in Utrecht and Amsterdam, this is the future of Indonesian cuisine in Holland. Service is skillful, the wait staff are a delight, and the *rijstaffel* dishes tasty and beautifully presented. See p. 75.
- **Envy, Amsterdam:** Currently enjoying a moment in fickle Amsterdam, Envy's specialty is tapas-style dining on multitudes of small dishes. There's an open kitchen and guest chefs often make surprise appearances. See p. 73.
- **Kee Lun Palace, The Hague:** Outside Amsterdam's Chinatown (p. 72), Chinese restaurants in The Netherlands generally do not make the grade. This one does; the place is heaving and although the service may be perfunctory the Singapore noodles and chili prawns are tasty and come in huge helpings. See p. 136.
- **Restaurant de Kas, Amsterdam:** One of Amsterdam's first organic restaurants, de Kas still keeps ahead of the pack with superlative cooking and a gorgeous setting by market gardens in the southern suburbs. Dining spreads out on to the terrace in summer. See p. 78.

best DUTCH OUTDOOR ACTIVITIES

- **Catching Some Rays in Amsterdam Parks:** Despite the intense urbanization of central Amsterdam, the city has many green spaces in which to catch your breath on sunny days, the Vondelpark (p. 94) and the Westerpark (p. 98) among them.
- **Cycling Anywhere in The Netherlands:** Cycling is the Dutch national obsession; it's healthy, it's green, and Holland is flat. Jump on a bike and explore the countryside. MacBike in Amsterdam rents out bicycles. See p. 101.
- **Enjoying Amsterdam's Beaches:** As a city without natural beaches, Amsterdam decided to create some. They are a haven for both visitors and local residents alike in summer. See p. 102.
- **Hiring a Canal Bike in Amsterdam:** Make up your own tourist itinerary and see the sights of Amsterdam from aboard a giant two- or four-seat paddleboat. See p. 100.

best DUTCH MUSEUMS

○ **Frans Hals Museum, Haarlem:** A destination of choice for many art lovers visiting The Netherlands, this museum is located in a splendid old almshouse, which is almost as much reason to visit as the stunning display of Frans Hals's civic guards portraits in the banqueting hall. See p. 116.

○ **Gemeentemuseum den Haag, The Hague:** The Hague's major museum showstopper is extensive enough to keep visitors going all day. Housed in a sparse brick gallery designed by feted architect H.P. Berlage, the treasures on show range from priceless Delftware to peerless contemporary painting. See p. 132.

○ **Het Grachtenhuis, Amsterdam:** Tucked away behind an elegant 17th-century facade, this is a little cracker of a museum that brings Amsterdam's history to life through clever interactive exhibits, sound, and film. It's an ideal place to start your exploration of the Canal Ring. See p. 89.

○ **Mauritshuis, The Hague:** Set in a former ducal palace, the Mauritshuis reopened in June 2014 after a thorough facelift and the building of more exhibition space underground. It has a small but stellar collection of Dutch Old Master paintings. See p. 132.

○ **Museum Boijmans Van Beuningen, Rotterdam:** Yet another of Holland's superlative art collections, Rotterdam's premier art museum is one of Europe's finest and relates the story of western art from medieval times to present day. Collections span works from Pieter Breughel to Man Ray. See p. 138.

○ **Rijksmuseum, Amsterdam:** With the finest collection of Dutch Old Masters in the world, the Rijksmuseum has had a long and expensive facelift and is once more, and deservedly so, the first stop for most visitors to Amsterdam. Just be sure to get there early to escape the lines or book in advance online to secure a time slot for your visit. See p. 92.

○ **Van Gogh Museum, Amsterdam:** The museum with the world's largest collection of works by tortured artist Vincent van Gogh—200 paintings and counting—is flooded with natural light and all the signage is multilingual. Everything a gallery should be. See p. 93.

best DUTCH CHURCHES

○ **Sint-Bavokerk (Church of St. Bavo), Haarlem:** The moment you enter Haarlem's main square, this massive church is revealed in all its Gothic splendor. It was the subject of many a 16th-century painting and Haarlem master painter Frans Hals is buried in its cavernous interior. The young Mozart played here in 1766. See p. 118.

○ **Westerkerk, Amsterdam:** The Westerkerk's tower, the Westertoren, is 85m (275 ft.) high, the tallest in Amsterdam, and provides a spectacular view of the city. Anne Frank could hear every note of the carillon's dulcet tones while in hiding from the Nazis in her house on Prinsengracht just around the corner. See p. 90.

best DUTCH SHOPPING

○ **Cheese:** Holland is world famous for its great round slabs of orange and yellow cheese, and cheese features on almost every menu—in fact, the Dutch dairy industry has revenues of more than seven billion euros annually. Most delis in the main cities will sell a selection of Goudas, Edam, and holey Maasdammer vacuum-packed and ready for export. See p. 105 and p. 120.

o **Delftware:** During the 16th century, Delft factories started decorating their pottery in elaborate blue patterns in mimicry of Chinese porcelain imported into The Netherlands. Delft Blue pottery became famous the world over, along with Makkumware from the town of Makkum. Delftware and Makkumware can be bought in Amsterdam's Spiegelkwartier (p. 103) and you can see Delftware being made in the Koninklijke Porceleyne Fles in Delft. See p. 128.

o **Flower Bulbs:** It's difficult to choose from the incredible variety of bulb shapes and colors offered in The Netherlands. In Amsterdam buy them from the **Bloemenmarkt** floating flower market on Singel canal (p. 82) or the **Tulip Museum** on Prinsengracht (p. 90). A great array can also be bought during the spring opening of **Keukenhof Gardens** in Lisse. See p. 123.

best BRUSSELS EXPERIENCES

o **Admiring Art Nouveau, Brussels:** Considering itself the world capital of Art Nouveau, Brussels was home to architect Victor Horta (1861–1947), who was its foremost exponent. Get up with the larks to beat the endless lines outside the colorful, sinuous Horta Museum at his former home. See p. 170.

o **Being Insulted by the World's Rudest Man, Brussels:** Don't let a visit to the sweetly old-fashioned Cantillon Brewery be spoiled by the curmudgeonly barman; he does it on purpose—especially now he has become a phenomenon on TripAdvisor—and it's all part of the fun of a visit to Belgium's last Lambic brewery. See p. 169.

o **Discovering Royal Brussels:** Much of Brussels was built under the stewardship of King Leopold I in the 19th century. Royal Brussels offers parks, museums, grand palaces, galleries, and gardens to explore. See p. 162.

o **Seeing the Grand-Place for the First Time, Brussels:** There's nothing quite like strolling onto the Grand-Place. You'll never forget your first look at this timelessly perfect cobbled square, surrounded by gabled guild houses or the Gothic tracery of the Hôtel de Ville (Town Hall) and Maison du Roi (King's House). See p. 158.

o **Standing in Front of the Lamb of God, Ghent:** Some fabled artworks disappoint when you finally get to see them in the flesh. The Van Eyck brothers' superb, glowing altarpiece in Sint-Bavokerk (St. Bavo's Cathedral) is categorically *not* one of these. It simply takes your breath away. See p. 118.

o **Touring Rubens's House, Antwerp:** Obviously a man with a euro or two going spare in his back pocket, the Dutch super-artist Rubens lived in some considerable style in an ornate mansion with an arcaded formal garden. See p. 210.

o **Visiting Kazerne Dossin, the Holocaust Centre, Mechelen:** Housed in a building constructed in 2012, this hard-hitting museum is on the site of a former holding center for Belgian Jewish deportees to the concentration camps of Germany and Poland. It acts as both memorial to those murdered in the Holocaust and as Europe's first Museum of Human Rights. See p. 230.

o **Walking the Illuminated Promenade by Night, Ghent:** See the beautiful historic heart of Ghent all lit up at night; if you don't want to follow the whole route through the city center, at least see the wildly gabled ancient guild houses along Graslei, all ethereally floodlit. See p. 219.

best BRUSSELS FAMILY-FRIENDLY EXPERIENCES

- **Cruising Antwerp Streets in the Touristram:** Take a whistle-stop tour of all Antwerp's major points of interest in a mini electric tram; you'll trundle through the Grote Markt and the cobbled lanes of the Old Town, venture through the main shopping thoroughfares, and potter along the Schelde riverfront. See p. 207.

- **Eating a Nose, Ghent:** Sample some of Ghent's iconic sweets; "noses" are conical and fruity, can be bought in an assortment of fruity flavors, and look for all the world like overweight, giant Jelly Babies. See p. 220.

- **Giggling at the Manneken-Pis, Brussels:** Heaven alone knows why this diminutive and distinctly underwhelming statue has become an icon of Brussels, but it has. Join the sniggering throng around the little fountain to photograph the city's famous peeing sculpture. See p. 165.

- **Laughing at the Cartoons in the Belgian Comic Strip Center, Brussels:** Here's a chance to understand the underlying skills of Belgian cartoonists, known to be some of the finest in the world. This is the place to catch up with old friends Tintin and the Smurfs in a showcase Art Nouveau gallery. See p. 163.

- **Seeing Ghent from atop the Belfort:** The 14th-century belfry rises 90m (300 ft.) above the city of Ghent, making it the tallest tower in Belgium. Whizz up to the top by elevator for unrivaled views over ancient rooftops and canals. See p. 192.

- **Spotting Tintin Artwork in Brussels:** Kids, keep your eyes peeled for Tintin graffiti on the walls of Brussels streets. For real aficionados, there's also a Tintin trail through the city. See p. 172.

best BRUSSELS HOTELS

- **Hotel Harmony, Ghent:** A family-run treasure in Patersol, Ghent's historic quarter, which is blessed with huge (even by U.S. standards) guestrooms at the front of the building, some with tiny balconies. It's all smartly kitted out in minimalist style and there's a natty little bar for early-evening drinks. See p. 220.

- **mo851, Antwerp:** Wow, what a stylish place! This intimate B&B has just a few rooms, all wonderfully decked out in contemporary fashion, and it's within staggering distance of the bars and restaurants in the old town as well as the city's upmarket shopping streets. See p. 210.

- **Hotel Amigo, Brussels:** One of the best, most luscious five-star hotels in the city. Despite its size, the Amigo manages to keep that personal touch often sadly lacking in big hotels. See p. 149.

best BRUSSELS RESTAURANTS & BARS

- **De Graslei, Ghent:** Wonderfully situated overlooking the canal on one of Ghent's loveliest streets, this is a truly romantic spot for dining after dark. As happens everywhere in this outgoing city, you'll soon end up deep in conversation with your dining neighbors. See p. 220.

- **Fanny Thai, Brussels:** Located in Brussels's trendy Danseart district, this is a stand-out Thai restaurant that's always full to bursting. Service borders on the hectic but the tom yam soup and pad Thai noodles are well spiced and heartwarmingly good. See p. 156.

- **Grand Café de Rooden Hoed, Antwerp:** The Red Hat is Antwerp's oldest, swishest brasserie, serving well-cooked Flemish staples including mussels and ginormous seafood platters. The wait staff deserves to be on the stage and do their best to make eating here a fun experience. See p. 211.

- **La Mort Subite, Brussels:** Old-fashioned and cavernous, this traditional Belgian bar serves its home-brewed beer to hundreds of thirsty punters hourly. Just watch the wait staff work and admire their friendly professionalism. See p. 178.

- **'t Dreupelkot, Ghent:** With no shortage of fine cafes, you can just about guarantee that any one you enter in Ghent will provide happy memories. 't Dreupelkot will leave you with a particularly warm glow of appreciation as it is the city's number-one spot for imbibing *jenever,* that mind-numbing ginlike liqueur. With 100 varieties to choose from, the atmosphere in the cafe soon ramps up. See p. 221.

best **BRUSSELS OUTDOOR ACTIVITIES**

- **Admiring the Flower Carpet, Brussels:** The Grand-Place turns into a complex, patterned carpet of flowers for one weekend in August every year for the city's famous flower festival. See p. 159.

- **Walking around the Serres Royales, Laeken, Brussels:** Out near the Atomium in Brussels's northern suburbs, the Art Nouveau Royal Greenhouses are a delight only too rarely seen. If you're in Brussels between April and May, be sure to catch the annual blaze of color. See p. 172.

best **BRUSSELS MUSEUMS**

- **Cinquantenaire Museum, Brussels:** With collections as vast as the V&A in London, this vibrant, well-curated museum looks at civilizations from Native American Indian to Indonesian, with a wonderful array of totem poles and wooden Balinese beds on display. Plan to spend several hours here or you'll miss half of it. See p. 167.

- **Design Museum Gent:** Tucked away behind the facade of a refined 18th-century townhouse, the stars of the show in Ghent's decorative arts museum are the cleverly pieced-together period Art Deco rooms and the range of *objets d'art* from Delftware tulip vases to Alessi tea services. See p. 215.

- **Koninklijk Museum voor Schone Kunsten Antwerpen (Royal Fine Arts Museum), Antwerp:** Antwerp's fine museum of Flemish Masters holds the largest group of Rubens masterpieces in existence. It is currently closed for refurbishment until late 2017. Selected showpieces from the collection are on loan to other Antwerp institutions. See p. 207.

- **Mechelen Toy Museum, Mechelen:** With a surprisingly extensive collection of toys that will have most of us descending into nostalgia, this entertaining toy museum is one of the largest in Europe and is as much loved by adults as by children. At last we know where all our old dolls and tin cars disappeared to. See p. 231.

o **Musée Hergé, Brussels:** Located 30km (20 miles) southeast of Brussels in Louvain-la-Neuve, this funky museum is dedicated to the works of Georges Remi, who breathed life into Tintin and his trusty terrier Snowy in 1927 under the name Hergé. See p. 172.

o **Musée Van Buuren, Brussels:** Secreted away in a posh Brussels suburb, this paean to Art Deco style hits the very apex of quality and sophistication. The house is not huge but it's been preserved with all its original furniture in situ; there's a lovely garden that is best seen in spring. See p. 169.

o **Musées Royaux des Beaux-Arts de Belgique, Brussels:** After much faffing about, closures, and lengthy re-organizations, Brussels finally has four fabulous museums showcasing paintings by the biggest Belgian names all assembled under one gigantic roof. That doesn't make the museum staff any more polite, however. See p. 166.

best BRUSSELS CHURCHES

o **Koekelberg National Basilica, Brussels:** One of Brussels's iconic landmarks, the Art Deco basilica of the Sacred Heart was built in the late 1920s out of reinforced concrete. Its calm, tranquil interior is so huge that it contains two museums, crypts, a business center, and cafes; it's quite a struggle to find them.

o **Sint-Pauluskerk (St. Paul's Church), Antwerp:** The gleaming white Gothic edifice of St. Paul's Church hides no fewer than four Rubens masterpieces; they adorn the interior of this lovely church along with masterly paintings by other prominent Flemish artists. See p. 210.

best BRUSSELS SHOPPING

o **Antiques, Brussels:** You'll need luck to score a bargain at the weekend antiques market on place du Grand Sablon—the dealers are well aware of the precise worth of each item in their stock and are calmly determined to get it. But it's still fun to wander the market, browsing and haggling, and who knows? You just might stumble on that hard-to-find affordable treasure. See p. 174.

o **Chocolates, Brussels:** The Swiss might wish to dispute this point, but the truth is that Belgian handmade chocolates, filled with various fresh-cream flavors, are the best in the universe. You won't go wrong if you buy chocolates made by Marcolini, Wittamer, Nihoul, Leonidas, and Neuhaus, available in specialty stores all over Belgium. See p. 34.

o **Diamonds, Antwerp:** Antwerp's Diamantkwartier (Diamond Quarter) is the center of the world's market in precious stones. Much of the trading is still carried out by members of the city's Hassidic Jewish community. See p. 209.

best BRUGES EXPERIENCES

o **Drinking Beer at an Outdoor Bar:** As long as you can dodge the hordes of European stag and hen parties that sully Bruges drinking holes, find a bar by a canal and set about sampling some local brews. See p. 189.

o **Eating Moules-Frites in Markt:** Yes, it's touristy but sit at any of the terrace restaurants around Bruges's expansive main square and you'll be rewarded with great plates of mussels and piles of crispy fries as well as fantastic views. See p. 185.

- **Hearing the "Last Post," Ypres:** Stand shoulder to shoulder with proud, be-medaled veterans and heroes of recent wars to hear the daily "Last Post" ceremony in tribute to the millions who died in Flanders Fields in World War I between 1914 and 1918. It's something you'll never forget. See p. 228.
- **Time-Traveling in Bruges:** Without a doubt, Bruges is one of Europe's most hand-some small cities. Its almost perfectly preserved center often feels like a film set or museum, with buildings that run the gamut of architectural styles from medieval times to the 19th century. The picturesque canals are the icing on Bruges's cake. See p. 189.
- **Touring Flanders Fields:** Whatever time of year you choose to take a tour of the World War I trenches, you'll be alternatively depressed at the folly of mankind and cheered by the apparent normality of Flanders as it exists today. Many old battle-fields are now under agriculture but still several people are killed every year by unexploded mines and shells left behind from the conflict. See p. 228.
- **Viewing the Holy Blood, Bruges:** One of the most revered Christian relics in Europe is housed in the ancient Basilica of the Holy Blood. It is revealed to visitors twice daily in a curiously moving but equally cynical money-grabbing ceremony. It's worth attending to see the blind faith that some believers invest in these relics as well as the over-the-top decoration of the church. See p. 193.

best BRUGES FAMILY-FRIENDLY EXPERIENCES

- **Making Belgian Chocolate:** Belgium is proud producer of some very fine chocolate and Bruges is the ideal place to discover how to make it. Various workshops in the gloriously messy art of chocolate-making take place daily at **Choco-Story** and are available by booking ahead online or occasionally on the day. See p. 195.
- **Speeding Past the Sights:** The streets of central Bruges ring out with the clip-clopping of horses' hooves as they circle the tourist routes endlessly at a smart trot. If you're time-impaired, taking a trip by pony-and-trap is a fun way to see every-thing in a short (sometimes very short) time, and kids love the novelty of the experi-ence. See p. 198.
- **Squeezing on to a Canal Cruise:** Bruges's ring of canals is nowhere near the size of Amsterdam's labyrinthine waterways, but the architecture and views are just as good. Pick up points for boat trips are dotted around the canals and tours are multi-lingual. See p. 199.
- **Visiting Child-Friendly Museums:** To say that Bruges is museum-rich is an under-statement; luckily among all the art museums there are plenty that will appeal to children, especially the **Fries Museum** (p. 196) and **Choco-Story** (p. 195). The gruesome surgical instruments in the **Sint-Janshospitaal** may have a certain maca-bre attraction too. See p. 197.

best BRUGES HOTELS

- **Egmond, Bruges:** Romantically located right next to the picturesque Minnewater (Lover's Lake), the Egmond is surrounded by private gardens and safely sited 10 minutes from the tourist bedlam of Bruges central. Staying here is like visiting a smart English country-house hotel but without the heart-stopping price tag that usu-ally accompanies it. See p. 185.

o **The Pand Hotel, Bruges:** Every creature comfort is supplied to weary sightseers at the Pand in a higgledy-piggledy series of bedrooms extending through two historic town houses. The suites are all elegantly fitted out with Ralph Lauren soft furnishings and the day always gets off to a flying start with a complementary glass of champagne over breakfast. See p. 184.

best BRUGES RESTAURANTS & BARS

o **2be:** With a "beer wall" behind glass purporting to contain all 1,132 Belgian beers, 2be is a popular canal-side spot in which to start a relationship with some of Bruges's local brews. See p. 189.

o **Breydel de Coninc:** Arguably the best fish restaurant in Bruges, this temple to mussels and lobster (served three different ways, no less!) is family owned and everything is cooked from scratch so you have to forgive the occasional delays. The dining halls are simple to the point of being sparse but the quality of the fish served here more than compensates for the canteen-level surroundings. See p. 188.

o **La Civière d'Or:** One of the best choices of the Markt restaurants for lunchtime pit stops involving bucket-loads of mussels served with tomatoes, roasted fennel, and saffron. It's actually three venues rolled into one, offering brasserie, cafe, and fine dining menus. See p. 189.

best BRUGES MUSEUMS

o **Expo Picasso:** Bruges's oft-overlooked collection of 20th-century artwork should not be missed by anyone with a love of modern art from the last 100 years. Sketches, prints, and lithographs from a roster of world-famous names including Picasso and Magritte are beautifully displayed in a former almshouse. See p. 196.

o **Groeningemuseum:** Simply the high point of an art-lover's visit to Bruges, the museum focuses on the Flemish Primitive, dating from the 15th century when Bruges was one of the most powerful trading cities in Europe. The highlight of the collection is the horrific "Last Judgment" by Hieronymous Bosch, painted in 1482. See p. 196.

o **Gruuthusemuseum:** Housed in the ornate former residence of an aristocratic Belgian family, the museum is cleverly laid out to highlight the historical handiwork of a number of Bruges's guilds. Don't miss the fabulous—and original—carved woodwork doors, floors, and ceilings dotted about the palace. See p. 194.

o **In Flanders Fields Museum, Ypres:** Clearly an awful lot of money has been expended on this thoughtful, interactive museum housed in Ypres's remodeled Cloth Hall (the medieval original was destroyed during the dark days of World War II). It's imaginative, poignant, and heart-rending by turn. Not to be missed! See p. 228.

best BRUGES CHURCHES

o **Onze-Lieve-Vrouwekerk (Church of Our Lady):** The spire of this church soars 122m (400 ft.) high and can be spotted for miles around Bruges. The church did hold a marble "Madonna and Child" by Michelangelo, a painting by Anthony van Dyck, and the 15th-century bronze tomb sculptures of Charles the Bold and Mary of Burgundy. At the time of writing it was under refurbishment although still open for visits. See p. 197.

best BRUGES SHOPPING

o **Beer:** With more than 400 breweries producing over a thousand varieties, Belgium is the European home of beer. It comes in many styles, from Trappist to white beer, and there are stores throughout Bruges selling a selection of bottles that can be wrapped for taking home in suitcases or couriered overseas. See p. 200.

o **Chocolate:** As in Brussels, there are dozens of confectioners creating exquisite handmade chocolates in Bruges. Sample the wares before you buy to find your favorite fillings. See p. 200.

o **Lace:** There are two kinds of Belgian lace: exquisitely handmade pieces or the machine-made stuff, which is of indifferent quality to meet the never-ending demand for souvenirs. Obviously the highest-quality lace is handmade and it is way more expensive; rummage around the many lace-selling stores in Bruges carefully to compare prices and quality before buying, and avoid the shops around Burg and Markt, which are aimed at the lower end of the market. See p. 199.

AMSTERDAM, BRUSSELS & BRUGES IN CONTEXT

Despite being buffeted by the worldwide economic storms associated with the early 2010s, both The Netherlands and Belgium escaped lightly in comparison with their Mediterranean counterparts. Both countries continue to enjoy an enviable standard of living and a quality of life that happily reflects that. Their societies become more multicultural by the day—a development that's seen most clearly in the region's main metropolises of Amsterdam and Brussels—and these countries are among the most urbanized on earth. For the most part, this has only added to their contemporary vibrancy, but the process has not been without stress. Even Amsterdam's famed tolerance is showing signs of strain as civic leaders press to clean up the Red Light District and limit the sale of drugs in the coffee shops (p. 111).

Belgium is a small country. Not so small that if you blink you'll miss it, like neighboring Luxembourg, but small enough that a couple of hours of focused driving will get you from the capital city Brussels to any corner of its realm. Yet the variety of culture, language, history, and cuisine crammed into this meager space would do credit to a land many times its size. Belgium's diversity is a product of its location at the cultural crossroads of western Europe. The boundary between Europe's Germanic north and Latin-language-speaking south cuts clear across the country's middle; the clash of culture has come home to roost in Brussels, where street signage is multilingual although the language most heard in the streets is French.

Like an Atlantis in reverse, The Netherlands has emerged over the centuries from the sea. Much of the country was once a pattern of islands, precariously separated from the North Sea by dunes. As time rolled past, these islands were patiently stitched together by Dutch ingenuity and hard work. The outcome is a canvas-flat, green-and-silver Mondriaan of a country, with nearly half its land and two-thirds of its 16 million inhabitants below sea level.

To make themselves even more welcoming and enjoyable than they already are, the cities of Amsterdam and Brussels are expanding their transport systems, redeveloping decayed inner-city or harbor zones, and revamping their cultural offerings. Amsterdam's Big Three museums have all received major facelifts, while Brussels is also busily upgrading its roster of attractions. The major Dutch satellite cities of Rotterdam and The Hague, plus Belgian Antwerp, are all the while nurturing, improving, and consolidating their attractions. The smaller cities of Bruges and Ghent are on the self-improvement bandwagon too; with Bruges opening several family-friendly museums and Ghent, once down at heel, scooting rapidly up the popularity stakes with a major cleanup of its many historical assets.

THE NETHERLANDS

Let's clear up some matters of nomenclature. "Dutch" is the result of a 15th-century misunderstanding on the part of the English, who couldn't distinguish too clearly between the people of the northern Low Countries and the various Germanic peoples living further south and east. So to describe the former, they simply corrupted the German *Deutsch* to Dutch.

The term "Holland," is also a misnomer as, strictly speaking, it refers only to the provinces of Noord-Holland and Zuid-Holland and not to the whole country. The Dutch themselves call their country *Nederland* (The Netherlands) and themselves *Nederlanders.* But they recognize that Holland and Dutch are popular internationally and are here to stay, so, being a practical people, they make use of them.

The Netherlands is small enough that a burst of vigorous driving will get you from one corner of the country to the other in a morning, and you can travel by train from Amsterdam to the farthest point of the rail network in an afternoon. The nation's 42,000 sq. km (16,500 sq. miles) are among the most densely populated in the world, holding 16 million people, or approximately 1,000 per square mile. The crowding is most noticeable in the Randstad, the heavily populated conurbation that includes the urban centers of Amsterdam, Rotterdam, The Hague, Leiden, Haarlem, Utrecht, and Delft and sprawls across the top half of the country. Elsewhere the land is much more sparsely populated.

The Netherlands is a constitutional monarchy headed by King Willem-Alexander of the House of Orange, who was inaugurated to the throne upon the abdication of his mother, Queen Beatrix on April 30, 2013. He is married to Argentinian Queen Máxima and they have three young daughters.

Dutch people have a passion for detail that would boggle the mind of a statistician—and a sense of order and propriety that sends them into a tailspin if you mess things up. They organize everything (people, land, flower beds, even the sea), and they love to make schedules and stick to them. They may allow you to indulge an occasional whim, though they haven't a clue what it means to "play it by ear."

AMSTERDAM TODAY

"The Dutch Disease" is what a conservative U.S. columnist called Holland's social liberalism. But not many of the hookers in Amsterdam's Red Light District are Dutch, and relatively few denizens of the smoking coffee shops are Dutch. If Amsterdam is a latter-day Sodom and Gomorrah, it's one mainly for visitors.

Sex & Drugs

The uniquely Dutch combination of tolerance and individualism impacts areas of personal and social morality that in other countries are still red-button issues. In 2001, the world's first same-sex marriage, with a legal status identical to that of heterosexual matrimony, took place in Amsterdam. The Dutch Parliament legalized regulated euthanasia in 2000, making The Netherlands the first country in the world to do so. And then there's prostitution and drug use.

Prostitution is legal in Holland, and prostitutes work in clean premises, pay taxes, receive regular medical checks, are eligible for welfare, and have their own trade union. Around about 2010, most of the girls working in Amsterdam's three red light districts (p. 87) hailed from the Far East, but by 2014 there had been a sea change, with the majority hailing from eastern Europe, lured into the city by the removal of border controls within the E.U.

Authorities are not duty bound to prosecute criminal acts, leaving a loophole for social experimentation in areas that technically are illegal. It has been wryly said that the Netherlands has one of the lowest crime rates in Europe because whenever something becomes a criminal problem, the Dutch make it legal. Don't laugh—at least not in Holland—or you may find you've touched the natives where they're tender. The Dutch will take aim at anyone, on any issue, outside their borders. Just so long as it's understood that everything *inside* has arrived at that hallowed state of perfection.

Popular belief notwithstanding, narcotic drugs are illegal in the Netherlands. But the Dutch treat drug use mainly as a medical problem rather than purely as a crime. The authorities distinguish between soft drugs like cannabis, which in some quarters are considered—rightly or wrongly—less likely to cause addiction and pose a minor health risk, and hard drugs like heroin and cocaine, which are highly addictive and pose significant risks to users' health. Both are illegal, but the law is tough on hard drug abuse. Ironically, improvements in Dutch cannabis cultivation techniques have increased the concentration of the active ingredient THC from 9 percent to 18 percent in the past 10 years.

The Netherlands has significantly lower rates of heroin addiction, drug use, and drug-related deaths than Britain, France, Germany, and other European countries that criticize Holland fiercely on this issue. Still, the Dutch "tradition" of allowing visitors to the country to pop into what's euphemistically known as a coffee shop to smoke an illegal but tolerated cannabis joint is under threat.

A legal ruling upheld the mayor of Maastricht's decision to end cross-border drugs tourism into his city by banning foreigners from its smoking coffee shops. Rosendaal and Bergen op Zoom, two other border towns plagued by drugs tourists, simply shut down all of their coffee shops in 2009. The most serious threat to Amsterdam came in 2010, when the government announced its intention to force all of the country's surviving coffee shops—their number reduced from a peak of close to 2,000 in 1997 to around 650, and are still falling—to become members-only clubs open only to residents of the Netherlands. This would have meant shutting out the tens of thousands of weed tourists who visit Amsterdam each year. With some coffee shops claiming that 99 percent of their customers are tourists—though an overall estimate of 40 percent is probably more accurate—many coffee shops would have closed if the proposals had become law. Not surprisingly, once the civic sums where done, these laws were quietly shelved, although the number of coffee shops in Amsterdam has continued to decline. Around 200 are still open and are strictly regulated: They all must be licensed and display the official green-and-white sticker in the window. Anyone caught carrying more than 5 grams (for personal use) of cannabis will be fined, and it is illegal to smoke dope in the streets, and also illegal for anyone under the age of 18 to buy drugs, even in the coffee shops. Ironically for venues that are already awash with the haze of dope smoke, smoking cigarettes is also illegal on the premises.

A Clash of Cultures

For the visitor, the very medieval heart of Amsterdam today presents much the same face it has over the centuries—a serene canalscape interwoven with a tangle of waterways, but around the extremities of the city, much is changing. Its industrious population still hangs on to the country's age-old traditions of tolerance and immigrants of all political, religious, and ideological persuasions are still welcomed. However, almost a million (6 percent) of the country's inhabitants are now Muslim and in recent years there have been indications that the welcome mat is wearing thin, thanks in part to threats from radical Islamists. Far-right-wing politician Geert Wilders has become a lightning rod for the racial tensions in contemporary Dutch society, inheriting the anti-Islam mantle of the gay populist politician Pym Fortuyn, assassinated in 2002 by a pro-Muslim Dutch activist; and also of filmmaker Theo van Gogh, murdered by a Dutch-Moroccan Islamist in 2004. Wilders heads Holland's fourth-largest party, the Party for Freedom (PVV), which in elections in 2010 increased its representation from 9 to 24 out of 150 seats in the Lower House of Parliament. The PVV views Dutch society, culture, European values, and public safety as threatened by the growth of the Muslim community and of radical Islam. Wilders, who has described the Koran as a "fascist book," and who wants Muslim migration into The Netherlands halted, lives under permanent police protection due to threats to his life. Various surveys of Dutch public opinion suggest a society that's split on his views. In 2014 Wilders and his party won four seats in the European Parliament, based in Brussels, in elections that saw right-wing MEPs sweep alarmingly into power all over Europe.

THE ORIGINS OF AMSTERDAM

The earliest inhabitants of what is now The Netherlands were three tribal groups who settled the marshy deltas of the Low Countries in the dawn of recorded history. They were the Belgae of the southern regions; the Batavii, who settled in the area of the Great Rivers; and the fiercely independent Frisii, who took up residence along the northern coast. Each tribe posed a challenge to Julius Caesar when he came calling in the 1st century B.C., but the Romans managed, after prolonged and effective objections from the locals, to get both the Belgae and the Batavii to knuckle under.

After the demise of the Roman Empire, the Frisians were still going strong. They repelled the next wave of would-be conquerors in the 5th century, when hordes of Saxons and Franks over-ran the Romano-Batavians. Although many northern European peoples embraced Christianity by the late 5th century, it was not until the late 8th century that the Frisians abandoned their pagan gods, and then only when the mighty Charlemagne, king of the Franks and ruler of the Carolingian Empire, compelled them to in a massive show of force.

Good for Business

By the 13th and 14th centuries, the nobility were busy building the castles and fortified manor houses throughout The Netherlands. Meanwhile the Catholic hierarchy grew both powerful and wealthy; the bishops of Maastricht and Utrecht played key roles in politics, and they preserved their legacy by erecting splendid cathedrals, abbeys, and monasteries.

During the 14th and 15th centuries, Holland's position at the mouths of three great west European rivers made it a focal point in power struggles. The House of Burgundy became the first major feudal power in the Low Countries, consolidating its hold on the region by acquiring fiefdoms one by one through the various means of marriage, inheritance, and military force. Its day soon passed, however, and the Austrian Habsburg emperor Maximilian acquired the Low Countries from the Burgundians by much the same means.

Amsterdam began its rise to commercial prosperity in 1323, when Floris VI, the Count of Holland, established the city as one of two toll points for the import of beer from Hamburg. The city's powerful merchants established guilds of craftsmen and put ships to sea to catch North Sea herring. Soon they had expanded into trading salted Baltic herring; Norwegian salted and dried cod, and cod-liver oil; German beer and salt; linen and woolen cloth from the Low Countries and England; Russian furs and candle wax; Polish grain and flour; and Swedish timber and iron.

Wars of Religion

Dutch citizens began to embrace the Protestant church at the same time that the Low Countries came under the rule of Charles V, the Catholic Habsburg emperor and king of Spain in 1506. Then known as the Spanish Netherlands, the country became a pressure point and fulcrum for the shifting political scene caused by the Reformation right across Europe. The rigorous doctrines of John Calvin and his firm belief in the separation of church and state began to take root in the country's psyche.

When Charles relinquished the Spanish throne to his son Philip II in 1555, the days darkened for the Dutch. As an ardent Catholic, Philip was determined to defeat the Reformation and set out to hunt heretics throughout his empire. He dispatched the infamous Duke of Alba to the Low Countries to carry out the Inquisition's "death to heretics" edict. The Dutch resented Philip's intrusion into their affairs and began a resistance movement, led by William of Orange, Count of Holland. Known as William the Silent, he declared: "I cannot approve of princes attempting to control the conscience of their subjects and wanting to rob them of the liberty of faith."

Only those towns that declined to join the ensuing fight were spared destruction when the Spanish invaded in 1568. Spanish armies marched inexorably through Holland, besting the defenses of each city to which they laid siege, with few exceptions. In an ingenious if desperate move in 1574, William of Orange saved Leiden by flooding the province, allowing his ships to sail right up to the city's walls.

This victory galvanized the Dutch in fighting for their independence. In 1579, the Dutch nobles formed the Union of Utrecht, in which they agreed to fight together in a united front. Although the union was devised solely to win the battle against Spain, consolidation inevitably occurred and by the turn of the 17th century, the seven northern provinces of what had been the Spanish Netherlands was declared the Republic of the Seven Provinces.

The struggle with Spain continued until 1648, but a new, prosperous era was soon to be ushered in.

The Golden Age

Over the first 50 to 75 years of the 17th century, that legendary Dutch entrepreneurial talent came into its own. These years have since become known as the Golden Age. It seemed every business venture the Dutch initiated during this time turned a profit and that each of their many expeditions to the unknown places of the world resulted in a new jewel in the Dutch trading empire. Colonies and trade were established to provide the luxury-hungry merchants at home with new delights, such as fresh ginger from Java, foxtails from America, fine porcelain from China, and flower bulbs from Turkey

Dutch in the English Lexicon

The 17th-century Dutch got up English noses by competing for maritime trade and, in 1667, by sailing boldly up the Medway near London and trashing the English fleet. So the English added verbal abuse to their arsenal. That's why we have "Dutch courage" (alcohol-induced courage), "Dutch treat" (you pay for yourself), "going Dutch" (everybody pays their share), and "double Dutch" (gibberish). Americans were kinder to their Revolutionary War supporters, speaking of "beating the Dutch" (doing something remarkable).

that produced big, bright, waxy flowers and grew quite readily in Holland's sandy soil—tulips.

The Netherlands was getting rich and Amsterdam soon grew into one of the world's wealthiest cities. In 1602, traders from each of the major cities in the Republic of the Seven Provinces set up the Vereenigde Oostindische Compagnie (V.O.C.), the United East India Company, which was granted a monopoly on trade in the east. It was wildly successful and established the Dutch presence in the Spice Islands (Indonesia), Goa, South Africa, and China.

This is the period that saw the planning and developing of the **Canal Ring** (p. 56) around the old heart of Amsterdam. The three great canals that form a concentric belt around the city center were years in the planning and construction, but were needed urgently as the original streets were overcrowded and disease-ridden thanks to the never-ceasing flow of immigrants into the city. Today Keizersgracht, Prinsengracht, and Herengracht stand as proud reminders of this great time of development, lined with mansions built by the nouveau riche of the Dutch Golden Age. Visit **Het Grachtenhuis** (p. 89) to learn how the canals were constructed.

Holland was becoming a refuge for persecuted groups. The Pilgrim Fathers stayed in Leiden for a dozen years before embarking for America from Delfshaven in Rotterdam in 1620, Sephardic Jews fled the oppressive Spanish and welcomed the tolerance of the Dutch, and refugees straggled in from France and Portugal. William of Orange had created a climate of tolerance in The Netherlands that attracted talented newcomers who contributed a great deal to the expanding economic, social, artistic, and intellectual climate of the country.

Golden Age Holland can be compared to Classical Greece and Renaissance Italy for the great flowering of wealth and culture that transformed society. "There is perhaps no other example of a complete and highly original civilization springing up in so short a time in so small a territory," wrote the British historian Simon Schama.

The End of the Golden Age

However, the country's luck was soon to change. The Dutch call 1672 the Rampjaar (Year of Disaster). France, under Louis XIV, invaded the United Provinces by land and the English attacked by sea. This war (1672–78) and the later War of the Spanish Succession (1701–13) drained both Holland's wealth and morale. The buccaneering, can-do, go-anywhere spirit of traders, artists, and writers began to ebb, replaced by conservatism and closed horizons.

Revolutionary France invaded Holland in 1794, capturing Amsterdam and establishing the Batavian Republic in 1795, headed by the pro-French Dutch Patriots. Napoleon brought the short-lived republic to an end in 1806 by setting up his brother, Louis

The Dutch as Giants

Maybe it's nature's way of compensating for their country being challenged size wise, but the Dutch are *tall*. The average man is 1.8m (6 ft.) and the average woman is 1.7m (5 ft., 7 in.), which in both cases is 5cm (2 in.) more than the European average. Not only that, but a government study showed that the average height of the Dutch increases by 1.5cm (½ in.) every decade.

Napoleon, as king of the Netherlands, and installed him in a palace that had been Amsterdam's Town Hall. Louis did such a good job of representing the interests of his new subjects that in 1810 Napoleon deposed him and brought the Netherlands formally into the empire.

When the Dutch recalled the House of Orange in 1814, it was to fill the role of king in a constitutional monarchy. The monarch was yet another William of Orange; however, because his reign was to be a fresh start, the Dutch started numbering their Williams all over again (which makes for a very confusing history). However, it was not until the Battle of Waterloo in 1815 that Napoleon was finally defeated and sent into exile.

In 1831 the Low Countries split entirely, with the southern provinces forming Belgium. The rest of the 19th century saw social reforms, an influx of Jews from Antwerp, who formed the backbone of the diamond-cutting industry in Amsterdam, and the building of more canals, waterways, and railway lines.

Modern Times

As the storm clouds gathered across Europe with the advent of World War I, The Netherlands escaped the worst ravages by maintaining strict neutrality. Holland shared in the wealth as Europe's condition improved after the war, but conditions were very bad during the 1930s, when widespread unemployment in Amsterdam brought on by the worldwide Great Depression caused the government to use the army in 1934 to control the unruly masses.

During World War II, Nazi troops invaded the country in 1940. An estimated 104,000 of Holland's 140,000 Jews were murdered, Rotterdam sustained heavy bombings, and the rest of the country suffered terribly at the hands of its invaders. The Dutch operated one of the most effective underground movements in Europe, which became an important factor in the liberation in 1945. Among those murdered in the Nazi terror was a teenage girl who came to symbolize many other victims of the Holocaust: Anne Frank (1929–45).

In the 1960s, Amsterdam was a hotbed of political and cultural radicalism. Hippies trailing clouds of marijuana smoke took over the Dam and camped out in the Vondelpark and in front of Centraal Station. Radical political activity, which began with "happenings" staged by a group known as the Provos, continued and intensified. In 1966, the Provos were behind the protests that disrupted the wedding of Princess Beatrix to German Claus von Amsberg in the Westerkerk; they threw smoke bombs and fighting broke out between protesters and police. The Provos disbanded in 1967, but many of their principles were adopted by the Kabouters (this translates into English as "Green Gnomes," a hardline anarchist group that won several seats on the city council before fading into obscurity).

The Provos and Kabouters had long advocated environmental programs such as prohibiting all motor vehicles from the city. They persuaded authorities to provide 20,000 white-painted bicycles free for citizens' use—this scheme was abandoned when most of the bicycles were stolen, to reappear in freshly painted colors as "private" property. But some of their other ideas very nearly came to fruition. In 1992, Amsterdam's populace voted to create a traffic-free zone in the center city, but this has yet to be realized.

THE LAY OF THE LAND

For all that the Bible says otherwise, the Dutch insist the Creation took 8 days, not 7—on the eighth day they reclaimed their country from the sea with their own hands. "God made the earth," they tell you, "and the Dutch made Holland."

The all-important dikes are designed to hold back the sea and began to evolve as far back as the A.D. 1st century, when the country's earliest inhabitants settled on unprotected coastal wetlands in the northern regions of Friesland and Groningen. These settlers first attempted to defend their land by building huge earthen mounds called *terpen,* on which they constructed their homes during recurring floods. Around the 8th and 9th centuries, they were building proper dikes; by the end of the 13th century, entire coastal regions were protected from the sea by dikes. Today they take the form of great mounds of earth and stone that extend for miles, and indeed, many of the roads you travel on around Amsterdam are built along the tops of dikes.

Around half of the country's land area has been reclaimed from the sea, lakes, and marshes. Some 2,600 sq. km (1,000 sq. miles) of The Netherlands was underwater just 100 years ago. Approximately 25 percent of Holland, an area that holds about two-thirds of its people, lies *below* sea level, protected from flooding only by sand dunes, dikes, and Dutch engineering ingenuity. That Amsterdam itself has not disappeared under the North Sea is largely due to this ingenuity, as most of the city is 5.5m (18 ft.) below sea level, built on piles, and shored up by a complex system of dams, canals, locks, and dykes.

In 1953, devastating North Sea storms broke through the dikes in many places along Holland's southwest coast, flooding significant areas and causing a substantial loss of life and property. To assure greater protection along its coastal areas, The Netherlands embarked upon the long-term Delta Works to seal off the river estuaries with a series of dams in the southwest of the country.

In flat Holland, wind is ever present, so it is not surprising that the Dutch have made use of windmills to do their hard labor, from pumping water off the land to drain polders, to milling grain, and sawing timber. Nowadays you're as likely to see the whirling blades of wind turbines, generating a growing proportion of the nation's electrical power.

Amsterdam still exists, despite worries about global warming and rising sea levels. However, the government is considering bolstering the sea defenses to handle a rogue super-storm, which would be a tenfold increase over the current defense systems. Should holding back the tides turn out to be a lost cause, a possible solution is floating homes. Several hundred are being constructed at the IJburg development east of Amsterdam, on the IJsselmeer's southern shore. Made from timber and aluminum on a base of polystyrene-filled concrete, floating homes might one day keep those ingenious Dutch heads above water.

AMSTERDAM IN THE ARTS
Visual Art

The 17th century was the undisputed Golden Age of Dutch art. During this busy time, artists were blessed with wealthy patrons whose support allowed them free reign for their talents. Art held a cherished place in the hearts of average Dutch citizens, too. The Dutch were particularly fond of pictures that depicted their world: landscapes, seascapes, domestic scenes, portraits, and still lifes. The art of this period remains some of the greatest ever created.

One of the finest landscape painters of all time was **Jacob van Ruysdael** (1628–82), who depicted cornfields, windmills, and forest scenes, along with his famous views of Haarlem. In some of his works, the human figure is very small, and in others it does not appear at all; instead the artist typically devoted two-thirds of the canvas to the vast skies filled with the moody clouds that float over the flat Dutch terrain. Today his works can be seen in many museums, including the Rijksmuseum (p. 92).

Frans Hals (1581–1666), the undisputed leader of the Haarlem School, specialized in portraiture. The relaxed relationship between the artist and his subject in his paintings was a great departure from the formal masks of Renaissance portraits. With the lightness of his brushstrokes, Hals was able to convey an immediacy and intimacy. Visit the Frans Hals Museum (p. 116) in Haarlem to study his techniques.

One of the geniuses of western art was **Rembrandt Harmenszoon van Rijn** (1606–69). This highly prolific and influential artist had a dramatic life filled with commercial success and personal tragedy. Rembrandt was a master at showing the soul and inner life of humankind, in both his portraits and illustrations of biblical stories. His most famous work, the group portrait known as "The Night Watch" (1642), is on view in the Rijksmuseum (p. 92) in Amsterdam.

A spirituality reigns over his self-portraits as well; Rembrandt painted about 60 during his lifetime. His masterly "Self-Portrait with Saskia" shows the artist with his wife during prosperous times and is now back on show in Museum Het Rembrandthuis (p. 84) in Amsterdam—where it was painted ca. 1635—along with others of his paintings and some 250 of his etchings.

Perhaps the best known of the "Little Dutch Masters," who mainly restricted themselves to one genre of painting, such as portraiture, is **Jan Vermeer** (1632–75) of Delft. The main subjects of Vermeer's work are the activities and pleasures of simple home life. Vermeer placed figures at the center of his paintings, and typically used the background space to convey a feeling of stability and serenity. He excelled at reproducing the lighting of his interior scenes; there are fine examples of his work at the Mauritshuis in The Hague (p. 132) and in the Rijksmuseum (p. 92).

If **Vincent van Gogh** (1853–90) had not failed as a missionary in the Borinage mining region of Belgium, he might not have turned to painting and become the greatest Dutch artist of the 19th century. "The Potato Eaters" (1885) was his first masterpiece. This rough, crudely painted work shows a group of peasants gathered around the table for their evening meal after a long day of manual labor. Gone are the traditional beauty and serenity of earlier Dutch genre painting.

In 1888, Vincent traveled to Arles in Provence, where he was dazzled by the Mediterranean sun. His favorite color, yellow, which to him signified love, dominated landscapes such as "Wheatfield with a Reaper" (1889). For the next 2 years, he remained in the south of France, painting at a frenetic pace in between bouts of madness. The Van Gogh Museum in Amsterdam (p. 93) has more than 200 of his paintings.

Before **Piet Mondriaan** (1872–1944) became an originator of De Stijl (or neoplasticism), he painted windmills, cows, and meadows. His Impressionistic masterpiece, "The Red Tree" (1909)—which looks as though it's bursting into flames against a background of blue—marked a turning point in his career. With Theo van Doesburg, Mondriaan began a magazine in 1917 entitled *"De Stijl"* ("The Style") in which he expounded the principles of neoplasticism: a simplification of forms or, in other words, a purified abstraction; an art that would be derived "not from exterior vision but from interior life." The world's leading collection of his work is found in the Gemeentemuseum in The Hague (p. 132).

Architecture

One of Amsterdam's most prominent architectural features is the gable. The landmark town houses and warehouses of the city's old center all have gables and it is easy to judge their age by their shape. Simple triangular, wooden gables came first, and then spout gables (see Keizersgracht 403) with a little point on top were used, mostly on warehouses, in the 14th century. These simply followed the pitch of the roof, but over time, more ornate designs crept in. Step gables were popular in the 17th century (see Brouwersgracht 2 in the Jordaan), and elegant, straight neck gables (see Herengracht 168) adorned with ornamental shoulders appeared between 1640 and 1780. Rounded bell-shaped gables (see Prinsengracht 359) were introduced in the late 17th century and remained popular until the end of the 18th century.

The hook sitting central on most of these gables is called a *hijsbalk* and was used with a rope and pulley system for hauling cumbersome items in and out of houses with steep, narrow staircases. Most of the canalside houses lean a tad forward to prevent loads crashing into the facades.

Hendrick de Keyser (1565–1621), an architect who worked in Amsterdam at the height of the Renaissance, is known for using decorative, playful elements in a way that was practical to the structure. For instance, he combined hard yellow or white sandstone decorative features with soft red brick, creating a visually stimulating multicolored facade. The Westerkerk (p. 90) is probably his finest work. **Philips and Justus Vingboons** were architects and brothers who worked in the Renaissance style; while walking along Herengracht, Keizersgracht, and Prinsengracht, you'll see many of their buildings, including the Bible Museum (p. 88).

Jacob van Campen (1595–1657) built the elaborate **Town Hall** at the Dam, now the Koninklijk Royal Palace (p. 84), and was probably the single most important architect of Amsterdam architecture's classical period.

Around 1665, **Adriaan Dortsman** (1625–82), best known for his classic restrained Dutch style, began building homes with balconies and attics, leaving off the pilasters and festoons that adorned earlier facades; see his designs at the Museum van Loon (p. 89) on Keizersgracht.

A further cultural flowering took place in the late 19th century, which saw the construction of Centraal Station (p. 82) and the Rijksmuseum (p. 92) by **P.J.H. Cuypers** in neo-revivalist style as well as **A.L. van Gendt**'s neo-classical splendor of the Concertgebouw (p. 110), still the city's finest concert hall. Between 1900 and 1940, Amsterdam architects purveyed many different styles of building. **H.P. Berlage** is regarded as one of the city's first modern architects, designing the stock exchange (p. 82) and the Gemeentemuseum in The Hague (p. 132). He paved the way for the Amsterdam School of architects, whose follower **Michael de Klerk** designed Museum Het Schip (p. 98), a massive yet fluid building featuring decorations such as stained glass, wrought iron, and corner towers.

Today the tradition of producing spectacular architecture continues in Amsterdam with the ever-changing horizons on the IJ waterway; **Science Center NEMO** (p. 96) was designed by Renzo Piano, while the gleaming-white, mantislike **EYE Film Institute** (p. 98) was the first public building to be constructed in Amsterdam Noord, giving a clear indication of where the Amsterdam of the future will be headed.

THE ARTS IN AMSTERDAM

Books

If a single individual may be said to "personify" the Holocaust—a status that is surely an unbearable burden—that person must be Anne Frank. Her diary, compiled as a series of letters addressed "Dear Kitty" and kept for more than 2 years until her arrest on August 4, 1944, has come to symbolize the plight of millions of Jews during the Nazi terror. "The Diary of a Young Girl" (1947) includes photos of Anne and the people she hid with, plus a map of the secret annex in the house on Prinsengracht (p. 88).

For a personal insight into Vincent van Gogh's life and art, read Ken Wilkie's "The van Gogh File: A Journey of Discovery" (1990). What began as a routine magazine assignment in 1972 to coincide with the opening of the Van Gogh Museum became exactly what the book's subtitle indicates: Wilkie followed Van Gogh's trail through the Netherlands, Belgium, England, and France. Along the way, he met some of the last surviving people to have met the artist.

Nicolas Freeling's "Love in Amsterdam" (1962) was the first in his series of Inspector Piet Van der Valk detective novels, and even though it's the Amsterdam of almost a half century ago, the city is easily recognizable, and something of a co-protagonist. Much the same could be said of Alistair MacLean's thriller "Puppet on a Chain" (1969). In 1980 Dutch novelist Cees Nooteboom set his finest work, "Rituals," on the streets of Amsterdam, while Sylvie Matton captures Rembrandt's descent into bankruptcy all too vividly in 1997's "Rembrandt's Whore."

For non-fiction, Simon Schama's "The Embarrassment of Riches: An Interpretation of Dutch Culture in the Golden Age" (1987) lets you inside Amsterdam's greatest period and is simultaneously lighthearted and scholarly. Most of the 700 pages feature works of art that are explained in the text. Schama succeeds in his intention "to map out the moral geography of the Dutch mind, adrift between the fear of deluge and the hope of moral salvage."

Film

Amsterdam-born film director Paul Verhoeven is probably the best-known Dutch filmmaker—although that doesn't mean that Verhoeven's Hollywood films, such as "Basic Instinct," "Robocop," and "Starship Troopers," contain anything inspired by his hometown. Closer to home is his wartime resistance drama "Soldier of Orange" (1977), starring Jeroen Krabbé and Rutger Hauer. Another wartime drama, "The Assault," won the Oscar for Best Foreign Language Film in 1986.

Amsterdam starred as the darkly atmospheric setting of the underworld in the thriller "Puppet on a Chain" (1972), based on the novel of the same name by Scottish writer Alistair MacLean—which contained a memorable chase sequence on the canals. And it played a supporting role in the James Bond movie "Diamonds Are Forever" (1971). In "Girl with a Pearl Earring" (2003), Scarlett Johansson and Colin Firth star in an appropriately moody interpretation of the "backstory" to the Vermeer painting, set and partly filmed in Delft.

Should you want to dine on a movie set, head for Chinese restaurant Nam Kee in Amsterdam (p. 72), which played a notable role in the Dutch red-hot romance flick *"De Oesters van Nam Kee"* ("The Oysters of Nam Kee"; 2002). Amsterdam also features in crime movies "Ocean's Twelve" starring George Clooney and "Layer Cake," starring a soon-to-be James Bond Daniel Craig—both were made in 2004.

Music

About the only well-known song in English to feature Holland in a starring role is "Tulips from Amsterdam" (1956), which was originally written in German. This dose of concentrated saccharine keeps the unlikely company of pot-smoking, sex-tourism, and gay parades as a popular image of the city. Kids might likely be more familiar with "A Windmill in Old Amsterdam" (1965), which tells a heart-warming tale of "a little mouse with clogs on, going clip-clippety-clop on the stair."

Amsterdam has been immortalized in a few pop songs, however, including "Ballad of John and Yoko" by John Lennon following the pair's notorious "bed-in" at the Amsterdam Hilton in 1969. And Neil Finn of New Zealand band Crowded House wrote the following lyrics after spending a wasted weekend in the coffeehouses of Amsterdam: "Lying in the streets of Amsterdam/Nearly fell under a tram," which are hardly going to win any prizes for sentiment but probably echo the experiences of many a newbie visitor to Amsterdam.

EATING & DRINKING IN AMSTERDAM

Dutch national dishes tend to be of the ungarnished, hearty, wholesome variety—solid, stick-to-your-ribs stuff. A perfect example is *erwtensoep,* a thick pea soup cooked with ham or sausage that provides inner warmth against damp Dutch winters and is filling enough to be a meal by itself. Similarly, *hutspot,* a potato-based "hotchpotch," or stew, is no-nonsense nourishment to which *klapstuk* (lean beef) is sometimes added.

Seafood, as you might imagine in this traditionally seafaring country, is always fresh and well prepared. Fried sole, oysters, and mussels from Zeeland, and herring (fresh in early June, pickled other months) are most common. In fact, if you happen to be in Amsterdam for the beginning of the herring season, it's an absolute obligation—at least once—to interrupt your sidewalk strolls to buy a "green" herring from a pushcart such as Stubbe's Haring (p. 72). The Dutch are uncommonly fond of *paling* (an oily freshwater eel) and Zeeland oysters and mussels known as *Zeeuwse oesters* and *Zeeuwse mosselen,* from September to March.

At lunchtime you're likely to find yourself munching on *broodjes,* small buttered rolls usually filled with ham and cheese or beef, although a *broodje gezond* (healthy sandwich) with cheese and vegetables is a good choice for vegetarians. Not to be missed are the delicious, filling pancakes called *pannenkoeken,* often eaten as a savory dish with bacon and cheese. *Poffertjes* are a sweet, lighter, penny-size version that are especially good topped with apples, jam, or syrup. Dutch *gebak* (pastries) are fresh, varied, and inexpensive; and you will notice the Dutch sitting down for a *koffie* and one of these delicious *hapjes* (small snacks, or literally, "bites") throughout the day.

The popular Indonesian *rijsttafel* (rice table), a feast of 15 to 30 small portions of different dishes eaten with plain rice, has been a national favorite ever since it arrived in the 17th century. If you've never experienced this mini-feast, it should definitely be on your "must-eat" list for Holland—the basic idea behind the *rijsttafel* is to sample a wide variety of complementary flavors, textures, and temperatures: savory and sweet, spicy and mild.

For authentic Dutch dishes, look for the NEERLANDS DIS sign, which identifies restaurants specializing in the native cuisine. You'll find numerous moderately priced restaurants and brown cafes (p. 72), which are cozy social centers with simple but tasty food, sometimes served outside on sidewalk tables in good weather. Sidewalk vendors, with fresh herring and the ubiquitous *broodjes* or other light specialties, are popular as well.

Although there's no such thing as a free lunch, there is the next best thing—a *dagschotel* (plate of the day) and *dagmenu* (menu of the day). Another way to combat escalating dinner tabs is to take advantage of the tourist menu offered by many restaurants. And these days, Amsterdam is increasingly a destination for fine dining, with Michelin-starred restaurants such as **Bord'Eau** (p. 61), **La Rive** (p. 78), and **Vinkeles** (p. 73) as well as stylish, mid-priced eateries.

Beer, Gin & Wine

What to drink when in Amsterdam? Beer, for one thing. As you make the rounds of the brown cafes, you can get regular brands such as Heineken, Grolsch, or Amstel, or you could try something different such as *witte* (white) beer, which is sweeter than *pils,* the regular beer.

Also popular is the potent native ginlike liqueur known as *jenever* (the name comes from the Dutch word for "juniper"), a fiery, colorless spirit distilled from grain or malt, served ice cold and drunk neat—without any mixer, or even ice. In the 16th century, it was the drink of the masses in Holland, as the drinking water was filthy and the *jenever* was believed to have medicinal properties. Dutch brands include Jonge Wees, Bols, Rembrandt Korewijn, and De Kuyper.

There are even some Dutch wines, perfectly respectable although produced in modest quantities by 150 wineries around the country. Total annual production is some 800,000 liters (211,000 U.S. gallons). Some of the finest Dutch wines include the sparkling Riesling and Gewurztraminers of Domein de Linie (www.delinie.nl) or the pinots of Hoeve Nekum (www.hoevenekum.nl), both near Maastricht.

BELGIUM TODAY

After a long history of occupation by foreign powers, Belgium has emerged as the elected heart of Europe, the country where European nations come together to rule over their divided continent in precarious harmony. Brussels hosts the headquarters of both the European Union and NATO and is now home to the world's largest concentration of international diplomats. However, all is not well in the kingdom of Belgium.

Modern Belgium is a parliamentary democracy under a constitutional monarch, King Philippe, who ascended the throne on July 21, 2013, after his father King Albert II abdicated. Philippe is married to Queen Mathilde and they have four children. The government exists in a more-or-less permanent state of crisis due to the cultural and linguistic divide that has torn away at the heart of Belgium since the late 19th century. Ambitious regional politicians, particularly in Flanders, often push the country to the brink of dissolution; many believe that partition and subsequent accession of French-speaking Wallonia to France and Flemish- or Dutch-speaking Flanders to The Netherlands may be the only way to solve the issue.

In 2010 Flanders once again threatened to break away and form its own government, in light of inconclusive election results and Wallonia's current weaker economic status.

Although the country survived that crises intact, 4 years later there are more and more signs that Flemish and Walloon are leading increasingly disparate lives; universities in Brussels that once were open to both communities are now segregated and the denizens of Flanders towns like Bruges, Mechelen (p. 229), and Lennik firmly see themselves as Flemish, not Belgian.

For a geographical understanding of Belgium's two ethnic regions, Flemish- or Dutch-speaking Vlaanderen (Flanders) and French-speaking Wallonie (Wallonia), draw an imaginary east-west line across the country just south of the capital city Brussels, which exists as an urban island between the two bickering factions. North of the line is Flanders, where you find the medieval cities of Bruges, Ghent, and Antwerp, and Belgium's North Sea coastline. South of the line is Wallonia.

It has been said that Belgium suffers severely from linguistic indigestion. The inhabitants of Flanders speak four variations of *Vlaams* (Flemish), two of which are considered as dialects of Dutch and two as separate, but closely connected, languages. Flanders inhabitants always claim to speak Flemish, never Dutch, although Dutch is the official language of the region. The citizens of Wallonia speak French, and a minority still speak an old Walloon dialect of French. In Brussels the two languages mingle, often to ridiculous effect (the police have both POLICE and POLITIE emblazoned on the back of their uniforms) but French has the upper hand. So strong is the feeling for each language in its own region that, along the line where they meet, it's not unusual for French to be the daily tongue on one side of a street and Flemish on the other. Throughout the country, road signs acknowledge both languages by giving multiple versions of the same place name—Brussel/Bruxelles or Brugge/Bruges, for example. There's even a small area in eastern Belgium where German is spoken. Belgium, then, has not one but three official languages: Dutch, French, and German.

In short, far from being a homogeneous, harmonious people with one strong national identity, Belgians take considerable pride in their individualistic attributes.

The vast majority of Belgians are Catholic, though there's more than a smattering of Protestants, a small Jewish community, and a rising proportion of immigrant Muslims and their locally born children. Down the centuries, Belgians—nobles and peasants alike—have proclaimed their Christian faith by way of impressive cathedrals, churches, paintings, and holy processions. The tradition continues today, and can be seen at Bruges's centuries-old Procession of the Holy Blood (p. 182), held every year in May.

Folklore still plays a large part in Belgium's national daily life, with local myths giving rise to some of the country's most colorful pageants and festivals, such as Ypres's **Festival of the Cats,** Bruges's **Pageant of the Golden Tree,** and the stately **Ommegang** in Brussels.

Undoubtedly, Belgians have a finely tuned appreciation for the good things in life; when expectations are met, watch Belgian eyes light up. Appreciation then moves very close to reverence, whether inspired by a great artistic masterpiece, a homemade mayonnaise of just the right lightness, or one of Belgium's many native beers (p. 169).

LOOKING BACK AT BELGIUM

Julius Caesar first marched his Roman legions against the ancient Belgae tribes in 58 B.C. For nearly 5 centuries thereafter, Belgium was shielded from the barbarians by the great Roman defense line on the Rhine.

From the beginning of the 5th century, Roman rule gave way to the Franks. In 800, Charlemagne, king of the Franks and ruler of the Carolingian Empire, instituted an era of agricultural reform, setting up local rulers known as counts who rose up to seize more power after Charlemagne's death. In 843, Charlemagne's grandsons signed the Treaty of Verdun, which split French-allied (but Dutch-speaking) Flanders in the north from the southern (French-speaking) Walloon provinces.

A Flemish mercenary known as Baldwin Iron-Arm rose to become the first Count of Flanders in 862 upon his marriage to Judith, the daughter of the King of West Francia; his house eventually ruled over a domain that included the Low Countries and lands as far south as the Scheldt (Escaut) in France. Baldwin was responsible for repelling the constant Viking incursions of the time. Meanwhile, powerful prince-bishops controlled most of Wallonia from their seat in Liège.

Flanders Rising

As Flanders grew larger and stronger, its cities thrived and its citizens wrested more and more self-governing powers. Bruges emerged as a leading center of European trade; its monopoly on English cloth attracted bankers and financiers from Germany and Lombardy. Ghent and Ypres (Ieper) also prospered in the wool trade. Powerful trade and manufacturing guilds emerged and erected splendid edifices as their ego-satisfying headquarters.

As medieval towns emerged as wealthy city-states, the once-mighty counts of Flanders steadily lost their power and in 1297, France's King Philip IV attempted to annex Flanders. However, he had not reckoned on the stubborn resistance of Flemish common folk. Led by Jan Breydel, a lowly weaver, and Pieter de Coninck, a butcher, they rallied to face the heavily armored French military; the decisive battle took place in 1302 in the fields surrounding Kortrijk in western Flanders. When it was over, victorious Flemish artisans scoured the bloody battlefield, triumphantly gathering hundreds of golden spurs from slain French knights. Their victory at the Battle of the Golden Spurs is celebrated by the Flemish to this day on July 11th.

The Burgundian Era

Philip the Good, who was Duke of Burgundy, gained control of virtually all the Low Countries in the mid-1400s, His progeny, through a series of dynastic marriages, consolidated their holdings into a single Burgundian "Netherlands," or Low Countries. Brussels, Antwerp, Mechelen, and Leuven attained new prominence as centers of trade, commerce, and the arts.

This era was one of immense wealth, much of which was poured into the fine public buildings, impressive mansions, and soaring Gothic cathedrals that survive in Brussels and Bruges to this day. Wealthy patrons made possible the brilliant works of Flemish artists such as Jan van Eyck, Hieronymus Bosch, Rogier van der Weyden, and German-born Hans Memling; Flemish opulence became a byword around Europe.

By the end of the 1400s, however, Charles the Bold, last of the dukes of Burgundy, had lost to the French king on the field of battle, and once more French royalty turned a covetous eye on the Low Countries. To French consternation, Mary of Burgundy, the duke's heir, married Maximilian of Austria and the provinces became part of the mighty Austrian Habsburg Empire.

A grandson of that union, Charles V, born in Ghent and reared in Mechelen, presided for 40 years over most of Europe, including Spain and its New World possessions. But he was beset by the Protestant Reformation, which created dissension among the once solidly Catholic populace. It all proved too much for the great monarch, and in 1556 he abdicated in favor of his son, Philip II of Spain.

The Spanish Invasion

Philip II ascended to power in an impressive ceremony at Coudenberg Palace (p. 164) in Brussels in 1555. An ardent Catholic who spoke neither Dutch nor French, he brought the infamous instruments of the Inquisition to bear on an increasingly Protestant—and increasingly rebellious—Low Countries population. The response from his Protestant subjects was violent: For a month in 1566, they went on a rampage of destruction; the *Beeldenstorm* (Iconoclastic Fury) saw churches pillaged, religious statues smashed, and other religious works of art burned.

An angry Philip II ordered the Duke of Alba (p. 18) to lead 10,000 Spanish troops in a wave of retaliatory strikes. The atrocities Alba and his Council of Blood committed as he swept through what was then known as the Spanish Netherlands are legendary. He was merciless—when the Catholic counts of Egmont and Hornes tried to intercede with Philip, he put them under arrest for 6 months, and then had them publicly beheaded on the Grand-Place (p. 158) in Brussels.

Instead of submission, this sort of intimidation gave rise to a brutal conflict that lasted from 1568 to 1648. Led by William of Orange (p. 18) and other nobles who raised private armies, the Protestants fought on doggedly until independence was finally achieved for the seven undefeated provinces in the north (p. 18), which became the fledgling country of The Netherlands. Those in the south remained under the thumb of Spain and gradually returned to the Catholic Church.

An Independent State

In 1795, Belgium wound up once more under the rule of France. It was not until Napoleon Bonaparte's crushing defeat at Waterloo (p. 20)—just miles from Brussels—that Belgians began to think of independence as a real possibility. Its time had not yet come, however; under the post-Napoleonic Congress of Vienna (1814–15) Belgium was once more united with the provinces of Holland. The Dutch soon learned that governing unruly Belgium was more than they had bargained for and the 1830 rebellion in Brussels was the last straw. A provisional Belgian government was formed with an elected National Congress. On July 21, 1831, Belgium officially became a constitutional monarchy when a German prince, Leopold of Saxe-Coburg and Gotha, became king.

The new country set about developing its coal and iron natural resources, and its textile, manufacturing, and shipbuilding industries. The country was hardly unified by this process, however, for most of the natural resources were to be found in the French-speaking Walloon region, where prosperity grew much more rapidly than in Flanders. The Flemish, while happy to be freed from the rule of their Dutch neighbors, resented the greater influence of their French-speaking compatriots. And here the present-day dissension has its roots.

War & Peace

It took another invasion to bring a semblance of unity. When German forces swept over the country in 1914, the Belgians mounted a defense that made them heroes of World War I—even though parts of the Flemish population openly collaborated with the enemy, hailing them as liberators from Walloon domination.

With the coming of peace, Belgium found its southern coal, iron, and manufacturing industries reeling, while the northern Flemish regions were moving steadily ahead by developing light industry, especially around Antwerp. Advanced agricultural methods yielded greater productivity and higher profits for Flemish farmers. By the end of the

1930s, the Flemish population outnumbered the Walloons by a big enough majority to install their beloved language as the official voice of education, justice, and civil administration in Flanders.

With the outbreak of World War II, Belgium was once more overrun by German forces. King Leopold III decided to surrender to the invaders, remain in Belgium, and try to soften the harsh effects of occupation. The Belgian Resistance was among the most determined and successful of the underground organizations that fought against Nazi occupation in Europe. On the other side, Flemish and Walloon quislings formed separate Waffen-SS formations that fought for the Nazis in Russia. By the war's end, the king was imprisoned in Germany and a regent was appointed as head of state. His controversial decision to surrender led to bitter debate when he returned to the throne in 1950, and in 1951 he stepped down in favor of his son, Baudouin.

Unity & Disunity

During King Baudouin's 42 years on the throne, much progress was made in achieving harmony among Belgium's linguistically and culturally diverse population. In the 1970s, efforts were made to grant increasing autonomy to the Flemish and Walloons in the areas where each was predominant, and to apportion power to each group within the national government and the political parties. Finally, in 1993, the constitution was amended to create a federal state, made up of the autonomous regions of Flanders and Wallonia (and its semiautonomous German-speaking community), together with the bilingual city of Brussels.

Baudouin died in 1993, removing one of the pillars of unity. His successor, his brother Albert II, won respect for his conscientious efforts towards unity but did not achieve the same personal connection with the people. How King Philippe will fare is yet to be seen.

BELGIUM & THE ARTS

Visual Arts

Despite its small geographic size, Belgium has exerted a significant influence on Western art. The works of Bosch, Brueghel, Rubens, Van Dyck, Van Eyck, and Magritte represent only a fraction of the treasures you see gracing the walls of the notable art museums in Brussels, Bruges, Ghent, and Antwerp.

The golden age of Flemish painting occurred in the 1400s, a century dominated by the so-called Flemish Primitives, whose work was almost always religious in theme, usually commissioned for churches and chapels, and largely lacking in perspective. As the medieval cities of Flanders flourished, more and more princes, wealthy merchants, and prosperous guilds became patrons of the arts.

Art's function was still to praise God and illustrate religious allegory, but **Jan van Eyck** (ca. 1390–1441), one of the earliest Flemish Masters, brought a sharp new perspective to bear on traditional subject matter. His "Adoration of the Mystic Lamb," created with his brother Hubert for Sint-Bavokerk (St. Bavo's Cathedral; see p. 118) in Ghent, incorporates a realistic landscape into its biblical theme. The Primitives sought to mirror reality, to portray both people and nature exactly as they appeared to the human eye, down to the tiniest detail, without classical distortions or embellishments. These artists would work meticulously for months—even years—on a single commission, often painting with a single-haired paintbrush to achieve a painstakingly lifelike quality. Many of their works are on display in the peerless **Groeningemuseum** (p. 196) in Bruges.

The greatest Flemish artist of the 16th century, **Pieter Brueghel the Elder** (ca. 1525–69), lived and worked for many years in Antwerp. From 1520 to 1580, the city was one of the world's busiest ports and banking centers, and it eclipsed Bruges as a center for the arts. Many of the artists working here looked to the Italian Renaissance Masters for their models of perfection. Brueghel, who had studied in Italy, integrated Renaissance influences with the traditional style of his native land. He frequently painted rural and peasant life, as in his "Wedding Procession," on view at the **Musée de la Ville** (p. 164) in Brussels.

In 1563, Brueghel moved to Brussels, where he lived at rue Haute 132. Here his two sons, also artists, were born. **Pieter Brueghel the Younger** (ca. 1564–1637) became known for copying his father's paintings; **Jan Brueghel the Elder** (1568–1625) specialized in decorative paintings of flowers and fruits.

Peter Paul Rubens (1577–1640) was the most influential baroque painter of the early 17th century. The drama in his works, such as "The Raising of the Cross," housed in the Antwerp cathedral, comes from the dynamic, writhing figures in his canvases. His renditions of the female form gave rise to the term "Rubenesque," which describes the voluptuous women who appear in his paintings.

Portraitist **Anthony van Dyck** (1599–1641), one of the most important talents to emerge from Rubens's studio, served as court painter to Charles I of England, although some of his best religious work remains in Belgium, including "The Crucifixion" in **Mechelen Cathedral** (p. 230). More paintings by the great names mentioned above can be seen in the **Musées Royaux des Beaux-Arts de Belgique** (p. 166) in Brussels.

Belgium's influence on the art world is by no means limited to the Old Masters. **James Ensor** (1860–1949) was a late-19th-century pioneer of modern art. One of his most famous works is "The Entry of Christ into Brussels." Ensor developed a broadly expressionistic technique, liberating his use of color from the demands of realism. He took as his subject disturbing, fantastic visions and images.

Surrealism flourished in Belgium, perhaps because of the earlier Flemish artists such as Pieter Brueghel with a penchant for the bizarre and grotesque. **Paul Delvaux** (1897–1989) became famous, but the best known of the Belgian surrealists is unquestionably **René Magritte** (1898–1967). His fantastical images of pipes that are not pipes, and bowler-hatted men who fall like black rain from the skies have become widely recognized images in popular culture. Many of these modern works can be seen in the Musées Royaux des Beaux-Arts (p. 166) in Brussels and will be seen once more in Antwerp's **Koninklijke Museum voor Schone Kunsten** (p. 216) when it reopens in late 2017.

Architecture

Examples of Gothic civic architecture abound in Belgium. The great ecclesiastical examples are **St. Michael's Cathedral** in Brussels (p. 162), in which the choir is the earliest Gothic work in Belgium, and the churches of **Our Lady** in Mechelen and **Sint-Bavokerk** in Ghent (p. 118). The **Onze-Lieve-Vrouwekathedraal** (Cathedral of Our Lady; see p. 209) in Antwerp is perhaps the most imposing example of late Gothic; it was begun in 1352 at the east end and the nave was completed in 1474.

Among the finest examples of commercial Gothic architecture are the Cloth Hall at Ypres (built 1200–1304), now beautifully converted in to the heart-rending **In Flanders Fields Museum,** the **Cloth Hall** in Mechelen, the **Butchers Guildhall** in Ghent, and the **Butchers Guildhall** in Antwerp (p. 208). Gothic style remained dominant until the early 16th century, when Renaissance decorative elements began to appear.

Around the turn of the 20th century, Belgium produced one of the greatest exponents of the new Art Nouveau style of architecture and interior design, the prime materials of which were glass and iron, worked with decorative curved lines and floral and geometric motifs. The work of **Victor Horta** (1861–1947) can be seen throughout Brussels and especially at his former home in the suburbs, now the **Musée Horta** (p. 169).

BELGIUM IN POPULAR CULTURE

Books

Belgium's most prolific man of letters—indeed, one of the most prolific authors of all time—is **Georges Simenon** (1903–89), whose prodigious output very nearly defies belief. The Liège-born author wrote some 200 novels and 150 novellas, along with other works from autobiographical books to magazine and newspaper articles, and still found time to produce dozens more novels under a variety of pseudonyms. He is undoubtedly best known for the 75 novels and dozens of short stories in the Inspector Maigret detective series, most of them set in Paris.

The two best-known Belgian novels would likely be *"Het Verdriet van België"* (**"The Sorrow of Belgium"**; 1983) by Hugo Claus, which deals with the Nazi occupation; and *"b-la-Morte"* (**"Dead Bruges"**; 1892) by Georges Rodenbach, which deals with themes of love and loss, but is perhaps best known for having put Bruges on the European map as a tourist destination.

Brussels-born author **Marguerite Yourcenar** (1903–88), the first woman to be elected to the French Academy, and who spent a considerable part of her life living in Maine, wrote "Alexis" (1929), "Memoirs of Hadrian" (1951), and "The Abyss/Zeno of Bruges" (1976) and more recently, English writer **Tracy Chevalier** set her 2004 historical novel in the tapestry workshops of Brussels.

Comics

Belgium produces 30 million comic-strip books annually, and exports 75 percent of them. The **Tintin** books alone have sold more than 200 million copies since the youthful adventurer and his little terrier Snowy first appeared in 1927, created by Georges Remi, who is better known to his readers as Hergé (the initials of his name reversed and written as they would be pronounced in French). You'll find examples of his work at the **Centre Belge de la Bande Dessiné** (p. 163) as well as **his eponymous museum** in the Brussels suburbs (p. 172).

Lucky Luke, the cowpoke who beats his shadow to the draw and whose horse, Jolly Jumper, plays a mean hand at poker, stars in more than 80 adventures—each of which ends with the hero riding into the sunset singing "I'm a poor lonesome cowboy"; it has been adapted for television and computer games. His creator, illustrator Morris (real name Maurice de Bevere), a native of Kortrijk, died at age 77 in 2001.

Film

Belgium is not one of the world's greatest movie powers. It's a rare Belgian film that's seen by more than about 10 people outside of the cast, the crew, and their relatives. Then again, Belgium has given the world a Hollywood star in **Jean-Claude "the Muscles from Brussels" Van Damme,** and **Agatha Christie**'s ageless fictional detective Hercule Poirot has also often graced the silver screen.

Dominique Deruddere's "Everybody Famous" was nominated in 2000 for the Academy Award for Best Foreign Language Film, but it didn't win. However, Bruges hit the jackpot alongside Colin Farrell, Brendan Gleeson, Ralph Fiennes, and Clémence Poésy in the 2008 international hit movie "In Bruges," about two contract killers who take refuge in the city when a hit goes wrong.

Several Belgian comic-strip characters have received the Hollywood treatment; **"The Smurfs Movie,"** featuring the irritating little blue creatures brought to life by Belgian cartoonist Peyo, was such a hit in 2011 that a sequel was released in 2013. Plans for a third Smurf movie have mercifully been shelved. Steven Spielberg made his first foray into animation in 2011 with **"The Adventures of Tintin: Secrets of the Unicorn,"** based on three of the Tintin tales written and illustrated by Belgian cartoonist Hergé (p. 172). It made over US$370 million worldwide and a further Tintin movie directed by Peter "The Hobbit" Jackson has been set for release at Christmas 2015.

Music

If it hadn't been for the Belgian designer of musical instruments **Adolphe Sax** (1814–94), there would be no saxophone—and then where would jazz be today? Probably missing the legendary Bruxellois jazz harmonica and guitar player **Jean "Toots" Thielemans,** who played theme music for movies such as "Midnight Cowboy" and "Jean de Florette," and is widely credited as the best harmonica player of the 20th century.

But Brussels's most famous musical son is easily the famed singer/songwriter **Jacques Brel** (1929–78), who brought unequalled passion to his performances of songs of love, comedy, and the low life. Born into an affluent family, Brel composed and sang from an early age but did not cut his first record until 1953. He then hit the big time and toured Europe almost non-stop for the next 13 years. Sentimental and caustic by turn, his songs soon captivated audiences around the world and he went on to enjoy a short movie career in the U.S. and a Broadway hit with his musical "Man of La Mancha." Brel's discography includes *"Quand On n'a que l'Amour"* ("If We Only Have Love") and *"Ne Me Quitte Pas"* ("If You Go Away"). Should you want to dig into Brel's Belgian oeuvre, listen to songs like *"Le Plat Pays," "l'Ostendaise," "Knokke-Le Zoute Tango," "Bruxelles,"* and *"Marieke."*

EATING & DRINKING IN BRUSSELS & BRUGES

Cuisine

Belgian chefs are some of the finest in the world, with Brussels considered one of the gastronomical capitals of Europe. Top Michelin-starred chefs are known for creating a delicious cuisine based on the country's regional traditions and fresh produce, such as asparagus, chicory (endive), and even the humble Brussels sprout.

Belgium is also known for its selection of simple treats like rich, syrupy waffles topped with cream or fresh fruit, which are sold by street vendors throughout the country. In fact, kids will be delirious with joy when eating out in Brussels or Bruges because Belgians dote on their *moules-* or *steak-frites,* available at virtually every restaurant—even when not listed on the menu. *Frites* can accompany almost anything you order in a restaurant and are also sold in paper cones on many street corners; they're at their best topped with lashings of mayonnaise.

Handmade **Belgian chocolates** (known generically as *pralines*) are also world-beaters in the taste stakes, so lethally addictive they ought to be sold with a government health warning. This applies in particular to those cream-filled delicacies made by artisanal **Chocolatier Mary** in Bruges (p. 175) and arty **Marcolini** in Brussels (p. 159), but more widely available brands like Godiva, Wittamer, Nihoul, Neuhaus, and Leonidas are just as enticing. Purchase them loose, in bags weighing from 100 grams, or boxes of 2 kilograms or more.

Seafood anywhere in Belgium is fresh and delicious. Almost every menu lists *tomates aux crevettes* (tomatoes stuffed with tiny, delicately sweet North Sea shrimp and light, homemade mayonnaise) and *moules* (mussels) are a specialty in Brussels, Bruges, and Antwerp. Ironically, Belgian mussels actually come from Zeeland in The Netherlands and may, in fact, be the only Dutch products Belgians will admit to being any good. *Homard* (lobster) comes in a range of dishes and in Brussels the garish concentration of restaurants along rue des Bouchers feature them in just about every guise you can imagine as part of vast seafood platters served on ice and encompassing crab, giant langoustines, clams, and oysters.

Don't miss the heavenly creation that is écrevisses à la liègeoise (crayfish in a rich butter, cream, and white-wine sauce), and eel, often served in a grass-green sauce, is popular in both Flanders (where it's called *paling in 't groen*) and Wallonia (*anguilles au vert*). One famous Flemish dish you'll see on almost every menu, particularly in Ghent, is the heartwarming souplike stew *waterzooï,* a seasoned, creamy mixture of chicken or fish with vegetables.

Native specialties also include *jambon d'Ardenne* (ham from the hills and valleys of the Ardennes to the south of Brussels) and savory *boudins* (succulent sausages mixed with herbs) from pigs raised on organic farms, and piles of mussels served in many different manners. A special treat awaits visitors in May and June in the form of fresh (and expensive) asparagus, and from October to March a seasonal treat is chicory, known as *endive/witloof* in Belgium.

Most Belgian restaurants offer both a *plat du jour/dagschotel* (dish of the day) and a good-value two- or three-course menu at lunchtime as well as in the evening. No matter where you eat, service will be professional (although sometimes very perfunctory in Brussels tourist haunts) but not necessarily speedy. Belgians don't just eat; they savor each course—so if you're in a hurry, you're better off heading for a street vendor or a fast-food dive, but then you'd be missing a rare, gourmet treat.

Drinks

What to drink with all those tasty dishes? You're in Belgium, so drink beer. Belgium is justly famous for its **brewing tradition,** and this tiny country has more than 100 breweries producing around 450 different brands. The majority are local beers, specialties of a region, city, town, or village. Some famous pilsners are Stella Artois, Jupiler, Maes, Primus, and Eupener; ales to look out for include Duvel, De Koninck, and Kwak. Hoegaarden is a well-known wheat beer. Unique to the country are lambic beers (beer produced by spontaneous fermentation and brewed only in Brussels and the surrounding area), such as *faro* (a lambic sweetened with sugar), *kriek* (a fruit lambic made with cherries), and *gueuze* (a blend of lambics). Then there are the heavenly tasting beers brewed by the six Trappist breweries left in the land: Chimay, Orval, Rochefort, Achel, Westmalle, and Westvleteren.

Each local beer has a distinct bottle and shape of glass, which is why you can instantly tell what everyone is drinking in a Belgian bar. Needless to say, with so many choices, it may take quite a bit of sampling to find a firm favorite.

For a *digestif,* you might try the ginlike liqueur (p. 72) known in Flanders as *jenever* (or, colloquially, as *witteke*), and in Wallonia as *genièvre* (colloquially as *pèkèt*); it's a potent spirit served in glasses little bigger than a thimble. Belgium's 70 *jenever* **distilleries** produce around 270 varieties, some flavored with juniper, coriander, or other herbs and spices. Among notable brands are Filliers Oude Graanjenever, De Poldenaar Oude Antwerpsche, Heinrich Pèkèt de la Piconette, Sint-Pol, and van Damme. *Jenever* in a stone bottle makes an ideal gift.

In recent decades, a few Belgian **vineyards** have appeared, reversing a loss that began with the onset of the Little Ice Age in the 15th century, which saw harsh winters causing long freezes and destroying an agriculture that had existed since Roman times. Most of the wineries, and five out of the seven officially recognized Belgian geographical wine regions, are in Flanders. Total annual output is less than 200,000 liters (53,000 U.S. gallons), which is not even a quarter of neighboring Holland's production. Among the country's best labels are those of Wijnkasteel Genoels-Elderen (www.wijnkasteel.com), northeast of Tongeren, and Château Bon Baron (www.chateaubonbaron.com), in the Meuse River valley between Dinant and Namur; both wineries are open for tours and tastings.

WHEN TO VISIT

Amsterdam, Brussels, and Bruges are fast-becoming all-year-around destinations with packed itineraries of festivals and public events to entice the visitor even throughout winter. Although clement weather can never be guaranteed in this little corner of northern Europe, summers are generally warm enough for T-shirts and shorts, and winters, while a mite damp from time to time, are rarely bitterly cold. All three cities witness an influx of tourist between April and September, when the weather is on its best behavior and little can beat settling down into an *al fresco* cafe to watch the world slip unhurriedly by. Miniscule Bruges, in particular, can feel swamped with visitors during the peak months of June and July, so if you would rather have the place (relatively) to yourself, plan your visit for spring or early fall.

Amsterdam Average Temperatures & Rainfall

	JAN	FEB	MAR	APR	MAY	JUNE	JULY	AUG	SEPT	OCT	NOV	DEC
HIGH (°F)	39	41	47	51	60	67	69	69	66	58	47	40
LOW (°F)	31	31	33	38	45	50	53	53	50	47	38	34
HIGH (°C)	7	8	9	11	16	19	20	20	18	14	9	7
LOW (°C)	0	0	1	2	8	10	11	11	10	8	3	0
RAIN (IN.)	3	1.5	2.8	1.5	2	3	3	2.5	3.3	3.5	3.8	3.1

Brussels & Bruges Average Temperatures & Rainfall

	JAN	FEB	MAR	APR	MAY	JUNE	JULY	AUG	SEPT	OCT	NOV	DEC
HIGH (°F)	40	42	50	58	65	70	70	70	69	60	48	40
LOW (°F)	30	31	37	40	44	50	52	52	50	45	38	31
HIGH (°C)	5	7	10	14	19	21	21	21	20	16	9	6
LOW (°C)	−1	0	1	6	8	10	11	11	10	8	3	0
RAIN (IN.)	3.6	3.1	2	2.5	1.9	2.8	4.1	3.6	3.2	3.9	3	3.1

Amsterdam & Beyond Calendar of Events

JANUARY

New Year. This celebration is wild and not always wonderful. Youthful spirits celebrate the New Year with firecrackers, which they throw at the feet of passersby. This keeps hospital emergency rooms busy. January 1.

International Film Festival, Rotterdam. More than 300 indie films are screened at theaters around town. Contact ℭ **010/890-9090;** www.filmfestivalrotterdam.com. Late January.

FEBRUARY

ABN AMRO World Tennis Tournament, Rotterdam. The world's top tennis players converge on the port city for this ATP Tour event. Contact **Ahoy Rotterdam** (ℭ **010/293-3300;** www.abnamrowtt.nl). Second week in February.

MARCH

Windmill Days, Zaanse Schans. All five working windmills (out of eight windmills in total) are open to the public at this recreated old village and open-air museum in the Zanstreek, just north of Amsterdam. Contact **Center Zaans Schans** (ℭ **075/681-0000;** www.dezaanseschans.nl). March through October.

Opening of Keukenhof Gardens ★★★, Lisse. The greatest flower show on earth blooms with a spectacular display of tulips and narcissi, daffodils and hyacinths, bluebells, crocuses, lilies, amaryllis, and many other flowers at this 32-hectare (79 acres) garden in the heart of the bulb country. Nearly eight million bulbs are planted every year. Contact **Keukenhof** (ℭ **0252/465-555;** www.keukenhof.nl). March to mid-May.

APRIL

Museumweekend. A weekend during which most museums in the Netherlands offer free or reduced admission and have special exhibits. Contact **Museumweekend** (ℭ **020/551-8910;** www.museumweekend.nl). Early April.

Bloemencorso van de Bollenstreek (Bulb District Flower Parade) ★★. Floats dressed to a different floral theme each year parade from Noordwijk through Sassenheim, Lisse, and Bennebroek to Haarlem. Contact **Postbus 115** (ℭ **0252/428-237;** www.bloemencorso-bollenstreek.nl). Mid-April.

Koningsdag (King's Day) ★★★. Countrywide celebration honoring the King's official birthday, with parades, street fairs, flea markets, and raucous street entertainment. Throughout The Netherlands, but best in Amsterdam. April 27.

MAY

Bevrijdingsdag (Liberation Day). Commemorates the end of World War II and Holland's liberation from Nazi occupation. Celebrated throughout the country, but best in Amsterdam. May 5.

National Windmill Days. Around two-thirds of the country's almost 1,000 working windmills spin their sails and are open to the public. Contact **De Hollandsche Molen** (ℭ **020/623-8703;** www.molens.nl). Second weekend in May.

Vondelpark Openluchttheater (Open Air Theatre). Runs right through the summer with weekend programs of rock and pop concerts, stand-up, drama, and dance. Contact **Stichting Vondelpark Openluchttheater** (ℭ **020/428-3360;** www.openluchttheater.nl). May through end of August.

JUNE

Holland Festival. The city's big cultural buffet of music, opera, theater, film, and dance. The schedule includes all the major Amsterdam venues plus international companies and soloists. Contact **Holland Festival** (ℭ **020/788-2100;** www.hollandfestival.nl). Throughout June.

Vlaggetjesdag (Flag Day), Scheveningen. The fishing fleet opens the herring season with a race to bring the first *Hollandse Nieuwe* herring back to port (the first barrel is auctioned for charity). Contact **Stichting Vlaggetjesdag Scheveningen** (ℭ **070/307-2900;** www.vlaggetjesdag.com). Mid-June.

Amsterdam Roots Festival. This festival features music and dance from around the world, along with workshops, films, and exhibits. One part is the open-air **Oosterpark Festival,** a multicultural feast of song and dance held in Amsterdam-Oost (East). Contact **Amsterdam Roots Festival;** www. amsterdamroots.nl). Mid-June.

Open Gardens Days. If you wonder what the fancy gardens behind the gables of some of Amsterdam's Canal Ring houses-turned-museums look like, this is your chance to find out. Six of the best are open to the public for 3 days. Contact **Grachten Musea** (✆ **020/320-3660;** www.grachten musea.nl or www.opengardendays.nl). Third week in June.

JULY

Over Het IJ Festival. Performers stage avant-garde theater, music, and dance in Amsterdam-Noord beside the IJ channel, at the old NDSM-Wharf, TT Neveritaweg 15. Contact **Over Het IJ Festival** (✆ **020/492-2229;** www.overhetij.nl). July.

North Sea Jazz Festival ★★, Rotterdam. One of the world's leading gatherings of top international jazz and blues musicians unfolds over 3 concert-packed days at the city's giant Ahoy venue. Last-minute tickets are scarce, so book as far ahead as possible. Contact **Ahoy Rotterdam** (www.north seajazz.com). July.

AUGUST

Amsterdam Gay Pride ★. This is a big event in Europe's most gay-friendly city. As many as 150,000 people turn out to watch the Boat Parade's display of 100 or so outrageously decorated boats cruising the canals. In addition, there are street discos, open-air theater, a sports program, and a film festival. Contact **Amsterdam Gay Pride** (www.amsterdamgaypride.nl). Early August.

Grachtenfestival (Canal Festival) ★★. A 10-day festival of classical music, on a different theme each year, plays at intimate and elegant venues along the city's canals and at the Muziekgebouw aan 't IJ. There's always a performance or two for children. The festival culminates in the exuberant

Prinsengracht Concert, which plays on a pontoon in front of the Hotel Pulitzer. Contact **Stichting Grachtenfestival** (✆ **020/421-4542;** www.grachtenfestival. nl). Mid-August.

Festival Oude Muziek (Festival of Early Music), Utrecht. Concerts of music from the Middle Ages to the Romantic era. Contact **Stichting Organisatie Oude Muziek** (✆ **030/232-9000;** www.oudemuziek.nl). Late August through early September.

Uitmarkt. Amsterdam previews its cultural season with this open market of information and free performances in Leidseplain and Museumplein, theaters, and concert halls. The shows run the gamut of music, opera, dance, theater, and cabaret. Contact **Uitmarkt** (✆ **020/626-2656;** www.uitmarkt.nl). Last weekend in August.

SEPTEMBER

Open Monumentendag (Open Monument Day). Get to see historic buildings and monuments in the major towns around the country that usually are not open to the public, and get in free. Contact **Open Monumentendag** (✆ **020/422-2118;** www. openmonumentendag.nl). Mid-September.

State Opening of Parliament ★, The Hague. On Prinsjesdag (Princes' Day), King Willem-Alexander rides in a splendid gold coach to the Ridderzaal in The Hague to open the legislative session by delivering the Speech from the Throne. Contact **Gemeente Den Haag** (✆ **070/353-3000;** www.denhaag.nl). Third Tuesday in September.

OCTOBER

Leidens Ontzet (Relief of Leiden). Procession commemorating the anniversary of the raising of the 1574 Spanish siege of Leiden. *Haring en witte brood* (herring and white bread) are distributed, just as the piratelike band of "Sea Beggars" did after helping drive the Spaniards away. Contact **Leidens Ontzet Secretariaat** (✆ **071/532-4724;** www.3october.nl/leidens_ontzet). October 3 (Oct 4 when the 3rd is a Sun).

NOVEMBER

Crossing Border, The Hague. Literature, poetry, and music are combined in this

4-day festival. Contact **Crossing Border** (𝄞 070/346-2355; www.crossingborder.nl). Mid-November.

Sinterklaas Arrives. Holland's Santa Claus (St. Nicholas) launches the Christmas season when he sails into Amsterdam, accompanied by black-painted assistants, called Zwarte Piet (Black Peter), who hand out candy to kids. During the next 2 weeks, he makes his way to towns across the country. Contact local tourist offices. Third Saturday in November. He arrives the next day in Amsterdam.

DECEMBER

Amsterdam Light Festival. The center of Amsterdam is illuminated with contemporary light installations. The festival kicks off with a boat parade around the canals. Contact **Amsterdam Light Festival** (𝄞 020/420-2060; www.amsterdamlightfestival.com). Early December through mid-January.

Sinterklaas. St. Nicholas's Eve is the traditional day in Holland for exchanging Christmas gifts. December 5.

Brussels & Bruges Calendar of Events

JANUARY

Brussels Antiques and Fine Arts Fair. The top Belgian antiques dealers and selected dealers from abroad get together to show off their wares in the Tour & Taxis Convention Center on avenue du port. Contact **BRAFA** (𝄞 02/513-4831; www.brafa.be). Last 10 days of January.

FEBRUARY/MARCH

Carnival ★★★, Binche, Hainaut. This is one of Europe's biggest, most colorful street carnivals, worth a day trip. On Shrove Tuesday it's led by a thousand sumptuously costumed Gilles de Binche, whose costumes are apparently modeled on Inca nobles. Contact **Office du Tourisme de Binche** (𝄞 064/33-6727; www.binche.be or www.carnavaldebinche.be).

Beer Festival, Bruges. A weekend of fun sampling some of Bruges's boutique beers. The congenial festival spreads around town. Contact www.brugsbierfestival.be. Mid-February.

MARCH

VW Spring Sessions, all over Belgium. This is a series of concerts celebrating music from around the world, from jazz to hip-hop. Venues are all over the country, from Brussels to Ghent and Antwerp. Contact www.vwspringsessions.be. March through June.

APRIL

Brussels International Fantastic Film Festival. Science fiction and fantasy films are screened at several movie theaters around the city. Contact **Peymey Diffusion** (𝄞 02/201-1713; www.bifff.net). Mid-April.

MAY

Queen Elisabeth International Music Competition ★, Brussels. For promising young musicians, with piano, violin, and singing competitions. Generally at Bozar (Palais des Beaux-Arts; see p. 177) and a few other venues. Contact Concours Reine Elisabeth (𝄞 02/213-4050; www.concours-reine-elisabeth.be). Throughout May.

Kunstenfestivaldesarts, Brussels. An arts festival famed across the cultural universe for its irritatingly scrunched-up name, which means "arts festival" in both Dutch and French. It spotlights stage events, putting an emphasis on opera, theater, and dance, but finds space for cinema, music concerts, and fine-arts exhibits. Auditoriums and venues around town. Contact **Kunstenfestivaldesarts**; www.kfda.be). Three weeks in May.

Kattenstoet (Festival of the Cats) ★★, Ypres (Ieper). During the traditional Festival of the Cats, toy cats (they used to use live ones!) are thrown from the town hall belfry. There are parades and street entertainment too. Contact **Toerisme Ieper** (𝄞 057/23-9220; www.kattenstoet.be). Every third year on the second Sunday in May (May 10, 2015).

Heilig-Bloedprocessie (Procession of the Holy Blood) ★★★, **Bruges.** The bishop of Bruges carries a relic of the Holy Blood through the streets, while costumed characters act out biblical scenes. Contact **Church of the Holy Blood** (✆ **050/33-6792**; www.holyblood.com). Ascension Day (fifth Thurs after Easter). Usually May (May 14, 2015).

Brussels Jazz Marathon. Enjoy a long weekend of jazz of all kinds at a slew of concerts on the Grand-Place, place du Grand Sablon, and place Ste-Catherine; at other open-air venues around town; and in jazz clubs, cafes, and hotel bars. Contact **Jazz Marathon** (✆ **02/456-0484**; www.brusselsjazzmarathon.be). End of May.

JUNE

Couleur Café Festival, Brussels. Three days of African, Caribbean, and Latin music and dance, ably supported by heaps of soul food at the Tour & Taxis Cultural Complex, in a former warehouse zone next to the Willebroeck Canal dock. Contact Couleur Café (www.couleurcafe.be). Late June.

Brussels Film Festival. A 9-day feast of European films, primarily of first or second features, and by independent directors, screened at the Flagey Cultural Center. Contact Brussels Film Festival (✆ **02/762-0898**; www.brff.be). Mid-June.

JULY

Ommegang ★★★, **Brussels.** A dramatic annual historical pageant that dates from the 13th century and represents the city guilds, magistrates, and nobles honoring the Virgin Mary. Participants wearing period costume from the time of the "joyous entry" of Emperor Charles V into Brussels in 1549, escorted by a mounted cavalcade and waving medieval banners, go in procession from place du Grand Sablon to the Grand-Place. Contact **Ommegang-Brussels Events** (✆ **02/512-1961**; www.ommegang.be). First Tuesday and Thursday in July.

Brosella Folk and Jazz Festival, Brussels. A small-scale specialized music fest that takes place over a weekend at the Théâtre de Verdure in Parc d'Osseghem. Contact

Les Amis de Brosella (✆ **02/474-0641**; www.brosella.be). Mid-July.

Cactus Festival, Bruges. A prickly summer rock festival unfolds over 3 days and attracts big names to the city. Contact Cactus Muziekcentrum (✆ **050/33-2014**; www.cactusfestival.be). Mid-July.

Belgian National Day, Brussels. Marked throughout Belgium but celebrated most in Brussels, with a military procession and music at the Palais Royal (p. 164). Contact City of Brussels Tourism (✆ **02/279-2211**; www.brussels.be). July 21.

Gentse Feesten (Ghent Festivities) ★. Free street entertainment of music, dance, theater, puppet shows, and general fun and games marks the annual Ghent Festivities. Contact www.gentsefeesten.be. Late July.

AUGUST

Visiting the Palais Royal, Brussels. The Royal Palace on place des Palais is open to free guided tours. King Philippe won't be there, however. Contact the Palais Royal (✆ **02/551-2020**; www.monarchie.be). Throughout August.

Planting of the Meyboom (May Pole), Brussels. Despite the name, this ceremony happens in August, on the eve of the Feast of St. Lawrence, at the corner of rue des Sables and rue du Marais, and celebrates Brussels's victory over Leuven in 1311 (nowadays it's more a celebration of summer). Contact City of Brussels Tourism (✆ **02/279-2211**; www.brussels.be). August 9.

Tapis des Fleurs (Carpet of Flowers) ★★★, **Grand-Place, Brussels.** The historic square is carpeted with two-thirds of a million begonias arranged in a complex patterned tapestry. Contact City of Brussels Tourism (✆ **02/279-2211**; www.brussels.be). Mid-August in even-numbered years.

Reiefeesten (Canal Festival) ★★, **Bruges.** Around 600 costumed participants celebrate the city's storied history with a series of concerts, spectacles, short theater pieces, and other events. Contact Visit Brugge (✆ **050/44-4646**; www.brugge.be). Every fourth year (Aug 2018).

Praalstoet van de Gouden Boom (Pageant of the Golden Tree) ★★★, Bruges. Some 2,000 costumed participants, along with giant mannequins and parade floats reenact the lavish spectacle that accompanied the wedding of the Duke of Burgundy, Charles the Bold (p. 182) and Margaret of York in 1468. Contact www.goudenboom stoet.be. Every fifth year (Aug 2017).

SEPTEMBER

Liberation Parade, Brussels. The **Manneken-Pis** statue (p. 165) is dressed in a Welsh Guard's uniform in honor of the city's liberation in 1944. Contact **City of Brussels Tourism** (℗ **02/279-2211;** www.brussels. be). September 3.

Journées du Patrimoine (Heritage Days), Brussels. Taking a different theme each year, this program allows you to visit some of the finest buildings in town that are usually closed to visitors. Contact City of Brussels Tourism (℗ **02/279-2211;** www. brussels.be). Third weekend in September.

OCTOBER

Ghent Film Festival, Ghent. Belgium's top international film festival, and an event that has grown in stature to become one of Europe's main movie showcases. As many as 150 full-length movies and 100 shorts are screened over 12 days. Contact **Film Fest Ghent** (℗ **09/242-8060;** www.filmfestival. be). Mid-October.

NOVEMBER

Snow & Ice Sculpture Festival ★, Bruges. Cool works of ice sculpture can be viewed on Stationsplein in front of the train station. There's an ice bar too. Contact Snow & Ice Sculpture Festival (www.ijssculptuur.be). Mid-November to early January.

DECEMBER

Christmas Market, Antwerp. Stands selling seasonal trinkets, craft items, and food and drink are set up on Grote-Markt. Contact **Visit Antwerp** (www.visitantwerpen. be). Throughout December.

Christmas Market, Brussels. Stands selling seasonal trinkets, craft items, and food and drink are set up on place Ste-Catherine. Contact City of Brussels Tourism (℗ **02/279-2211;** www.brussels.be). Throughout December.

Christmas Market, Bruges. Seasonal trinkets, craft items, and food and drink, alongside an ice-skating rink, are for sale on stalls throughout the Markt. A second market is on Simon Stevinplein, daily 11am to 7pm. Contact Visit Brugge (℗ **050/44-4646;** www.brugge.be). Throughout December.

Christmas Market, Ghent. Stands selling seasonal trinkets, craft items, and food and drink are set up on Sint-Baafsplein. Contact Visit Gent (℗ **09/210-1010;** www.gent.be). Throughout December.

Nativity Scene and Christmas Tree, Grand-Place, Brussels. The crib on display at this Christmas nativity scene has real animals. Contact **City of Brussels Tourism** (℗ **02/279-2211;** www.brussels.be). Throughout December.

Winter Fun, Brussels. An ice-skating rink and a big wheel are set up on the Marché aux Poissons; there's a carousel on neighboring place Ste-Catherine. Contact City of Brussels Tourism (℗ **02/279-2211;** www. brussels.be). Throughout December.

SUGGESTED ITINERARIES

The quintessential Belgium and Holland experience is an urban one; not many foreign visitors come for the Belgian beaches and even fewer for the Dutch mountains. On the other hand, their main cities—big and small—stand out even among Europe's gloriously over-endowed cities for their cultural and historical glories. This doesn't mean there are no places of scenic beauty; there are many, from the rolling hills of the Belgian Ardennes to the dune-backed North Sea islands of The Netherlands, but they don't always feature highly on tourist itineraries.

Getting around Belgium and Holland is remarkably easy, both on the intense network of high-speed Thalys or an InterCity Express and by road, although the main arteries are becoming increasingly choked with heavy-goods vehicles and commuter traffic. What will be difficult is sandwiching everything you want to see into your itinerary, so bring as much time with you as you can afford; plan carefully; book tickets online ahead of time for the Rijksmuseum and Anne Frank Huis in Amsterdam, plus the Ridderzaal in The Hague; and book a multi-based vacation to see even more of The Netherlands and Belgium.

THE COUNTRIES IN BRIEF

Taken together, the nations of Belgium and The Netherlands cover a mere 72,400 sq. km (27,380 sq. miles)—around one-fifth the size of neighboring Germany, and not much larger than West Virginia. But no other comparably sized area in Europe compresses so many points of interest. Topping the list are artistic masterpieces, cultural events, and substantial reminders of a long and colorful history. Space remains for scenery that, while mostly lacking in drama, can still be lyrically beautiful. Then there are the more mundane advantages of convenience, economy, and friendly populations (yes, even occasionally in Brussels), not to mention a host of other travel delights—the exquisite food and drink of Brussels, the unadulterated gorgeousness of Bruges, and the exuberant sociability of Amsterdam.

BELGIUM For a graphic image of Belgium's two ethnic regions, Dutch-speaking Vlaanderen (Flanders) and French-speaking Wallonie (Wallonia), draw an imaginary east-west line across the country just south of Brussels. North of the line is Flanders, where you find the medieval cities of Bruges, Ghent, and Antwerp, and Belgium's North Sea coastline. South of the line is Wallonia. The art cities of Tournai and Mons, and the scenic resort towns of the Meuse River valley and the Ardennes are the attractions of this region. Then there's Brussels, the capital, roughly in the geographic middle, and going off on a trajectory of its own as the HQ of the European Community.

THE NETHERLANDS   What you see is what you get in Holland. There are no dramatic canyons or towering peaks. The nation's highest point wouldn't top the roof of a New York City skyscraper, and its average altitude is just 11m (37 ft.) above sea level. This makes for few panoramic vantage points—most of those are manmade in the cities—and you can't see the canals and lakes until you're about to fall into them. Does this mean the views are boring? The answer is a vehement "no!" As the famous 17th-century Dutch landscape painters showed the world, vistas in Holland are among the most aesthetic anywhere, giving wide-angle views of green pastures dotted with tiny houses, church spires, and grazing cattle silhouetted against the horizon. With the exception of Rotterdam, all Holland's cities are aeons old; but all without exception are vital, alive, and stuffed to the gunnels with fine art and great architecture.

BELGIUM & THE NETHERLANDS IN 1 WEEK

Few countries can boast of cities more justly celebrated than Amsterdam, Brussels, and Bruges, with a raft of smaller, but no less impressive, destinations not far behind. They are all bursting with wonderful museums, galleries, shops, and restaurants and this whistle-stop tour will allow you to see their main attractions—just about. For this is a week where you'll barely be able to catch your breath. Travel between all the cities is easy—get around by car or ride Belgium and Holland's excellent network of trains.

Day 1: Arrive in Amsterdam ★★★

Arrive on an early flight and get going—time is of the essence this week! First up is a 1-hour **canal cruise** (p. 99). This is the Dutch capital's tourist trap par excellence, but it is also the very best way to view much of this canal-threaded city in a reasonable time. Now choose *just one*—a tough decision that will depend on your own interests—from Amsterdam's three standout museums: the **Van Gogh Museum** (p. 93), the **Rijksmuseum** (p. 92), or the **Stedelijk** (p. 93). A stroll around **Museumplein** (p. 92) will clear your head, then follow up with drinks with **Café Cobra** (p. 75). Dine in the evening at a traditional Dutch brown cafe like **'t Smalle** (p. 72) or an Indonesian restaurant like **De Blauw** (p. 75).

Day 2: The Hague ★★

The Dutch seat of government is a 50-minute train ride from Amsterdam. Parliament is in the heart of town, in the **Binnenhof** and **Ridderzaal;** you can take a guided tour if you've planned ahead (p. 130). Visit the superb collection of **Dutch Old Masters** (p. 132) in the **Mauritshuis,** then hop on a tram and take a short ride to the seacoast at **Scheveningen** (p. 135), where you can breathe fresh sea air and have afternoon tea at the splendid **Steigenberger Kurhaus Hotel** (p. 136). Take the tram back into The Hague to catch an early-evening InterCity train to Brussels from The Hague's Hollands Spoor railway station.

Day 3: Brussels ★★★

If you don't want to be packing and unpacking every day, lodge in Brussels and visit Belgium's other historic cities as easy day trips. In the "capital of Europe," start out at the **Grand-Place** (p. 158), taking time to absorb the magnificent old square's architectural details and animated spirit. A date with Rubens, Brueghel, Magritte, and other notable Belgian artists awaits you in the elegant **Musées Royaux des Beaux-Arts de Belgique** (p. 166). Next you might want to stroll amid trees, fountains, and lawns in the **Parc de Bruxelles** (p. 152), and view the **Palais Royal** (p. 164) and the Belgian Parliament building, the **Palais de la Nation,** on opposite sides of the park. In the evening, have a beer at **La Morte Subite** (p. 178) and dine at any of the multi-ethnic restaurants in the trendy Dansaert district.

Day 4: Bruges ★★★

By train, Bruges is an hour from Brussels. Once you arrive, hire wheels at the rail station as you can easily tour the city by **bicycle** (p. 183). A must-do is a **canal cruise** (p. 199), as you'll get to see a lot in a short time. Later, stroll around the connected medieval central squares **Burg** (p. 193) and **Markt** (p. 192). On the Burg, visit the **Basiliek van het Heilig-Bloed** (p. 193) for a glimpse of a relic that's said to be drops of Christ's blood; on the Markt, climb the **Belfort** (p. 192) for splendid city views. Next, head to the **Kantcentrum** (p. 197) to see Bruges's handmade lace being crafted.

Day 5: Ghent ★★

Just a half-hour train ride from Brussels, Ghent is a buzzing university town with a thoroughly Flemish vibe. Get your bearings by taking the elevator up above the city's rooftops to the viewing platform of the 14th-century **Belfort** (p. 214). Next stop has to be **Sint-Bavokerk** (p. 217) for its great medieval artwork: Jan van Eyck's altarpiece "The Adoration of the Mystic Lamb" (1432). From the cathedral, stroll to the medieval inner harbor along **Korenlei** and **Graslei** (both p. 219), which are both lined with spectacular medieval guild houses. From here, pick up a cruise boat to check out the canals or head for the restored medieval district of **Patershol** (p. 215).

Day 6: Antwerp ★★

Forty minutes by train from Brussels, Antwerp is Belgium's second-largest city. Visit the **Grote Markt** (p. 206) to view the dramatic Brabo Fountain and glorious, lacy guild houses, and then stop for a *bolleke* (round glass) of Antwerp's De Koninck beer at the grand old tavern **Café den Engel,** also on the square. Antwerp means Rubens; to learn more about the artist, go to his former home, the **Rubenshuis** (p. 210), and view his four masterly paintings at the Gothic **Sint-Pauluskerk** (p. 210). Back at Antwerp Centraal Station, stroll briefly around the city's celebrated (although not exactly handsome) **Diamond Quarter** (p. 209) before catching your train.

Day 7: Back to Amsterdam ★★

If you have an early flight home from Amsterdam's **Schiphol Airport,** you'll be happy to know that Thalys high-speed and InterCity express trains to Amsterdam from Brussels and Antwerp stop at Schiphol. If you have time to kill in Amsterdam but don't want to stray too far from Centraal Station, take a taxi to Prinsengracht to the **Anne Frank Huis** (p. 88)—but you'll have to book tickets in advance online to avoid wasting time in the long lines. More time might permit you to squeeze in a visit to historic **Haarlem** (p. 115).

A 2-WEEK HOLLAND & BELGIUM ITINERARY

If you have 2 weeks in your itinerary to dedicate to Amsterdam and Brussels and all stops in between, you'll breathe more easily. You can stroll where you might otherwise have needed to hop on a city tram or bus, and you'll sink into the city vibe more thoroughly as well as heading off the beaten track a little. This itinerary is designed for travel by car, but most of it can be managed by train and an occasional bus. You'll just need to modify some elements to allow for the additional time it will take to get around.

Day 1: Arrive in Amsterdam ★★★

With 2 weeks, you can take your time exploring the delights of Amsterdam. As ever the first thing to do is step onboard a **cruise boat** (p. 99) for an hour's cruise around the canals. Afterward, stroll along the 17th-century Golden Age **Canal Ring** (p. 56)—comprising the Herengracht, Keizersgracht, and Prinsengracht canals—starting out at the **Westerkerk** (p. 90) and going by way of **Leidseplein** to **Rembrandtplein.** For dinner, head to the smart canal-side restaurant **Envy** (p. 73).

Day 2: More of Amsterdam's Best ★★★

This morning you have to make a choice between the **Van Gogh Museum** (p. 93), the **Rijksmuseum** (p. 92), or the **Stedelijk** (p. 93); all three are close together on Museumplein. Visit the **Anne Frank Huis** next, but be sure to book tickets online in advance; otherwise you'll be waiting for precious hours outside. In the afternoon, tour the **Red Light District** (p. 86) and then wander through the old artisans' district of **Jordaan** (p. 91), now prettily gentrified. For a light supper, try **'t Smalle** (p. 72) a traditional Dutch brown cafe, or **De Blauw** (p. 75) for an Indonesian feast.

Day 3: Amsterdam Again ★★★

Today's the day for going off piste in Amsterdam to see smaller attractions; start your day at the wonderful **Het Grachtenhuis** (p. 89) for an entertaining explanation of how the 17th-century Canal Ring was built, then nip into the **Tulip Museum** (p. 90) to learn about Amsterdam's historical obsession with tulips. In the afternoon take the free ferry across the IJ River to **EYE Film Institute** (p. 98) to see its amazing architecture and the burgeoning new city north of the waterway. If you happen to visit on a summer weekend, spend the evening at an open-air concert in the **Vondelpark** (p. 94); otherwise take in an evening's comedy at **Boom Chicago** (p. 111).

Day 4: Drive to Haarlem ★★★

Get on the road today for the short hop west to Haarlem. Head straight for the **Grote Markt** (p. 206) to admire the splendor of its gabled, medieval buildings, dominated by the great spire of **Sint-Bavokerk** (p. 217), where a 10-year-old Mozart played an organ recital in 1766. Spend a couple of hours in the **Frans Hals Museum** (p. 116), located in a dreamy former almshouse, noted for its exceptional collection of Hals's civic portraits. From there, move on to the oldest museum in The Netherlands, the **Teylers** (p. 119), established in 1778, for its eccentric displays of minerals and scientific instruments. Scour the pretty tangle of streets around the Grote Markt to find a restaurant for supper.

Day 5: Drive to The Hague ★★

If you are traveling in spring, detour today to take in the blaze of color of the world-famous gardens at **Keukenhof,** near Lisse (p. 123) and tour the bulb fields of the Bloembollenstreek. Otherwise drive on to The Hague, where your first stop should be the fine medieval buildings of the **Binnenhof** and **Ridderzaal** (p. 130) at the home of the Dutch Parliament (book guided tours in advance). Visit the superb collection of **Dutch Old Masters** (p. 132) in the Mauritshuis, then hit **Chinatown** for supper (p. 72).

Day 6: A Day in Scheveningen ★★

Visit the extraordinary Panorama Mesdag for its "painting in the round" of 19th-century **Scheveningen** (p. 135), then hop on a tram and take the short ride to the seacoast to see the 21st-century reality of Scheveningen. Breathe in the brisk sea air and head for the **Museum Beelden aan Zee** (p. 135) for its cluster of modern sculpture strewn alongside the boardwalk. Take afternoon tea at the splendid **Steigenberger Kurhaus Hotel** (p. 136) and enjoy supper in one of the promenade fish restaurants before catching the tram back to The Hague.

Day 7: Drive to Rotterdam ★★

Rotterdam is normally less than an hour away from The Hague but the traffic is often clogged up on the expressways, so leave early to get there in time to take a **boat trip** (p. 140) around the world's third largest natural harbor. From there, head up **Euromast** (p. 138) to see the city laid out far below. In the afternoon, choose between the works of Jan van Eyck and other art treasures in the **Museum Boijmans van Beuningen** (p. 138) or the vibrant ethnographic collections from Indonesia and the Americas in the **Wereldmuseum** (p. 138). Take a water taxi to **Hotel New York** (p. 141) across the River Maas for super and riverside views.

Day 8: Brussels ★★★

Today, you'll scoot along the expressway to Belgium's capital. The magnificent **Grand-Place** (p. 158) is an ideal starting point for your sightseeing. You might also want to fit in a "pilgrimage" to the miniscule **Manneken-Pis** statue (p. 165) nearby. Following this, stop off at the **Musées Royaux des Beaux-Arts de Belgique** (p. 166) to view works by Rubens, Brueghel, Magritte, and other notable Belgian artists. Then stroll amid Masonic symbols in the **Parc de Bruxelles** (p. 152), stopping to view the **Palais Royal** (p. 164) and the **Palais de la Nation** on opposite sides of the park. In the evening, enjoy a Belgian beer on the Grand-Place and then dive into the maze of touristy pedestrian streets around rue des Bouchers for a seafood supper.

Day 9: Brussels ★★★

Go window-shopping in the 19th-century **Galeries Royales St-Hubert** (p. 177), then make your way to the **Cathédrale des Sts-Michel-et-Gudule** (p. 162). Go up to rue Royale and take a tram to **place du Grand Sablon** (p. 159) to browse its antiques stores and the weekend antiques market. Cross over rue de la Régence to tranquil **place du Petit Sablon** (p. 159) and stop a while by the fountain. In the afternoon, take a trip to the **Atomium** (p. 172) on Brussels's northern edge or to the **Cantillon Brewery** (p. 169), just southwest of the city center. Take your pick of restaurants in Dansaert for supper.

Day 10: Bruges ★★

Not much more than an hour on the fast dual carriageways, Bruges is Belgium's prime medieval showpiece. Take a **canal cruise** (p. 199) to acquaint yourself with the city's layout and character before strolling around the interconnected medieval squares of **Burg** (p. 193) and **Markt** (p. 192). On the Burg, visit the **Basiliek van het Heilig-Bloed** (p. 193) for a glimpse of the relic that purports to be drops of Christ's blood; on the Markt, climb the **Belfort** (p. 192) for splendid city views. In the late afternoon, go to the **Kantcentrum** (p. 197) to see how Bruges's handmade lace is crafted and later enjoy sampling some Belgian boutique beers in the canal-side **2be** (p. 189).

Day 11: More of Bruges's Best ★★★

Visit the **Groeningemuseum** (p. 196) to view its outstanding collection of works by the Flemish Primitives. Next, explore the historical collection in the **Gruuthusemuseum,** housed in a 15th-century palace (p. 194). Stop off at **Expo Picasso** (p. 196) for sketches and prints by great names such as Magritte and Miró as well as Picasso before walking down to the pretty **Begijnhof** (p. 198) and romantic Minnewater lake. By night join all the other tourists for a supper of moules-frites in the gaggle of restaurants on Markt.

Day 12: Ghent ★★

Today move on to the edgy university city of Ghent, around an hour southeast of Bruges. Get your bearings by taking the elevator up the 14th-century **Belfort's** (p. 214) viewing platform to see the city's rooftops spread out below. Just across the elegant Sint-Baafsplein is the barnlike **Sint-Bavokerk** (p. 217), which offers Ghent's most spectacular medieval artwork: Jan van Eyck's glowing altarpiece "The Adoration of the Mystic Lamb" (1432). From the cathedral, it's a short stroll to the medieval inner harbor along **Korenlei** and **Graslei** (both p. 219), past the forbidding **Gravensteen** castle (p. 215), and on to explore the restored medieval district of **Patershol** (p. 215), where there are dining options aplenty.

Day 13: Antwerp ★★

Next it's on to Antwerp, an easy drive from Ghent. Visit the **Grote Markt** (p. 206) to view its central Brabo Fountain and the glorious, lacy guild houses, before stopping off for beer at the grand old tavern **Café den Engel,** also on the square. Antwerp was the home of Rubens and to learn more about this great artist, tour his splendid former home, the **Rubenshuis** (p. 210), and view his four masterly paintings at the Gothic **Sint-Pauluskerk** (p. 210). For the story behind Antwerp's growth as a trading port and its 21st-century role within Europe, head down to the revitalized docks to the innovative **Museum aan de Stroom** (p. 207), better known as MAS. Head back to the Old Center to eat at **De Rooden Hoed** (p. 211), a typical Antwerp brasserie.

Day 14: Back to Amsterdam ★★

From Antwerp, Amsterdam's Schiphol Airport is just a couple hours up the expressway. If you have time before your flight, consider stopping off in **Mechelen,** an as-yet-unsung Belgian town of stunning beauty with a lovely Grote Markt to chill out in, a canal to cruise upon, and the hard-hitting **Holocaust Centre** to discover.

AMSTERDAM, BRUSSELS & BRUGES FOR FAMILIES

Kids will be pleased to learn there's masses more to Holland and Belgium than gazing at Old Master paintings and looking at yet another Gothic church; eating mussels and raw herring; or struggling with French, Dutch, and Flemish. You certainly don't need to worry about the lingo since most natives of these multilingual cities speak English, and there are hundreds of fun family-friendly options to see and do, just as there are plenty of choices on the menus beyond mollusks—don't forget that fries and chocolate are almost the national dish of Belgium, while immense piles of child-friendly sweet pancakes sate the Dutch national sweet tooth.

Day 1: Brussels ★★★

Whenever the kids step out of line in Brussels, threatening a visit to the European Union administrative buildings should bring them back in to line. They (and you) would almost certainly prefer a tram ride out to the space-age **Atomium** (p. 172). And while you're in the city's northern Bruparck district, you might consider touring **Mini-Europe** (p. 173), but it's slim pickings in comparison with U.S. theme parks. Back in the center of town, treat the kids to an exposé of bold little **Manneken-Pis** (p. 165); grown-ups usually wonder what all the fuss is about, but kids love him.

Day 2: More of Brussels ★★

Boys—and their fathers—will want to take a look under the hood of **Autoworld** (p. 167) and most kids will enjoy discovering the cavernous underground excavations at **Coudenberg** (p. 164) underneath the Palais Royale. Both genders will likely agree that the comic strips and characters at the **Centre Belge de la Bande-Dessinée** (p. 163), where you'll meet Tintin and the Smurfs, are pretty cool.

Day 3: Bruges ★★★

In this historic Flemish city you can swerve past Old Masters, Gothic architecture, and mussel-slurping diners in one fast move. Achieve this satisfying feat by visiting the **Boudewijn Seapark** or take a canal cruise on an open-topped boat (p. 199) to see the city from the water. It's also completely safe to get around

Bruges by rented **pedal-bike** (p. 183) and even more exciting to see the sights by pony and trap (p. 199).

Day 4: Rotterdam ★★

Today make your way up the **Euromast** (p. 138) for the best views of Rotterdam. Afterward, you'll probably need to choose between a **boat tour** (p. 140) through the city's vast harbor and a visit to the outstanding **Blijdorp Zoo,** but if you have time for both, by all means squeeze them in. If you're staying overnight in Rotterdam, there are several floating boat-hotels to pique the excitement of kids.

Day 5: Amsterdam ★★★

Getting around Amsterdam by **tram** (p. 57) is safe fun for the whole family, as is **seeing the sights by canal** (p. 83). Steer away from cycling around the city center, as the resident cyclists are utterly ruthless and often downright dangerous. A visit to the **Anne Frank Huis** (p. 88) is thought provoking for older children and there is a clutch of other **museums,** from marine to science, that are specifically designed for youngsters (p. 103) as well as the **Artis Zoo** (p. 94) in De Plantage.

Day 6: Enkhuizen ★★

Get out of the city to Enkhuizen on the western shore of the IJsselmeer, a freshwater lake that until 1932 was part of the North Sea. The superb **Zuiderzee Museum** (p. 122) is located here and recreates traditional Dutch life in a series of reconstructed rural homes, farms, and windmills where displays of typical crafts are exhibited.

Day 7: Back to Brussels ★★

The easiest way to break the monotony of a 3-hour drive back ("are we there yet?") to Brussels from Amsterdam is to call in at the cluster of UNESCO World Heritage-listed windmills at **Kinderdijk** (p. 140), close to Rotterdam.

AN ART LOVER'S TOUR

A tour of the world-class art offerings of Amsterdam, Brussels, Bruges, and several other cities in between could take weeks. Here's how to shoehorn a lifetime's dose of culture into just a week. Pick and choose according to your itinerary or go dive in and see the lot.

Day 1: Amsterdam ★★★

Two world-beaters in 1 day is pushing it a bit, but if you book ahead of time for the **Rijksmuseum** (p. 92), and cherry pick your way through the acres and acres of magnificent Dutch art, silverwork, and the glorious glass- and Delftware, before ending up at Rembrandt's "The Night Watch" in the second-floor Gallery of Honor, you might just have time and energy left over for **Van Gogh** (p. 93). His eponymous museum is just a step away across the Museumplein (p. 92), and offers up the world's biggest collection of his works.

Day 2: Drive to Haarlem ★★★

It's back to Museumplein this morning for a trawl around the **Stedelijk Museum** (p. 93), for stellar modern work from a roster of great international names including Chagall, Warhol, Pollock, Mondriaan, and Lichtenstein. In the afternoon train it or drive out to Haarlem to admire the peerless Frans Hals civic guards portraits and other Old Master showstoppers in the **Frans Hals Museum** (p. 116).

Day 3: The Hague ★★

Quite apart from the curious **Panorama Mesdag** (p. 133), The Hague houses the world's leading collection of works by Piet Mondriaan in the H.P. Berlage-built **Gemeentemuseum Den Haag** (p. 132). You'll also find a sterling collection of Old Masters by the likes of Vermeer and Holbein in the sparkling **Mauritshuis** (p. 132), reopened in June 2014 after extensive refurbishment.

Day 4: Rotterdam ★★

Rotterdam furthers the roster of world-class art galleries with the **Museum Boijmans van Beuningen** (p. 138), which displays the cream of two collections running from Old Dutch Masters to contemporary glassware: Entrepreneur F.J.O. Boijmans donated his priceless art works to the city in 1847 and D.G. van Beuningen followed suit in 1955. Almost next door in the Museumpark is the **Kunsthal Rotterdam** (p. 139), where Rem Koolhaas's spacious white galleries serve up temporary exhibitions of contemporary artworks.

Day 5: Brussels ★★★

Only one day to see all the art treasures in Brussels? You can do no better than heading for the four masterpiece galleries at the **Musées Royaux des Beaux-Arts de Belgique** (p. 166); plan on staying there all day. You'll see Breughel, Rubens, Van Dyck, Magritte, and Christo all under one very huge roof.

Day 6: Bruges ★★★

Start your Bruges art tour at the **Groeningemuseum** (p. 196) to view the world-beating collection of works by the Flemish Primitives. After that, stop off at **Expo Picasso** (p. 196) for sketches and prints by great names such as Magritte and Miró and of course its namesake, Picasso. Pop in to **Sint-Janshospitaal** (p. 197) to catch the golden Shrine of St. Ursula by Hans Memling, then wind up your day at the **Dalí Xpo-Gallery** (p. 192) in the Belfort.

Day 7: Amsterdam via Ghent ★★

This one's dependent on your flight times. Leaving Bruges with the larks in the morning, head into Ghent to see Jan van Eyck's gleaming, glowing 13-section altarpiece of "The Adoration of the Mystic Lamb" (1432) in **Sint-Bavokerk** (p. 217). If time does not permit this, head straight for Schiphol and content yourself with a quick visit to the Rijksmuseum's airport outpost (p. 232), which houses a few treasures from the state collection.

A MINI MILITARY MEMORIAL TOUR OF BELGIUM

Belgium has been the scene of some of the world's fiercest battles three times in the last 200 hundred years. First of all, Napoleon carved up the region south of Brussels, then the advent of World War I saw more than 500,000 Allied and German soldiers killed in the trenches of Flanders. Sadly the country saw action again just 20 years later, with heavy fighting between Allied troops and the German army in the Ardennes.

Day 1: Waterloo ★

South of Brussels, the French emperor Napoleon Bonaparte met final defeat at the **Battle of Waterloo,** in 1815. A tour of this largely preserved battlefield and a visit to the Duke of Wellington's military HQ, now the **Musée Wellington** both afford a fascinating insight into the great and decisive battle.

Day 2: Drive to Ypres (Ieper) ★★★

A 2-hour drive north from Brussels brings you to the medieval cloth town of **Ypres** (p. 226), a crucible of fighting on the World War I Western Front that claimed the lives of 500,000 Allied and German soldiers in just 100 days in 1917. The now peaceful Flanders fields are sprinkled with a few remaining sections of trenches and plenty of military cemeteries, including Tyne Cot, which is the largest Commonwealth War Graves cemetery in the world. Don't miss Ypres's superb **In Flanders Fields Museum** (p. 228) or the emotional Last Post ceremony held at the **Menin Gate** (p. 228) daily at 8pm.

Day 3: Bastogne & World War II ★★

Drive southeast from Brussels past Tournai and Mons to the River Meuse at Namur. Continuing eastward into the rolling Ardennes hills, you'll pass many scenes of hard-fought action from the Battle of the Bulge in the winter of 1944 to 1945, at places such as Marche-en-Famenne, Rochefort, and La Roche-en-Ardenne. None was harder than the epic struggle U.S. troops fought to hold the strategic crossroads town of **Bastogne** in those closing days of World War II. The greatest memorial to American soldiers can be found at the star-shaped **Mardasson Memorial,** where the thoughtfully presented Bastogne War Museum opened in 2014.

AMSTERDAM

Open-hearted, welcoming, and prosperous, Amsterdam is a good-time city that merrily opens its arms to all comers. It embraces its tourists, its cyclists, its boat-folk, and its multicultural community. It is friendly, unflappable, and approachable; a city confident in its own skin but with one eye fixed on the future, buzzing with creativity and bonhomie.

But it is also a city of surreal juxtapositions; an elegant cityscape of 165 waterways, 1,280 bridges, and thousands of venerable 17th-century mansions exist side by side with the sleazy alleyways of the Red Light District. A city with some of the most impressive art museums in the world that tolerates sex clubs and dope smoking; that has one of Europe's best concert halls but also a gritty nighttime scene springing up around Westerpark and NDSM-Wharf; and a city that offers Michelin-starred restaurants alongside grungy brown cafes.

It's a long-outdated cliché to regard Amsterdam as some sort of latter-day Sodom and Gomorrah, for the winds of change are blowing through the streets. Tolerance may be embedded deeply in the Dutch psyche, but even the most open-minded of people can run out of patience. The very existence of Amsterdam's notorious coffee shops and red-light haunts is now threatened as the city fathers toil to improve its quality of life; druggie haunts have been closed down as have some of the prostitutes' infamous windows, and smart restaurants, bars, and upmarket independent stores are starting to move in to the pretty side streets of the Rosse Buurt (Red Light District), which ironically hides some of the most unspoiled architecture in Amsterdam.

In any case, Amsterdammers themselves have never drifted around town in a drug-induced haze. They are all too busy revitalizing rundown areas like the Jordaan, filling it with offbeat art galleries and cool hotels; or redeveloping the derelict harbor waterfront along the IJ waterway into a shiny, futuristic city that's light years away from the refined spirit of the Golden Age. Between dips into Amsterdam's artistic and historical treasures, be sure to give yourself time out to absorb the freewheeling spirit of Europe's most vibrant city.

4

ESSENTIALS

Arriving

BY PLANE Amsterdam Airport Schiphol (© **0900/0141** for general and flight information, 31-20/794-0800 from outside Holland; www.schiphol.nl; airport code AMS), 14km (9 miles) southwest of Amsterdam is pronounced *Skhip*-ol and is universally regarded as one of the best airports in the world for its ease of use, its massive duty-free shopping center, and its outpost of the Rijksmuseum (p. 92). Located southwest of the city

Amsterdam

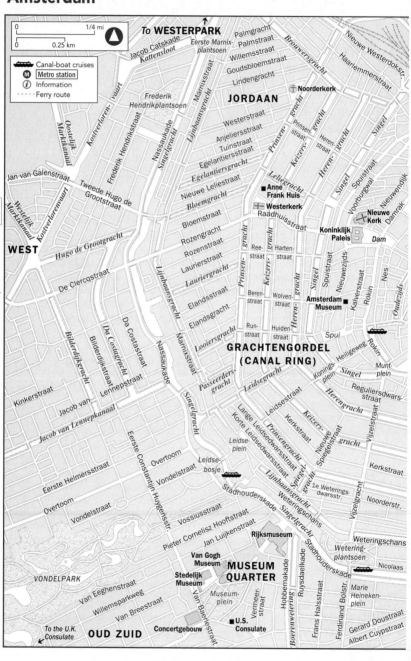

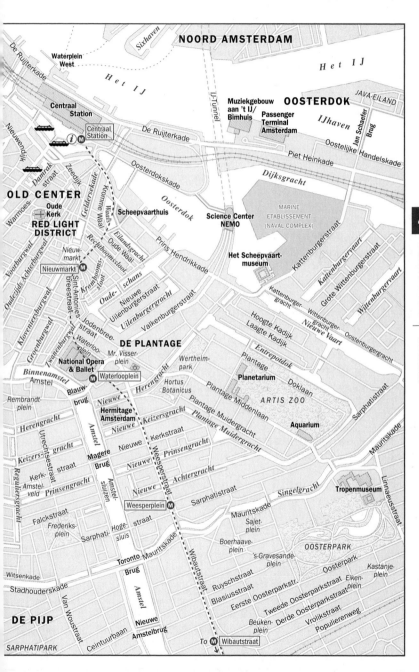

center, it is the main airport in The Netherlands, handling the country's international arrivals and departures.

There are three terminals close together and imaginatively numbered 1, 2, and 3. Moving walkways connect passengers with the Arrivals Hall and Passport Control, Baggage Reclaim, and Customs. Conveniences like free luggage carts, currency exchange, ATMs, restaurants, bars, shops, baby rooms, restrooms, and showers are all on tap. Beyond Customs is Schiphol Plaza, a one-stop destination that combines tourist office, transport ticket office, rail station access, Hotel Schiphol Airport and Mercure Hotel Schiphol Terminal for transit passengers, a shopping mall, bars and restaurants, restrooms, baggage lockers, airport and tourist information desks, car-rental, and hotel-reservation desks all in the one location. Bus and shuttle stops plus a taxi stand are just outside the terminal.

For tourist information and to make hotel reservations, go to Iamsterdam's **Visitor Information Center** in Schiphol Plaza (𝄐 **020/702-6000**); it is open daily 7am to 10pm.

BY CAR   A network of major international highways crisscrosses The Netherlands. European expressways E19, E35, and E231 converge on Amsterdam from France and Belgium to the south and from Germany to the north and east. These roads also have Dutch designations; as you approach the city they are, respectively, A4, A2, and A1. Amsterdam's ring road is A10. Distances between destinations are relatively short. Traffic is invariably heavy and delays are frequent but road conditions are otherwise pretty good, service stations are plentiful, and highways are plainly signposted.

BY CRUISE SHIP   Cruise-ship passengers arrive in Amsterdam at the **Passenger Terminal Amsterdam,** Piet Heinkade 27 (𝄐 **020/509-1000;** www.ptamsterdam.nl; tram 26), on the IJ waterway within easy walking distance of Centraal Station, where all modes of transport can be picked up to travel anywhere in the city.

BY FERRY   **DFDS Seaways** (𝄐 **0871/522-9955** in Britain, 44/330-333-0245 outside the UK; www.dfdsseaways.co.uk) has daily car-ferry services between Newcastle in northeast England and Ijmuiden, west of Amsterdam on the North Sea coast. The overnight travel time is 15.5 hours. From IJmuiden, you can go by bus to Amsterdam Centraal Station.

P&O Ferries (𝄐 **08716/642121** in Britain, 020/200-8333 in Holland; www.po ferries.com) has daily car-ferry service between Hull in northeast England and Rotterdam Europoort. The overnight travel time is 10 to 11 hours. Ferry-company buses shuttle passengers between the Europoort terminal and Rotterdam Centraal Station, from where there are frequent trains to Amsterdam Centraal Station.

Stena Line (𝄐 **08447/707-070** in Britain; www.stenaline.co.uk) has a twice-daily car-ferry service between Harwich in southeast England and Hoek van Holland (Hook of Holland) near Rotterdam. The travel time is 6 hours, 45 minutes for the daytime crossing, and 7½ hours overnight. Frequent trains depart from Hoek van Holland to Amsterdam Centraal Station.

BY TRAIN   Rail services to Amsterdam from other cities in the Netherlands and elsewhere in Europe are frequent and fast. International trains arrive at Centraal Station from Brussels, Paris, Berlin, Cologne, and other German cities, and from the main cities in Austria, Switzerland, Italy, and Eastern Europe. **Nederlandse Spoorwegen** (**Netherlands Railways;** www.ns.nl) trains arrive in Amsterdam from towns and cities all over The Netherlands. Service is frequent to many places around the country and trains are modern, clean, and punctual. Schedule and fare information on travel by train is available by calling ✆ **0900/9292** (0.70€ per minute) for national service, and 0900/9296 for high-speed international services (0.35€ per minute); or by visiting www.ns.nl.

The burgundy-colored **Thalys high-speed train,** with a top speed of 300kmph (186 mph), connects Paris, Brussels, Amsterdam, and (via Brussels) Cologne. Travel time from Paris to Amsterdam is 3 hours, 20 minutes, and from Brussels 1 hour, 50 minutes. For Thalys information and reservations, call ✆ **32-070/667-788,** 0.17€ per minute, or visit www.thalys.com. Tickets are also available from railway stations and travel agents.

On **Eurostar** high-speed trains (top speed 300kmph/186 mph), the travel time between London St. Pancras Station and Brussels's Bruxelles-Midi Station (the closest connecting point for Amsterdam) is around 2 hours. Departures from London to Brussels are approximately every 2 hours at peak times. For Eurostar reservations, call ✆ **08432/186186** in Britain; ✆ 44/1233-617-575 from outside the UK; www.eurostar. com.

BY BUS International coaches arrive at the bus terminal opposite the Amstel rail station (Metro: Amstel) in the south of the city. Eurolines operates coach services between London Victoria Bus Station and Amstel Station (via ferry), with up to five departures daily in the summer. Travel time is just over 12 hours. For reservations, contact **Eurolines** (✆ **08717/818-178** in Britain or 31/88-076-1700 in Holland; www. eurolines.com). From here, you can go by train or Metro to Centraal Station, or by tram no. 12 to the Museumplein area and to connecting points for trams to the center city. For the Leidseplein, take the Metro toward Centraal Station, get out at Weesperplein, and take tram 7 or 10.

Visitor Information

TOURIST OFFICES Amsterdam's main **Visitor Information Center** is run by Iamsterdam and is located at Stationsplein 10, right outside Centraal Station (✆ **020/702-6000;** www.iamsterdam.com); in our 24-hour world it has annoyingly short opening times, being Monday through Saturday 9am until 5pm, Sunday from 9am until 4pm; as a result is always crammed with hordes of backpackers. In spite of this, the hard-pressed staff could not be more charming and helpful. There's also a branch in Schiphol Plaza at the airport, with the same phone number but sensible opening times: daily from 7am until 10pm.

For last-minute admission to shows and events in the city, head for Iamsterdam's **Last Minute Ticketshop** in the Stadsschouwburg at Leidseplein 26 (www.lastminute ticketshop.nl; Mon–Sat 10am–6pm; tram: 1, 2, 5, 7, or 10), which sells half-price tickets for same-day performances after 10am every morning. You can buy tickets for any venue in town and pick up schedules for all Amsterdam's cultural events. There's a nominal booking charge of between 2€ and 5€ for all tickets. The Visitor Information Center Stationsplein 10 also has a branch of the Last Minute Ticketshop, and there's a third in the Amsterdam Public Library on Oosterdokskade 143 (Mon–Fri 10am–7:30pm, Sat–Sun 10am–6pm).

City Layout

Amsterdam is not a huge city and its central district, where most of the tourist attractions are concentrated, can be walked easily. The canals and streets fan out in a series of concentric circles from the historic city center. However, despite its size, this city is very diverse in mood and style, changing in feel almost from one street to another.

The Neighborhoods in Brief

The Old Center The oldest, most central district of Amsterdam centers on the rackety Dam Square, Oude Kerk (p. 85), and the Nieuwmarkt and is probably best known for containing the infamous Red Light District (p. 86 and 87), which lies between the two canals Oudezijds Voorburgwaal and Oudezijds Achterburgwaal. Despite its seedy reputation, it is safe and well policed. A recent gentrification policy has seen more restaurants and design stores moving into the area.

Canal Ring The concentric band of three canals that surround the Old Center was built in the 17th century as the cramped, disease-ridden old city drastically needed to expand. Herengracht, Keizersgracht, and Prinsengracht today form an aristocratic enclave of grand town houses overlooking the three canals. Some of the city's smartest hotels and many major attractions lie within this belt, including the Westerkerk (p. 90), the Anne Frank Huis (p. 88), the Canal House Museum, and the Willet-Holthuysen Museum (p. 91) along with more niche attractions like the pipe (p. 87) and biblical museums (p. 88).

Jordaan This area of formerly artisanal housing lining narrow canals interspersed with hump-backed ridges is now the favored residential area of Amsterdam's intelligentsia. There are lots of bars and traditional brown cafes to discover as well as innovative art galleries and design studios. Jordaan also has scores of canal-house hotels tucked into its pretty lanes, a world away from the Red Light District yet only a 10-minute walk.

Museum Quarter Housing Amsterdam's triumvirate of heavyweight art museums, the Rijksmuseum (p. 92), Stedelijk Museum (p. 93), and the Van Gogh Museum (p. 93), this quarter is also home to the Concertgebouw concert hall (p. 110), embassies, and upmarket stores as well as one of the city's most glorious public spaces, the Museumplein (p. 92). The Heineken Brewery is close by (p. 91).

Oud Zuid Adjoining the Museum Quarter and the Vondelpark (p. 94), Amsterdam's poshest residential area is also its most exclusive shopping district, with top international brands and jewelry stores packed along PC Hoofstraat. Luxury apartments abound along with exclusive hotels and a general air of wealth.

De Pijp Multi-ethnic and beguiling, De Pijp is choked with well-priced restaurants producing cooking from every nationality across the globe and features the city's best street market along Albertcuypstraat. Although the area is smartening up with the arrival of a few smart hotels and restaurants, it is still a natural home of immigrants, students, and Amsterdam's least-known red light district along Ruysdaelkade (p. 87).

De Plantage Incorporating the Artis Royal Zoo (p. 94), the Hortus Botanicus (p. 95), and Amsterdam's Jewish Quarter, Plantage is an area of wide boulevards surrounded by residential streets. It's the costly home to aspiring professional families with young families. The Jewish Museum (p. 96) and Portuguese Synagogue (p. 96) mark the district's western limits, the housing developments around Oosterdok its northern edges.

Noord Amsterdam The opening of EYE Film Institute started the migration across the IJ waterway to this new bastion of cool, an alternative area of graffiti, street art, and low-key housing that has seen industrial dilapidation of the old docks repurposed into new cultural centers such as the Tolhuistuin, housed in an abandoned Shell factory. A free ferry leaves from Waterplein West at the back of Centraal Station.

Westerpark Westerpark is a funky corner of the city, home to formerly working-class housing that has largely been turned into apartments. Its focal point is the trendy entertainment complex that has seen the old Westergasfabriek turned into one of the city's biggest leisure destinations.

Oosterdok Amsterdam's new residential areas consists of manmade islands redeveloped from the ruins of former dockyards. The housing stock is low-level and contemporary, with plenty of on-trend cafes, bars, and design boutiques along the IJ-front promenades. Residents are mainly a young bunch working in creative industries. The Scheepvaartmuseum (p. 92) and Science Center NEMO (p. 96) are close by.

Outlying Areas Amstelveen lies south of Amsterdam, a primarily middle-class suburban area that has little to distinguish itself other than for being the home of the exceptional Cobra Modern Art Museum (p. 99).

Getting Around

BY PUBLIC TRANSPORT Public transportation in Amsterdam uses an electronic card called the **OV-chipkaart.** There are two main types of OV-chipkaart that are useful for visitors: "personal" cards can be used only by their pictured owner, while "anonymous" cards can be used by anyone, but not at the same time. The personal and anonymous cards, both valid for 5 years, cost 7.50€ and can be loaded and reloaded with up to 50€. Reduced-rate cards are available for seniors and children. Electronic readers on Metro and train station platforms and onboard trams and buses deduct the correct fare—just hold your card up against the reader at both the start and the end of the ride. These cards are valid throughout The Netherlands.

Another option for short-term visitors who plan to use public transportation a lot is a **1-day or a multiday card** from GVB: 24 hours (7.50€), 48 hours (12€), 72 hours (17€), 96 hours (21€), 120 hours (26€), 144 hours (30€), and 68 hours (32€).

The central information and ticket sales point for GVB Amsterdam, the city's public transportation company, is **GVB Tickets & Info,** Stationsplein (✆ **0900/8011** for timetable and fare information and other customer services; www.gvb.nl), in front of Centraal Station, open Monday to Friday from 7am to 6pm, Saturday and Sunday from 10am to 6pm. In addition, cards are available from GVB and Netherlands Railways ticket booths in Metro and train stations, ticket machines (automats) at Metro and train stations, and ticket machines onboard some trams.

BY TRAM Half the fun of Amsterdam is walking along the canals. The other half is riding the blue-and-gray trams that roll through most major streets. There are 16 tram routes, 10 of which (lines 1, 2, 4, 5, 9, 13, 16, 17, 24, and 26) begin and end at Centraal Station, so you know you can always get back to that central point if you get lost and have to start over. The city's other tramlines are 3, 7, 10, 12, and 14. Lines 3, 5, 12, and 24 are useful for visiting the sights south of the city around Museumplein, while 4, 9, 14, 16, and 24 serve the city center.

Trams have one access door that opens automatically, normally toward the rear; arrowed indicators point the way to the door. To board a tram that has no arrowed indicators, push the button beside the door on the outside of any car. To get off, you may need to push a button with an "open-door" graphic or the words DEUR OPEN. Tram doors close automatically, and they do so quite quickly, so don't hang around. Always remember to hold your card against the reader as you get on and off the tram. *Note:* If you don't "check out" as you get off, your card will carry on being charged and will run out of credit.

BY BUS An extensive bus network complements the trams, with many bus routes beginning and ending at Centraal Station, but it's generally much faster to go by tram. Some areas of the city are served only by bus.

If you're keen on your green credentials, use a bike taxi or rickshaw to get around the city. They're clean, relatively comfortable, and can nip along the cobbled streets giving Amsterdam's lethal cyclists a run for their money. Luckily they're all fully insured. The rickshaws are easy to spot all over the city, but especially around Centraal Station, Leidseplein, Museumplein, and Waterlooplein, or you can order your eco-taxi in advance. Contact **Amsterdam Bike Taxi** (✆ **645/412-725;** www.amsterdam biketaxi.info). Charges are 30€ per half hour per rickshaw.

BY METRO   Although it can't compare to the labyrinthine systems of Paris, London, and New York, Amsterdam does have its own Metro, with four lines—50, 51, 53, and 54—that run partly over ground and transport commuters in and out from the suburbs, running between 6am and midnight daily. From Centraal Station, you can use Metro trains to reach both Nieuwmarkt and Waterlooplein in the old city center.

The new Noord-Zuidlijn Metro line 52 is currently under construction to link Amsterdam-Noord (North), under the IJ waterway with the city center and Amsterdam Zuid station. It's due to be completed in 2017.

BY FERRY   Free GVB ferries (www.gvb.nl) for passengers and two-wheel transportation connect the center city with Amsterdam-Noord (North), across the IJ waterway. The short crossings are free, which makes them ideal micro-cruises as they afford fine views of the harbor. Ferries depart from Waterplein West behind Centraal Station. One route goes to Buiksloterweg on the north shore, with ferries every 6 to 12 minutes around-the-clock. A second route goes to IJplein, a more easterly point on the north shore, with ferries every 8 to 15 minutes from 6:30am to around midnight. A third ferry goes west to NDSM-Werf, a 14-minute trip. A fourth ferry runs between the Azartplein on Java/KNSM Island to the east of Centraal Station and Zamenhofstraat on Noord; and three others from Houthavenveer, west of the city, across to Noord.

BY TAXI   It used to be that you couldn't simply hail a cab from the street in Amsterdam but nowadays they often stop if you do. Otherwise, find one of the taxi stands sprinkled around the city, generally near the luxury hotels, at major squares such as the Dam, Spui, Rembrandtplein, Westermarkt, and Leidseplein, and of course at Centraal Station. Taxis have rooftop signs and blue license plates, and are metered. Hotel reception staff can easily order a cab for you, too.

Fares are regulated citywide and all cabs are metered; the meter starts at 2.89€ and there is a charge of 2.12€ per kilometer. A generally reliable service is **Taxi Centrale Amsterdam (TCA;** ✆ **020/650-6506;** www.tcataxi.nl). The fare includes a tip, but you may round up or give something for an extra service, like help with your luggage or for a helpful chat. In fact most Amsterdam cab drivers like to talk and are pretty knowledgeable about their city, so take full advantage of them.

BY CAR   If you're staying in Amsterdam, either leave your car at home or park up and save it for day trips into the Dutch countryside. There are limited **parking facilities** in the city itself but plenty of Park + Ride options in the suburbs, with rates of 8€ per 24 hours. Useful P+R parking lots include Olympisch Stadion and RAi in the southern city, and Sloterdyk and Zeeburg in the north; all are near public transport facilities. If you insist on parking in town, there are 14 designated car parks centrally, the most useful for tourists being at Waterlooplein 8 or Beursplein 15 and charging 2.50€ to 5€ per hour.

Don't risk leaving your car on the street as the limited public parking in the city is managed with a gauntlet-grip by Cition (www.cition.nl), who will **tow your car away** at the drop of a hat for the slightest parking violation and then whack you with a 420€ fine; cash payments not accepted. If you do have the misfortune to get towed, the collection depot is at Daniël Goedkoopstraat 9 and it's open daily 7am until 11pm.

There's no point whatsoever in hiring a car if you are intending to stay in Amsterdam and not venture out of the city, as the public transport system works efficiently and most attractions are within walking distance of each other. In addition, the streets are narrow, many are one-way, some are pedestrianized, and all are crowded with bonkers cyclists; in short, driving in the city is a nightmare. However, if you are travelling outside Amsterdam, it's usually cheapest to book a rental car online before you leave home. Try **Hertz** (www.hertz.com), **Avis** (www.avis.com), **Budget** (www.budget.com), or **Enterprise** (www.enterprise.com).

[Fast FACTS] AMSTERDAM

ATMs The easiest and cheapest way to get cash overseas is through an ATM—the **Cirrus and Plus** networks span the globe. Although some debit and credit cards can be used overseas without incurring charges, most banks charge a fee for international withdrawals—check with your bank before you leave home, and find out your daily limit. There are ATMs all over Amsterdam, and many are open 24/7, although you'll want to be a bit cautious about withdrawing cash in quiet areas after dark.

Business Hours Stores usually open from 9:30am to 6pm Tuesday, Wednesday, Friday, and Saturday. Many are closed on Monday morning, opening at 1pm, and most shops outside the center close all day Sunday. Some stay open until 8 or 9pm on Thursday. Most museums close 1 day a week (often Mon), but open some holidays, except for Koningsdag (King's Day on Apr 27; see p. 84), Christmas, and New Year's Day. (Even then, the Rijksmuseum is open every day of the year, regardless of public holidays.)

Consulates The **U.S. Consulate:** Museumplein 19 (✆ **020/575-5330;** http://amsterdam.usconsulate.gov; tram 3, 5, 12, 16, or 24). **The U.K. Consulate:** Koningslaan 44 (✆ **020/676-4343;** www.britain.nl; tram 2). The Australian, Canadian, Irish, New Zealand, UK, and U.S. embassies are all in The Hague (p. 129).

Emergencies For any **emergency** (fire, police, ambulance), the number is ✆ **112** from any land line or cellphone. For 24-hour urgent but **nonemergency** medical or dental services, call ✆ **088/0030-600;** the operator will connect you to an appropriate doctor or dentist. To **report a theft,** call ✆ **0900/8844.** Residents of E.U. countries must have a European Health Insurance Card (EHIC) to receive full health-care benefits in The Netherlands.

Internet Access Most hotels in Amsterdam offer Wi-Fi access as a matter of course, although some of the more expensive ones charge a daily (rip off) fee. **KPN hotspots** are scattered throughout the city; cost starts at 1.50€ for 15 minutes **(http://portal.hotspotsvankpn.com).**

Pharmacies In The Netherlands, a pharmacy is called an *apotheek* and sells both prescription and nonprescription medicines. Regular open hours are Monday to Saturday from around 9am to 6pm. A centrally located pharmacy is **Dam Apotheek,** Damstraat 2 (✆ **020/624-4331;** www.dam-apotheek.nl; tram 4, 9, 14, 16, or 24), close to the

National Monument on the Dam. Pharmacies post details of nearby **all-night and Sunday pharmacies** on their doors.

Post Office The city of Amsterdam doesn't have post offices as such anymore; instead various branches of newsagents, supermarkets, and grocery stores have postal points run by **PostNL** (www.post.nl). The stationers Gebroeders Winter (Rozengracht 62), the branch of Albert Heijn supermarket at Jodenbreestraat 21, and Ako newsstand (Reguliersbreestraat 19) all have postal points where you can mail a parcel or postcard home. Stamps can also be purchased from your hotel reception and any newsstands that sell postcards.

WHERE TO STAY

Whether you are after glitzy luxury with every conceivable amenity, a cozy townhouse hotel, family-friendly facilities, or bare-bones bed and board that frees up hard-earned cash for party purposes, Amsterdam will have just the right accommodation for you.

The city's not a great business destination, so you won't pick up great deals for weekend stays but most hotels offer rate reductions between November and March simply to fill their rooms—with the notable exception of the Christmas and New Year periods of course. Amsterdam is fast becoming an all-year-around destination and has many charms in the off season, such as empty museums, slashed prices during sales in the stores, and a full calendar of winter cultural events (p. 36).

In a world where almost everybody is online, it's easy to book accommodations well in advance of your trip. However, should you come unstuck and arrive in Amsterdam without a bed for the night, the **Iamsterdam Visitor Information Centers** at Schiphol Airport and outside Centraal Station will certainly be able to find you a port in a storm; ℂ **020/702-6000;** www.iamsterdam.com.

Self-Catering in Amsterdam

If you don't fancy staying in a hotel but would prefer to have a space to call your own in the city, self-catering doesn't come much better than in Amsterdam, where the accommodations stock includes dreamy canal-side townhouses, spacious studios, houseboats out in the IJ, and barges moored up along the Canal Ring. Look no further than the agency website **www.luxury-apartments-amsterdam.com** for countless smart, fully equipped apartments with all the fluff from Wi-Fi to flowers, and short- or long-term lets, while **www.houseboat-rental-amsterdam.com** and **www.house boathotel.nl** both hire out boats and studios by the water.

RECOMMENDED ACCOMMODATION AGENCIES

Couchsurfing (www.couchsurfing.org) connects travelers with folks willing to share their room/sofa/apartment for free or a very minimal charge.

AirBnB (www.airbnb.com) has thousands of Amsterdam properties on its books, from houseboats to studio apartments in sumptuous canal houses and miniscule bolt holes in windmills. Prices typically range from 75€ to 185€ per night.

IHA (www.iha.com) is a rental agency letting hundreds of Amsterdam apartments, cabins on barges and houseboats, or rural barns for up to 1,000€ per week.

TravelZoo (www.travelzoo.com) is a discount website offering cut-price, last-minute accommodation bargains in hotels as well as tickets for events and vouchers for restaurants. There are also British and European versions of the site.

All four recommended agencies have their own apps for download on to Android, iPhone, and other mobiles.

The Old Center

VERY EXPENSIVE

Hotel de l'Europe ★★   The grande dame of Amsterdam's luxury hotels occupies a prime location overlooking the Binnenamstel and is the final word in ostentatious splendor. The rooms are sumptuous and spacious, and flooded with light, all with barn-sized marble bathrooms. A new innovation for 2014 was the introduction of the all-suite Dutch Masters Wing, with every extravagant apartment boasting a copy of a famous oil painting from the Rijksmuseum. On top of double-Michelin-starred restaurant Bord'Eau, the spa, and the summer terrace with river views, l'Europe also boasts the award-wining Freddy's cocktail bar and what might well be Amsterdam's last *fumoir,* where the smoking of (only) cigars is still very much permitted.

Nieuwe Doelenstraat 2-14, 1012 CP Amsterdam. ✆ **020/531-1777.** www.leurope.nl. 111 units. 450€–720€ double. Parking 57€/day. **Amenities:** 2 restaurants, 2 bars, sauna, spa, free Wi-Fi.

Renaissance Amsterdam Hotel ★★   With a ghetto-fabulous new facelift completed in 2013, the Renaissance has risen phoenixlike from its drab former ashes and now is a standout among the city's soulless business hotels. Tucked away behind an historic facade on a quiet canal just a 5-minute walk from Centraal Station, the reception and lobby are now funky and welcoming, with a strikingly warm color scheme that continues into the guest rooms with bold, contrasting soft furnishings. The bathrooms are now state of the art, with marble fittings and power showers. On-site facilities include the Mediterranean-style bistro Scossa, a clubby bar kitted out in dark wood, and several meeting rooms in the historic and adjacent Koepelkerk (Dome Church).

Kattengat 1, 1012 SZ Amsterdam. ✆ **020/621-2223.** www.marriott.com. 402 units. 259€–799€ double. Parking 58€/day. **Amenities:** 2 restaurants, bar, business center, fitness room, free Wi-Fi.

EXPENSIVE

Mauro Mansion ★★★   Currently riding high on the Amsterdam list of hot hotels, Mauro Mansion is the antithesis of a bland city chain hotel. This little gem is a nine-room treasure-trove of quirky design hidden in a 16th-century canal house overlooking Geldersekade and is run by an equally offbeat couple. Several bedrooms have views over the canal and all are a stylish clash of old and new—wardrobes made of industrial piping, hammocks, beds swathed in net, shiny rubber flooring, and pristine white-tiled bathrooms. Children 11 and under are not allowed and breakfast is optional, costing 5€ per person and served between 8:30 and 11am, but such is its current popularity that you'll need to book well in advance. The only real drawback? There's no elevator.

Geldersekade 16, 1012 BH Amsterdam. ✆ **061/297-4594.** www.mauromansion.com. 9 units. 130€–250€ double. **Amenities:** Breakfast room, free Wi-Fi.

MODERATE

Blue Sheep B&B ★★   This stylish, family-run gem is found in a gorgeous canal house on a car-free street in a tranquil backwater of the old city center. There's no elevator and some of the pristine bathrooms are shared, but airy rooms furnished in styles from antique to contemporary and a standout mega-breakfast make this place the perfect choice for anyone chasing stylish accommodation without breaking the bank. And the amenable young owners Jan and Novella must be doing something right as their empire has grown to incorporate a selection of beautifully appointed apartments and suites close by suitable for romantic couples or families with young kids—but be

Amsterdam Hotels

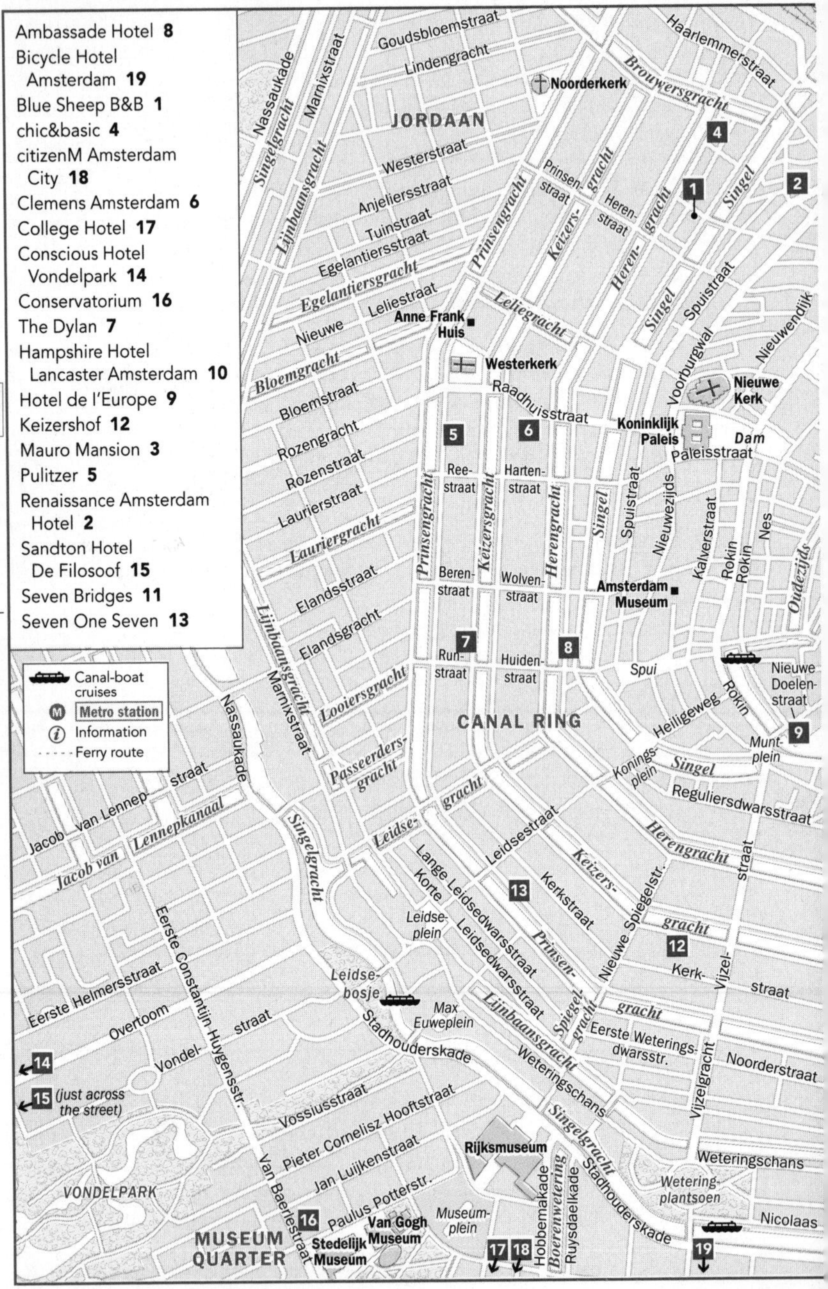

Canal-boat cruises

Ⓜ **Metro station**

ⓘ Information

- - - - Ferry route

JORDAAN

† **Noorderkerk**

Anne Frank Huis

Westerkerk

Nieuwe Kerk

Koninklijk Paleis *Dam*

Amsterdam Museum

CANAL RING

Max Euweplein

Rijksmuseum

VONDELPARK

MUSEUM QUARTER

Van Gogh Museum

Stedelijk Museum

(just across the street)

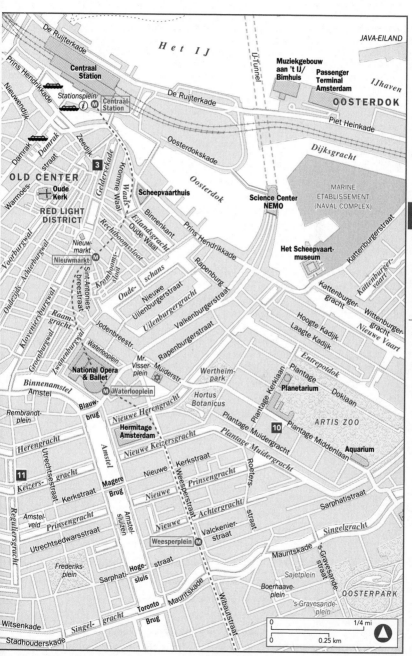

warned, all these options have very steep stairs and are not suitable for people with mobility issues.

Korsjespoortsteeg 3, 1015 AP Amsterdam. ✆ **06/2962-3499.** www.thebluesheep.net. 13 units. 119€–249€ double. Rates include full breakfast. Paid public parking nearby. **Amenities:** Breakfast room, supper on request, free Wi-Fi.

Canal Ring
VERY EXPENSIVE
The Dylan ★★★ Offering truly individual guest rooms with stripped oak floors, exposed beams, blindingly white bathrooms, and four-poster beds that you could lose a family in, Amsterdam's glossiest boutique hotel is located in a former 17th-century theater on lively Keizersgracht and well deserves its accolades. The never-ending list of facilities includes a concierge service, dinner cruises in the hotel's boat, a terrace for afternoon tea and evening drinks, and light-filled top-floor suites. As if that's not enough, the fabulous Michelin-starred restaurant Vinkeles (p. 73) also has its home in the Dylan. For a hotel so upmarket, the ambience is surprisingly chilled and informal, but with room rates starting at 350€ it is a very special treat.

Keizersgracht 384, 1016 GB Amsterdam. ✆ **020/530-2010.** www.dylanamsterdam.com. 39 units. 350€–1,400€ double. Rates include continental breakfast. Parking 80€/day. **Amenities:** 2 restaurants, bar, gym, on-boat catering, free Wi-Fi.

Pulitzer ★★★ Voted Dutch Hotel of the Year 2013 and awarded a place in the prestigious Condé Nast list of the top-25 hotels in northern Europe, the Pulitzer offers its lucky guests pure luxury without sinking into ostentation. Long considered the boutique hotel of choice in Amsterdam, it has a superior location on the side of Prinsengracht in between the charming Jordaan and the tourist hotspots of the Old Center, and it's right there among the retail delights of the buzzy Nine Streets (p. 106). The rooms and suites are smartly furnished and decorated in soothing creams and beiges, there's a lush spa, and the much-lauded **Restaurant Keizersgracht 238** has a perfect summer-time terrace, making this place a number-one spot for romantic weekend dalliances.

Prinsengracht 315-331, 1016 GZ Amsterdam. ✆ **020/523-5235.** www.pulitzeramsterdam.com. 230 units. 309€–706€ double. Parking 55€/day. **Amenities:** Restaurant, 3 bars, on-boat catering, art gallery, pet friendly, gym, Wi-Fi 19€/day.

EXPENSIVE
Seven One Seven ★★ Hardly a budget option, this magical, suite-only and award-wining temple of style is wonderfully furnished in lavish 19th-century style, complete with antique furnishings and with every possible amenity on tap. With views either over the canal or a leafy patio to the rear, there's no bad choice of room here. An elegant drawing room, a sun-spot terrace, views over the canal, a flower-filled breakfast room, and smooth service all contribute to making this a truly unforgettable experience in Amsterdam, far removed from impersonal chain hotels. A little irritant is the extra charge for breakfast over and above an already expensive stay.

Prinsengracht 717, 1017 JW Amsterdam. ✆ **020/427-0717.** www.717hotel.nl. 9 units. 275€–450€ double. Public parking nearby. **Amenities:** Breakfast room, free Wi-Fi.

MODERATE
Ambassade Hotel ★★ A far cry from the minimalist styling adopted by so many city hotels, the designers of the Ambassade evidently believed that more is best; the 10 17th- and 18th-century gabled townhouses sandwiched together to form this

Staying in an elegant 17th-century canal house in the UNESCO World Heritage-listed district may offer all the charm and atmosphere you could possibly dream of, but the fact remains that it's nigh on impossible to shoehorn an elevator into the cramped confines of most of these multi-story, narrow buildings. And it's expensive, in fact way beyond the means of most moderate and budget hotels, so many simply don't have them. If that's a problem, ask for a room on a low floor or choose another hotel where elevators are installed and working.

elegant frippery are gaily festooned with swags of curtain, chandeliers, and antiques—plus a collection of priceless CoBrA artwork (p. 99). The guest rooms have statement color palettes, fancy gilt mirrors, and walls filled with Dutch paintings. The five joyfully appointed suites all have views over the canal, as does the first-floor apartment; a few doors down at Herengracht 321, you'll find the hotel's blissful Koan Float massage center. Although not all rooms are accessible by elevator, plenty are; breakfast is not included in the room rate.

Herengracht 341, 1016 AZ Amsterdam. ℂ **020/555-0222.** www.ambassade-hotel.nl. 58 units. 186€–225€ double. Parking 45€/day. **Amenities:** Breakfast room, spa, free Wi-Fi.

Seven Bridges ★★★   Quite simply one of the most gorgeous hotels in the city, with individually decorated room boasting genuine antique furnishings in a variety of opulent Biedermeier, Art Deco, or rococo styles with original 17th-century wooden floors. The attic rooms have sloped ceilings and exposed wood beams and provide the perfect romantic hideaway for couples. Breakfast is served in the guest rooms as there are no public spaces beyond the entrance lobby, which cuts overhead and may explain the exceptionally reasonable prices for a hotel of such comfort and opulence. As with so many Canal Ring hotels, there's no elevator.

Reguliersgracht 31, 1017 LK Amsterdam. ℂ **020/623-1329.** www.sevenbridgeshotel.nl. 11 units. 95€–205€ double. **Amenities:** Free Wi-Fi.

INEXPENSIVE

Keizershof ★   Offering quite exceptional value for your money in the expensive city center, the Keizershof occupies a four-story, narrow canal house that dates back to 1672, so of course there's no elevator. Guestrooms are beamed and plain with simple, modern furnishings, and only two have private bathrooms; they either overlook the bustle of the canal or a tranquil pocket-size, flower-filled courtyard to the rear, where breakfast is served in summer. Downstairs a TV lounge shares its space with a grand piano, but what makes this place memorable is the warm welcome from its owners, the hospitable De Vries family, who will go that extra mile to make your stay comfortable.

Singel 301, 1012 WH Amsterdam. ℂ **020/622-2855.** www.hotelkeizershof.nl. 6 units. 95€–130€ double. Rates include breakfast. **Amenities:** Breakfast room, TV lounge, free Wi-Fi.

Jordaan
MODERATE

chic&basic ★   An example of the winds of change blowing through the Amsterdam hotel world, this newish and ultra-cool boutique hotel is part of a European chain

4

AMSTERDAM | Where to Stay

Despite there being thousands of rooms in more than 550 hotels up for grabs in Amsterdam, it can be nigh on impossible to find a room between May and September, when the weather is at its best and there are plenty of festivals and events kicking off. If you get really stuck for accommodation, the best bet is to contact the **Iamsterdam visitor information centers** (p. 55) at Stationsplein 10 or in Schiphol Plaza at the airport (© **020/702-6000;** www.iamsterdam.com), or you could consider staying in Haarlem (p. 115), which is only a 15-minute train ride from Amsterdam city center.

enjoying great success for it simple styling and decent prices. It's tucked away behind a canal-house facade, and the compact bedrooms are gaily decorated with homely touches like patchwork quilts or wackily upholstered comfy chairs, while the public spaces in the hotel are all smooth and contemporary. Best of all is the light-filled loft apartment with glorious views across the canal—but there's no elevator.

Herengracht 13–19, 1015 BA Amsterdam. © **020/522-2345.** www.chicandbasic.com. 28 units. 135€–190€ double. Rates include continental breakfast. **Amenities:** Breakfast room, coffee bar, free Wi-Fi.

BUDGET

Clemens Amsterdam ★★   A little hotel that packs a big punch, the Clemens is a budget choice that has been recently extensively upgraded. As befits a two-star establishment, it's not long on amenities but the refurbed (in 2013) rooms are all pristine and welcoming with wet rooms. Bear in mind when booking that the Clemens sits on one of the city's main thoroughfares, although the rooms at the front of the building do have the added pull of cute wrought-iron balconies to perch on. Typically for a small hotel in central Amsterdam, it occupies four floors in a narrow townhouse and there's simply no place to put an elevator, but the hotel is fantastically located near the Anne Frank Huis and the Westerkerk.

Raadhuisstraat 39, 1016 DC Amsterdam. © **020/624-6089.** www.clemenshotel.nl. 14 units. 85€–100€ double. Rates include continental breakfast. **Amenities:** Breakfast room, free Wi-Fi.

Museum Quarter
VERY EXPENSIVE

Conservatorium ★★   The new kid on the block of competitive upmarket hotels in Amsterdam, the Conservatoriun opened in 2011 and occupies the former neo-Gothic Sweelinck Conservatory of Music. It is owned by bespoke hotel chain The Set and certainly sets a new benchmark for luxury with 12 stylish suites with vaulted ceilings, wooden floors, and sleek marble bathrooms, plus several eating options under the stewardship of super-chef Schilo van Coevorden. It is mere steps away from the Museumplein attractions, although when you spy the gorgeous Akasha Holistic spa, it'll be a toss up between spending the day floating around in there or elbowing your way through the crowds to stand in front of Rembrandt's fabled "The Night Watch" in the Rijksmuseum.

Van Baerlestraat 27, 1071 AN Amsterdam. © **020/570-0000.** www.conservatoriumhotel.com. 129 units. 345€–945€ double. Parking 65€/day. **Amenities:** 2 restaurants, bar, pool, spa, gym, free Wi-Fi.

EXPENSIVE

College Hotel ★★   A sleek and urbane boutique hotel found in a former school (hence the name), the College is a couple of minutes from Amsterdam's Big Three museums, the Rijksmuseum, Stedelijk, and Van Gogh. It's also dangerously close to the shockingly expensive designer stores on PC Hoofstraat so you'll get to spy on plenty of self-consciously glam 30-something European professionals among the vaguely Art Nouveau surroundings of the hotel's luscious, shady courtyard and bar. The guest rooms are the last word in contemporary cool, in soothing beiges and tans, with stacks of pillows, smart fixtures and fittings, and plenty of space to swing a cat.

Roelof Hartstraat 1, 1071 VE Amsterdam. ⓒ **020/571-1511.** www.thecollegehotel.com. 40 units. 125€–230€ double. Parking 50€/day. **Amenities:** Restaurant, bar, free Wi-Fi.

Sandton Hotel De Filosoof ★★   A staple on the Amsterdam hotel scene for decades, the Filosoof was the city's first theme hotel, decked out as it is with a series of guestrooms decorated in themes loosely pertaining to various gentleman philosophers, which means that a smattering of quotes and portraits adorn the walls. Housed in a graceful 19th-century townhouse in refined residential environs a step away from the Vondelpark, rooms are small and some are in need of a makeover, but they are cheerily idiosyncratic with crooked walls and madly sloping floors. A tiny bar is tucked into the lobby and a tranquil patio garden lurks behind the hotel for coffee or drinks on a sunny day. There's no elevator to the suites.

Anna van den Vondelstraat 6, 1054 GZ Amsterdam. ⓒ **020/683-3013.** www.sandton.eu. 38 units. 120€–195€ double. Rates include breakfast. Public parking nearby. **Amenities:** Breakfast room, bar, free Wi-Fi.

De Pijp
BUDGET

Bicycle Hotel Amsterdam ★★   Homely and basic, the Bicycle Hotel is fiercely proud of its sustainable ethos; it is powered by solar heat, has a "green" roof, and uses recycled furniture wherever possible. The miniscule bedrooms are no great shakes in terms of luxury but are spotlessly clean; be warned, however, that the very cheapest rooms at 30€ don't stretch to private bathroom. A few have kitchenettes for self-catering stays and there are also a couple of triples for families. Amazingly for these prices, a decent Dutch breakfast of bread, ham, and cheese is included in the room rate. Foolhardy guests who choose to explore Amsterdam by bike can rent cycles for 7.50€ per day. There's no elevator and payment is preferred in cash.

Van Ostadestraat 123, 1072 SV Amsterdam. ⓒ **020/679-3452.** www.bicyclehotel.com. 16 units. 50€–120€ double. Rates include breakfast. **Amenities:** Breakfast room, free Wi-Fi.

Oud Zuid
MODERATE

citizenM Amsterdam City ★★   One of the new gaggle of no-frills accommodation options that seem to be flooding European cities, CitizenM has washed up close to the World Trade Center and RAi and caters largely to short-stay business travelers, although there's the fast Tram 5 service right into the city center for sightseers. Check in is automated, barista-standard coffee is on tap 24/7, and a canteen serves up sushi and salads at lunch. The zingy, ultramodern room designs include podlike showers, touch-screen remotes, huge, comfortable beds, and free movies; breakfast is extra at

11€ if ordered in advance, 3€ more on the day. There's another outpost within spitting distance of Schiphol airport.

Prinses Irenestraat 30, 1077 WX Amsterdam. ℂ **020/811-7090.** www.citizenm.com. 215 units. 89€–150€ double. **Amenities:** 24/7 snack room, bar, free Wi-Fi.

Conscious Hotel Vondelpark ★★   A new arrival on the Dutch accommodation scene that shouts its green credibility throughout, with living plant walls, eco-roofs, and green energy. It's run by a young, handsome, and very cool staff who go the whole hog to help and make recommendations on where to eat and what to see. They let their collective hair down at the weekends when every night is party night, with music and dancing in the bar. Bedrooms are compact and wittily adorned with pithy slogans on energy conservation, and the breakfast bar is an organic delight. Tram Line 1 stops right outside the hotel and is in the city center in under 5 minutes. The sister hotel is near Museumplein and ideally placed for visiting the Rijksmuseum and Van Gogh Museum.

Overtoom 519, 1054 LH Amsterdam. ℂ **020/820-3333.** www.conscioushotels.com. 81 units. 90€–175€ double. Parking 23€/day. **Amenities:** Breakfast room, bar, discounted gym next door, free Wi-Fi.

De Plantage
MODERATE
Hampshire Hotel Lancaster Amsterdam ★   Located on the eastern, gentrified side of the city, a world away from the leery Red Light District, this hotel is perfectly placed for family visits to Artis Zoo, the Tropenmuseum, and the Botanical Gardens. Even better, it's just a 10-minute ride on trams 9 or 14 to all the central amenities and action. Prices are reasonable (although Wi-Fi is 13€ per day and breakfast is also extra) with spacious bedrooms furnished in neutral, inoffensive tones and gigantic black-and-white images over the beds. If you're traveling with kids, there are several triple rooms available.

Plantage Middenlaan 48, 1081 DH Amsterdam. ℂ **020/535-6888.** www.edenlancasterhotel.com. 91 units. 138€–188€ double. Public parking nearby. **Amenities:** Breakfast room, restaurant, bar.

WHERE TO EAT

Amsterdam's cuisine is a perfect mirror image of the city itself; multi-ethnic, warming, and exciting. As a trading city with tentacles that spread all over the world, Amsterdam has welcomed immigrants from the Far East, South America, Africa, and Eastern Europe ever since the Golden Age days of the 17th century, a phenomenon reflected in the diverse cooking styles seen in its many restaurants. In Amsterdam, it seems, you can eat in any language and certainly at any price, taking your pick from Michelin-starred gastronomic feasts, multi-plated Indonesian *rijstaffel* banquets, or comforting snacks of Dutch *bitterballen.*

As with most northern European countries and certainly in comparison with Spain and Italy when families are still munching away at midnight, Amsterdam eats early. Even the smartest restaurants open around 6pm, which makes dining out a family-friendly experience.

Old Center
EXPENSIVE
Bloesem ★ MEDITERRANEAN   Now serving an almost completely organic menu, trendy Bloesem is screaming up the restaurant ratings in Amsterdam. This is a

romantic little spot with gilt-framed mirrors and rust-colored walls just off work-a-day Haarlemmerdijk, where rising-star Chef Marco Deegen decides what to cook each day according to market and season; in other words, after preferences or allergies have been checked, there's no choice. The gastronomic bent is European fusion, with offerings such as beef tenderloin with walnut, cocoa sauce, and pumpkin.

Binnen Dommersstraat 13–15. ⓒ **06/1445-6644.** www.restaurant-bloesem.info. Fixed-price menus 33€–43€. Tues–Sun 6–10:30pm.

MODERATE

Kapitein Zeppos ★★ FISH   A casual cafe tucked away down a little alley off Spui, Zeppos offers cheeses, salads, and great pots of mussels by day and feasts of Portuguese *mariscos* (mixed seafood platter), paella, or Coquille St.-Jacques by night. It's popular with students from the University of Amsterdam across the street and has a slightly cheesy decor that's compounded when the equally cheesy 1980s disco music starts up late on weekend nights. There's live music most evenings (not Sun) and kitschy sing-alongs around a grand piano the first Sunday brunch of the month in winter.

Gebed Zonder End 5, Spui. ⓒ **020/624-2057.** www.zeppos.nl. Mains 17€–24€. Daily noon–1am (Fri–Sat till 3am).

Restaurant-Café In de Waag ★★ DUTCH   Bang in the middle of vibrant Nieuwmarkt, the historic Waag buzzes day and night; its outdoor cafe is filled to bursting all afternoon and it serves late-night snacks of nachos and Dutch cheeses to soak up any surfeits of alcohol. The restaurant inside the Waag is made for romance, with a candlelit dining room and long trestle tables ideally suited to one of Amsterdam's oldest buildings. The menu is short and predictable, offering Aberdeen Angus steaks and fish of the day, but the cooking is skilled and the atmosphere chilled.

Nieuwmarkt 4. ⓒ **020/422-7772.** www.indewaag.nl. Mains 19€–25€. Daily 10am–10:30pm.

Supperclub Amsterdam ★ FUSION   Having been on the list of things to do in Amsterdam for years, Supperclub has now spread across the world, with branches in San Francisco and Dubai. This stark, white, wildly popular restaurant-cum-cocktail bar has two tricks up its sleeve: Diners lounge on couches and cushions to listen to whatever the DJ is playing, and there is no menu—you will be served a five-course feast of whatever is available seasonally. Inform your waiter of any dietary restrictions and sit back to see what arrives. Post-supper is party time with live music and wild dancing. Reservations required.

Jonge Roelensteeg 21. ⓒ **020/344-6400.** www.supperclub.com. Mains 20€, fixed-priced menus 69€. Daily 8pm–late.

Visrestaurant Lucius ★★ SEAFOOD   A top choice for fresh fish in Amsterdam, Lucius is decked out like a traditional fishmongers with tiled walls and marble tabletops, wooden seating, and ceiling fans. It has been going great guns for 40 years. The spectacular seafood platter includes piles of fresher-than-fresh mussels, oysters, clams, and shrimp, plus a half lobster, and there's a reasonably priced set menu for 40€, consisting of three courses that could include langoustines, mackerel, or earthy pike perch. Cooking styles are unfussy, allowing the true taste of the fish to shine on the plate. Reservations are recommended on the weekend.

Spuistraat 247. ⓒ **020/624-1831.** www.lucius.nl. Mains 22€–30€, fixed-price menu 40€, seafood platters to share 63€–115€. Daily 5pm–midnight.

4

AMSTERDAM | Where to Eat

Amsterdam Restaurants

Bloesem **2**
Bordewijk **4**
Brasserie Plancius **21**
Café Cobra **15**
Café de Sluyswacht **23**
Café Restaurant
  Mamouche **17**
Envy **9**
EYE Bar-Restaurant **26**
Golden Temple **18**
Het Ketelkeuken **1**
Kapitein Zeppos **11**
Koffiehuis de Hoek **8**
La Rive **19**
Le Garage **16**
Miss Korea Barbecue **17**
Nam Kee Chinatown **25**
Pancake Bakery **6**
Restaurant Blauw **14**
Restaurant de Kas **20**
Restaurant-Café
  In de Waag **24**
Soen **7**
Stubbe's Haring **5**
Supperclub
  Amsterdam **10**
Tapas & Crazy
  Cocktail Bar **22**
Toscanini **3**
Vinkeles **13**
Visrestaurant Lucius **12**
Wilhelmina-Dok **27**

0 _____ 1/4 mi
0 _____ 0.25 km

Canal-boat cruises
M Metro station
ⓘ Information
······ Ferry route

Goudsbloemstr.
Haarlemmerstraat
Frederik Hendrik-plantsoen
Lindengracht
Brouwersgracht
Noorderkerk
Marnixstraat
JORDAAN
Westerstraat
Prinsen-straat
Heren-straat
Singel
Singelgracht
Nassaukade
Lijnbaansgracht
Anjeliersstraat
Tuinstraat
Egelantiersstraat
Egelantiersgracht
Leliegracht
Heren
Singel
Spuistraat
Nieuwe
Leliestraat
Anne Frank Huis
Bloemgracht
Westerkerk
Nieuwe Kerk
Bloemstraat
Raadhuisstraat
Koninklijk Paleis
Dam
Paleisstraat
Rozengracht
Ree-str.
Harten-straat
Voorburgwal
Nieuwendijk
Rozenstraat
Laurierstraat
Lauriergracht
Herengracht
Singel
Spuistraat
Nieuwezijds
Kalverstraat
Rokin
Rokin
Nes
Oudezijds
Elandsstraat
Beren-straat
Wolven-straat
Amsterdam Museum
Elandsgracht
Lijnbaansgracht
Marnixstraat
Run-straat
Huiden-straat
Spui
Nieuwe Doelen-straat
Looiersgracht
CANAL RING
Heiligeweg
Rokin
Passeerders-gracht
Konings-plein
Singel
Munt-plein
Nassaukade
Leidse-gracht
Leidsestraat
Keizers-gracht
Kerkstraat
Herengracht
Reguliersdwarsstraat
Lange Leidsedwarsstraat
Korte Leidsedwarsstraat
Prinsen-gracht
Nieuwe Spiegelstr.
gracht
straat
Leidse-plein
Leidse-bosje
Spiegel-gracht
Kerk-straat
Vijzel-straat
Eerste Constantijn Huygensstr.
Overtoom
Max Euweplein
Lijnbaansgracht
Eerste Weterings-dwarsstr.
Vijzelgracht
Noorderstraat
Overtoom
straat
Stadhouderskade
Weteringschans
Singelgracht
Vondel-
Vossiusstraat
Pieter Cornelisz Hooftstraat
Rijksmuseum
Weteringschans
Jan Luijkenstraat
Wetering-plantsoen
VONDELPARK
Van Baerle-
Paulus Potterstr.
Museum-plein
Hobbemakade
Boerenwetering
Ruysdaelkade
Stadhouders-
Nicolaas
MUSEUM QUARTER
Museum
Van Gogh Museum
Stedelijk Museum
kade

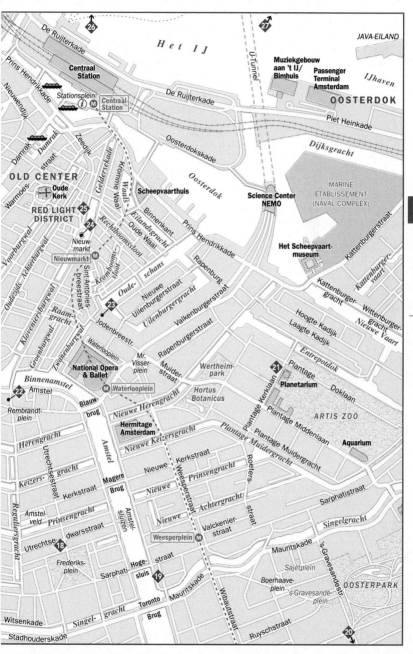

Traditional Dutch taverns or "brown cafes" are great places to mix with local Amsterdammers, as they are the very embodiment of *gezellighied*, that particularly Dutch mixture of charm, conviviality, and comfort all wrapped into one splendid welcoming package. Some brown cafes date right back to Rembrandt's day; all are warm and cheery, with dark interiors and simple wooden furniture and bars. Some have kitchens where short-order chefs rustle up all manner of moderately priced breakfasts, all-day dishes, *broodjes* (sandwiches), and simple suppers. Opening hours are anywhere between 8 and 10am and 1 and 3am the following day.

Hoppe ★★ is an ancient brown cafe that dates back to 1670. It has a convivial, English-pub atmosphere, and is standing-room-only in the early evening, when the place fills up with a merry after-work bunch. Things can become a bit rowdy after a couple of samplings of Dutch *jenever*, a ginlike liqueur with recipes dating back to the 18th century. Main dishes are 7.50€ or less. It's open daily 8am to 1am (Sat–Sun till 2am). You'll find it at Spui 18–20 (ℂ **020/420-4420;** www.cafe-hoppe.nl).

't Smalle ★★★ is on the edge of the cute Jordaan area. It's a traditional locals' cafe decked out in wood and glass and offering a small menu of snacks (dishes 3.50€–8.75€). The primary business here is the beer, so grab a glass and join the local drinkers at the bar, or on warm evenings sit outside on the decking over the canal. 't Smalle is on Egelantiersgracht 12, and open daily 10am to 1am (ℂ **020/623-9617;** www.t-smalle.nl).

INEXPENSIVE

Café de Sluyswacht. ★★ DUTCH   Tilting at a precarious angle over the Oudeschans canal, this former 17th-century lock-keeper's cottage is one of the oldest and most famous pubs in Amsterdam. Inside all is crooked, with wooden bars and uneven stone floors. Sample the *wit bier* (white beer) and a plate of strong Dutch cheese and enjoy the tiny, crowded terraces with views over the canal or towards the Museum Het Rembrandthuis.

Jodenbreestraat 1. ℂ **020/625-7611.** www.sluyswacht.nl. Mon–Thurs 12:30pm–1am, Fri–Sat 12:30pm–3am, Sun 12:30–7pm. Mains 7.50€–18€.

Nam Kee Chinatown ★★★ CHINESE   The most famous restaurant in Amsterdam's burgeoning Chinatown is also one of its best; this family-run venue looks like nothing from the outside and frankly not that much in the neon-lit sparse interior but it's always packed out with local Chinese families as well as tourists. The plates piled high with noodles, Peking duck, and beef spare ribs dripping in honey simply fly out of the kitchen. There are now two more equally successful outposts of Nam Kee at Geldersekade 117 and Marie Heinekenplein 4. If you don't fancy eating out, there's also a delivery service.

Zeedijk 111–113. ℂ **020/624-3470.** www.namkee.net. Daily noon–11pm. Mains 7.50€–25€.

Stubbe's Haring ★★ FISH   Raw herring is a Dutch specialty, and there are dozens of *haringhuis* stands in town, but this one is regarded as the best. Located on a bridge near Centraal Station, the stall is something of a local institution and long lines form here come lunchtime. It's a great spot to sample raw herring served in a bread roll with pickles and sweet onions; tip your head back and try and eat the fish whole for a quintessential Amsterdam experience.

Nieuwe Haarlemmersluis. ℂ **020/623-3212.** Sandwiches 5.50€. Midday–evening. No credit cards.

Tapas & Crazy Cocktail Bar ★ SPANISH   This quirky place is decked out in madcap tiles and colors like something Gaudí would have designed in Barcelona, but it is just off Rembrandtplein in the heart of Amsterdam's nighttime action. Part of the charm has to be the Catalan owner Dhillon and his oddball Georgian partner, who are outgoing party people, because although the tapas (garlic prawns, *albondigas* meatballs, tortilla) are decent they're certainly not the world's best and the restaurant doesn't get going until after 11pm. However, when the cocktails start coming across the bar—which is stacked with Spanish brandies and South American tequilas–you can forgive the food as the partying flows out into the streets. Friday and Saturday are salsa nights.

Halvemaansteeg 8, off Rembrandtplein. ℂ **020/777-9090.** Tapas 6€–9€. Daily noon–1am (Fri–Sat till 3am).

Canal Ring
VERY EXPENSIVE
Vinkeles ★★ FRENCH   Housed in the converted bakery of a 17th-century almshouse that is now the Dylan, Amsterdam's top boutique hotel, Vinkeles has been overseen by top Michelin-star chef Dennis Kuipers since 2006. He whips up unusual signature dishes such as sea bass with cannabis seed, Iberico ham, and baby squid. Should you decide to splash out and eat at the Chef's Table, the bill will set you back a trauma-inducing 490€ for two; for that you get to feast on seven extravagantly tasty courses teamed with exquisite wine pairings as recommended by sommelier Grosse Hollander.

Dylan Hotel, Keizersgracht 384. ℂ **020/530-2010.** www.vinkeles.com. Mains 34€–60€, fixed-price menus 105€–135€. Mon–Sat 7–10:30pm.

MODERATE
Envy ★★ MODERN ITALIAN   The emphasis at this matte-black citadel of Zen is grazing on small plates of food, tapas-style. Small but perfectly formed tuna, crab, risotto, sausage, and entrecôte dishes are all created in the open kitchen and most of the ingredients are organic. Guest chefs often make their appearance, and it's on its way to getting a coveted Michelin star.

Prinsengracht 381. ℂ **020/344-6407.** www.envy.nl. Mains 10€–13€, tasting menu 35€. Daily 6pm–1am, Fri–Sun noon–3pm.

Golden Temple ★★ VEGETARIAN   This is one of the best vegetarian, vegan, and raw-food options in town. Housed in a narrow, candle-lit dining hall with an open kitchen, low-slung tables, and rugs as decoration, the menu goes one step beyond the normal veggie affairs with its unlikely roster of Indian and Middle Eastern plates, mung bean salads, and Italian pizza. Mixed *thalis* and *mezze* are the delicious way to go but there is also a choice of chunky salads using ingredients such as quinoa, tempeh, and soba noodles. If anything, the ethnic music can sometimes get a bit irksome and there's no alcohol; sadly it's closed at lunchtime, as this would make a great sightseeing pit stop.

Utrechtsestraat 126. ℂ **020/626-8560.** www.restaurantgoldentemple.com. Mains 14€–21€. Daily 5:30–9:30pm.

INEXPENSIVE

Koffiehuis de Hoek ★ DUTCH   An old-style Amsterdam cafe on the corner of the Nine Streets shopping enclave and overlooking the canal, this place positively bursts at the seams with local workers at lunchtime. Grab a table for an all-day breakfast or a Dutch snack of croquettes or bitterballen washed down with an excellent espresso; take a rain check on the acidic house wine and try a local beer instead. If you don't fancy sharing a table, join the line for takeaway sandwiches piled high with salami and salad.

Prinsengracht 341. ✆ **020/625-3872.** www.koffiehuisamsterdam.nl. Snacks from 5€. Tues–Fri 7:30am–4pm, Sat 9am–3:30pm.

Pancake Bakery ★ PANCAKES   There are many, many pancakes houses in Amsterdam but this is one of the best. A 17th-century canal warehouse houses the simple eatery where you can sample yummy pancakes with your choice of 70 toppings and stuffings, from Indonesian chicken to honey, nuts, and whipped cream. The selection of cracking breakfast options includes organic muesli, scrambled eggs, and giant omelets. The bakery is a boon if you're traveling with children as they seem to have insatiable appetites for pancakes, plus it's on Prinsengracht and suitably placed for a treat after a visit to the sobering Anne Frank Huis.

Prinsengracht 191. ✆ **020/625-1333.** www.pancake.nl. Pancakes 6€–17€. Daily 9am–9:30pm.

Soen ★★ THAI   A relative newcomer on the block, this stripped-down, wooden-floored Thai joint is somewhere between a local cafe and sophisticated restaurant. Thai delicacies such as spicy *tom yum* soup and pad Thai noodles are offered with a choice of meats, fish, or vegetarian options and in a variety of chili heats from cowardly to head blasting. The chefs also offer a takeaway delivery service and hampers stuffed full of goodies for picnics on canal cruises. A great choice for casual dining in the evening and one of the few places open after 9pm during the week in this area.

Prinsengracht 178. ✆ **020/334-2247.** www.soen.thai-food.nl. Mains 14€–18€. Daily 5:30–10pm.

Jordaan

MODERATE

Bordewijk ★★ MODERN FRENCH   Regarded as one of the best French restaurants in Amsterdam, Bordewijk is patronized by locals in the know for its affordable prices and the casual vibe of the minimalist restaurant, which is sparsely but stylishly kitted out with wooden floors and spindly tables. In true French style there's not much here for vegetarian diners—the menu inhabits the world of suckling pig and tripe, all deliciously cooked by consummate chef Wil Demandt. His creative French cuisine is paired with a superb wine list and service is relaxed, so expect dinner here to last all night. There's a terrace for alfresco dining alongside the canal in summer. Reservations recommended.

Noordermarkt 7. ✆ **020/624-3899.** www.bordewijk.nl. Mains 20€–30€, fixed-price menus 39€–54€. Tues–Sat 6:30–10:30pm.

Toscanini ★ ITALIAN   The chefs at Jordaan's superlative Italian restaurant make almost everything on the premises, from the organic bread to the pasta, which comes in myriad shapes and colors. The vaulted restaurant leads on to an open kitchen that operates like clockwork, with piles of *carpaccio,* mixed salads, fettuccine with artichoke, seafood risotto, veal cutlets, and chargrilled steaks constantly pouring forth. Recently quibbles about the service have crept into reviews but my last visit there was

Popular snacks include **bitterballen** (fried meatballs) available in most bars and bistros and served with cold beer, or **patat** (fries) bought from street vendors and eaten dunked in mayonnaise, straight from the paper cone.

Haring (herring) is the most popular fish in Amsterdam, traditionally eaten whole and pickled from street vendors such as the famous Stubbe's Haring (p. 72) in Nieuwe Haarlemmersluis.

For sweet Dutch street food options, see p. 78.

as good as ever. While the tasting menu is a little pricey, it's possible to eat comparatively cheaply, and very well, from the a la carte menu.

Lindengracht 75. ℂ **020/623-2813.** www.restauranttoscanini.nl. Mains 14€–26€, tasting menu 48€. Mon–Sat 6–10:30pm.

Museum Quarter
EXPENSIVE
Le Garage ★ POSH BRASSERIE Once the hottest restaurant in town and awarded a Michelin Bib Gourmand, Le Garage has been under scrutiny recently for slipping standards of service; the jury is still out on this but the food is certainly holding up. Try tuna pizza or piles of oysters or go for the astonishingly good-value six-course menu that offers brasserie favorites including fish croquettes, veal cutlet, and crème brûlée. It's such a sparkly, glitzy restaurant, with bright lights, big mirrors, and bright-red banquettes somehow reminiscent of Las Vegas that is feels rude not to pull on the glad rags to go eat there. Reservations recommended.

Ruysdaelstraat 54–56. ℂ **020/679-7176.** www.restaurantlegarage.nl. Mains 23€–38€, fixed-price lunch 27€, fixed-price dinner 36€. Mon–Fri noon–11pm, Sat–Sun 6–11pm. Jul–Aug closed for lunch and Sun.

MODERATE
Café Cobra ★★ DUTCH Little beats sitting outside at Café Cobra on a sunny afternoon, watching the great and good of Amsterdam come out to play for Sunday brunch. The food is not top-drawer but the spicy croquettes and *bitterballen* (meatballs) accompanied with fat fries, mayo, and a glass of Prosecco certainly hit the spot. By day, the light-filled cafe interior is always heaving with tourists as amazingly it is the only restaurant adjacent to the Rijksmuseum, Stedelijk, and Van Gogh museums, but the young wait staff cope admirably with the multilingual crowds and service is always impeccable and smooth. In winter there's an ice rink outside.

Hobbemastraat 18. ℂ **020/470-0111.** www.cobracafe.nl. Daily 10am–7pm. Mains 7€–20€.

Oud Zuid
EXPENSIVE
Restaurant Blauw ★★★ INDONESIAN Part of the new breed of Asian restaurants in The Netherlands, De Blauw may serve traditional Indonesian dishes but its minimalist decor and service from the beautiful, charming wait staff are thoroughly 21st century, and there's even a decent wine list—a rarity in Indonesian eateries. It's filled to the rafters on two noisy floors every night of the week and even then people line up for the chance of a table. The *rijsttafel* consists of an amazing 17 plates,

Thanks to the influx of immigrants from across the world into The Netherlands, anything goes in the country's cuisine, particularly in the capital Amsterdam and the port city of Rotterdam (p. 136). Chinese, Surinamese, Turkish, Indian, Indonesian, Italian, and Mediterranean cooking has been accepted into the Dutch gourmet lexicon since immigration first began in the 17th century. Indonesian *rijstaffel* (meaning "rice table") is virtually a staple national dish, originating with Dutch plantation overseers in what was then called the East Indies.

The basic concept of *rijstaffel* is to sample many different tastes on one plate, relying on a backdrop of plain rice to help blend textures and flavors.

Restaurants in Amsterdam offer a shared feast of up to 30 small plates; these can include *loempia* (classic Chinese-style egg rolls); *satay* or *sateh* (small kabobs of pork, grilled and served with a spicy peanut sauce), *perkedel* (meatballs), *gado-gado* (vegetables in peanut sauce), *daging smoor* (beef in soy sauce), *babi ketjap* (pork in soy sauce), *kroepoek* (crunchy, puffy shrimp toast), *serundeng* (fried coconut), *roedjak manis* (fruit in sweet sauce), and *pisang goreng* (fried banana).

One of the best Indonesian restaurants in the city is **De Blauw** in Oud Zuid (p. 75); other tasty alternatives include **Kantjil en de Tiger** on Spiustraat (www.kantjil.nl) and **Long Pura** on Rozengracht (www.restaurant-longpura.com).

including pickles, fried and sticky rice, pork balls, plantain, satay, and chili-laden beef, pork, chicken, and fish dishes. Other tasty mains include chicken cooked with lime and soy, or slow-braised beef in coconut sauce. Heaven! Remember to book ahead.

Amstelveenseweg 158–160. ℘ **020/675-5000.** www.restaurantblauw.nl. Mon–Thurs 6–10:30pm, Fri 6–11pm, Sat 5–11pm, Sun 5–10:30pm. Mains 21€–27€, *rijstaffel* 26€–32€.

De Pijp

MODERATE

Café Restaurant Mamouche ★★ MOROCCAN   The styling of this intimate little restaurant is a romantic blend of French brasserie (mirrors, smartly laid tables) and North African (tagines and candlesticks) flourishes, and that is reflected in the trans-Mediterranean menu—a happy blending of North African dishes and French influences. Hence confit of duck, grilled fish with *charmoula* (a spicy Maghreb marinade), and couscous *mechoui* often appear on the brief menu. Locals and overseas visitors alike have been known to visit more than once simply to experience the specialty of the house: a delicious lamb tagine with prunes, almonds, beans, and coriander. Unusually for a restaurant, the bar staff can whip up a punchy cocktail too.

Quellijnstraat 104. ℘ **020/670-0736.** www.restaurantmamouche.nl. Mains 16€–24€. Daily 5–10:30pm.

Miss Korea Barbecue ★★ KOREAN   Another interesting choice among De Pijp's multicultural restaurants, Miss Korea is smartly designed with bare brick walls illuminated by unusual mood lighting, and straggles through three adjoining townhouses. A positive sign is that the restaurant is always packed out with Korean families happily tucking in to their tabletop BBQ of top-quality meats and seafood with as many side dishes, including kimchi and pickles, as they can eat. Despite the crowds, the wait staff is happy to explain the intricacies of the menu—there's a set price for the main courses, which is halved for kids, and you choose three items per person for as many courses as you can stuff down in 2½ hours.

Albertcuypstraat 66–70. ℂ **020/679-0606.** www.misskorea.nl. Fixed-price menu Mon–Wed 25€, Thurs–Sun and public holidays 27€. Daily 4–11pm.

De Plantage
MODERATE

Brasserie Plancius ★★ BRASSERIE   The perfect spot for sitting outside on a sunny day right opposite the Artis Royal Zoo and next door to the Dutch Resistance Museum, the cavernous interior of Plancius fills up quickly with wealthy local families and glamorous women loudly treating each other to lunch. Lunchtime menus offer carefully constructed brasserie-style dishes such as *croque-monsieur,* organic burgers, satay chicken salad, or steak and fries, and there's a calorific afternoon tea, plus two sittings for dinner (at 5:30 and 8:10pm). Excited kids who are impatient to visit the zoo get their own junior menu (pancakes, fries) and a coloring book to distract them from pestering their parents.

Plantage Kerklaan 61. ℂ **06/2324-4069.** www.brasserieplancius.nl. Mains 3€–19€. Daily noon–10:30pm.

Noord Amsterdam
INEXPENSIVE

EYE Bar-Restaurant ★★ INTERNATIONAL   The spectacular, smooth planes of the EYE form one of the coolest buildings in Amsterdam (p. 98), with views through great glass windows over the ever-changing architectural horizons of the IJ waterway. Currently one of the hottest tickets in Amsterdam, with the suntrap terrace tables being the hottest of all, the bar-restaurant gets two stars for its location (take the free ferry from Buiksloterweg at Centraal Station; see p. 58), but one star for its gourmet offerings: insubstantial and predictably Dutch dishes are served during the day, offering aged Gouda cheeses, salads, soups, and quiches. The evening offerings are a little more imaginative, incorporating fish curries, steaks, and vegetarian risottos, but flickering nighttime views across the harbor more than compensate.

IJpromenade 1. ℂ **020/589-1402.** www.eyebarrestaurant.nl. Tues–Thurs and Sun 10am–1am, Fri–Sat 10am–2am. Main courses lunch 4.50€–8.50€, dinner 18€–€25.

Wilhelmina-Dok ★ CONTINENTAL   With an orange, cuboid shape and glass-walled terrace right on the ship channel, this laid-back cafe-restaurant was something of an alternative hangout but it has now been discovered for the incredible views of passing motor boats and the PTA cruise ship terminal on the south shore of the IJ. Those bustling views and a children's menu should also keep kids happy. Summer days see a vast range of *broodje* (tasty open sandwiches) and lots of foragings from the Mediterranean buffet being consumed on the terrace; expect to share long trestle tables. The a la carte dinner always includes an off-beat vegetarian option such as cannelloni stuffed with feta and almond, plus seasonal fish and meat dishes of the day. *Note:* Wilhelmina-Dok does not accept cash, so be sure to have a debit or credit card with you.

Noordwal 1. ℂ **020/632-3701.** www.wilhelmina-dok.nl. Mains 13€–18€. Daily 11am–midnight. No cash.

The Dutch have a particularly sweet tooth and happily devour *pannenkoek* (pancakes) and thick, sweet *poffertjes* served with heart-busting butter and sprinkled with sugar at any given opportunity. Other calorie-laden treats include *stroopwafels* (treacle wafers oozing with caramel) and deep-fried *oliebollen* (donuts) filled with raisins and dusted with sugar, which can be bought on street stalls all over the city center.

Amsterdammers also have a thing for chocolate sprinkles, which you'll find shaken over breakfast rolls as well as all sorts of *broodjes* (sandwiches), sweet and savory; a favorite combination is chocolate sprinkles with salty peanut butter. Or you could try adding a dollop of thick, syrupy *appelstroop* made from sugar and apple, to your lunchtime cheese *broodje* (sandwich).

4

Westerpark

INEXPENSIVE

Het Ketelkeuken ★ DUTCH   An industrial-chic hangout at the avant-garde Westergasfabriek movie theater, with rough plaster walls and concrete floors. A daytime menu sees lashings of organic cheeses and salamis, organic bread and tapenade, or homemade soups of the day served up with wheat beers and frothy cappuccino. Sturdier options including organic steaks with spicy pepper sauce or interesting seasonal salads are available between 5:30 and 9pm. The cool clientele often includes Dutch movie actors, and in summer the action spreads out onto the cool alleyways around the cultural complex. Service can be a bit offhand although that doesn't seem to impact the weekend crowds who pack into this bastion of cool in their grungy hundreds.

Pazzanistraat 4. ✆ **020/684-0090.** www.ketelhuis.nl. Mon–Tues and Thurs 4pm–1am, Wed 2pm–1am, Fri 2pm–3am, Sat noon–3am, Sun 10:30–1am. Mains 4€–14€.

Oost

VERY EXPENSIVE

La Rive ★★★ FRENCH/MEDITERRANEAN   Michelin-starred master chef Rogér Rassin has been at the very top of his game since 2008 and consistently puts out superlative cooking using the very finest of seasonal ingredients. Located in Amsterdam's spiffy InterContinental Hotel, La Rive's dining rooms have the unruffled ambience of an English gentlemen's club but the service from the accomplished waiting staff is happily unstuffy; however, it is advisable to look smart when you visit. The food itself is a thing of unparalleled beauty, each plate a delicate masterpiece of peerless modern cooking. Every night two menus are presented with three courses in each; dishes vary seasonally and may include Wagyu beef with Hollandaise, sea bass, or langoustines in a mild curry sauce. Reservations required.

InterContinental Hotel Amstel, Professor Tulpplein 1. ✆ **020/520-3264.** www.restaurantlarive.nl. Fixed-price menu 95€–115€. Mon–Sat 6:30–10pm, Sun 5–9pm.

South of Amsterdam

EXPENSIVE

Restaurant de Kas ★★★ INTERNATIONAL   Award-winning de Kas was one of the first organic restaurants in Amsterdam when it opened in 2001, and is run on totally green principles and supplied with fruit, vegetables, and herbs grown in the nursery next door. The spacious, light-filled dining rooms inhabit former greenhouses and in summer, the huge patio is filled with fragrances from the herbs. Chef Jarno van den Broek cooks a short prix-fixe menu each day, dependent on what's available in the market or garden; his skillful, beautifully presented gastronomic repertoire may conjure up BBQ-ed lobster claw, scallops with samphire, or lamb shoulder accompanied by feta and rosti. Imaginative vegetarian alternatives are always available. Each course is carefully paired with quality wines. Reservations are required, and must be booked at least a week ahead to feast at the chef's table with the kitchen brigade.

Kamerlingh Onneslaan 3, Park Frankendael. © **020/462-4562.** www.restaurantdekas.nl. Fixed-price lunch 39€, fixed-price dinner 50€, chef's table 130€. Mon–Fri noon–2pm, Mon–Sat 6:30–10pm.

EXPLORING AMSTERDAM

Where to start in this city of 165 canals, 1,250 bridges, countless cobbled streets, the UNESCO World Heritage-listed Canal Ring (p. 56), and more than 40 beckoning museums? The answer to that question is easy. Your first adventure in Amsterdam should be a canal cruise (p. 99), both to get your bearings and acquire a feel for the city's carefree vibe. The magnificence of the elegant canal houses, the mystique of the labyrinthine waterways, and the call of world-class art will spark your curiosity to explore the myriad wonders on offer. Whatever your interest or itinerary, culture vulture or low-brow, Amsterdam welcomes you with open arms and rarely disappoints. Tram lines 3, 5, 12, and 24 are useful for visiting the sights south of the city around Museumplein, while 4, 9, 14, 16, and 24 serve the city center sights.

Old Center

Amsterdam Museum ★★ MUSEUM   The city's historical museum is partly housed in a former convent and partly in a 17th-century orphanage and is pleasantly situated around a cobbled courtyard. Telling the story of Amsterdam's progression from simple fishing village to world power in the 17th-century Golden Age, the displays kick off superbly with the interactive exhibition Amsterdam DNA, which takes a whistle-stop tour through the main stages of the city's history, illustrated by Old Dutch Master paintings, maps, tools, armor, and religious sculpture. After that, however, things tail off as you are led through gallery after gallery of poorly organized artifacts; one highlight is the 1677 scale model of the Koninklijk Paleis (p. 84). The Schuttersgalerij (Civic Guards Gallery; see p. 86) stands outside the museum entrance.

Kalverstraat 92. © **020/523-1822.** www.amsterdammuseum.nl. Admission 11€ adults, 5€ children 5–18. Daily 10am–5pm. Closed Apr 27, Dec 25.

Begijnhof ★★ HISTORIC BUILDING   Entered through an ornate gate off Spui, this cluster of photogenic gabled houses around a leafy garden courtyard is the perfect place to feel the ambience of old Amsterdam. Built as a *hofje* (almshouse; see p. 88) intended to offer *beguines* (devout women) the option to live independently of husband and children, but without becoming a nun, the 47 houses of the Begijnhof today provide sheltered residence for elderly people. Amsterdam was a destination for religious pilgrims and an important Catholic center before the Calvinist rebellion and Alteration in 1578. It remained in operation for centuries after the changeover of the city from Catholicism to Protestantism and the last *beguine* died in 1971 at the age of 84. In the southwest corner of the cloister, at no. 34, stands Het Houten Huys, one of

Amsterdam Attractions

Amsterdam Dungeon **9**
Amsterdam Museum **10**
Amsterdam Pipe
  Museum **19**
Anne Frank Huis **3**
Artis Royal Zoo **44**
Begijnhof **15**
Beurs van Berlage **28**
Bijbels Museum **14**
Bloemenmarkt **16**
Centraal Station **26**
De Waag **33**
Erotic Museum **32**
EYE Film Institute **25**
FOAM **17**
Hash Marihuana &
  Hemp Museum **31**
Heineken Experience **24**
Hermitage Amsterdam **38**
Het Grachtenhuis **13**
Het Scheepvaartmuseum **35**
Hollandse Schouwburg **42**
Hortus Botanicus **41**
Huis Marseille Museum
  voor Fotografie **12**
Joods Historische
  Museum **39**
Koninklijk Paleis **7**
Madame Tussauds **8**
Museum Het
  Rembrandthuis **36**
Museum Het Schip **1**
Museum Ons' Lieve
  Heer op Solder **29**
Museumplein **21**
Museum Van Loon **18**
Nieuwe Kerk **6**
Oude Kerk **30**
Portuguese Synagogue **40**
Rijksmuseum **20**
Science Center NEMO **34**
Sexmuseum Amsterdam **27**
Stedelijk Museum **23**
Stedelijk Museum
  Bureau Amsterdam **5**
Tropenmuseum **45**
Tulip Museum **2**
Van Gogh Museum **22**
Verzetsmuseum **43**
Westerkerk **4**
Westerpark **1**
Willet-Holthuysen
  Museum **37**
Woonbootmuseum **11**

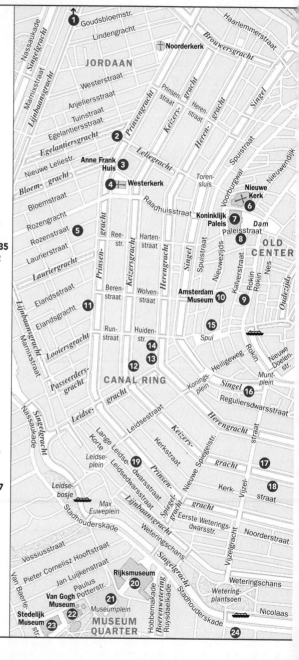

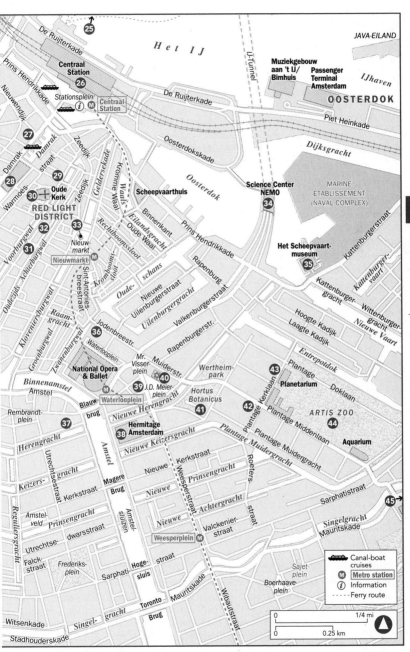

De Ruijterkade

25

Het IJ

JAVA-EILAND

Muziekgebouw
aan 't IJ/
Bimhuis

Passenger
Terminal
Amsterdam

IJhaven

OOSTERDOK

Prins Hendrikkade

Centraal
Station
26

Stationsplein
(i) Ⓜ Centraal
Station

De Ruijterkade

Piet Heinkade

Nieuwendijk

Oosterdokskade

Dijksgracht

Oosterdok

27

Damrak

Damrak

Zeedijk

Kromme Waal

Gelderskade

Scheepvaarthuis

Prins Hendrikkade

Science Center
NEMO
34

MARINE
ETABLISSEMENT
(NAVAL COMPLEX)

Kattenburgerstraat

28

Warmoesstraat

Oude
Kerk
29

30

RED LIGHT
DISTRICT

32

33

Zeedijk

Waals

Binnenkant

Eilandsgracht

Oude Waal

Het Scheepvaart-
museum
35

Kattenburger-
gracht

Kattenburger-
vaart

Voorburgwal

Achterburgwal

31

Nieuw-
markt

Ⓜ Nieuwmarkt

Rechtboomssloot

Kromboomssloot

Sint-Antonies-
breestraat

Oude-
schans

Nieuwe
Uilenburgerstraat

Rapenburg

Kattenburger-
gracht

Hoogte Kadijk

Laagte Kadijk

Wittenburger-
gracht

Nieuwe Vaart

Oudezijds Achterburgwal

Raam-
gracht

Jodenbreestr.

Uilenburgergracht

Valkenburgerstraat

Rapenburgerstr.

Entrepotdok

Kloveniersburgwal

Twaaenburgwal

36

Waterlooplein

National Opera
& Ballet

Mr.
Visser-
plein

Muiderstr.

40

Wertheim-
park

Plantage

43

Doklaan

Plantage Kerklaan

Planetarium

Binnenamstel

Amstel

Ⓜ Waterlooplein

39 J.D. Meijer-
plein

Hortus
Botanicus
41

42

Plantage Middenlaan

ARTIS ZOO

44

Groenburgwal

Rembrandt-
plein

37

Blauw-
brug

Nieuwe Herengracht

38 Hermitage
Amsterdam

Nieuwe Keizersgracht

Plantage Muidergracht

Plantage Muiderlaan

Aquarium

Herengracht

Utrechtsestraat

Amstel

Nieuwe Kerkstraat

Kerkstraat

Roeters-
straat

Keizers-
gracht

Kerkstraat

Magere
Brug

Nieuwe Prinsengracht

Weesperstraat

Sarphatistraat

45

Amstel-
veld

Prinsengracht

Nieuwe Achtergracht

Valckenier-
straat

Singelgracht
Mauritskade

Reguliersgracht

Utrechtse- dwarsstraat

Amstel-
sluizen

Ⓜ Weesperplein

Falck-
straat

Frederiks-
plein

Sarphati-
sluis

Hoge-
sluis

straat

Sajet-
plein

Boerhaave-
plein

Witsenkade

Singel- gracht

Toronto
Brug

Mauritskade

Wibautstraat

Stadhouderskade

Canal-boat
cruises

Ⓜ Metro station

(i) Information

· · · · Ferry route

0 _____ 1/4 mi
0 _____ 0.25 km

Amsterdam's pair of surviving timber houses, built around 1425. The Engelse Kerk (English Church) dates to 1607 and is used today by British ex-pats. Opposite the church, at no. 30, is the Begijnhofkapel, a secret Catholic chapel dating from 1671 that's also still in use today.

Spui and Gedempte Begijnensloot. Free admission. Daily 9am–5pm.

Beurs van Berlage ★★ HISTORIC BUILDING   Amsterdam's red-brick former stock exchange was built in 1903 by Hendrik Berlage and is now an occasional concert venue. This monumental building was one of the precursors of the Amsterdam School and is exceptional for its use of patterned brickwork and clean lines, which broke away from the fancy Dutch Revivalist styles of the time (as seen at the Stedelijk Museum and Centraal Station). A frieze decorates the facade of the building showing man's (questionable) evolution from Adam to 20th-century stockbroker. It's rarely open, so you'll have to content yourself with looking from the outside.

Beursplein 1. ⓒ **020/530-4141.** www.beursvanberlage.nl.

Bloemenmarkt (Flower Market) ★★ HISTORIC MARKET   Amsterdam's last remaining floating market is also the world's only floating flower market; this explosion of color is now a permanent fixture housed on a row of moored barges along the Singel canal. This is the place to purchase seeds, bulbs, gardening tools, and houseplants. Yes, these days the market is touristy, but the seasonal displays are always a pleasure to look at, especially over Christmas and during the spring when the stalls burst with riots of bright tulips and daffodils.

Singel between Koningsplein and Muntplein. Free admission. Mon–Sat 9am–5:30pm, Sun 11am–5:30pm.

Centraal Station ★★ HISTORIC BUILDING   Amsterdam's humongous main railway station is an architectural masterpiece in its own right. Designed by Dutch architect P.J.H. Cuypers, who also built the Rijksmuseum, it was built between 1884 and 1889 on three artificial islands in the IJ waterway. Amsterdammers thoroughly disliked the building when it debuted, but now it is loved for its extravagantly ornate, two-tone Dutch Revivalist facade covered in allegorical tributes to Amsterdam's maritime past. The left-hand tower is adorned with a gilded weathervane; the right one with a clock. Apart from being the jumping-off point for thousands of adventures in Amsterdam, the terminus also acts as a transport hub, with trams, buses, and taxis leaving from Stationsplein outside and ferries departing from the piers behind the building.

Iamsterdam City Card

This euro-saving sightseeing card provides free entry into most of Amsterdam's museums and free travel on public transport. It also entitles cardholders to a free canal cruise (p. 99), discounts in certain stores and restaurants, admission to attractions outside Amsterdam including Zaanse Schans (p. 121) and the museums in Haarlem (p. 116), a free city map, and 2.50€ of admission to the Rijksmuseum (p. 92). Prices in 2014: Iamsterdam City Card for 24 hours 47€, 36 hours 57€, 72 hours 67€. You can buy the passes at Iamsterdam at Stationsplein 10, right outside Centraal Station (ⓒ **020/702-6000;** www.iamsterdam.com), open daily 9am to 5pm (Sun till 4pm), or at the branch in Schiphol Plaza at the airport (same phone number), open daily 7am–10pm.

TOURING THE canals—AMSTERDAM'S ESSENTIAL EXPERIENCE ★★★

Come to Amsterdam and stay up until the wee hours mingling with the locals in an ancient brown cafe. Visit the Rijksmuseum to bask in Rembrandt's finest masterworks. Go sample the beer in the Heineken Brewery. But whatever else you choose to do, don't miss out on a **canal tour**. It's absolutely the best way to soak up Amsterdam's spirited atmosphere and orient yourself to this dynamic and historic city. Tours are free with your **Iamsterdam City Card** (see above), and there are plenty of specialty cruises available for a reasonable price (see p. 99 for details). So what are you waiting for? Hop onboard now!

The main Iamsterdam Visitor Center is in Stationsplein, and it is the starting point for canal cruises. It's worth catching your breath here and taking time to absorb the buzz that swirls around the station in a blur of people, backpacks, bikes, trams, buses, vendors, pickpockets, and junkies. The air of crazy chaos is augmented by the station being in a fairly constant state of renovation.

Stationsplein, off Prins Hendrikkade. Free admission. Open 24/7.

De Waag ★★ HISTORIC BUILDING   You'll find Amsterdam's only surviving medieval fortified gate on the fringe of Chinatown. The many-towered, squat Waag was constructed in 1498 of red-and-white brick and is now the oldest secular building still standing in Amsterdam. The building had many functions over the centuries; it was the sight of public executions before morphing into a public weigh house for merchandise brought into the city and later becoming a guild house. One of the wealthy, powerful guilds that lodged here was the Surgeon's Guild; a fact that is immortalized in Rembrandt's graphic painting "The Anatomy Lesson" (1632), which depicts a dissection being conducted in the upper-floor Theatrum Anatomicum. Thankfully the function of the Waag today is purely dedicated to pleasure; it's the perfect spot for people watching from the buzzy outdoor bar of the historic Restaurant-Café In de Waag (p. 69).

Nieuwmarkt 4. Free admission. Daily 10am–10:30pm (when restaurant is open).

Erotic Museum ★ MUSEUM   Even less erotic than the (unsexy) Sex Museum (p. 86), this ludicrous attempt at an homage to erotica is spread over five dusty floors, with one entirely dedicated to some rather alarming aspects of S&M; here you'll find a photo opportunity complete with handcuffs and whips, which does at least raise a smile. Otherwise there are tons of lewd antique figurines on display, some sketches by John Lennon, and a flea-bitten re-creation of a red-light window complete with half-dressed waxwork prostitute. A new addition is the Sexy Art Gallery, which shows and sells provocative drawings and paintings featuring soft porn.

Oudezijds Achterburgwal 54. ℂ **020/627-8954.** www.erotisch-museum.nl. Admission 7€. Sun–Thurs 11am–1am, Fri–Sat 11am–2am.

Hash Marihuana & Hemp Museum ★★ MUSEUM   Along one of the Red Light District's main drags, this museum was extensively reworked and the new exhibitions reopened in 2012; it's not a bad place to start for anyone curious about the history of soft drugs and modern-day medicinal applications of hemps. There's the predictable display of pipes—some beautifully carved—and bongs, some lovely old paintings depicting 16th-century farmers smoking dope, and lots of items made out of hemp. If you're after a smoke, drugs are not sold here nor is their use promoted.

Oudezijds Achterburgwal 148. ℂ **020/624-8926.** www.hashmuseum.com. Admission 9€ adults, free for children 12 and under (must be accompanied by adult). Daily 10am–11pm. Closed Apr 27.

Koninklijk Paleis ★★ HISTORIC BUILDING   The behemoth building plonked in the middle of Amsterdam's focal Dam Square is the official residence of the reigning Dutch House of Orange (p. 15), although these days the Royal Family prefers to reside in The Hague. This palace was originally designed by Jacob van Campen in 1655 as the City Hall and has a solid, neoclassical facade. It was repurposed into a royal palace by Louis Bonaparte, brother of the better-known Napoleon, when he was crowned king of Holland in 1806, and its public rooms are now open to view. The interior is crammed with early-19th-century furniture, chandeliers, sculptures, and vast oil paintings reflecting Amsterdam's wealth during the Golden Age in the 17th century. Highlights include the highly ornate Council Chamber, and the high-ceilinged Burgerzaal (Council Chamber), where maps inlaid on the marble floors place Amsterdam at the center of the world. The palace is closed to visitors during periods of royal residence and state receptions.

Dam, off Damrak. ℂ **020/620-4060.** www.paleisamsterdam.nl. Admission 10€ adults, 9€ seniors and students, free children 17 and under. Daily 11am–5pm (check website before visiting, as there are frequent changes and closures).

Museum Het Rembrandthuis ★★★ MUSEUM   The former home of Rembrandt van Rijn, Dutch Old Master artist extraordinaire, was on the edge of the former Jewish quarter and proved to be his downfall. He bought this elegant town house in 1639 when his career as Amsterdam's premier portrait painter was flying but overstretched himself with a massive mortgage that plagued his life for years. The house brought him little personal happiness as his adored first wife Saskia died here in 1642 and subsequently he was declared bankrupt in 1656. Rembrandt's belongings were all sold off and he moved to a smaller house on Rozengracht, where he died in 1669. This house was re-opened as a museum in 1911, furnished faithfully in period thanks to a notary's inventory of his possessions. The layout of the house is typical of the 17th century, with servants' quarters in the basement, and three floors atop that. Rembrandt's hallway served as his gallery, with his dealing room off this, and the family's living quarters are hung with his masterful oil paintings. Upstairs you'll find his cabinet of curiosities and the airy studio where he painted "The Night Watch." Bequests of his prints and paintings continue to grow and in 1998 a new wing was built to display them all.

Jodenbreestraat 4. © 020/520-0400. www.rembrandthuis.nl. Admission 13€ adults, 10€ students, 4€ children 6–17. Daily 10am–6pm. Closed Apr 27, Dec 25.

Museum Ons' Lieve Heer op Solder (Our Lord in the Attic) ★★

MUSEUM   One of Amsterdam's best-kept historical secrets is tucked away on Oudezijds Voorburgwal. Following the Alteration (p. 79) and the sacking of all Catholic churches in 1578, practicing Roman Catholicism was banned, so the Catholics had to find ways to worship in secret. Between 1661 and 1663, the wealthy Catholic merchant Jan Hartman bought this stately town house and two others behind it, converting all three attics into a clandestine but lushly decorated Catholic chapel. Worshipers entered from a side street and climbed the narrow stairs to the hidden third-floor chapel, which could accommodate a congregation of 150. Renovated in 2012, the secret chapel is once more resplendent with its Baroque flourishes, organ, marble columns, and oil paintings behind the altar once more shining like new. A visitor center is being built in the adjoining house and rooms decorated in period style are opening up on the lower floors to enhance the museum.

Oudezijds Voorburgwal 40. © 020/624-6604. www.opsolder.nl. Admission 8€ adults, 4€ students and children 5–18. Mon–Sat 10am–5pm, Sun and holidays 1–5pm. Closed Apr 27.

Nieuwe Kerk (New Church) ★★

CHURCH   This beautiful church is the most important in The Netherlands. It was built in the last years of the 14th century, and in 1814, King William I first took the oath of office and was inaugurated here (Dutch royalty are not crowned). It still retains its relevance into the modern era, with His Majesty King of the Netherlands Willem-Alexander marrying Argentinian Princess Máxima here in 2002. Although many of its original priceless treasures were removed or painted over in 1578 when it passed into Protestant hands, much of its original grandeur has since been recaptured. The church has a stately arched nave, an elaborately carved altar, a great pipe organ that dates from 1645, several noteworthy stained-glass windows, and sepulchral monuments for many of Holland's most revered poets and naval heroes. It's also the venue for a lively program of events and exhibitions; see the website for more information.

Dam, off Damrak. © 020/626-8168. www.nieuwekerk.nl. Admission varies with events; free when there's no exhibit. Daily 10am–5pm. Closed Dec 25, Jan 1.

Oude Kerk (Old Church) ★★

CHURCH   This late-Gothic, triple-nave church has its origins in 1250 but was only completed with the extension of the bell tower in 1566. Its exterior is encrusted with 17th- and 18th-century houses and the barnlike

---

The Narrow View

The **narrowest house** in Amsterdam is at **Singel 7.** It's just 1m (3.3 ft.) wide—barely wider than the front door. However, it's a cheat. Only the front facade is really so narrow; behind this it broadens out to more usual proportions. The genuine narrowest house is **Oude**

Hoogstraat 22, near Nieuwmarkt. With a typical Amsterdam bell gable, it's 2m (6½ ft.) wide and 6m (20 ft.) deep. A close rival is nearby at **Kloveniersburgwal 26,** the cornice-gabled **Kleine Trippenhuis,** 2.4m (8 ft.) wide.

interior was stripped of all its adornment in the Alteration of 1578. Rembrandt's beloved first wife lies in vault 28K, which bears the simple inscription "Saskia Juni 1642." The magnificent 1728 organ is regularly used for recitals. You can take a guided tour up the church tower between 1 and 5pm on Thursday to Saturday from April through September for fantastic views across the rooftops, canals, and spires of Amsterdam and the Red Light District.

Oudekerksplein 23. Church: ⓒ **020/625-8284;** tower: 020/689-2565. www.oudekerk.nl. Church admission 7.50€ adults; 5€ seniors, students, and children 13–18; tower admission: 7€. Mon–Sat 10am–6pm, Sun 1–5:30pm. Closed Jan 1, Apr 30, Dec 25.

Rosse Buurt (Red Light District) ★★★ HISTORIC AREA   A few steps away

from the Oude Kerk and De Waag and you're immersed in the sleazy underbelly of Amsterdam's infamous Red Light District. Here barely clad prostitutes advertise themselves behind illuminated glass windows along the medieval canals and alleyways; if the curtains are closed, then you know that a deal has been struck, but if they are open, sometimes you can even glimpse the stark beds upon which the deal is done. Currently most of the girls seem to be from Eastern Europe and some (although by no means all) are exceptionally beautiful. Needless to say, throngs of testosterone-driven men circle these tiny alleyways egging each other on either to visit a prostitute or one of the live, hardcore sex shows that leave nothing to the imagination.

Despite all this, the Red Light District is seedy rather than dangerous; although you should keep an eye out for pickpockets, the area is generally safe. However, a word of warning: Don't photograph the prostitutes; it might be tempting to take pictures of half-naked women posing in windows but it will not be appreciated by the thuggish bouncers who parade the area, and you may well find your camera in the canal. Dusk is the best time to visit, before the drunken/stoned hordes of Euro-trash youth arrive to ogle the girls.

Along Oudezijds Achterburgwal and surrounding alleyways. Free admission. Daily 24/7.

Schuttersgalerij (Civic Guards Gallery) ★ MUSEUM   Outside the entrance

to the Amsterdam Museum, this narrow, glass-roofed walkway links Kalverstraat to the Begijnhof and has been transformed into a public art gallery currently displaying 15 bigger-is-better, 17th-century portraits of the city's heroic musketeers, the Civic Guards. Elegantly uniformed and coiffed, these militia companies once played an important role in the city's defense but degenerated into little more than decadent banqueting societies. Their portraits are accompanied by a vast wooden sculpture of Goliath and a miniscule David, plus photographs of Amsterdam's contemporary elite side by side with the magical Barbara Broekman carpet representing the 179 nationalities of Amsterdam.

Kalverstraat 92 ⓒ **020/523-1822.** www.amsterdammuseum.nl. Free admission. Daily 10am–5pm. Closed Apr 27, Dec 25.

Sexmuseum Amsterdam ★ MUSEUM   Located on scruffy Damstraat, Amster-

dam's so-called "Venustempel" opened in 1985 and is the oldest sex museum in the world. Thanks to its position on the edge of the Red Light District, it attracts more than half a million giggling visitors per year, who wander in a bemused manner around the muddled layouts, bumping into each other up and down stairs in two medieval houses that have been grafted together. There's not much about the history of sex here, just lots of erotic ephemera such as a Delft blue tile showing a man playing cards with an erection, Chinese and Japanese figurines in compromising positions, and wax work figures in various states of undress and decay. These include a rather random diorama of Marilyn Monroe in the famous scene from The Seven Year Itch in which her skirt is blown up by a subway vent. The most interesting display is of early erotic photography, around which red-faced teenagers stand sniggering.

Damrak 18. ⓒ **020/622-8376.** www.sexmuseumamsterdam.com. Admission 4€ ages 16 and over (15 and under not admitted). Daily 9:30am–11:30pm. Closed Dec 25.

Waterlooplein Flea Market ★★ MARKET   Amsterdam's best-known and biggest flea market sprawls in a ramshackle fashion around Waterlooplein. Two canals were filled in 1882 to form a market square that by 1893 lay at the heart of the Jewish Quarter. Before World War II this was a daily market central to Jewish life, but as Amsterdam's Jews were deported it fell into disrepair. During the 1960s the market was reborn when dazed hippies floated in from all over Europe in the haze of their summers of love to sell bongs, water pipes, and doubtless lots of dope. Today the market has around 300 stalls flogging anything from knock-off DVDs to piles of vintage clothes, plastic jewelry, and (ironically) Nazi pilot leather jackets. If you take time to scrabble deeply around the stalls, you may even find some decent second-hand books.

Waterlooplein 2. www.waterloopleinmarkt.nl. Mon–Fri 9am–5:30pm, Sat 8:30am–5:30pm.

Canal Ring

Amsterdam Pipe Museum ★★ MUSEUM   For what sounds like a museum of fairly niche appeal, the pipe museum turns out to be actually quite good fun. The eccentric curator-owner is an entrancing character and also runs the curiously old-fashioned Smokiana shop in the basement, which sells pipes and books about pipes. Go up the steps to the museum and you'll be treated to a guided tour of the world's largest collection of Dutch clay pipes, intricately carved and bejeweled Meerschaum pipes, and bronze cast pipes from Cameroon in Africa. You'll also get to drink in the rarified atmosphere of the traditional 17th-century house renovated in 19th-century fashion.

Prinsengracht 488. ⓒ **020/421-1779.** www.pijpenkabinet.nl. Admission 8€ adults, 4€ children 18 and under. Wed–Sat 12–6pm. Closed Jan 1, Apr 27, Dec 25.

4

AMSTERDAM | Exploring Amsterdam

Amsterdam has many secret courtyards surrounded by almshouses—they could be considered an early form of care in the community where the poor or disadvantaged of the parish could be housed and supported. The best known is the **Begijnhof** (p. 79), where a community of pious women lived for several centuries. The **Hermitage Amsterdam** (p. 95) is also housed in a former *hofje*, where homes were provided for elderly women of slender means. **Zon's Hofje** at Prinsengracht 159–171 is an example of a tranquil *hofje* with courtyard garden; the outer door is open Monday through Saturday between 10am and 5pm, and you can walk quietly through the passageway to the serene courtyard. A walk around the pretty streets of the Jordaan will reveal several *hofjes*, including the **Raepenhofje** at Palmgracht 28-38, and the **Suyckerhofje** at Lindengracht 149-163.

Anne Frank Huis ★★★ MUSEUM   This is one of Amsterdam's most popular sights for the insights it provides into the incarceration of 13-year-old Anne Frank and her Jewish family during the Nazi occupation of Amsterdam in World War II. This would have gone largely unremarked had she not embarked upon writing a diary of her time in the secret attic, which was published by her father Otto after her death. Otto Frank took his family and other Jewish refugees into hiding behind his jam-making factory on July 6, 1942; they remained there for 2 years until they were betrayed to the Nazis by people unknown and deported, Anne to Bergen-Belsen and her parents to Auschwitz in Poland. Along with her sister, Anne died of typhus just months before Liberation and only their father survived the war.

The apartments where the family hid carry sad reminders of their life there; the posters Anne put up to decorate her bedroom, the height marks against the wall, the steep, creaking stairs, and claustrophobic rooms. Sound bites from her diary and a heartrending final word from her father augment the somber atmosphere. Despite the crowds filing around the rooms, this haunting museum has the power to silence everyone.

If you don't want to join the crowds waiting patiently for admission outside this nondescript canal house on Prinsengracht for hours, apply for tickets online about a month before your visit.

Prinsengracht 263–267. ℂ **020/556-7100.** www.annefrank.org. Admission 9€ adults, 4.50€ children 10–17. Nov–Mar Sun–Fri 9am–7pm, Sat 9am–9pm; Apr–June and Sept–Oct Sun–Fri 9am–9pm, Sat 9am–10pm; Jul–Aug daily 9am–10pm. Closed Yom Kippur.

Bijbels Museum (Biblical Museum) ★ MUSEUM   Two of a group of four majestic 1660s houses (nos. 364–370 Herengracht) with delicate neck gables house the Biblical Museum. The houses are notable for being designed by architect Philips Vingboons for wealthy timber merchant Jacob Cromhout, but the museum itself is nothing to write home about. Despite a couple of ceiling frescoes by Jacob de Witt, it suffers from a ramshackle layout and the few exhibits are odd in the extreme—a model of the temple in Jerusalem, some religious tapestries, and a few dusty bibles in a little room on the extravagantly carved wooden staircase. Two floors are under renovation and there's just not that much to see. However, the house itself is beautiful so be sure to check that out.

Herengracht 366–368. ℂ **020/624-2436.** www.bijbelsmuseum.nl. Admission 8€ adults, 6€ students, 4€ children 5–18. Tues–Sat 10am–5pm, Sun and holidays 11am–5pm. Closed Jan 1, Apr 27.

FOAM ★ MUSEUM   Dedicated to contemporary photography, this cool gallery is tucked behind a traditional canal-house facade. Its interior has been partly stripped out to reveal a warren of white exhibition rooms that form the perfect backdrop to show off the work of established photographers like the highly graphic, highly colored war images of American photographer Richard Mosse or the work of newly discovered Dutch talent. There's a smart bookshop flogging coffee-table art books and a little cafe tucked underneath the galleries.

Keizersgracht 609. (℃) **020/551-6500.** www.foam.org. Admission 10€ adults, 7€ seniors and students, free children 10 and under. Sat–Wed 10am–6pm, Thurs–Fri 10am–9pm. Closed Apr 27.

Het Grachtenhuis (Canal Museum) ★★★ MUSEUM   Take the tram to Herengracht on the Grachtengordel (Canal Ring) to the elegant mansion housing the Canal Museum. This brilliant museum shares the secrets of Amsterdam's expansion through a cleverly curated series of interactive displays. First off, a sound-and-light show centers on a model of the city in medieval times; it was grim, overcrowded, and with little concession to hygiene. By the 17th century, expansion became imperative. The planning and construction of the ring of three canals around the medieval city is dealt with in a lively series of interactive displays, films, models, and holograms; the final exhibit romps home with an all-singing, all-dancing celebration of multi-cultural Amsterdam today. You couldn't wish for a more instructive or entertaining introduction to the city and its social and cultural development.

Herengracht 386. (℃) **020/421-1656.** www.hetgrachtenhuis.nl. Admission 12€ adults, 6€ children 6–17. Tues–Sun 10am–5pm.

Huis Marseille Museum voor Fotografie ★★ MUSEUM   One of two Amsterdam photography museums (see also FOAM, above), the Marseille is privately owned and housed in a spectacularly neck-gabled aristocratic merchant's house along Keizersgracht (the Emperor's Canal). Six galleries alternate photos from the museum's permanent collection with worthy exhibitions of contemporary images that change every 3 months. As with so many Amsterdam galleries and museums in the Canal Ring, the building is part of the attraction; this one dates from the 17th century and takes its name from the plaque on the front of the house that depicts a map of Marseille harbor in France. The interior maintains many original features, including fireplaces, wooden floors, and plaster moldings as well as a ceiling fresco by Jacob van Campen. Out the back there's a summer cafe in the delightful leafy courtyard garden.

Keizersgracht 401. (℃) **020/531-8989.** www.huismarseille.nl. Admission 8€ adults, 4€ seniors and students, free children 17 and under. Tues–Sun 11am–6pm. Closed Jan 1, Apr 27, Dec 25.

Museum Van Loon ★ MUSEUM   The Museum Van Loon is housed in an elegant mansion first owned by Ferdinand Bol, who was a student of Rembrandt. Between 1884 and 1945 it was the property of the Van Loons, who were founders of the Dutch East India Company and one of the richest families in Amsterdam. Although this is a beautiful house with a double frontage and vast dimensions as befits the family's social standing, its grand rooms now have a vague air of neglect. Nevertheless, it's worth stopping by to see the style in which the Dutch aristocracy lived among the scores of family portraits (but not the ghastly modern ones by Katinka Lampe upstairs), the Louis XV furniture, and the marble staircase with its ornately curly brass balustrade. Out back there is a formal knot garden that needs a good weeding and a coach house modeled on a Greek temple that houses a rudimentary cafe; there are occasional opera recitals in the gardens. If you're short on time, the Willet-Holthuysen Museum (see below) has more to offer in terms of content.

Keizersgracht 672. ℭ **020/624-5255.** www.museumvanloon.nl. Admission 8€ adults, 6€ students, 4€ children 6–18. Wed–Mon 11am–5pm. Closed Jan 1, Apr 27, Dec 25.

Tulip Museum ★★ MUSEUM   The revamped Tulip Museum is just across Prinsengracht from the Anne Frank Huis, and is the perfect antidote if you need cheering up after a visit. It's a cheery, contemporary, and informative slant on the story of Amsterdam's obsession with tulips, which were imported from the Himalayas and nearly brought the country down when trade in the bulbs collapsed in 1637. It's all showcased in a short, well-designed basement exhibition with superb poster-sized photos of swathes of tulips and cleverly designed woodcuts showing the journey of tulips from the Far East into The Netherlands. On ground level is a top-quality souvenir store selling bulbs, pretty plant holders, and other classy tulip-related ephemera.

Prinsengracht 116. ℭ **020/421-0095.** www.amsterdamtulipmuseum.com. Admission 6€ adults, 4€ students. Daily 10am–6pm. Closed Apr 27, Dec 25.

Westerkerk ★★ CHURCH   Just round the corner from the Anne Frank Huis, the Protestant Westerkerk is yet another ecclesiastical masterpiece by the Dutch celebrity architect of the 17th century, Hendrick de Keyser (who also designed the Noorderkerk and the Zuiderkerk), as part of the new development of the Grachtengordel (Canal Ring). The foundation stone was laid in 1620 (de Keyser died a year later), and the tower was finally completed in 1638; it is more than 85m tall (270 ft.) and is topped with the gilded Crown of Maximilian. Every 15 minutes the carillon bells ring out across the city but the church itself is austere inside; in chime with the Calvinist beliefs of the time there is no altar, but the gold and silver pipes and Baroque sculpture adorning the organ make up for the lack of ornamentation. It is the burial place of Rembrandt—although no one knows where his grave is on the unmarked stone floor— as well as his wife Saskia and son Titus. It is also the venue for several royal weddings. The Westerpass gives access to computerized information inside the church.

Prinsengracht 281. ℭ **020/624-7766.** www.westererkerk.org. Free admission (4€ for Westerpass guide). Mon–Sat 10am–3pm; Sun services only.

Amsterdam's Historic Buildings

The **Munttoren** on Muntplein sits at a busy traffic intersection on the Rokin and Singel canals. In 1487, the Mint Tower's base was part of the Reguliers Gate in the city wall. In 1620, Hendrick de Keyser (p. 23) topped it with an ornate, lead-covered tower, from which a carillon of Hemony brothers bells sings out gaily every hour and plays a 1-hour concert on Fridays at noon. The tower got its present name in 1672, when it housed the city mint.

The tilting **Montelbaanstoren** is known as the "Leaning Tower of Amsterdam," a fortification at the juncture of the Oudeschans and Waalseilandsgracht canals that dates from 1512. It's one of only a few surviving elements of the city's once-powerful defensive works. In 1606, Hendrick de Keyser added an octagonal tower and spire. The building now houses local Water Authority offices.

Willet-Holthuysen Museum ★★★ MUSEUM   This is a wonderful museum with a pristine interior dating from the 19th century in a perfectly restored canal house that shouts money. It's redolent of the sybaritic lifestyle of Amsterdam's prosperous merchant classes and every curtain, every piece of furniture displayed, and every scrap of wallpaper, down to the deep-blue fabric in the gentleman's parlor, is in keeping with the period. Displays include an introduction to the aristocratic family who lived here, and a collection of painstakingly detailed silver figurines. There's an exquisite formal knot garden at the rear of the house.

Herengracht 605. ℂ **020/523-1822.** www.willetholthuysen.nl. Admission 8€ adults, 6€ students, 4€ children 5–18. Mon–Fri 10am–5pm, Sat–Sun 11am–5pm. Closed Apr 27, Dec 25.

Woonbootmuseum (Houseboat Museum) ★ MUSEUM   The Houseboat Museum is found on board the Hendrika Maria, a freighter that was built in 1914, and was busily transporting sand up until the 1960s. A tour won't take more than 15 minutes as there's not that much to see but it gives punters the opportunity to glimpse life aboard one of Amsterdam's 2,500 houseboats. The Hendrika Maria was renovated in 2008 and its inner living spaces reveal a surprisingly roomy timber-roofed living space with box beds, a couple of 1950s armchairs, and a tiny cafe.

Prinsengracht 296k. ℂ **020/427-0750.** www.houseboatmuseum.nl. Admission 3.75€ adults, 3€ children 5–15. Daily 11am–5pm. Closed Jan 1 and 2 weeks in Jan, Apr 27, Dec 25–26, Dec 31.

Jordaan

Stedelijk Museum Bureau Amsterdam ★★ ART GALLERY   This micro-outpost of the Stedelijk Museum (p. 93) is an innovative gallery designed to give a leg up to the careers of promising Amsterdam artists. Regarded in The Netherlands as the place to watch for new young talent, the gallery has a bland, white exhibition space perfect for showing off oft-changing exhibitions of photography, video, abstract works, bizarre installations, and occasionally intense performance art.

Rozenstraat 59. ℂ **020/422-0471.** www.smba.nl. Free admission. Wed–Sun 11am–5pm. Closed Jan 1, Apr 27, Dec 25–26.

Museum Quarter

Heineken Experience ★★ BREWERY   The Heineken is one of Amsterdam's most popular attractions and so is always crowded with multi-national youngsters eager to get their hands on the beer. It's housed inside the red-brick former brewery, which functioned from 1867 until 1988 before production was moved to modern

4

AMSTERDAM | Exploring Amsterdam

The Day Watch?

Contrary to popular belief, Rembrandt's "The Night Watch" (1642) actually shows a daytime scene. Centuries of grime dulled its luster until restoration revealed sunlight glinting on the militia company's arms.

facilities in The Hague and Den Bosch. The intro to Heineken the company, delivered by human hologram from behind a well-stocked bar, sets the pace for a rollicking journey through the growth of the brand from micro-brewery to multi-million-euro, international company with liberal use of interactive exhibits and funny simulated rides. The tour also incorporates the original copper brewing vats, malt silos, and vintage brewing equipment, plus a stable full of Shire horses used to pull the promotional drays. The ultimate goal for most is to glug back Heineken beer at the bar so expect a bit of a scuffle when trying to get served at the bar, which is usually standing-room only and awash with lager.

Stadhouderskade 78. © **020/523-9435.** www.heinekenexperience.com. Admission 18€ adults (includes 2 beers), 13€ children 12–17, free children 10 and under. Sept–June Mon–Thurs 11am–7:30pm, Fri–Sun 10:30am–9pm; Jul–Aug daily 10:30am–9pm.

Museumplein ★★★ PARK   After the crush of the Rijksmuseum, take a breather in the spacious Museumplein, home to all three of Amsterdam's great art museums. At press time, the Van Gogh was being extended but work on the Stedelijk, including its incongruous "bathtub" extension, is complete. The elaborate facade of **Het Concertgebouw** (p. 110) faces the Rijksmuseum across the piazza, which has become a buzzing public space with lawns, buskers playing South American pan pipes, the brilliant open-air terrace of **Café Cobra** (p. 75), museum stores, and a kids' playground. In winter the area in front of the Rijksmuseum is transformed into a fairytale ice rink, backed by one of Amsterdam's iconic Iamsterdam signs, which normally has scores of kids clambering all over it.

Museumplein. Free admission. Daily 24/7.

Rijksmuseum ★★ MUSEUM   After a 10-year refurbishment, this grand old dame of the Amsterdam museum scene reopened to worldwide fanfare in 2013. The Rijksmuseum is the world's biggest repository of Dutch Golden Age treasures, stacked over four sprawling floors in the red-brick P.J.H. Cuypers monolith opened in 1855. The refurbishment has done a spectacular job in sprucing up the elegant Cuypers decorations in the central Voorhal (Great Hall) but the layout of the museum remains confusing. It's almost sacrilegious to criticize this venerable institution, but to my mind the biggest mistake made in laying out the displays is crowding all the famous **Dutch Old Masters ★★★** together in the Gallery of Honour on the second floor. Over 2 million people visit this museum annually and they all want to see Rembrandt's "The Night Watch" from 1642 (or, to give it its official title, "The Militia Company of Captain Frans Banning Cocq and Lieutenant Willem van Ruytenburch") and the wonderful works by Jan Steen, Jan Vermeer, and Frans Hals, so be prepared for impenetrable throngs. "The Milkmaid" and "The Merry Drinker" are truly mesmerizing close up, so you'll have to bear with the crowds.

Elsewhere in the museum are glorious collections of tulip vases, fine silver, glassware, and Delftware, forming the greatest collection of Dutch Golden Age treasures in the world. There are endless galleries stuffed with Asian and Indonesian artifacts brought back by marauding Dutch trading vessels, and two rare furnished 17th-century dollhouses should be a highlight for children. In a nod to more modern times, there are works by CoBrA artist Karel Appel and De Stijl designer Gerrit Rietveld. Don't forget the sculpture exhibitions in the gardens. Lines are always long so either reserve a ticket online before your visit or turn up on the dot of opening time. And—like everywhere else in Amsterdam—watch out for the bikers who stream through the museum's under-pass with little regard for milling tourists.

Museumstraat 1. ℂ **020/674-7000.** www.rijksmuseum.nl. Admission 15€ adults, 7.50€ students, free children 18 and under. Daily 9am–7pm.

Stedelijk Museum ★★★ MUSEUM   This is the second of the triumvirate of great art museums in Amsterdam. Devotees of contemporary art will instantly fall in love with this place and hopefully all visitors will be instant converts to its delights. The stark original 1895 building by A.W. Weissman has been renovated and a curious bathlike extension has been appended to its flank, which now houses temporary exhibitions and the new foyer and ticket office. The Stedelijk's interior is bright and white, all the better to show off its stellar collections of works by the most famous names of the 19th to 21st centuries. Things get off to an excellent start with the sparkly mural by CoBrA artist Karel Appel in the first gallery, and the roster of great names exhibited here includes Mondriaan, Chagall, Van Gogh, Spencer, Matta, Newman, Pollock, and Pop Artists Warhol and Liechtenstein. The museum's design collection is less success-ful as the layout is cramped, but there are many stand-out pieces here, including De Stijl designer Gerrit Rietveld's famous painted chair and Jeff Koons' kitsch "Ushering in Banality" (1988).

Museumplein 10. ℂ **020/573-2911.** www.stedelijk.nl. Daily 10am–6pm (Thurs till 10pm). Admis-sion 15€ adults, 7.50€ students, free children 17 and under.

Van Gogh Museum ★★★ MUSEUM   The third of Amsterdam's heavyweight art museums is being expanded at the time of writing but it's still very much up for business. The museum was opened in 1973 and designed by Gerrit Rietveld, the lead-ing exponent of the Dutch De Stijl movement; it has three floors of white space in which to show off the tortured artist's ethereal works to their best advantage. Vincent van Gogh was born in 1853 in Groot-Zundert in the south of Holland and during his short life he produced over 800 paintings. More than 200 of his portraits, landscapes, and still lifes, plus more than 500 drawings, are held in the collections here, forming the biggest cache of Van Gogh in the world. Displays start with various works from different points in Vincent's career hung alongside contemporary work by Pissarro, Gauguin, and Monet to provide useful historical context.

The exhibition on the second floor shows the artist finding his way stylistically and this is where you'll see Van Gogh's seminal paintings as his career is tracked from his early still lifes through his Japanese stage to his untimely death at Arles in 1890. Van Gogh was extraordinarily prolific in his last years and world-famous examples of his brilliance on display here include the gloomy "Potato Eaters" (1885); "Bedroom at Arles" (1888); and an 1889 version of "Sunflowers." The museum's bulbous Exhibi-tion Wing by Kisho Kurokawa was opened in 1999 and houses temporary exhibitions; the grand new entrance now under construction is set to open summer 2015.

Paulus Potterstraat 7. ℂ **020/570-5200.** www.vangoghmuseum.nl. Admission 15€ adults, free children 16 and under. Mar–Sept 1 and Dec 27–Dec 31 daily 9am–6pm; Sept 2–Dec 26 daily 9am–5pm; year-round Fri till 10pm.

When the Germans arrived in Amsterdam on May 16, 1940 after a day of intense bombing that all but destroyed Rotterdam (p. 136), they were cautiously welcomed into The Netherlands. But slowly the Nazis clamped down on the city and its open-minded people; more brutal laws were enforced taking away individual freedom, and underground resistance to the Nazis mounted. The 10 percent of the population that was Jewish were persecuted, forced to wear yellow Stars of David, and stripped of their jobs. In 1942, the roundup of Jewish families began; thousands of people were taken to the Hollandse Schouwburg (p. 95) before being deported to labor camps—Bergen-Belsen in Germany, or Auschwitz in Poland. Of the 140,000 Sephardic and Ashkenazi Jews who lived in Amsterdam before WWII, fewer than 30,000 survived until Liberation on May 5, 1945. The most famous Dutch victim of the Holocaust was Anne Frank, whose tragic story is told at the Anne Frank Huis (p. 88) on Prinsengracht. To learn more about opposition to the German occupation of Amsterdam, visit the Resistance Museum (p. 97).

4

Vondelpark ★★ PARK   A 5-minute stroll from the Van Gogh down Van Baerlestraat (head down to P.C. Hooftstraat to gawp at the expensive stores; see p. 103) brings you to Amsterdam's biggest, greenest public park, providing 44 hectares (109 acres) of peace and quiet. This is a cherished open space crammed with trees, lawns, lakes, and bridges criss-crossed with walking, biking, and jogging tracks, although as usual cyclists take precedence, so watch your step. Summer sees the lakeside restaurants (p. 75) filling up and open-air festivals and concerts (p. 113).

Entrance gate on Van Eeghenlaan at the corner of Jacob Obrechtstraat. Free admission. Daily 24/7.

Plantage/Oost

Artis Royal Zoo ★★ ZOO   Amsterdam's wonderfully family-friendly zoo was established in 1838 and covers more than 14 hectares (35 acres) of tree-lined pathways and landscaped gardens. It has more than 900 species of animal, successfully combining 19th-century layout and buildings with a 21st-century commitment to conservation and breeding. Buy a map and a list of the current feeding times from the Artis office at the zoo's entrance to negotiate the animal enclosures—where lions, leopards, elephants, giraffes, and gazelles range fairly freely—the ticket price grants admission to Artis's Aquarium, the Insect House, Geological Museum, and Planetarium where 3D films on the birth of the planet are shown. There's also a children's farm, where kids can pet assorted small animals. There are daily keeper talks, vulture and lion feeding sessions, playful sea lions, and elephant training to fit in to your day as well, plus late-night sessions at the zoo on Saturdays between June and the end of August.

Plantage Kerklaan 38–40. ✆ **0900/278-4796.** www.artis.nl. Admission 20€ adults, 17€ children 3–9. Nov–Feb daily 9am–5pm, Mar–Oct daily 9am–6pm.

Dockworker Statue ★★ MONUMENT   Just to the left side of the Portuguese Synagogue complex is Jonas Daniël Meijerplein, where many Dutch Jews were herded together while awaiting deportation to concentration camps in Germany and Poland. The bronze figure is always surrounded by wreathes of flowers; it was created by Mari Andriessen and was erected in 1952 in commemoration of the February 1941 strike by workers protesting against the Jewish deportations, which was violently suppressed by Amsterdam's Nazi occupiers and ended in a bloodbath.

Jonas Daniël Meijerplein. Free admission. Daily 24/7.

Hermitage Amsterdam ★★ MUSEUM

The Amsterdam branch of St. Petersburg's Hermitage is a delight to visit; it's housed in the Amstelhof, a former almshouse for elderly women built in 1680 behind a serene neoclassical facade. Centered on a giant courtyard and all but surrounded by canals and the Amstel River, the building has been beautifully transformed into a state-of-the art gallery displaying the rich pickings from the Russian state collection. Two exhibitions run simultaneously for about 6 months, so check online before you visit, but with the Hermitage's holding more than 3 million works of art, chances are the current exhibition will be spectacular.

Amstel 31. ℂ **020/530-7488.** www.hermitageamsterdam.nl. Admission 15€ adults, 12€ seniors and students, 5€ children 6–16. Daily 10am–5pm. Closed Apr 27, Dec 25.

Het Scheepvaartmuseum (National Maritime Museum) ★★ MUSEUM

Housed in a mammoth, Venetian-style 17th-century arsenal, Amsterdam's Maritime Museum is a gem of a museum, completely remodeled and reopened in 2011; its displays showcase the importance of Amsterdam's maritime history. There are many paintings and models of ships, seascapes, navigational instruments, cannons, and other weaponry scattered through the displays, which have all been spruced up with the clever use of interactive light, sound, multimedia, and audio-visual aids. The best exhibits detail the growth of the Dutch East India Company and sensitively address the slave trade and today's whaling issues. Special exhibits aimed at kids tell the story of lots of naval derring-do but the main point of a trip to this museum is for youngsters to get on board the gaily painted, full-size replica of the merchant ship Amsterdam, moored on the quay outside. Everything on board is as it was in 1749 when the original boat foundered on its maiden voyage to the East Indies (present-day Indonesia). Actors playing the part of sailors fire cannons, sing sea shanties, mop the deck, hoist cargo on board, and attend a solemn burial at sea. Kids can join sail makers and rope makers at work and see the cook prepare a shipboard meal in the galley.

Kattenburgerplein 1. ℂ **020/523-2222.** www.scheepvaartmuseum.nl. Admission 15€ adults, 7.50€ students and children 5–17. Daily 9am–5pm.

Hollandse Schouwburg ★★ MUSEUM/MEMORIAL

The imposing white Hollandse Schouwburg was originally a theater, but in World War II hundreds of Dutch Jewish families were forcibly detained here before deportation to the concentration camps of Poland. The former theater is now the official memorial to the Nazi Holocaust in Amsterdam, with a deeply moving documentary highlighting the persecution of the Jews through a series harrowing interviews with victims. The small museum on the upper floor is mainly notable for its pictures of the ingenious hiding places used to conceal Jewish people from the Nazis. However, it is the monument out in the rear courtyard that grabs attention—a simple cast column scattered with flowers.

Plantage Middenlaan 24. ℂ **020/531-0310.** Admission with ticket from Jewish Historical Museum 12€ adults, 6€ students and children 13–17, 3€ children 6–12. Daily 11am–5pm. Closed Apr 27, Rosh Hashanah, and Yom Kippur (check online as dates change).

Hortus Botanicus (Botanical Garden) ★★ PARK

The treasure-trove of tropical plants, steamy hot houses, and exotic palm trees planted in these soothing, tranquil gardens have their origins in former Dutch colonies across the world.

Established in 1682, the gardens are packed with 115,000 rare plants and trees; in summer the landscape explodes with the colors and scents of more than 250,000 flowers. The three-climate greenhouse gets progressively warmer as you walk through it—most of the plants in there come from Australia and South Africa. There's also an herb garden, a desert greenhouse, a tree-spotting route through the gardens, and a butterfly house with free-flying giant butterflies that kids love.

Plantage Middenlaan 2A. ℂ **020/625-9021.** www.dehortus.nl. Admission 8.50€ adults; 4.50€ seniors, students, and children 5–14. Daily 10am–5pm. Closed Jan 1, Dec 25.

Joods Historische Museum (Jewish Historical Museum) ★ MUSEUM

This vast complex was central to Jewish life in Amsterdam between the 17th and mid-20th centuries and it originally consisted of four synagogues. Built by Ashkenazi Jewish refugees from Germany and Poland in the 17th and 18th centuries, it was sheer luck that the synagogues survived the Nazi occupation in World War II. They have now been turned into a museum relating the story of the Jewish community in Amsterdam from the 17th century to present day and displaying some of the artifacts looted from Jews by the Nazis during the war; some attempts have been made to enliven the displays with interactive screens and personal commentary, but generally the standard of display is pretty dull. The adjoining **Kindermuseum (Children's Museum)** ★★ is much better, cleverly set up as the home of a traditional Orthodox Jewish family, giving kids the chance to bake matzos, learn Yiddish, or celebrate the Sabbath, but that's strictly a child-only zone. Museum tickets are also valid in the Portuguese Synagogue and Hollandse Schouwburg.

Nieuwe Amstelstraat 1. ℂ **020/531-0310.** www.jhm.nl. Admission 12€ adults, 6€ students and children 13–17, 3€ children 6–12. Daily 11am–5pm. Closed Apr 27, Rosh Hashanah, and Yom Kippur (check online as dates change).

Monument of Jewish Gratitude ★ MONUMENT

This white limestone memorial was given in thanks by the Jewish community to the people of Amsterdam for supporting them against the Nazis in World War II. It sits on Weesperstraat at the rear of the Hermitage Amsterdam (p. 95).

Weesperstraat. Free admission. Daily 24/7.

Portuguese Synagogue ★★ SYNOGOGUE

Europe's largest synagogue was built in 1675 by Sephardic Jews who moved to Amsterdam from Spain and Portugal. The building was restored in the 1950s and today it looks pretty much as it did 3 centuries ago. The women's gallery on the upper floor of the synagogue is supported by 12 stone columns representing the Twelve Tribes of Israel, and the large, low-hanging brass chandeliers together hold 1,000 candles. In the courtyard complex that surrounds the synagogue, effectively cutting it off from the rest of the city, are the mikvah ritual baths; the mourning room complete with a coffin stand; and the synagogue's treasure chambers containing precious menorahs, torahs, and ornate clerical robes.

Mr. Visserplein 3. ℂ **020/531-0380.** www.portugesesynagoge.nl. Admission with ticket from Jewish Historical Museum 12€ adults, 6€ students and children 13–17, 3€ children 6–12. Apr–Oct Sun–Thurs 10am–5pm, Fri 10am–4pm; Nov–Mar Sun–Thurs 10am–4pm, Fri 10am–2pm. Closed Apr 27, Rosh Hashanah, and Yom Kippur (check online as dates change).

Science Center NEMO ★★★ MUSEUM

More children's play station than museum, NEMO is the number one place to hit with kids if it's a rainy day. This accessible, hands-on, interactive science center is housed in a magnificent, pale green, ship-shaped building designed by Renzo Piano in 1997. Its aim is to introduce science and technology to kids in an understandable and interesting form. It's a great experience for kids 7 or older, but even ages 4 to 6 can go through a "Shadow World" especially designed for expanding young minds. Through games, experiments, and demonstrations, kids learn how chain reactions work, search for ETs, blow a soap bubble large enough to stand inside, and much more fun stuff. There's a lab for supervised experiments, displays on harnessing green energies, and even simple explanations of Big Bang. NEMO's broad, stepped, and sloping roof is an attraction in itself; a place to hang out, have a beer or catch the sun in summer, and take in the views. At the top, you are 30m (100 ft.) above the IJ waterway and have sweeping views over the Old Harbor and Eastern Dock, plus the fast-changing new architectural horizon around the River IJ. Snacks are served in Café DEK5, which has a grand outdoor terrace, and modest menus in Café Renzo Piano.

Oosterdok 2. ✆ **020/531-3233.** www.e-nemo.nl. Admission 15€, free for children 4 and under. Tues–Sun 10am–5pm. Closed Jan 1, Apr 27, Dec 25.

Tropenmuseum ★★★ MUSEUM   The museum is out in the boondocks of Oosterpark in eastern Amsterdam, but can easily be reached by tram. Holland's Royal Institute for the Tropics owns this unusual museum devoted to the study of the cultures of tropical areas around the world. Breathing life into the sights, smells, and sounds of the tropics and sub-tropics, this superb anthropological museum originally took as its central theme the role of The Netherlands as colonial power across the Far East, South America, and the Dutch Caribbean. Today the displays go far beyond this colonial-era mindset to embrace contemporary issues such as the causes of poverty in the developing world and the depletion of the world's tropical rainforests. And they start them young; the Tropenmuseum Junior's new MixMax Brasil is an interactive display encouraging kids between 6 and 13 to understand different cultures. Among the museum's collection of 250,000 artifacts, youngsters love the walk-through peasant house in Java, the Arab souk, the Mongolian yurt, and the elaborate wedding costumes from Thailand. The building itself is noteworthy for its ornamented 1920s facade bristling with turrets, step gables, arched windows, and delicate spires.

Linnaeusstraat 2. ✆ **020/568-8200.** www.tropenmuseum.nl. Admission 13€ adults; 8€ seniors, students, and children 4–17. Tues–Sun 10am–5pm. Closed Jan 1, Apr 27, Dec 25.

Verzetsmuseum (Dutch Resistance Museum) ★★★ MUSEUM   With its entrance right opposite Artis Royal Zoo (see above), Amsterdam's Resistance Museum has clever dioramas and interactive exhibits that neatly chart the absorbing story of the gradual rise of Dutch resistance to their Nazi occupiers from 1940 until the end of World War II. Printing presses, ID cards, and touching personal artifacts like the Christmas tree made out of blackout curtains add to this impressive exhibition. Along with the 140,000 Jews sent to concentration camps and murdered, around 20,000 Dutch nationals were sent to labor camps in Germany; of those 2,000 were executed and several thousand more did not survive the appalling conditions. The Resistance Museum Junior is found in a new wing of the museum and focuses on the experience of Dutch children under Nazi occupation.

Plantage Kerklaan 61. ✆**020/620-2535.** Admission 8€ adults, 4.50€ children 7–15. Tues–Fri 10am–5pm, Sat–Sun 11am–5pm. Closed Jan 1, Apr 27, Dec 25.

Wertheim Park ★ PARK   The little scrap of grass overlooking Nieuwe Herengracht canal houses one of Amsterdam's most poignant commemorations of the Holocaust. In the center of Wertheim Park is a 1993 memorial by sculptor Jan Wolkers, dedicated to the millions killed at Auschwitz. Six large cracked glass shards lie flat on the ground reflecting a shattered sky and covering a buried urn that contains ashes of the dead from the concentration camp. The glass legend reads NOOIT MEER AUSCHWITZ ("Never Again, Auschwitz"), with the words reflecting back from the glass.

Plantage Middenlaan. Free admission. Daily 24/7.

Amsterdam Noord

EYE Film Institute ★★★ MUSEUM/MOVIE THEATER   The pristine white shape of Amsterdam's new film museum hovers over the north bank of the River IJ like a mantis. Built in 2012 by Austrian firm Delugan Meissl Associated Architects, the EYE is the first major public building to be constructed north of the river. Its gleaming complex houses four movie theaters, exhibitions, a store, and a restaurant with a sought-after terrace with views back to Centraal Station. Although there's an admission fee for the movies and temporary exhibitions, the 360-degree Panorama film display in the basement is free to access. EYE is a totally cash-free zone so make sure you go armed with plastic.

IJpromenade 1. ℰ **020/589-1400.** www.eyefilm.nl. Admission movies: 10€ adults, 8.50€ students; exhibitions: 9€ adults, 7.50€ students. Sun–Thurs 10am–10pm, Fri–Sat 10am–11pm. Take free ferry across IJ waterway from Waterplein West dock behind Centraal Station to Buiksloterweg.

NDSM-Werf (NDSM-Wharf) ★★ CULTURAL CENTER   The Nederlandsche Dok en Scheepsbouw Maatschappij (Netherlands Dock and Shipyard Corporation) had been long derelict before it was taken over by an artists' community known as Stichting Kinetisch Noord, who have spruced up the dilapidated buildings and strewn the streets with recycled sculpture and heavy-duty graffiti. Among this urban jungle, studios and galleries have sprung up as well as a theater, forming a cutting-edge cultural center that is growing in reputation as the Westergasfabriek becomes more mainstream. Here, too, is the Amstel Botel, the city's only floating hotel. The elegant old triple-masted schooner *Pollux* is moored up alongside the Botel, and Greenpeace's retired environmental warrior of the seas, *Sirius,* is berthed across the dock from the Botel. The *Pannenkoekenboot* (Pancake boat; see p. 100) sorties from here to prowl the harbor laden with pancake-munching kids.

NDSM-Werf. Free admission 24/7. Take free ferry across IJ waterway to NDSM-Werf from behind Centraal Station.

Westerpark

Museum Het Schip ★★ MUSEUM   The city's most famous example of Amsterdam School architecture is a bus ride west to Zaanstraat. The movement's designs were influenced by the socialist ideals of architect Hendrik Berlage and are epitomized by heavy use of brickwork, elaborate masonry, spiky towers, painted glass, and wrought-iron work. Michel de Klerk (1884–1923) was the leading exponent of the school and designed his seminal building Het Schip to resemble an ocean liner; the brick complex incorporated social housing, a school, and a post office. The latter is the only one of De Klerk's interiors currently open to the public but at the time of press the school was being restored and is set for opening in late 2014.

Spaarndammerplantsoen 140. ℰ **020/686-8595.** www.hetschip.nl. Admission 7.50€ adults, 5€ students. Tues–Sun 11am–5pm. Closed Jan 1, Easter, Apr 27, Dec 25. Bus: 22.

Westerpark ★★ PARK   Until the early 2000s the Westerpark was a scrubby patch of green in the otherwise grimy industrial wasteland around the gas works that lay on its western flank, which became redundant and fell into disrepair after the advent of North Sea gas in the 1960s. Since then new life has been breathed into the area with the Westerpark remodeled to include open lawns and shady trees, tennis courts, skate parks, and play areas for kids. The gasworks have been repurposed into the Westergasfabriek, one of Amsterdam's coolest entertainment venues, with plenty of chances for beer or coffee as well as exhibition spaces, design studios, and Het Ketelhuis movie theater. Summer sees plenty of free open-air concerts here and there's often a fair for kids.

Westerpark, off Haarlemmerweg. ⓒ **020/586-0710.** www.westergasfabriek.nl. Free admission 24/7.

Amstelveen

Cobra Modern Art Museum ★★ MUSEUM Art lovers will find this breathtakingly contemporary museum worth the trek to its off-the-beaten-path location. The most enjoyable way to get here is the 20-minute Tram 5 ride from Amsterdam city center, giving you a chance to see leafy, suburban Amstelveen as you rattle through the streets. The museum is a light-filled brick-and-glass affair with plenty of white space for framing the artwork; it was designed by Dutch architect Wim Quist and opened in 1995. The collection overflows with the post–World War II abstract expressionist art and ceramics of the short-lived CoBrA Group, named for the initials of the founding artists' home cities: Copenhagen, Brussels, and Amsterdam. Karel Appel (1921–2006) and Constant (1920–2005) were the Dutch proponents, both controversial painters, sculptors, and ceramicists whose work, like their fellow CoBrA artists, have a childlike quality, employing strong colors and abstract shapes, seen in Constant's oil painting "Figure of the Night" and Appel's delightfully simple ceramics. There's a cafe here for coffees but it's no great shakes on the food front.

Sandbergplein 1, Amstelveen. ⓒ **020/547-5050.** www.cobra-museum.nl. Admission 10€ adults; 6€ seniors, students, and children 6–18. Daily 10am–5pm. Closed Jan 1, Dec 25.

Organized Tours

BUS TOURS For many travelers, a quick bus tour is the best way to launch a sightseeing program in a strange city, and though Amsterdam offers its unique alternative—canal boat cruises—you might want to get your bearings on land. The hop-on, hop-off circular bus tour run by **City Sightseeing** stops at all the major sights and buses run every 15 to 20 minutes from 9:15am to 7:20pm (ⓒ **020/420-4000;** www.citysightseeingamsterdam.nl). Prices start at 18€ (9€ for children) for 24 hours of access to the service.

   Viator (ⓒ **888/651-9785** in the U.S.; www.viator.com) and **Keytours** (ⓒ **020/305-5333;** www.keytours.nl) run bus tours around the city and also across The Netherlands. A favorite trip from March to May is out to the Keukenhof bulb fields at Lisse (p. 123). Rates vary with the particular tour on offer, but typical half-day tours begin around 30€ and full-day tours around 50€.

CANAL CRUISES There's no better way to discover Amsterdam than from its waterways. **Holland International** (ⓒ **020/217-0501;** www.canal.nl/en/holland-international-canal-cruises) canal cruises leave from the pier to the left of Centraal Station and are free with the Iamsterdam City Card (p. 82). During the summer season (Mar 20–Nov 2), tours leave daily every 15 minutes from 9am to 6pm, and every 30 minutes from 6 to 10pm. In winter, departures are every 45 minutes from 10am to 4pm. Cruises loop northwards into the IJ, which is bordered by the gleaming contemporary architecture of EYE Film Institute (p. 98), Muziekgebouw aan 't IJ (p. 110), and

Science Center NEMO (p. 96) before entering the Canal Ring and passing along the eastern canals, giving sight of the Magere Brug (Skinny Bridge) connecting Keizersgracht and Prinsengracht and illuminated at night with hundreds of lights. Then it's up Herengracht past mighty mansions to the "Nine Bridges" viewpoint, which actually permits sight of 15 bridges on the corner of Reguliersgracht. There's a rather lackluster commentary in English on board the boat, but it is still an entertaining way to learn about Amsterdam in a short time.

Other canal tour-boat lines are: **Amsterdam Canal Cruises** (℃ 020/679-1370; www.amsterdamcanalcruises.nl), **Gray Line** (℃ 303/394-6920; www.grayline amsterdam.com), **Reederij P Kooij** (℃ 020/623-4186; www.reederijkooij.nl), **Rederij Lovers** (℃ 020/530-1090; www.lovers.nl), **Rederij Plas** (℃ 020/624-5406; www. rederijplas.nl), and **Blue Boat Company** (℃ 020/679-1370; www.blueboat.nl). Prices vary from company to company, but a basic hourlong tour is around 15€ for adults, 8€ for children 4 to 12, and free for children 3 and under. Evening tours are available through most of these companies; 3-hour candlelit dinner cruises are among the most popular.

Still other canal cruising options include the hop-on, hop-off **Canal Bus** (℃ 20/217-0500; www.canal.nl), which stops at (or near) all the major attractions and allow you to build your own sightseeing itinerary. After a lunchtime treat for the kids? Try the **Pannenkoekenboot** (**Pancake Boat;** ℃ 020/638-88170; www.pannenkoekenboot.nl) for unlimited servings of pancakes with sweet or savory fillings with your boat trip. **Evening tours** are also available through most of the companies mentioned above; 3-hour candlelit dinner cruises are among the most popular.

CYCLING TOURS   Cycling in flat old Amsterdam would be fun if it wasn't for the local cyclists, but there's safety in numbers and there are several tour companies offering tours of the city by bike. **Yellow Bike** (℃ 020/620-6940; www.yellowbike.nl) and **Viator** (℃ 888/651-9785 in the U.S.; www.viator.com) both offer multiple options, from 2-hour canal jaunts to all-day rides out into the country past windmills and through nature reserves. Prices start at around 25€.

HORSE & CARRIAGE TOURS   These romantic, family-friendly vehicles run by **Karos Citytours** (℃ 020/691-3478; www.karos.nl) depart from just outside the Royal Palace on the Dam for traipses through the Old Center, along the canals, and into the Jordaan. Tours operate April to October daily 11am to 6pm (July–Aug to 7pm), and on a limited schedule in winter. Rides are 35€ for 20 minutes, 45€ for 30 minutes, and 65€ for 45 minutes.

WALKING TOURS   It's easy enough to make up your own walking tour of Amsterdam and include all the important sights, but if you need guidance, the tourist office has several suggested routes to follow. For 3€, you can purchase a brochure outlining one of three walking tours: City Center, Jewish Amsterdam, and the Jordaan; a fourth brochure, which costs 1€, covers the De Pijp district. The brochures are available at the Visitor Information Center outside Centraal Station and Schiphol airport.

A lot of companies offer themed walking tours around the city. One of the best is **Viator** (see "Cycling Tours," above) offering a range of guided walks (Red Light District, foodie tours of the markets, diamond factories) costing around 25€ per head.

WATER BIKE TOURS   If the canal-boat cruise whets your appetite to ramble the canals on your own, you can rent sturdy paddleboats called canal bikes from **Canal** (℃ 020/217-0500; www.canal.nl). They seat two or four and come with a guidebook with map and route suggestions. The Canal Bike moorings are at Leidseplein; Westerkerk, near the Anne Frankhuis; and Stadhouderskade, beside the Rijksmuseum. Rental is 8€ per person hourly plus a deposit of 20€.

Outdoor Activities

BOATING & SAILING Sailboats, kayaks, and canoes can be rented on the Sloterplas Lake from **Watersportcentrum De Duikelaar,** Noordzijde 41 (𝄢 **06/8146-6991;** www.deduikelaar.nl). From mid-March to mid-October, you can go to the Loosdrecht lakes, southeast of Amsterdam, to rent sailing equipment from **Ottenhome,** Zuwe 20, 1241 NC Kortenhoef (𝄢 **035/582-3331;** www.ottenhome.nl). Canoes can be rented in **Amsterdamse Bos,** south of the city, for use in the park lakes.

CYCLING Amsterdam is flat, flat, flat, but you take your life in your hands trying to ride a bike in the center of the city—local cyclists take no prisoners. Luckily there are plenty of options for enjoying a bike ride. Cycle along the canals; follow the path of the River Amstel south to Amstelpark and out to the photogenic village of Ouderkerk aan de Amstel; head into the Amsterdamse Bos; or venture further afield to the UNESCO-listed Amsterdam Stelling; this former defense line is 10km (8 miles) out of the city and gives 135km (85 miles) of scenic cycling past nature reserves and waterways. **MacBike** (𝄢 020/428-7005; www.macbike.nl) is the best-known cycle hire company. You'll need passport ID and a 50€ deposit per bike (cash or credit card). Rates (with insurance) are 9€ for 3 hours and 13€ for 1 day for a pedal-brake bike, 13€ and 18€ respectively for a bike with a handbrake. MacBike is open daily 9am to 5:45pm. A range of bikes is available, including tandems, six-speed touring bikes, and smaller ones for kids. There are five MacBike rental outlets (same web details)—on Waterlooplein, Stationsplein outside Centraal Station, Oosterdokskade 149, Weteringschans 2 at Leidseplein, and Marnixstraat 220.

GOLF Among public courses in or near Amsterdam are: 9-hole **Golfbaan Sloten,** Sloterweg 1045 (𝄢 **020/614-2402;** www.golfbaansloten.nl); 18-hole **Waterlandse Golf Club,** Buikslotermeerdijk 141 (𝄢 **020/636-1010;** www.waterlandsegolfclub.nl); and **Golfbaan Spaarnwoude,** Het Hoge Land 2, 1981 Velsen-Zuid (𝄢 **023/538-5599;** www.golfbaanspaarnwoude.nl).

HORSEBACK RIDING If you want to see the countryside from horseback, options include **Sonnenburgh Stables,** Nieuwe Kalfjeslaan 25 (𝄢 **020/643-1342;** www.sonnenburghstables.nl); or nearby **Manege Nieuw Amstelland,** Jan Tooropplantsoen 17 (𝄢 **020/643-2468;** www.nieuwamstelland.nl).

ICE-SKATING If temperatures drop low enough for long enough in winter, the canals of Amsterdam become sparkling highways through the city and the Dutch get their skates on. Classical music plays over the ice and kiosks are set up to dispense warming liqueurs. There are very few places that rent out skates, however. One that does is **Jaap Eden IJsbanen,** Radioweg 64 (𝄢 **0900/724-2287;** www.jaapeden.nl); you can rent skates here from November to February.

JOGGING The two main jogging areas are **Vondelpark** in the center city and **Amsterdamse Bos** on the southern edge of the city. You can run along the Amstel River. If you choose to run along the canals, watch out for uneven cobbles, loose paving stones, and dog poop.

ROLLER BLADING You can hire blades from **De Vondeltuin** (𝄢 **06/275-65576;** www.devondeltuin.nl) on the southwest side of the Vondelpark, near the western gates

Amsterdam has no natural beaches of its own, so it decided to create some. And what's even better is that admission is free to all their facilities and daily entertainment programs. **Blijburg aan Zee ★★★** is out at IJburg Zuid (Muiderlaan 1001; © **020/416-0330**; www.blijburg.nl; tram 26) in the eastern suburbs. Backed by a manmade sandy strip, it has a bohemian vibe, campfires, and late-night summertime clubbing. Party central for the young and hip of the city is **Strand West ★** at Stavangerweg 900 ((© **020/682-6310**; www.strand-west.nl), just north of the Westerpark and 15 minutes from Centraal Station by bus 22 or 48; here you'll find parasols, volleyball, beach bars, night-time DJs, and dance parties. Sophisticated **Strandzuid ★★** at Europaplein 22 ((© **020/639-2589**; www.strand-zuid.nl) is the preserve of a rather more mature clientele, with a restaurant, chill-out lounge, and cocktail bar on the wooden boardwalk. It's south of De Pijp; catch tram 4.

leading on to Amstelveenseweg. That's all the better to join the hundreds of skaters who skate on Amsterdam's regular—and free—**Friday Night Skate** (www.fridaynightskate.com). This event begins at 8:30pm, weather permitting. Meet at 8pm in summer and 8:15pm in winter outside the VondelCS cultural center in the Vondelpark, and take a circular route of around 20km (12½ miles) through the city. It's a sensible idea to wear a helmet and knee protection.

SWIMMING   Amsterdam's state-of-the-art swimming facility is **Het Marnix,** Marnixplein 1 (© **020/524-6000**; www.hetmarnix.nl), which has two heated pools along with a fitness center and spa, and a cafe-restaurant. The **Zuiderbad,** Hobbemastraat 26 (© **020/252-1390**), is a handsome, refurbished place close to the Rijksmuseum and built in 1911; it even has times set aside for those who like to swim in their birthday suit. **De Mirandabad,** De Mirandalaan 9 (© **020/252-4444**), features an indoor pool with wave machines, slides, and other amusements, and an outdoor pool that's open May to September.

TENNIS   Find indoor courts at **Frans Otten Stadion,** IJsbaanpad 43 (© **020/662-8767**; www.fransottenstadion.nl), close to the Olympic Stadium. For indoor and outdoor courts, try **Sportcentrum Amstelpark,** Koenenkade 8, Amsterdamse Bos (© **020/301-0700**; www.amstelpark.nl), which has 32 courts.

Especially for Kids

Despite the obvious considerations, Amsterdam caters brilliantly for children. The city offers modern, interactive museums carefully designed to appeal to youngsters; canal trips; trams to ride; and bikes to hire. With playgrounds in all the parks, kids' shows in several theaters, and pancakes on almost every menu, there's always something to do when youngsters get fractious or it pours with rain. However, as anyone with toddlers will tell you, pushing baby strollers across all those cobbles ain't much fun.

Best options for a happy family day out include **canal cruises;** if you don't think they'll last an hour without getting bored, you might like to blackmail them into behaving by promising a lunchtime treat aboard the *Pannenkoekenboot* (**Pancake Boat;** see above) for unlimited pancakes with sweet or savory fillings. There are family-size **Canal Bikes** to hire (see above), and bikes with baskets or little carts behind them from **MacBike** (see above). Even **riding the trams** can be quite a novelty.

And as for **museums,** there are plenty to choose from. The **Tropenmuseum** (p. 97) is full of color and noise while teaching about culture and race in an unpreachy manner; the hands-on **Science Center NEMO** (p. 96) cleverly unravels the mysteries of science; and all kids will fall in love with the sea lions and penguins at **Artis Royal Zoo** (p. 94). The tales of piratical derring-do aboard the good ship *Amsterdam* at **Het Scheepvaartmu-seum (National Maritime Museum;** p. 95) will enthrall most kids too.

The heartache of **Anne Frank Huis** (p. 88) will challenge and interest children 9 and older but can confuse younger kids, and it is not at all stroller-friendly. **Madame Tus-sauds** (Dam 20; ℂ 020/522-1010; www.madametussauds.nl) is perennially popular with older kids for its waxwork models of Johnny Depp, the uncoupled Gwyneth Paltrow, and Portuguese soccer star Ronaldhino; it costs 22€ adults, 18€ children 5 to 15, and free for children 4 and under. It's open daily 10am to 6:30pm (closed Apr 27). Although the **Amsterdam Dungeon** (Rokin 78; ℂ **020/530-8500;** www.thedungeons.com/amsterdam) may well terrify youngsters, teens will adore it for the gory interpretations of the Spanish Inquisition and burning witches at the stake. Admission is 22€ adults, 18€ children 5 to 15, and free for children 4 and under. It's open daily 11am to 5pm.

SHOPPING

Although Amsterdam is no Paris or Milan in the shopping stakes, it's no slouch either. Ignoring the tatty souvenir stores selling plastic tulips and mass-produced clogs around Dam Square, **Rokin** and pedestrianized **Kalverstraat** offer mainstream shopping brands that can be seen anywhere in the world. **Leidsestraat** and **Koningsplein** are among the most popular shopping spots, with mid-range boutiques and design stores. Upping the ante are young designers changing the face of the retail scene around the **Nine Streets** (p. 106) and in the **Museum Quarter,** where independents are giving the international designers such as Louis Vuitton and Gucci a run for their money on exclusive shopping streets Pieter Cornelisz Hooftstraat and van Baerlerstraat. The **Spie-gelkwartier** at the south end of the Canal Ring is famous for its antiques and art stores, and is the place to head for genuine blue-and-white Delftware. Typically Dutch prod-ucts such as cheese and flower bulbs are bargains, as diamonds can be if bought care-fully from a reputable dealer such as Gassan (p. 109).

Art & Antiques

Antiekcentrum Amsterdam ★★   The largest indoor antiques market in The Netherlands is situated in Jordaan. Formerly known as De Looier, it's a cornucopia of Delftware, porcelain, silverware, wonderfully restored furniture, and bizarre statuary straggling through several old warehouses. There are 46 dealers with permanent stalls here, specializing in anything from Bakelite phones to priceless pocket watches. Wednesday, Saturday, and Sunday sees dealers from all over the country bring their wares to a table market just outside the antiques center; get their early and you just might find that elusive Old Master oil painting. Open Monday, Wednesday, and Friday 11am to 6pm, and Saturday and Sunday 10am to 5pm. Elandsgracht 109. ℂ **020/624-9038.** www.antiekcentrumamsterdam.nl.

Art Plein Spui ★   Sundays in the Old Center see a gathering of local artists who show their works under canvas just off the busy street of Spui. Standards and subject matter vary considerably as 25 artists from a pool of 60 exhibit each week. As well as predictable canal-side views badly executed in watercolor, you might find lovely ceramic bowls by Marc Wensma or wacky etchings from Janny Endstra, handmade ethnic jewelry, or silk-screen printing. You have to take potluck. Spui.✆ **06/2499-2403.** www.artplein-spui.org.

Galerie Lieve Hemel ★★   Located in the exclusive Spiegelkwartier in the Canal Ring, Lieve Hemel is a refined gallery selling the very best of contemporary Dutch art from a carefully selected gaggle of fine artists who may prove to be the Damien Hirsts of the future. Styles range from slightly surreal to 21st-century takes on the 17th-century still-life genre. Also on sale here is a charming selection of contemporary silverware, including vases, bowls, and tea services. Nieuwe Spiegelstraat 3.✆ **020/623-0060.** www.lievehemel.nl.

Mathieu Hart ★★   Still family owned and considered one of the leading experts in fine art since 1878, Erik Hart's antiques emporium in the Old Center is stuffed to the gunnels with rare prints of Dutch cities, elaborate French Empire chandeliers and candlesticks, top-quality 18th-century Delftware, priceless Chinese porcelain, and an array of loudly ticking clocks. A courier service is available for shipping overseas. Rokin 122.✆ **020/623-1658.** www.hartantiques.com.

Premsela & Hamburger ★★   Opened in 1823, this historic store in the Old Center deals in antiquities at the luxury end of the market. Although some modern jewelry is sold here, the shop specializes in antique silver and gold collectables, from beautifully crafted 17th-century galleons under full sail to exquisite pre-loved diamond rings. It's a reputable choice if you're considering buying gemstones, gold, or jewelry in Amsterdam. Rokin 98.✆ **020/624-9688.** www.premsela.com.

Van Gogh Museum Shop ★★★   One of the better Amsterdam museum shops, selling hundreds of items smothered with Van Gogh's familiar artworks. There's a choice of books detailing the story of the tortured artist's life and postcards and posters by the hundred as well as puzzle books for kids and pretty silk scarves patterned with sunflowers. Slightly less successful are the T-shirts bearing one of Van Gogh's wretched-looking self-portraits. Paulus Potterstraat 7. ✆ **020/570-5200.** www.vangogh museum.nl.

Amsterdam Shop Opening Hours

Shops normally open from 9:30am to 6pm Tuesday, Wednesday, Friday, and Saturday. Some stay open until 8 or 9pm on Thursday. Many close on Monday morning, opening at 1pm, and most stores around the city center also open Sunday around midday; outside the center many are closed all day Sunday.

Books

American Book Center ★   From best-selling novels to travel guides, remaindered titles, and the latest celeb magazines, this vast bookstore is handsomely stocked. Book readings are frequent, there are discount vouchers for students, and if you are an aspiring author, there's even a self-publishing advisory service. This main branch is in the Old Center, but there is another branch in The Hague (p. 129). Spui 12. ✆ **020/625-5537.** www.abc.nl.

If you want to get high without smoking a joint or eating a space cake made with hash, head for Amsterdam's smart shops, which sell natural stimulants such as *guarana* and supposed aphrodisiacs such as *ginkgo biloba*, as well as magic mushrooms, growing kits for weed, and seeds. Check out **Nightlife** (Nieuwendijk 42), the **Magic Mushroom Gallery** (Spuistraat 249), or **Azarius** on Kerkstraat behind the Leidseplein.

Evenaar ★ In the Canal Ring, Amsterdam's first stop for travel literature is a beguiling, cramped warren of travel maps, mainstream guides, and gorgeous coffee-table tomes containing stunning color photography. There's also a section on armchair travel and anthropology as well as antique travel books. Singel 348. ℂ **020/624-6289.** www.evenaar.net.

Cheese

De Kaaskamer van Amsterdam ★★★ Amsterdam's most famous cheese emporium is in the cutesy Nine Streets shopping district in the Canal Ring. This deli delight lets you choose from more than 300 cheeses, including wheels of aged Gouda, creamy goats' cheeses, and variety packs of up to six selections of organic cheeses with prices starting around 45€ (they will vacuum-pack for travelers). Runstraat 7 (at Keizersgracht). ℂ **020/623-3483.** www.kaaskamer.nl.

Delftware

Galleria d'Arte Rinascimento ★★ Buying authentic Dutch Delftware can be a problem in Amsterdam, but you'll never have an issue here as all the blue-and-white pottery on sale is authenticated. Dealing in pottery old and new, the gallery has a fine collection of antiquarian Delft tiles depicting Dutch views that make perfect gifts to take back home. The cream of the crop is the pricey, exquisite, and subtly multicolored Makkumware from Koninklijke Tichelaar Makkum. Prinsengracht 170 (at Bloemstraat). ℂ **020/622-7509.** www.delft-art-gallery.com.

Jorrit Heinen Royal Delftware ★★ There are three Amsterdam and three Delft branches of this family-owned chain that makes and sells its own-brand porcelain as well as being official dealers in fine De Porcelyne Fles and leaded crystal. It's the go-to place for many-spouted tulip vases, the legacy of 17th-century tulip madness, as well as cute Delftware charm bracelets and cufflinks. One store is based in the historic Muntoren. Prinsengracht 440 (at Leidsestraat). ℂ **020/627-8299.** www.delftsblauwwinkel.nl.

Department Stores

de Bijenkorf ★★ Amsterdam's answer to Harrods and Bloomingdales is a four-story shopping addict's dream in the Old Center, selling anything from Gucci belts to Chanel headphones under one roof. The city's most prestigious and expensive department store is a luxurious delight, with high-brand designs such as Missoni and Alexander Wang for women as well as Petit Bateau and Hilfiger for kids, and Armani or Nike sports gear for men-about-town. A duty-free shopping service allows overseas visitors to claim their tax back on leaving the country. Dam 1. ℂ **0800-0818.** www.de bijenkorf.nl.

The Negen Straatjes—Amsterdam's Nine Streets

Tucked away between the historic Old Center and the bohemian Jordaan, the Nine Streets are a classy one-stop shopping destination crisscrossing the western side of the 17th-century Canal Ring between Reestraat and Runstraat. The streets provide a welcome relief from the tatty souvenir stores of Dam Square, as they offer chic stores selling designer labels, artisan jewelry, offbeat vintage fashions, and luxury toiletries, all interspersed with plenty of stylish bars and restaurants.

Fashion store **Van Ravenstein** (𝄐 **020/639-0007;** www.van-ravenstein. nl) sells on-trend Belgian designers Ann Demeulemeester and Dries van Noten. **L'étoile de Saint Honoré** (Oude Spiegelstraat 1; 𝄐 **020/330-2419;** www. etoile-luxuryvintage.com) is the best place for vintage handbags, **Anecdote** (Wolvenstraat 15; 𝄐 **020/427-9156;**

www.anecdote.nl) for simple, stylish fashion, and **Spoiled** (Wolvenstraat 19; 𝄐 **020/626-3818;** www.spoiled.nl) offers arguably the best selection of denim labels in Amsterdam. **United Nude** (see below) sells cool shoes and boots for women, **Parisienne** (Berenstraat 4; 𝄐 **020/428-0834;** www.nlstreets.nl/EN/shop/parisienne) offers lovely vintage jewelry, and **MINT Mini Mall** (Runstraat 27; 𝄐 **020/627-2466;** www.mintminimall.nl) sells cushions, pottery, and furniture in all shades of pastel. **Skins Cosmetic** (Runstraat 11; 𝄐 **020/528-6922;** www.skins.nl) is the place for organic toiletries, and **La Savonnerie** (Prinsengracht 294; 𝄐 **020/428-1139;** www.savonnerie.nl) for handmade soaps. For more information about the Nine Streets in English, visit **www.theninestreets.com**.

Peek & Cloppenburg ★★   No doubt given a shot in the arm by the closure of the lovely old Metz & Co. department store, this elegant shop is in pole position just off Amsterdam's main square, the Dam. It does fashion for both sexes brilliantly at a range of price levels, from designer brands such as D&G and Armani to the less pricey Fred Perry and Geox. With stores now in 15 European countries, P&C is introducing more European clothing lines to its repertoire. Dam 20. 𝄐 **020/623-2837.** www.peek-cloppenburg.nl.

Design

Pol's Potten Amsterdam B.V. ★★   Housed in a former warehouse right at the coal face of Amsterdam regeneration in the eastern docks, this funky design store concentrates on selling simple, stark designs for the home. From colorful glassware to plastic kitchen utensils and desk accessories, the shop's style is reminiscent of an upmarket Swedish Ikea. A visit might unearth funky Italian furniture, dog-shaped watering cans, and pretty sets of tinted glasses. KNSM-Laan 39. 𝄐 **020/419-3541.** www.polspotten.nl.

Fashion

Azzurro Due ★★   With four stores now open in chi-chi PC Hoofstraat, Azzurro has got the job of dressing men, women, kids, and fashion-conscious youngsters—the latter at the on-trend Four Azzurro at no. 127—all wrapped up. The shiny, sleek flagship store Azzurro Due showcases young Dutch designers such as Marjon Hoogervarst alongside stellar international names like Rachel Zoe, Isabel Marant, and Roland Mouret. Pieter Cornelisz Hooftstraat 138. 𝄐 **020/671-9708.** www.azzurrofashiongroup.nl.

De Maagd & De Leeuw ★★   A pretty boutique in the lovely shopping enclave of the Nine Streets, selling jeans and stylish tops for off-duty wear, smart day dresses, and elegant gowns for the evening, all sourced from the latest Paris fashions on a monthly basis. There's also a selection of stylish shoes and boots, belts in many colors, and leather bags at reasonable prices. Hartenstraat 32. ℭ **020/428-0047.** www.demaag dendeleeuw.nl.

Episode ★★★   This was one of Amsterdam's original thrift stores and has been a huge eco-friendly success story, adhering to principles of sustainability that see almost nothing thrown away. Everything sold here is secondhand—tatty old jeans are up-cycled into shorts, gauzy evening frocks given a new lease on life, and fresh items of clothing are cleverly created out of old. Two more stores are found at Berenstraat 1 in the Nine Streets, and at Nieuwe Speigelstraat 61. Waterlooplein 1. ℭ **020/320-3000.** www. episode.eu.

Megazino ★★★   One of Amsterdam's few discount stores, this designer outlet in the Nine Streets is always crammed with fashionistas searching for that elusive bargain. Discounted brands that are featured include Prada, Hugo Boss, and Christian Dior; new styles are discounted to 30 percent off, but there's also a whole floor dedicated to fashion from bygone seasons that come at a whopping 50-percent reduction. Rozengracht 207–213. ℭ **020/330-1031.** www.nlstreets.nl/NL/winkel/megazino-store.

Redlight Fashion Amsterdam ★★   With the ongoing cleanup of the Red Light District, several of the prostitutes' windows in De Wallen have been closed and shops, exhibition spaces, galleries, and studios have appeared among the tawdry sex shops. Run by talented independent designers as part of the project Redlight Fashion Amsterdam, stores to check out include Code on Oudezijds Achterburgwal for hot menswear designers at decent prices, and Jouw Stoute Schoenen on the same street for über-cool footwear. Oudezijds Achterburgwal. www.redlightfashionamsterdam.com.

Webers Holland ★★   A scream of a shop hidden behind the facade of one of Amsterdam's narrowest houses. Yes, the 17th-century Klein Trippenhuis (Little Trippenhuis) in the Old Center is the unlikely venue for the wacky, outlandish fetish designs of Désirée Webers, who has been creating rubber and leather outfits since 1995. Apart from huge, stacked platforms by Pleaser and cat suits with cut outs, not all her clothes are so out there; a recent collection of black hand-knit dresses and Tees was even quite demure. Kloveniersburgwal 26. ℭ **020/638-1777.** www.webersholland.nl.

Flea Markets

Noodermarkt op Zaterdag (Northern Market on Saturday) ★★   The Noorderkerk (North Church) was built in 1623, the final masterpiece of Hendrik de Keyser (p. 23). The square surrounding the church is the site of a sprawling flea market on Saturday, where stalls are a mixed bag of decent paintings, a few antiques, handmade jewelry, rugs, and old books at rock-bottom prices. Everything starts to close up around 2pm so get there at 9am to snap up some great vintage finds. The Boerenmarkt (see below) is adjacent. Noordermarkt. No phone. www.noordermarkt-amsterdam.nl.

Waterlooplein Flea Market ★   The big daddy of Amsterdam street markets has around 300 stands flogging anything and everything from rubbishy oil paintings to jugglers' balls by way of knock-off DVDs, beat-up army jackets, and dainty ethnic jewelry. You can still find genuine treasures under all the second-hand tat but you have to look hard; be prepared to bargain, but accept that Dutch speakers will probably get a better deal. Whether you turn up that vintage Burberry trench or not, Waterlooplein makes for a great hour or two rummaging around in what is effectively other people's cast-offs. It's open Monday through Friday 9am to 5:30pm, and Saturday 8:30am to 5:30pm. Waterlooplein. No phone. www.waterloopleinmarkt.nl.

Flowers

Bloemenmarkt (Flower Market) ★★ A permanent fixture along the Singel, the Bloemenmarkt (p. 82) is partly housed on riverboats. The massive plant-and-flower bonanza has been in its present position since 1883 and runs from the Koningsplein shopping street along the canal to Muntplein. Always festooned in a blaze of color, the flower market really explodes into psychedelic overdrive in springtime when the tulip bulbs and hyacinths arrive. It also looks fetching around Christmas under a carpet of fake snow and sparkly baubles. Admire the swathes of cut flowers and plants, but restrict your buying to gardening tools, seeds, and bulbs ready packed and stamped for export if you expect to take them out of the country. Open Monday to Saturday 9am to 5:30pm, Sunday 11am to 5:30pm. Along the south bank of Singel btwn. Muntplein and Koningsplein. No phone.

Gerda's Bloemen & Planten ★★★ Among the scores of enticing flower shops in the center of Amsterdam, this is one of the best. Recent commissions have seen the store's florists produce elegant bouquets for Tom Ford's fashion shows, and they have a regular gig creating all the flower arrangements for the Grachtenfestival (see below). Every day there's a fresh selection of riotously colored blooms for sale in the stylish store, and a delivery service spans the city. Runstraat 16. ✆ **020/624-2912.** www.thenine streets.com/gerda.html.

Food Markets

Albert Cuypmarkt ★★★ Amsterdam's biggest street market stretches for 1km (½ mile) and takes place Monday through to Saturday from 9am to 5pm. Although it is fast becoming a tourist attraction in its own right, the market still functions as the daily food market for De Pijp residents. Reflecting the multi-ethnic nature of the district, everything is on sale here from raw herring to sweet baklava pastries and rice noodles. It's also the place to stock up on cheery patterned sarongs, flip-flops, daft headgear, and kitchen mops. Albert Cuypstraat btwn. Ferdinand Bolstraat and Van Woustraat. No phone. www.albertcuypmarkt.nl.

Boerenmarkt (Farmers Market) ★ Amsterdam's premier organic market is known locally as **the Bio** and runs alongside Saturday's flea market on Noordermarkt. As it has a captive audience of middle-class shoppers from genteel Jordaan, the market's quality produce has proved a great hit and, despite the high prices, it is fast expanding. This is the spot for you if you're after an al fresco picnic lunch; search out delicious organic breads, homemade salads, luscious fresh fruit and vegetables, salamis, and cheeses, then scarf down the lot on a tranquil Jordaan canal bank. Open Saturday 9am to 4pm. Noordermarkt. No phone. www.boerenmarktamsterdam.nl.

Gifts

Condomerie ★ The world's first condom shop is cleverly sited on the edge of the Red Light District for those little emergencies in life. Even though it's notorious the world over, the store is surprisingly small, but it packs in all manner of protection in numerous flavors, patterns, and shapes from common brands to flashing or sparkly

oddities as well as a variety of other sex aids. Warmoesstraat 141. ℂ **020/627-4174.** www.
condomerie.com.

't Curiosa Winkeltje ★★★   A deeply eccentric store in the Canal Ring where
you're sure to find an unusual gift, be it a glitzy gold tea service, a 1960s record player,
plastic tulips in plastic pots, and children's toys from the 1950s. It's worth having a
good scrabble around to come up with that truly unique present for your beloved. Prinsengracht 228. ℂ **020/625-1352.**

Smokiana ★★   Like a relic of a bygone age, this odd little store underneath the
bizarrely compelling and informative Amsterdam Pipe Museum (p. 87) offers tobacco
in a multitude of flavors, snuff, and smoking memorabilia as well as an enormous
selection of wooden and clay pipes from across the world. An anachronism in an era
where smokers are virtually alienated from society, the store carries on regardless of
popular opinion. Prinsengracht 488. ℂ **020/421-1779.** www.pijpenkabinet.nl.

Van der Donk Fine Chocolates ★★   Located in a handsome store a step away
from the Rijksmuseum, Van der Donk is run by a pair of keen, connoisseur chocolatiers who have conjured up their ambrosial confections since 2012. You can try before
you buy and first among equals are the taste-tingling white champagne truffles. Other
yummy international brands of chocolate are available, from NYC's Dean & DeLuca
to Spanish ChocoLate Orgániko. Nieuwe Speigelstraat 72. ℂ **020/620-2777.** www.vander
donkchocolates.nl.

Jewelry

Gassan Diamonds ★★★   An international company of some repute, Gassan's
jewelry stores have spread into airports across the world, but their HQ is still based in
the remarkable Amsterdam School building designed by J.N. Meyer in 1897, overlooking the Oudeschans canal. It is here that the founder of Gassan first learned to cut
diamonds; free, guided tours of the factory are available daily and incorporate a visit
to the onsite Choices by DL Flagship boutique, where whopping great precious stones
are sold at whopping great prices. There are three other stores in Amsterdam, one at
Rokin 1–5 in the Old Center, plus two more out at Schiphol airport. Considering the
company's size and standing, it is one of the better options to head for if you are thinking of investing in gemstones. Nieuwe Uilenburgerstraat 173–175. ℂ **020/622-5333.** www.
gassandiamonds.nl.

Kids

Tinkerbell ★★★   *The* place in Amsterdam to purchase traditional wooden toys,
puzzles, and gentle learning tools for kids 9 and under. Located in the exclusive Spie-
gelkwartier among the antiques shops, there's a refreshing lack of plastic in favor of
quality and sustainability. Best sellers include cuddly teddy bears, model farm animals,
books, and animal glove puppets. Spiegelgracht 10. ℂ **020/625-8830.** www.tinkerbelltoys.nl.

Malls

Magna Plaza ★★   Housed in the city's former main post office, which dates back
to 1899, this elegant mall has just been through a multimillion-euro facelift, and its
attractive, colonnaded, and arcaded interior looks as good as new. Arranged around
three levels under a soaring vaulted roof, the 21 mid-range stores include the gleaming
crystals animals of Swarovski and the cool Spanish fashion chain Mango, as well as

Lacoste and America Today. There's also a Megastore Fame selling movies and music, a branch of UK's top-notch hairdresser Tony and Guy, and a couple of food outlets. Nieuwezijds Voorburgwal 182. ☏ **020/570-3570.** www.magnaplaza.nl.

Shoes

United Nude ★★   On the outer reaches of the corner of the Nine Streets shopping area, this wackily designed boutique is owned by avant-garde designer Rem D Koolhaas, who has pushed boundaries in shoe design in the same way that his uncle of the same name storms forward with his architecture. A recent collaboration with Iranian-English architect Zaha Hadid has produced a series of gravity-defying boots, but more practical and wearable styles include multi-striped court shoes and dainty flats with ankle straps. Spuistraat 125a. ☏ **020/626-0010.** www.unitednude.com.

ENTERTAINMENT & NIGHTLIFE
The Performing Arts

Amsterdam's top orchestra—indeed, one of the world's top orchestras—is the renowned **Royal Concertgebouw Orchestra** (www.concertgebouworkest.nl), whose home is the **Concertgebouw** ★★★, Concertgebouwplein 2–6 (☏ **0900/671-8345;** www.concertgebouw.nl), which first opened its doors in 1888 and still touted as one of the most acoustically perfect concert halls in Europe. The Netherlands Philharmonic Orchestra and the Netherlands Chamber Orchestra are also based here, and both have the same contact details (☏ **020/521-7500;** www.orkest.nl). World-class orchestras and soloists line up for the chance of appearing in the hallowed Grote Zaal (Great Hall) of the Concertgebouw thanks to its perfect sound quality. Chamber and solo recitals are given in the smaller Kleine Zaal (Little Hall). Tickets cost 18€ to 100€. The main concert season is September to mid-June, with the Robeco SummerNights concert series running during July and August and featuring world-class artists but with much-reduced seats priced 10€ to 35€. A mixed-bag of free concerts are held at the Concertgebouw every Wednesday at 12:30pm.

At the other end of the musical spectrum, lovers of avant-garde and experimental music should head to the **Muziekgebouw aan 't IJ,** Piet Heinkade 1 (☏ **020/788-2000;** www.muziekgebouw.nl), which opened in 2005 on the ever-expanding IJ waterfront east of Centraal Station. It's the hub of modern and old jazz, electronic, and non-Western music in Amsterdam, as well as small-scale musical theater, opera, and dance. The waterside terrace of the cafe-restaurant is one of the most idyllic in town. Tickets are 10€ to 28€. Right next door is the Bimhuis, Piet Heinkade 3 (☏ **020/788-2188;** www.bimhuis.com), Amsterdam's much-loved improvisational jazz and blues club, where ticket prices range from 10€ to 25€.

Artistic director Pierre Audi, who until 2014 was also in charge of the Holland Festival (see below), has established the **Dutch National Opera** (www.dno.nl) as one of the leading companies in Europe. They perform at the **Dutch National Opera & Ballet,** Waterlooplein 22 (☏ **020/625-5455;** www.operaballet.nl). The box office is at Amstel 3, and the theater is also home to the **Dutch National Ballet** (www.operaballet.nl), which offers both classical ballet repertoire and contemporary works. The **Netherlands Dance Theater** (www.ndt.nl), known for its contemporary repertoire,

Amsterdam's reputation as a party town is due in part to its tolerance toward soft drugs. But in fact the practice is technically illegal. Whereas it's fine to carry 5 grams (⅙ oz.) for personal use, it's not fine to buy dope anywhere other than in a **coffee shop.** These are licensed and controlled venues where you can purchase marijuana or hashish, and can sit and smoke all day if you want to. Although around 200 coffee shops still exist in Amsterdam (most concentrated around the Red Light District; **The Bulldog** at Oudezijds Voorburgwal 88 is the best known), many have been closed down since 2010 as civic leaders have tried to clean up the city's act. There was even talk back in 2012 of introducing an ID system for coffee shop users that would have banned overseas tourists from utilizing them, but this was rather cynically vetoed as financially unviable for the city. However, it is still illegal to smoke dope in the streets, to buy drugs in the streets, and to buy drugs at all if you are under 18. And don't be tempted to take any drugs out of the country with you.

also stages productions here, although its home is in The Hague. Most performances begin at 8:15pm and tickets cost between 15€ and 155€, depending on the program.

Theater

Royal Theatre Carré ★★★ A lovely old theater that was once Amsterdam's circus arena; these days a circus performs here only over Christmas. The theater hosts a few English-language productions of opera, contemporary dance, and ballet, as well as best-selling big-name shows such as "War Horse." International acts (Neil Finn, Glenn Miller Orchestra) also perform here from time to time. Amstel 115–125. ✆ **0900/252-5255.** www.carre.nl. Tickets 5€–140€.

Stadsschouwburg ★★ Amsterdam's foremost venue for mainstream Dutch theater is a 950-seat municipal theater showcasing homegrown productions that are almost always in Dutch. Opera and ballet performances are occasionally staged here, as are the occasional classic and modern plays in English. Ticket prices vary according to production, but average between 10€ and 50€. The Last Minute Ticketshop (p. 55) for tickets to events at venues all over town is on the ground floor. Leidseplein 26. ✆ **020/624-2311.** www.stadsschouwburgamsterdam.nl.

Comedy Theater

Boom Chicago ★ Amsterdam's foremost comedy theater has moved from the Leidseplein but continues to bring delightful English-language improvisational comedy to the city. The partly scripted, partly improvised humor takes potshots at life in Amsterdam, politics, tourists, and any other available target. Dutch audiences seem to enjoy the English comedy as much as anyone and in fact often seem to get the point ahead of the native English-speakers in attendance. There's a ginormous bar and the audience sits at candlelit tables during the show. Tickets are 7.50€ to 35€ not including dinner, which must be booked in advance. Boom Chicago has teamed up with three local restaurants to deliver Asian, Italian, or Arabic chow right to your table. The box office is open daily from 4pm until show time, with doors opening at 8pm. Rosengracht 117. ✆ **0900/266-6244.** www.boomchicago.nl.

4

AMSTERDAM

Entertainment & Nightlife

New Year's Eve sees raucous parties on the streets, with the **Amsterdam Light Festival** running concurrently and illuminating the streets around the Amstel with wacky light installations. February sees street parades and firework displays in honor of **Chinese New Year,** and March brings the film-and-dance festival **Cinedan** at the EYE Film Institute (p. 98). Spring heralds the bulb frenzy at **Keukenhof Gardens** at Lisse (p. 123), which open from March to mid-May. June marks a month of drama and music at the **Holland Festival** (www.hollandfestival.nl/en), which runs for the entire month.

Another much-loved summer institution is **Vondelpark Open Air Theater** (www.openluchttheater.nl/theater), in its 41st year in 2015 and offering a repertoire of plays, concerts, films, and stand-up comedy June through August. August in Amsterdam is festival city;

Uitmarkt (www.amsterdamsuitburo.nl/uitmarkt/english) is the biggest cultural festival in The Netherlands with 450 performances from 2,000 international artists, and the **Grachtenfestival (Canal Festival;** www.grachtenfestival.nl) celebrates classical music with a series of outdoor concerts.

Fall sees the **State Opening of Parliament** in The Hague (p. 129) by King Willem-Alexander on the third Tuesday in September. Winter's great family-friendly event is the appearance of **Sinterklaas** on the third Saturday in November to check on the behavior of the city's kids. He arrives by boat at Centraal Station pier, accompanied by black-painted assistants called Zwarte Piet (Black Peter), who hand out candy to kids before proceeding in stately horseback procession through Amsterdam to be given the keys to the city in Dam Square.

Bars & Pubs

Bubbles & Wines ★★   An oh-so-sophisticated champagne and wine bar in the Old Center that was voted Amsterdam's wine bar of the year in 2011 and makes a little oasis of hushed red decor and subdued lighting among the chaos of the city's tourist heartland. Along with the extensive and reasonably well-priced selection of new and old world wines, there are also champagnes sold by the glass. Some of the most delicious tapas bites in the city are served as accompaniment to the wines, but with prices starting at 23€ for a tiny dollop of caviar, you'd be better off sticking to the delicious jamon Iberico or Wagyu beef. Nes 37. ☎ 020/422-3318. www.bubblesandwines.com.

Café Pollux ★★   A real treasure in the Dam area, primarily due to the charismatic and slightly bonkers owner Frits and his enigmatically smiling wife. It has a garish scarlet interior reminiscent of an old-fashioned American diner on acid, and a simple menu of Dutch favorites like *bitterballen* and croquettes is served all day. Come evening, there is often live music—but if not, you can fall back on rock 'n' roll from the 1950s jukebox and dance around the stripper's pole. It's often open very late, dependent on the mood of Frits. Prins Hendrikkade 121. ☎ 020/624-9521. www.cafepollux.com.

Chocolate Bar ★★   A hip hangout in De Pijp, with a sparse, orange-and-brown retro 1970s look, this is a contemporary take on Amsterdam's traditional brown cafes. With a clientele culled from local residents and young foreign visitors, a good time to hit the place is early evening for fruity cocktails and the really good Thai beef salad. Thursday through Saturday sees live music from local DJs, and there's a terrace for cocktails and supper when the weather's clement. Disappointingly for cocoa addicts, the chocolate theme does not extend beyond the name. Eerste Van der Helststraat 62A. ⓒ **020/675-7672.** www.chocolate-bar.nl.

De Drie Fleschjes ★★★   There's sawdust on the floor and wooden barrels line the walls in this traditional *proeflakaal* (tasting room), which is a real find and a welcome escape from the Red Light District hinterland. De Drie Fleschjes is run by informed and relaxed bartenders who are only too pleased to pass on their secrets for sampling *jenever* (a ginlike liqueur) in wholesome, old-fashioned surroundings. Although one or two tourists may find their way in here, most of your fellow drinkers will be Dutch. Gravenstraat 18. ⓒ **020/624-8443.** www.dedriefleschjes.nl.

De Jaren ★★   Overlooking the Binnenamstel waterfront, this perennial Amsterdam favorite has panoramic upper-floor terraces perfect for reading newspapers on sunny Sunday afternoons or meeting up with the girls for lunch. There's an enormous bar, a yummy salad buffet, and a traditional English high tea with scones and clotted cream served every afternoon. Nieuwe Doelenstraat 20–22. ⓒ **020/625-5771.** www.cafe-de-jaren.nl.

Vesper ★★★   One of a new breed of super-smooth and super-friendly cocktail bars with some wacky and wonderful concoctions, Vesper is currently widely regarded as employing the coolest mixologists in Amsterdam. In Jordaan, it's one step beyond the usual fare of mojitos and gin slings as the bar tenders go off piste to create new wonders in a cocktail glass. The little wooden bar is also the original home of the alcoholic high tea, which puts a pleasant new slant on scones with clotted cream. Vinkenstraat 57. ⓒ **020/846-4458.** www.vesperbar.nl.

Dance Clubs & Live Music

Jimmy Woo ★★   An Asian-themed club with a posh clientele who happily sit around quaffing champagne all night. Things don't start to heat up until around 1am, when the music cranks up downstairs and the elegant crowds stalk on to the dance floor. Dress up, as the fashion police can be quite picky. Korte Leidsedwarsstraat 18. ⓒ **020/626-3150.** www.jimmywoo.com. Admission 10€–20€.

Paradiso ★   An Amsterdam institution, Paradiso is based in a former church that has converted well into a majestic, multi-purpose club with lofty ceilings and high balconies encircling the dance floor. Big-name DJs and theme nights keep bringing the punters in at the weekend, and in recent times Arcade Fire, Robbie Williams, and Adele have all played here. Weteringschans 6–8. ⓒ **020/626-4521.** www.paradiso.nl. Admission 10€–25€.

Vondelpark Openluchttheater (Open Air Theater) ★★★   Summer is festival and party time in Amsterdam, and May through August see al-fresco fun kick off in the Vondelpark with a series of concerts at the moon-shaped open-air stage. There are Sunday afternoon jazz sessions plus a program of pop, rock, Latin, classical music, and stand up as well as special shows for kids. Best of all everything is free, although a small donation of around a euro is requested. Bring a picnic or eat at 't Blauwe Theehuis before the concert starts. Vondelpark. ⓒ **020/428-3360.** www.openlucht theater.nl. Free admission.

WesterUnie ★★   Secreted away in the Westergasfabriek cultural complex west of Centraal Station, WesterUnie is a venue of three parts. By day it's an industrial-chic, cavernous bar and cafe with a suntrap terrace, but at night it morphs into either a concert hall or a heavy-duty music club that gets packed with fans of hip-hop, garage, and pretty much anything danceable. Numerous DJ parties are held here over summer, when the action goes on until the wee, wee hours; it's becoming the go-to club of choice for the post-, post-party crowd. Westergasfabriek, Klönneplein 4–6. ✆ **020/684-8496.** www.westerunie.nl. Admission free–75€.

Gay & Lesbian

Saarein ★★   A happy-go-lucky, essentially lesbian environment that is open to all comers, straight, bi, or gay, Saarein is typical of the Jordaan's brown cafes (p. 72) in that the bar staff and clientele are cheery, welcoming, and happy to talk. With a decent selection of draught and bottled beers, live music, DJs, and one of the few pool tables in the Jordaan, the bar becomes the center of much of the action during Amsterdam Gay Pride. Elandsstraat 119. ✆ **020/623-4901.** www. saarein.info.

SoHo Amsterdam ★   The city's quintessential gay venue is a typical pub during the week, but hits party time at the weekend. Nothing really gets going until after 11pm, and there are DJ nights and themed parties right in the heart of Amsterdam's gay area in the Old Center. Reguliersdwarsstraat 36. ✆ **020/638-5700.** www.soho-amsterdam.com.

Amsterdam Gay Pride

The summer's biggest street party is the riotous Amsterdam Gay Pride, which normally takes place the last week of July. A celebration of the open-hearted, welcoming, and tolerant culture of The Netherlands, Pride kicks off with a canal parade of lavishly decorated barges around the Canal Ring and the week that follows is a non-stop round of street parties, concerts, and drag queen Olympics. The Amsterdam Gay Pride program is available on the website (www.amsterdamgaypride.org).

Entertainment & Nightlife

AMSTERDAM

SIDE TRIPS FROM AMSTERDAM

The Netherlands may start with Amsterdam, but it certainly doesn't end there. This crowded little country has much more up its sleeve, from the stately pleasures of genteel Hague, which is after all the country's political capital, to the laid-back charm of Haarlem. You can step back in time to visit a Holland almost forgotten at the open-air museums of Zuiderzee and Zaanse Schans, or look to the future among the gritty, urban architecture of Rotterdam. There are chart-topping art museums to discover in virtually every city, beaches to stroll in Scheveningen, and blazes of color to admire in the bulb fields of Lisse.

Most of the side trips suggested below can be achieved as a day out from Amsterdam; however if you really want to get a feel for the ultra-modern vibe of Rotterdam or the provincial gentility of The Hague, then a stay of at least 1 night is recommended, so a couple of eating and sleeping options have been included in both cities. You might choose to spend an entire day among the flower displays at Keukenhof (only open btwn. Mar and May) but others may prefer to see iconic Holland in a day, combining Keukenhof with a visit to the exceptional Frans Hals Museum in Haarlem. Likewise a jaunt to the pottery factory at Delft or the botanical gardens at Leiden can easily be appended to a stay in either The Hague or Rotterdam.

HAARLEM

18km (11 miles) W of Amsterdam

Haarlem is the little sister of Amsterdam; it's thoroughly provincial, prosperous, and gets along just fine without the big-city hassles of Amsterdam, which is only a 15-minute train commute away. The micro-city (pop. 150,000) was founded around the 10th century, so technically it is older than Amsterdam, but has a similar 17th-century ambience. You can easily get around this quaint, quiet center of music and art—it's home to one of Holland's premier art museums—on foot.

Being so close to Amsterdam, there's no need to make an overnight stopover in Haarlem, but there is a scattering of classy restaurants to choose from around the tangle of pedestrianized streets in the old city center. Options include **Dijkers** (Warmoesstraat 5–7; ✆ **023/551-1564;** www.restaurantdijkers.nl) in the chic shopping streets south of the Grote Markt, **Grand Café Xo** (Grote Markt 8; ✆ **023/551-1350;** www.

xo-haarlem.nl) near the tourist office, or the glamorous **Brasss Haarlem de Brasserie** (Korte Veerstraat 1; © **023/542-7804;** www.brassshaarlem.com) for high-end lobster dishes.

Essentials

GETTING THERE   Trains for Haarlem depart at least every half-hour from Amsterdam Centraal Station; the ride takes 15 minutes. A round-trip ticket is 8€. For more details, visit **www.ns.nl**.

By **car** from Amsterdam, take N200/A200 west; parking is around 3€ an hour.

VISITOR INFORMATION   VVV Haarlem, Grote Markt, 2; (© **023/531-7325;** www.haarlemmarketing.nl), is housed in the Stadhuis, one of the city's oldest buildings. The office is open April through September Monday to Friday from 9:30am to 5:30pm, Saturday 10am to 5pm, and Sunday noon to 4pm; October through March Monday 1 to 5:30pm, Tuesday to Friday 9:30am to 5:30pm, and Saturday 10am to 5pm.

Exploring Haarlem

Granted municipal status by Count Willem II of Holland in 1245, this is where Frans Hals, Jacob van Ruisdael, and Pieter Saenredam were living and painting their famous portraits, landscapes, and church interiors at the same time that Rembrandt was working in Amsterdam.

The old center of Haarlem is a 10-minute walk from the graceful Art Nouveau rail station dating from 1908, most of it via pedestrian-only shopping streets. First-time visitors generally head straight for the **Grote Markt ★★★**, the beautiful central market square adjacent to **Sint-Bavokerk** (p. 118). The monumental buildings around the tree-lined square date from the 15th to the 19th centuries and are a microcosm of the development of Dutch architecture. The glorious 15th-century **Stadhuis (Town Hall)**, Grote Markt 2 (© **023/511-5115**), has an ornate bell tower, gables, and elaborate balconies. It was once a hunting lodge of the Counts of Holland and is now—rather prosaically—the home of the tourist information office.

Frans Hals Museum ★★★ MUSEUM   Quite simply the highlight of many art lovers' trips to Holland, this museum is housed in the elegant former Oudemannenhuis, a home for retired gentlemen dating from 1608 during the Dutch Golden Age. Consequently, the wonderful paintings by Frans Hals (1580–1686) and other masters of the Haarlem School hang in a setting reminiscent of the 17th-century houses they were intended to adorn. The dynamic permanent exhibition, "The Hals Phenomenon," provides an informative introduction to this great artist, who earned a living by painting portraits of members of the local guilds.

Five of his civic-guard pictures are on display in the museum, lining the walls of the former refectory, which is set up as for a Golden Age banquet, with a long wooden table piled high for a feast. This is where Hals's consummate "A Banquet of the Officers of the Civic Guard of St. George" (1616) is hung. Other showcase pieces include landscapes by Jacob van Ruisdael, Gerrit Berckheyde's famous "Grote Markt" (1696), and the disturbing "The Monk and the Beguine" (1591) by Cornelisz van Haarlem, depicts a monk tweaking a nun's bare breast. Among other highlights of the collections are a superb wooden replica of a merchant's town house from around 1750 and fine collections of antiques, silver, porcelain, and clocks.

Groot Heiligland 62. © **023/511-5775.** www.franshalsmuseum.nl. Admission 13€ adults, 6€ students 19–24, free for children 18 and under. Tues–Sat 11am–5pm, Sun noon–5pm. Closed Jan 1, Apr 27, and Dec 25.

Western Netherlands

Haarlem

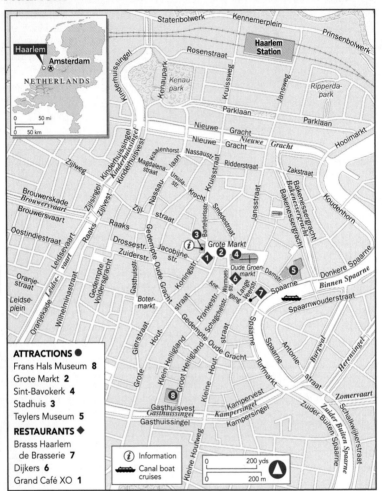

ATTRACTIONS ●
Frans Hals Museum **8**
Grote Markt **2**
Sint-Bavokerk **4**
Stadhuis **3**
Teylers Museum **5**

RESTAURANTS ◆
Brasss Haarlem
  de Brasserie **7**
Dijkers **6**
Grand Café XO **1**

ⓘ Information

🚢 Canal boat
    cruises

Sint-Bavokerk (St. Bavo's Church) ★★ CHURCH   The tall spire of St. Bavo's Church, also known as the Grote Kerk (Great Church), looms over the central pedestrianized streets like a beacon; once in the Grote Markt, it's revealed in all its massive splendor. The colossal late-Gothic church was begun in 1445 under the direction of Antwerp's city architect, Evert Spoorwater. It was complete by 1520 and has a pleasing unity of structure and proportion. The interior is light and airy, with whitewashed walls and sandstone pillars. Its elegant wooden tower is covered with lead sheets and adorned with gilt spheres.

The Grote Kerk was so popular as a subject with 16th- and 17th-century Dutch painters that it immediately feels familiar; Gerrit Berckheyde and Pieter Saenredam repeatedly featured it in their work. And indeed Haarlem's greatest artist, Frans Hals, was buried under a simple stone slab near the choir stalls in 1666. The famous Christian Müller organ, built in 1738, is considered one of the best in Europe; when the precocious prodigy Mozart played this magnificent instrument in 1766 at just 10 years old, he is said to have shouted for joy. Handel, Mendelssohn, Schubert, and Liszt also visited Haarlem to play the organ. Free organ concerts are held at 8:15pm every Tuesday between mid-May and mid-October, and there's a program of services, festivals, and concerts running throughout the summer; check the website for details.

Grote Markt 22. ℂ **023/553-2040.** www.bavo.nl. Admission 2.50€ adults, 1.25€ children 12–16, free for children 11 and under. June–Sept Mon–Sat 10am–5pm, Sun 10am–7pm; Oct–May Mon–Sat 10am–4pm.

Teylers Museum ★ MUSEUM   Strange but oddly compelling for its very eccentricity, this museum was the very first to open in The Netherlands, in 1784. It's named after the 18th-century merchant Pieter Teyler van der Hulst, who willed his entire fortune to the advancement of art and science. You'll find a diverse collection in the galleried display rooms: drawings by Michelangelo, Raphael, and Rembrandt (which are shown in rotation); fossils, minerals, and skeletons; instruments of physics; and an odd assortment of wacky inventions plus some ancient globes showing Holland at the apex of the world.

Spaarne 16. ℂ **023/531-9010.** www.teylersmuseum.eu. Admission 11€ adults, 2€ children 6–17. Tues–Sat 10am–5pm, Sun noon–5pm. Closed Jan 1 and Dec 25.

VOLENDAM & MARKEN ★

Marken: 16km (10 miles) NE of Amsterdam; Volendam: 18km (12 miles) NE of Amsterdam

Volendam and Marken are in the area north of Amsterdam labeled the "Waterland" and have long been combined on bus-tour itineraries from Amsterdam as a kind of pre-packaged "clogs, cheese, and windmills" day trip. Many people even attach that damning label "tourist trap" to these two lakeside communities. Yes, they're touristy in the summer months, but you're a tourist, for heaven's sake. It's still possible to have a delightful day in the bracing air there, and you might even see a few residents in traditional dress.

Essentials

GETTING THERE   R-Net (www.rnet.nl) and **EBS** (www.ebs-ov.nl) buses depart every 15 to 30 minutes from the upper bus terminal behind Amsterdam Centraal Station. Nos. 110, 118, and 316 go to Volendam and no. 111 goes on to Marken. The ride to Volendam takes 35 minutes and to Marken 45 minutes. The round-trip bus fare is 10€ for the all-day "Waterland Ticket."

By **car,** go north on N247. When driving to Marken, which was once an island, you cross a 3km (2-mile) causeway from the quiet backwater Monnickendam. Leave your car in a parking lot outside the main village before walking through the narrow streets to the harbor. April to October, **passenger-and-bike ferry** *Marken Express* (ℂ 0299/363-331; www.markenexpress.nl) sails every 45 minutes daily 10:30am to 6:45pm between Volendam and Marken. The ride takes 30 minutes, and fares are 10€ round-trip and 7.50€ one-way for adults, 7€ round-trip and 5€ one-way for children 4 to 11, and free 3 and under; bicycles are carried for an additional 1.50€ one-way.

VISITOR INFORMATION   VVV Volendam, Zeestraat 37 (ℂ **0299/363-747;** www.vvv-volendam.nl), is just off Julianaweg in the heart of town. The office is open

The cheese markets that were once a weekly occasion in many Holland towns are now largely defunct with the exception of the colorful summer-time happenings in Edam and Alkmaar.

Just 18km (11 miles) northeast of Amsterdam and a fraction north of Volendam, self-effacing **Edam** (pronounced Ay-dam) was a whaling port during the 17th-century Golden Age and today is a pretty town centered around its canals. It's quiet enough most of the year but Edam's major claim to fame is its world-renowned Edammer cheese. Things really heat up with the tourists when the historic *kaasmarkt* (cheese market; www.kaasmarktedam. nl) is on. You'll be lucky to catch it as the market only takes place on Wednesday in July and August, from 10:30am to 12:30pm on Kaasmarkt. Nowadays it is little more than a shameless tourist attraction but nevertheless it's a colorful event, taking place with much ringing of church bells, stirring music from local bands, hand clapping, and overly dramatic "bargaining" by the straw-boater-and-clog-clad cheese carriers. Most of the action takes place outside the gaily frescoed **Kaaswaag (cheese weigh house),** which dates from 1592 and features cheese-making displays over summer. By the way, don't expect to see the luscious rounds of cheese in its familiar red skin—that's purely for export. In The Netherlands, the Edammer's skin is always canary yellow.

Edam can be reached on **R-Net** (www.rnet.nl) and **EBS** (www.ebs-ov.nl) buses departing every 15 to 30 minutes from the upper bus terminal behind Amsterdam Centraal Station. Nos. 110, 118, 314, 316, and 317 go to Edam. By **car,** go north on N247 via Volendam (p. 121). **Tourist information** is at **VVV**

Edam in the Stadhuis (Town Hall), Damplein 1 (© **0299/315-125;** www. vvv-edam.nl), in the center of town. Should you wish to tour a local Edammer cheese factory, this is where you get the details.

Alkmaar is 30km (19 miles) north of Amsterdam and its famous cheese market takes place every Friday morning between April and September, when a torrent of tourists pour in to this handsome, canal-lined town founded in the 10th century. At 10am precisely the white-uniformed cheese carriers enact an ancient scene in the Waagplein. There's much rushing around with brightly painted wooden cheese hoppers, which are weighed under supervision and rushed to the market square to be laid out in rows in front of the ancient **Waaggebouw (weigh house).** Haggling over price and quality is conducted with much hand clapping and good-natured shouting. Get there by 9:30am for the kickoff at 10am, otherwise you won't see a thing thanks to the crowds. There's also a small cheese museum, the **Hollands Kaasmuseum,** in the Waaggebouw, Waagplein 2 (© 072/ 511-4284; www.kaasmuseum.nl). April to October it's open Monday to Saturday from 10am to 4pm (Fri 9am–4pm; closed Apr 27), November to March Saturday 10am–6pm. Admission is 3€ for adults, 2€ for children 4 to 12, and free for 3 and under.

Get to Alkmaar on trains departing every 15 minutes or so from Amsterdam Centraal Station; the ride takes around 40 minutes. A round-trip ticket is 15€. By **car** from Amsterdam, take A8, N246, N203, and A9 north. Tourist information is at the **VVV Alkmaar** at Waagplein 2 (© **072/511-4284;** www.vvvalkmaar.nl).

mid-March to September Monday to Saturday 10am to 5pm, and Sunday 11am to 4pm; October Monday to Saturday 10am to 5pm; and November to mid-March Monday to Saturday 10am to 3pm.

WHAT TO SEE & DO

A small, Catholic town on the mainland, **Volendam** lost most of its fishing industry to the enclosure of the Zuiderzee. It now makes its living from tourism, and has plenty of souvenir and gift stores, boutiques, cafes, and restaurants. Lots of people come to pig out on the town's near-legendary *gerookte paling* (smoked eel) and to visit such attractions as the fish auction, diamond cutter, and clog maker. Still, Volendam's boat-filled harbor, tiny streets, and traditional houses have an undeniable charm. If you must have a snapshot of yourself in the traditional Dutch costume—local women wear white caps with wings—this is the place to do it.

Volendam's rival in today's tourism tables is **Marken,** historically Protestant and an insular island until a narrow causeway connected it to the mainland in 1957. Smaller and less in-your-face than Volendam, it is rural, with clusters of farmhouses dotted around the polders. Half of Marken village is called Havenbuurt and consists of green-and-white houses on stilts grouped around a tiny harbor. A **clog maker** works in summer in the village car park. Four old smokehouses in the other half of the village, Kerkbuurt, serve as the **Museum Marken,** Kerkbuurt 44–47 (© **0299/601-904;** www.markermuseum.nl), which displays traditional furnishings and costumes. The museum is open April to September daily 10am to 5pm, and October daily 11am to 4pm. Admission is 2.50€ for adults, 1.25€ for children 5 to 12, and free 4 and under.

Marken does not go overboard for its tourists. It merely feeds and waters them and allows them to wander its pretty streets gawking at the locals as they go about their daily routines of hanging out laundry, washing windows, and shopping for groceries. Some residents occasionally wear traditional dress—for women, caps with ribbons and black aprons over striped petticoats—as much to preserve the custom as for you.

ZAANSE SCHANS

16km (10 miles) NW of Amsterdam

Incorporated into the town of Zaandam on the east bank of the River Zaan, Zaanse Schans is an historic area dedicated to replicating 17th- and 18th-century village life in northern Holland. This living, working slice of history is made up of houses, windmills, and workshops that were moved to the 8-hectare (20-acre) site when industrialization leveled their original locations; pictures of the windmills and green-painted houses grace many a Netherlands tourist website.

The Zaanstreek (Zaan District) was historically a shipbuilding area and its backstory is told in the contemporary, glass-and-brick **Zaans Museum & Verkade Pavilion ★**, Schansend 7 (© **075/681-0000;** www.zaansmuseum.nl), at the entrance to the site. The museum is open daily 9am to 5pm (closed Jan 1 and Dec 25). Admission is 9€ adult, 5€ children aged 4 to 7. Pick up a brochure here to identify all the buildings outside and enjoy a self-guided tour of the area.

At one time, the Zaanstreek had more than 600 windmills; of those only 15 have survived. You'll discover ten here, including a sawmill, and mills specializing in producing paint, vegetable oil, and Zaanse mustard, all prettily located on the Zaan riverside.

Tucked among the gabled wooden houses are several excellent museums exhibiting traditional crafts, including the **Bakkerijmuseum (Bakery Museum),** Zeilenmakerspad 4, where cookies and candy are made to old recipes, and the **Nederlandse Uurwerk (Dutch Clock) Museum,** Kalverringdijk 3, which displays timepieces from the period 1500 to 1900, and also has a functioning workshop. Lovingly showcasing every Dutch cliché are the **Klompenmakerij (Clog Maker's Workshop),** a workshop where wooden *klompen* (clogs) are made and sold; and **De Catherina Hoeve Kaasmakerij,** which does likewise with cheese. And for an idea of how a well-heeled Zaan resident lived, visit **Museum Het Noorderhuis,** Kalverringdijk 17, a merchant's house from 1670 containing furnishings, utensils, and traditional costumes.

Most of these mini museums are open April to October daily 11am to 5pm, and November to March Saturday and Sunday 11am to 5pm. Admission varies from free to 10€.

In summer, 45-minute **river cruises** on the Zaan River aboard **Rederij de Schans** tour boat (① **065/3294-467;** www.rederijdeschans.nl) depart from a dock next to the De Huisman mustard mill, April to September hourly Tuesday through Sunday from noon to 3pm (July and Aug btwn. 11am and 4pm). Trips are 6€ for adults, 3€ for children 3 to 12.

Trains depart around every 15 minutes from Amsterdam Centraal Station via Zaandam to Koog-Zaandijk station near Zaanse Schans, from where it's a 1km (⅔-mile) walk, across the Zaan River, to Zaanse Schans. The train ride takes 20 minutes, and a round-trip ticket is 6€. Or take **Connexxion bus** no. 391 (www.bus391.nl) from bus platform C at Amsterdam Centraal Station for the 40-minute ride. Fares are 10€ return. By **car** from Amsterdam, take A8 north and then switch to A7/E22 north to exit 2, from where you follow the signs to Zaanse Schans. Parking is 8€ per day.

Zuiderzee Museum at Enkhuizen ★★ MUSEUM   The economy of several coastal towns was devastated when the Afsluitdijk was constructed in 1932, transforming the Zuiderzee into the freshwater IJsselmeer. To commemorate a lifestyle long gone, the Zuiderzee Museum showcases the 19th-century fishing-based industry on which the ports around the former seacoast depended. Split into two sections, the museum features the **Binnenmuseum** ★★, housed in a 17th-century Dutch Renaissance building that once served as warehouses of the Dutch East India Company. Here you'll find a display of the fishing boats that provided an income for the Zuiderzee folk. The open-air **Buitenmuseum** ★★★ stands on the IJsselmeer shore; more than 130 historic buildings—farmhouses, public buildings, stores, a church—were shipped here intact from defunct lakeside communities across northern Holland and furnished in period style. Among others, two bottle-shaped limekilns, a working windmill, and a functioning smokehouse also pay tribute to the area's industrial heritage, alongside a chandler, an apothecary, a cheese warehouse, and a steam laundry. Just south of the Buitenmuseum is a recreation of Marken's old harbor, with smokehouses for preserving herring and eels standing on the dike, and fishing boats tied up at the dock. Cafes and restaurants are found on site.

Wierdijk 12–22. ① **0228/351-111.** www.zuiderzeemuseum.nl. Admission 15€ adults, 14€ seniors, 9€ children 4–12, free for children 3 and under, 40€ family. Binnenmuseum: Daily 10am–5pm. Buitenmuseum: Apr–Oct daily 10am–5pm. Trains from Amsterdam Centraal Station to Enkhuizen run every 30 min., taking an hour, for 21€ round trip. Apr–Oct a free ferry departs every 15 min. from dock next to Enkhuizen station to Buitenmuseum, otherwise it's a 10-min. walk from station. Car parking is 5€/day.

KEUKENHOF & THE BULB FIELDS

35km (22 miles) W of Amsterdam

The heaviest concentration of the tulip bulb fields that contribute millions of euros to the Dutch economy lie in the **Bloemenbollenstreek (Bulb District)** ★, a strip of land 16km (10 miles) long and 6km (4 miles) wide between Haarlem and Leiden. In the spring, it's a frenzied Dutch rite of passage to traipse through this colorful district and view the massed, varicolored regiments of tulips on parade. Every year from around the end of January to late May, the fields are covered at various times with tulips, crocuses, daffodils, narcissi, hyacinths, and lilies.

Viewing the flowers is easy. Just follow all or parts of the circular, signposted **Bollenstreek Route** (60km/37 miles) by car or bike—although you could find your way there by the trail of roadside stalls flogging bunches of cut flowers, garlands, and bulbs. To get to the bulb fields from Amsterdam, drive to Haarlem, then go south on N206 through De Zilk and Noordwijkerhout, or on N208 through Hillegom, Lisse, and Sassenheim. There are also scores of **bus tours** leaving for Keukenhof from all the main cities, including Amsterdam, Rotterdam, and The Hague; Viator (© **888/651-9785** in the U.S.; www.viator.com) provides several different Keukenhof tours, even offering a package including a flight over the bulb fields. Special seasonal buses transport eager-beaver visitors on the direct service no. 858 from Schiphol Airport, and tourists staying over in Leiden can catch bus service no. 854 from Leiden Central train station.

Keukenhof ★★★ GARDEN   Open for barely 2 months between March and May when the flowers are at their peak, Keukenhof is the most-visited attraction in The Netherlands. Every year more than 800,000 flower fans from all across the world flock to see eight million bulbs explode into life in intricate patterns in gardens that are a scented, visual paradise (such is the rush to get here that buses run directly from the airport). The meandering, 32-hectare (79-acre) estate in the heart of the bulb-producing region is all-too-briefly a riot of tulips and narcissi, daffodils and hyacinths, bluebells, crocuses, lilies, and amaryllis. Swathes of color are seen in greenhouses, beside brooks and shady ponds, along paths, in neat little plots, and helter-skelter on lawns. There's also a boat tour of the neighboring bulb fields; lines are inevitably long. Keukenhof claims to be the greatest flower show on earth, and certainly it is Holland's annual spring gift to the world. The spectacular annual **flower parade** (p. 36) takes place in early May. There are four decent cafes on-site where you can grab a quick bite and contemplate your bulb purchases.

Stationsweg 166A, Lisse. © **0252/465-555.** www.keukenhof.nl. Admission 15€ adults, 7.50€ children 4–11, free children 3 and under. Parking 6€. 3rd week of Mar to 3rd week of May daily 8am–7:30pm. Bus: no. 858 from Schiphol airport, no. 854 from Leiden Central.

Flower Power

During Holland's 17th-century "tulip mania" when trading in bulbs was a lucrative business and prices soared to ridiculous heights, a single tulip bulb could be worth as much as a prestigious Amsterdam canal house, with the garden and coach house thrown in.

LEIDEN

36km (22 miles) SW of Amsterdam; 20km (12 miles) NE of The Hague

Stately yet bustling, the old heart of Leiden is classic Dutch, filled with handsome, gabled brick houses along canals spanned by graceful bridges. The Pilgrim Fathers lived here for 11 years before sailing to North America from Delfshaven in Rotterdam. Leiden's proudest moment came in 1574, when it became the only Dutch town to withstand a Spanish siege, although William of Orange *was* forced to flood the land around the city to win that battle. The town is also the birthplace of Rembrandt, the Dutch tulip trade, and the oldest university in the Netherlands (founded in 1575). The 12th-century citadel of De Burcht stands on a mound in the town center between two branches of the Rhine, the Oude and Nieuwe, providing a great view of the surrounding rooftops. And with a choice of 14 museums, covering antiquities, natural history, anatomy, clay pipes, windmills, and coins, Leiden seems perfectly justified in calling itself Holland's *Museumstad* (Museum City).

Rembrandt in Leiden

In 1606, the great artist Rembrandt van Rijn was born in Leiden. He later moved to Amsterdam, where he won fame and fortune—and later suffered bankruptcy and obscurity. In his hometown, a **Rembrandt Walk** takes in the site of the house (since demolished) where he was born, the Latin School he attended as a boy, and the first studio where he worked. A booklet outlining the walk route is available from Leiden Visitor Centre for 3€.

Essentials

GETTING THERE Up to eight **trains** per hour run from Amsterdam Centraal Station to Leiden Centraal Station. The ride takes around 35 minutes, and the round-trip fare is 17€. The center of Leiden is a walk of around 1.5km (1 mile) south from the station. For more details, visit **www.ns.nl**. By **car**, take A4/E19.

VISITOR INFORMATION **Leiden Visitor Centre,** Stationsweg 41 (© **071/516-6000;** www.vvvleiden.nl), is just outside the train station. The office is open Monday to Friday 7am to 7pm, Saturday 10am to 4pm, and Sunday 11am to 3pm.

Exploring Leiden

Hortus Botanicus der Rijksuniversiteit (University Botanical Garden) ★★

GARDEN Leiden's botanical gardens were established by the University of Leiden in 1590 to cultivate tropical trees and plants such as banana plants, ferns, and flesh-eating plants brought back from overseas trading forays. Carolus Clusius, who was the first professor of botany at Leiden University, was also the man responsible for first introducing tulip bulbs into The Netherlands, and in so doing he may have brought about the abrupt end of the Golden Age. Such was their popularity that they quickly became a status symbol among the Dutch aristocracy and the crazy trading in tulip bulbs led to the downfall of the economy in 1637. Today may of the original specimens are still thriving in the Clusiustuin, a garden dedicated to the botanist.

Rapenburg 73 (at Nonnensteeg). © **071/527-7249.** www.hortus.leidenuniv.nl. Admission 7€ adults, 3€ children 4–12. Apr–Oct daily 10am–6pm, Nov–Mar Tues–Sun 10am–4pm. Closed Jan 1, Oct 3, and last week of Dec.

Museum De Lakenhal Leiden ★★ MUSEUM   Located in Leiden's fine cloth hall, dating from 1640, the city's civic museum focuses on a fine collection of paintings by Dutch artists of the 16th and 17th centuries including Rembrandt and Jan Steen. The masterpiece of the exhibits is the masterly "Last Judgment" triptych by Lucas van Leyden, which was rescued from Leiden's main church, the Pieterskerk, during the Alteration of 1578. In among the guild silverware and decorative arts found in the museum's modern wing, purpose-built in the 1920s, is a bronze cooking pot believed to have belonged to William of Orange himself.

Oude Singel 28–32. ✆**071/516-5360.** www.lakenhal.nl. Admission 7.50€ adults, 4.50€ seniors and students, free for children 18 and under. Tues–Fri 10am–5pm, Sat–Sun noon–5pm. Closed Jan 1, Apr 27, and Dec 25.

Rijksmuseum van Oudheden (National Museum of Antiquities) ★★★ MUSEUM   Quite simply one of the best museums in The Netherlands, so if you're short of time in Leiden, make this your priority for the collection of Egyptian, Near Eastern, Greek, and Roman treasures. Opened in 1818, the showpiece of the museum is the Egyptian Temple of Taffeh, dedicated to Isis, the Egyptian Goddess of Fertility; it was assembled here in 1978. Other highlights include treasures from Dutch Bronze Age graves, statuary from Roman villas, and ancient Greek amphorae. With so much to see, it's sensible to follow one of the suggested themed routes through the collections.

Rapenburg 28. ✆**071/516-3163.** www.rmo.nl. Admission 9.50€ adults, 7.50€ seniors, 3€ children 5–17, free for children 4 and under, 22€ family. Tues–Sun 10am–5pm (during school holidays also Mon 10am–5pm). Closed Jan 1, Oct 3, and Dec 25.

Rijksmuseum Volkenkunde (National Ethnological Museum) ★ MUSEUM   Housed in a grand town house dating from 1837, this enchanting ethnographical museum is founded on a superb collection of thousands of *objets d'art* squirreled together between 1823 and 1830 by German-born Philipp Franz von Siebold, who was the physician at the Dutch trading post on Deshima Island in Nagasaki Bay in Japan. From this beginning, the displays have grown to include intriguing artifacts from across the world, such as Inuit snowshoes, Balinese *gamelans,* and a roomful of Chinese Buddhas. An ever-changing series of temporary exhibits might include anything from rare black-and-white images to interactive displays about world music.

Steenstraat 1. ✆**071/516-8800.** www.volkenkunde.nl. Admission 11€ adults, 8€ ages 13–18, 5€ children 4–12. Tues–Sun 10am–5pm. Closed Jan 1, Apr 27, May 5, Oct 3, and Dec 25.

GOUDA

40km (25 miles) S of Amsterdam; 25km (16 miles) NE of Rotterdam

Essentials

GETTING THERE   There's frequent train service from Amsterdam to Gouda, with up to six trains an hour (some are direct, while others require a change in Utrecht) and six an hour from Rotterdam. The direct ride from Amsterdam takes 45 minutes, and a round-trip ticket is 22€. From Rotterdam it's around 20 minutes, and fares are 10€ round trip. For more details, visit **www.ns.nl**.

By **car,** the town is just off the A13/E19 expressway from The Hague to Rotterdam.

Exploring Gouda

Today Gouda (pronounced *Khow*-dah) is famous for its cheese, its summer cheese markets, and its candle festival in mid-December, which sees the Markt and **Stadhuis (Town Hall)** illuminated by flickering candlelight. This handsome town stands on two rivers, which helped it become a wealthy brewing center in the 15th century; the legacy of that is a series of fine public buildings bristling with gables and pinnacles in decorative Gothic style.

Visit on Thursday morning from 10am to 12:30pm between the third week in June and the first week in September to catch the lively and traditional **Goudse Kaasmarkt (Gouda Cheese Market)** ★. This brings farmers into town driving wagons painted with bright designs and piled high with round cheeses in orange skins; sample them at stalls near the Stadhuis, which is festooned with step gables and red shutters. It is reputed to be Holland's oldest town hall, and parts of its Gothic facade date from 1449.

The foremost reason to visit Gouda is the assembly of outstanding **stained glass windows in Sint-Janskerk** ★★. The church is a step away from Markt and easily identified by its ornate spire peeking above the rooftops. As well as being the longest church in The Netherlands at 23m (76 ft.), this 15th-century Gothic beauty hides some of Europe's loveliest stained-glass windows, considered so beautiful that they were even spared destruction in the Protestant Alteration of 1578. They were donated to the church by a series of rich patrons and number 64 in total, with a total of 2,412 panels depicting biblical scenes and contemporary scenes. To see the contrast between the stained glass of times past and contemporary work, take a peek at the most recent window, no. 28A, commemorating the World War II years in Holland. Sint-Janskerk is located at Achter de Kerk 16 (© **0182/514-119;** www.sintjan.com). Admission is 3.50€ adults, 2.50€ students and seniors, and 2€ kids 5 to 12. It is open March to October Monday to Saturday 9am to 5pm, and November to February Monday to Saturday 10am to 4pm.

Adjacent to Sint-Janskerk, the **Museum Gouda** ★ is housed in the Catharina Gasthuis, a former almshouse built in 1665. It showcases a charming mix of Hague School landscape painting, silver guild relics, altarpieces that survived the Alteration, and original sketches for the stained-glass windows in Sint-Janskerk. You'll find it at Achter de Kerk 14 (© **0182/331-000;** www.museumgouda.nl). Admission is 7€, free for ages 18 and under. The museum is open Wednesday through Friday 11am to 5pm.

DELFT

55km (34 miles) SW of Amsterdam; 10km (6 miles) SE of The Hague; 14km (9 miles) NW of Rotterdam

Minute Delft is perhaps the prettiest town in all of Holland. The facades of the Renaissance and Gothic houses here reflect age-old beauty, a sense of tranquility pervades the air, and linden trees bend over its gracious canals. Indeed, it's easy to understand why Old Master painter Jan Vermeer chose to spend most of his life surrounded by Delft's gentle beauty in the 17th century.

A hefty part of Dutch history is preserved in Delft. William of Orange, who led the Dutch insurrection against Spanish rule, was assassinated in the Prinsenhof and now

Porcelain from the factories at Delft is beautiful to look at but it certainly doesn't come cheap. It is produced predominantly, but not exclusively, by three Delft-based firms: **De Koninklijke Porceleyne Fles** (see below); **De Delftse Pauw,** Delftweg 133, Rijswijk (℃ **015/212-4920;** www.delftpottery.com); and **De Candelaer,** Kerkstraat 13 (℃ **015/213-1848;** www.candelaer.nl).

Genuine Delftware is for sale in specialized stores through The Netherlands (p. 105) but it is fascinating to visit a workshop and see it being made. Production methods have changed little down the centuries and most of the decorating is still done by hand, which of course accounts for the breathtaking price tags. Some copies of Delftware

nearly equal its quality, while most miss the delicacy of the brush strokes, the richness of color, or the sheen of the glazes that make this porcelain so highly prized.

To be sure that you're looking at a *real* Delft vase from De Koninklijke Porceleyne Fles, check on the bottom for the distinctive 3-part hallmark: an outline of a small pot, above an initial "J" crossed with a short stroke, above the scripted word DELFT. For De Delftse Pauw, look for three blue stars separated by a drafting compass, above the scripted text D.P. DELFT. And for De Candelaer, there will be the company's candle-and-candlestick symbol, the scripted text D.C. DELFT, and the initials of the artist.

rests in a magnificent tomb in the Nieuwe Kerk; every member of the Royal House of Oranje-Nassau has since been brought here for burial.

Of course, to many visitors, Delft means only one thing—the prized blue-and-white earthenware still produced by the meticulous methods of yore. Every piece of genuine Delftware is hand-painted by skilled craftspeople; a trip to Delft really should encompass a visit to a porcelain factory.

Essentials

GETTING THERE   There are six trains an hour to Delft from Amsterdam (one is direct; transfer in Rotterdam for the others) and eight an hour from Rotterdam. The ride from Amsterdam takes around 1 hour; a round-trip ticket is 25€. From Rotterdam, it's 15 minutes and 6€. From The Hague, the train journey is a 15-minute ride that costs 5€ round trip. For more details, visit **www.ns.nl**.

By **car,** the town is just off the A13/E19 expressway from The Hague to Rotterdam.

VISITOR INFORMATION   Delft's **Touristen Informatie Punt (TIP)** is at Kerkstraat 3 (℃ **015/215-4051;** www.delft.nl) in the center of town near the Nieuwe Kerk. April to September, opening hours are Monday and Saturday 10am to 5pm, Tuesday to Friday 9am to 6pm, Sunday 10am to 4pm; October to March, Tuesday to Saturday 10am to 4pm, Sunday 11am to 3pm.

Exploring Delft

The best way to absorb Delft's special ambience is by strolling its streets. Around every corner and down every street, you step into scenes that might have been composed for the canvas of a great artist. Supplement your walks with a leisurely tour of the canals via the numerous water taxis that operate during the summer. The town's large main square, the Markt, is a zoo on market day (Thurs), but on quieter days, you get space to see how picturesque it is.

De Koninklijke Porceleyne Fles (Royal Delft) ★★★ WORKSHOP

If you love Delftware porcelain, you'll be in heaven at the Royal Delft workshop. A visit to the factory entails a firsthand view of the business of painting porcelain; a visit to the Delft museum, which features antique, multi-spouted tulip vases; and the obligatory showroom where factory seconds can be bought at relative bargain prices. And if you thought that Delftware only came in its trademark blue-and-white color scheme, you'll be surprised to see exquisite multicolored patterns. The highlights of any visit are the workshops where you can paint your own porcelain, which is fired, glazed, and ready for pickup (or shipping overseas) in 48 hours. The price quoted for the workshops includes materials but not shipping costs; courses must be reserved at least 24 hours in advance. Your purchases and your creations can both be shipped home directly from the factory.

Rotterdamseweg 196. ℂ **015/251-2030.** www.royaldelft.com. Tour 12€ adults, free for children 11 and under. Workshops 40€. Mid-Mar to Oct daily 9am–5pm; Nov to mid-Mar Mon–Sat 9am–5pm, Sun 12–5pm. Closed Jan 1 and Dec 25–26.

Museum Het Prinsenhof ★★ MUSEUM

The Prinsenhof (Prince's Court), on the banks of Delft's oldest canal, Oude Delft, dates from the late 1400s and was originally a convent backed by tranquil gardens that make a pleasant spot to wander. William of Orange, the "Father of the Dutch Nation," maintained his battle HQ here during all the years he fought the Spanish to found the Dutch Republic, and also where an assassin's bullets ended his life in 1584. The musket-ball holes are still visible on the stone stairwell. Three permanent exhibitions look at the life of William of Orange and highlight his influence on modern-day Holland; chart the Dutch entrepreneurial spirit from Golden Age to present day; and examine the creative genius of the nation with impressive tapestries, silverware, pottery, Golden Age glassware, and paintings—including five versions of the "View of Delft" painted by contemporaries of Jan Vermeer.

Sint-Agathaplein 1. ℂ **015/260-2358.** www.prinsenhof-delft.nl. Admission 10€ adults, 5€ students and children 12–16, free for children 11 and under. Tues–Sun 11am–5pm (May 24–Oct 26 also Mon 11am–5pm). Closed Jan 1, Easter Mon, Apr 27, and Dec 25.

Nieuwe Kerk (New Church) ★ CHURCH

The fine spire that graces the Delft skyline belongs to the New Church, which isn't new at all—it was begun in 1383 and completed in 1510. Inside is the magnificent tomb of William of Orange; it was designed by Hendrick de Keyser and is decorated with a sculpture of William in full battle gear as well as figures representing Liberty, Justice, Valor, and Religion. The royal dead of the House of Orange-Nassau lie in a crypt beneath the remains of the founder of their line. The 109m-high (360-ft.) church tower is the second tallest in the country after Amsterdam's Westerkerk (p. 90); climb it for marvelous views over the town's red rooftops.

Markt 80. ℂ **015/212-3025.** www.nieuwekerk-delft.nl. Church: Mon–Sat 9am–6pm. Tower: Jan Mon–Fri 11am–4pm, Sat 10am–5pm; Feb–Mar Mon–Sat 10am–5pm; Apr–Oct Mon–Sat 9am–6pm; Nov–Dec Mon–Fri 11am–6pm, Sat 10am–5pm. Admission church: 3.50€ adults, 2€ students 12–19, 1.50€ children 6–11, free 5 and under; tower: 3.50€ adults, 2€ students 12–19, 1.50€ children 6–11, free 5 and under.

THE HAGUE

50km (31 miles) SW of Amsterdam; 22km (14 miles) NW of Rotterdam

Stately and dignified, The Hague is an easy day trip from Amsterdam, but some travelers prefer it as a more relaxed sightseeing base. 's-Gravenhage, to give the city its full name, or more commonly Den Haag, is a cosmopolitan town bursting with style and culture, full of parks and elegant homes. Its 18th-century French vibe suits its role as a world-class diplomatic center and the site of the International Court of Justice, housed in the famous Peace Palace.

Essentials

GETTING THERE

BY PLANE   Amsterdam's **Schiphol Airport** (p. 51), 40km (25 miles) away, also serves The Hague. Trains run directly from the airport to The Hague, with up to six trains an hour during the day and one an hour at night; the ride takes around 35 minutes, and round-trip fare is 16€. A taxi from Schiphol to The Hague city center takes 40 minutes in reasonable traffic and costs around 100€.

BY TRAIN   The Hague has excellent rail connections from Amsterdam, with fast InterCity trains that take around 50 minutes. The city has two main stations, **Den Haag Centraal Station** and **Den Haag HS;** most city sights are closer to Centraal Station, but some trains stop only at HS. The round-trip fare from Amsterdam is 22€. For more details, visit **www.ns.nl**.

BY CAR   From Amsterdam and the north, take A4/E19. You'll want to avoid all three *snelwegen* (expressways) during the morning and evening commuter hours, when traffic grinds to a halt. At other times, you should be able to drive to The Hague from Amsterdam in under an hour.

VISITOR INFORMATION

Tourist information is at **VVV Den Haag,** Spui 68 (© **070/361-8860;** www.denhaag.nl), close to the Binnenhof (Parliament). The office is open Monday noon to 8pm, Tuesday to Friday 10am to 8pm, Saturday 10am to 5pm, and Sunday noon to 5pm. There are additional tourist information points at Lange Voorhout 58B (Tues–Sun 9am–5pm) and Wagenstraat 193 (Mon–Fri 9:30am–5pm, Sat 10am–5pm, and Sun 10am–2:30pm).

GETTING AROUND

Public transportation in The Hague is operated by **HTM** (www.htm.net). Centraal Station is the primary interchange point for bus and tram routes, and HS station is the secondary node. Going by **tram** is the quickest way to get around town, but some points are served only by **bus.** Tram no. 1 is useful for sightseers as it travels from the North Sea coast at Scheveningen through The Hague and all the way to Delft. For details on using the **OV-chipkaart** stored-value card for getting around by public transportation in The Hague as well as the rest of The Netherlands, see p. 57.

Regulated taxis wait at stands outside both main rail stations and at other strategic points around town; you can also hail them in the streets. A new eco-friendly service is provided by **gCab** (www.g-cab.nl), who operate a fleet of electric buggies and charge a flat fee of 5€ throughout the city.

Exploring The Hague

One of the pleasures of spending a day or more in The Hague is walking through its genteel streets, matching your pace to the unhurried leisure that pervades the city. Stroll past the mansions that line Lange Voorhout, overlooking a broad avenue of poplar and elm trees, and you'll be struck by how these spacious, restrained mansions differ from Amsterdam's gabled, ornamented canal houses. Take time out in more than 30 sq. km (12 sq. miles) of parks, gardens, and other green spaces within the city limits or head out to The Hague's sophisticated seacoast resort, Scheveningen, on Tram no 1.

Binnenhof & Ridderzaal (Inner Court & Hall of the Knights) ★★ HISTORIC BUILDING

The imposing Binnenhof is one of the oldest buildings in The Netherlands and was originally the 13th-century hunting lodge of the counts of Holland. When Count Willem II was crowned king of the Romans and emperor-elect of the Holy Roman Empire in 1248, he appointed the Binnenhof as his official royal residence. Today it forms the hub of Dutch political life in a series of offices and ceremonial halls around a vast cobbled courtyard, including the First and Second Chamber of the Staaten-Generaal (States General), the two houses of the nation's Parliament.

At the courtyard's heart is the beautiful, twin-towered Ridderzaal (Hall of the Knights), which was the last building to be added to the Binnenhof in 1280 by King Floris V, who was the son of Willem II. Measuring 38×18m (125×60 ft.) and soaring 26m (85 ft.) to its oak roof, its immense interior is adorned with provincial flags and leaded-glass windows depicting the coats of arms of Dutch cities. Since 1904, the hall has hosted the King's annual address to Parliament on Prinsjesdag (Prince's Day; see p. 37) and a multitude of official receptions. Adjacent to the Ridderzaal are the former quarters of the Stadhouder (Head of State).

Book in advance online to join a 45-minute guided tour of the hall and (depending on parliamentary business) one of the chambers of Parliament. Frankly the Ridderzaal is much more interesting so don't worry if you don't get to peek behind the political scenes.

Binnenhof 8A. ℂ070/757-0200. www.english.prodemos.nl. Courtyard free admission; 8€ guided tours (book in advance online). Mon–Sat 10am–4pm. Closed holidays and special events at short notice.

Escher in Het Paleis (Escher at the Palace) ★ MUSEUM

Located on The Hague's swish boulevard of Lange Voorhout and kitted out with a series of lavishly appointed rooms, this palace is also adorned with an Art Nouveau staircase that was installed in 1901 and glimmering stained-glass windows in the skylights of the main hall as well as crystal chandeliers in the shape of boats and animals by Hans van Bentem.

Behind its elegant neoclassical 17th-century facade, the palace was formerly the winter residence of Queen Emma of the Netherlands and later the home of Dutch graphic artist **M.C. Escher.** He lived from 1898 to 1972 and traveled throughout Europe, living in Italy and Switzerland and drawing on influences as far apart as the Alhambra in Granada and the bucolic landscape of Tuscany. Escher became famous for his slightly demented lithographs, woodcuts, and engravings as well as drawings and prints. His eccentric works with twisted perspectives are exhibited throughout his former home.

The museum opened in 2002 and has the world's largest collection of Escher's madcap designs. Highlights include the circular woodcut "Metamorphosis III" as well as the permanent "In the Eye of Escher" exhibition on the second story, where games

The Hague & Scheveningen

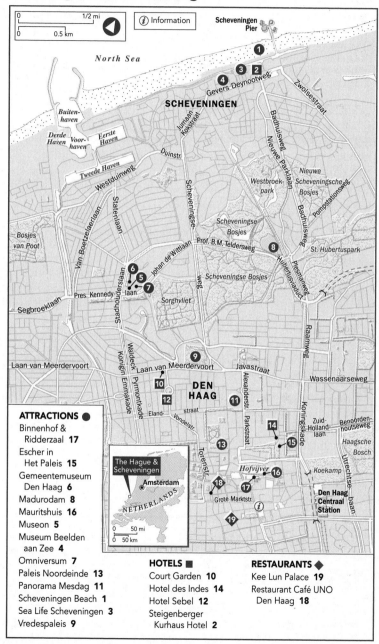

Scheveningen
Pier

(i) Information

0   1/2 mi
0   0.5 km

North Sea

SCHEVENINGEN

Gevers Deynootweg

Zwolsestraat

Buiten-
haven

Derde
Haven   Voor-   Eerste
haven   Haven

Duinstr.

Jurriaan
Kokstraat

Badhuisweg

Nieuwe Parklaan

Nieuwe
Scheveningsche
Bosjes

Nieuwe Scheveningsche weg

Pompstationsweg

Westbroek-
park

Badhuisweg

Tweede Haven

Westduinweg

Statenlaan

Van Boetzelaerlaan

Scheveningse weg

Scheveningse
Bosjes

Prof. B.M. Teldersweg

St. Hubertuspark

Plesmanweg

Hubertusviaduct

Bosjes
van Poot

Scheveningseweg

Johan de Wittlaan

Scheveningse Bosjes

Segbroeklaan

Pres. Kennedylaan

Stadhouderslaan

Sorghvliet

Raamweg

Laan van Meerdervoort

Laan van Meerdervoort

Javastraat

Wassenaarseweg

Waldeck Pyrmontkade

Koningin Emmakade

DEN
HAAG

Eland-
straat

Vondelstr.

Alexanderstr.

Parkstraat

Koningskade

Zuid-
Holland-
laan

Benoorden-
houtseweg

Haagsche
Bosch

Torenstr.

Grote Marktstr.

Hofvijver

Koekamp

Utrechtse-baan

Den Haag
Centraal
Station

The Hague &
Scheveningen

Amsterdam

NETHERLANDS

0   50 mi
0   50 km

ATTRACTIONS ●

Binnenhof &
  Ridderzaal **17**
Escher in
  Het Paleis **15**
Gemeentemuseum
  Den Haag **6**
Madurodam **8**
Mauritshuis **16**
Museon **5**
Museum Beelden
  aan Zee **4**
Omniversum **7**
Paleis Noordeinde **13**
Panorama Mesdag **11**
Scheveningen Beach **1**
Sea Life Scheveningen **3**
Vredespaleis **9**

HOTELS ■

Court Garden **10**
Hotel des Indes **14**
Hotel Sebel **12**
Steigenberger
  Kurhaus Hotel **2**

RESTAURANTS ◆

Kee Lun Palace **19**
Restaurant Café UNO
  Den Haag **18**

5

SIDE TRIPS FROM AMSTERDAM | The Hague

are played with perspective using mirrors and kaleidoscopes. Permanent displays include his early Italian landscapes, family portraits, and many prints and woodcuts with ingenious optical illusions.

Lange Voorhout 74. (C) **070/427-7730.** www.escherinhetpaleis.nl. Admission 9€ adults, 8€ children 7–15, free children 6 and under, 25€ family. Tues–Sun 11am–5pm. Closed Jan 1, Apr 27, Whitsun, and Dec 25.

Gemeentemuseum Den Haag (The Hague Municipal Museum) ★★★

MUSEUM   The Gemeentemuseum forms part of a museum complex surrounding a small lake along with the science-themed Museon (see below), the Omniversum 3D movie theater (see below), the Den Haag Museum of Photography, and the Museum of Contemporary Art. Housed in a honey-hued brick building finished in 1935 by architect H.P. Berlage, and with an interior of harmonious curves and pale yellow and white tiles, this is an outstanding gallery with so much excellence to discover that several hours are required to do the vast displays justice.

Top billing goes to the world's biggest hoard—more than 50 works—by De Stijl artist Piet Mondrian, including his last painting, the unfinished "Victory Boogie Woogie" (1944), an abstract representation of New York. Other permanent exhibitions are equally strong; for example, "Discover the Modern" covers the very best of 20th-century art from Kandinsky and Schiele to Kirchner, Monet, and Picasso.

Decorative arts are covered in detail with ceramics from Delft, China, and the Middle East; Dutch and Venetian glass; silver; period furniture; and an intricate wooden dollhouse dating from 1743. The music department has antique instruments from around the world and an impressive library of scores, books, and prints, as well as underground galleries hosting temporary fashion exhibits such as dresses by Chanel. A new innovation is the child-friendly interactive exhibition "Wonderkamers," in which kids effectively become part of a space-age computer game as they explore the gallery.

Stadhouderslaan 41. (C) **070/338-1111.** www.gemeentemuseum.nl. Admission 14€ adults, 10€ students, free for children 18 and under. Tues–Sun 11am–5pm. Closed Jan 1, May 5, and Dec 25.

Mauritshuis ★★★ ART GALLERY

Once the residence of Count Johan Maurits van Nassau-Siegen, a scion of the ruling House of Orange, this small but delightful neoclassical mansion from 1637 sits astride the Hofvijver lake just outside the Binnenhof complex. One of the greatest art galleries in The Netherlands, it was closed for 2 years for refurbishment, reopening to great fanfare in June 2014.

Completed in 1644 to the designs of Jacob van Campen, the main facade of the Mauritshuis was extensively refashioned according to his original specs, and the pediments and delicate plasterwork are once more gleaming. A new foyer and underground galleries now connect the museum with the Art Deco-style Royal Dutch Shell Wing, more than doubling exhibition space.

At the time of press, details of exactly what is in store in the new gallery have not been released. What is certain is that the Mauritshuis collections previously included a stunning collection of 15th- to 18th-century Low Countries art donated to the nation by King Willem I in 1816. Famous works from this collection have been on display in galleries across the city, and indeed across the world, so it's a rare treat to anticipate seeing them all under one roof again. Great names to look out for include Rembrandt, Frans Hals, Jan Vermeer, Jan Steen, Peter Paul Rubens, and Hans Holbein. The standout pieces from a standout collection are Rembrandt's "The Anatomy Lesson of Dr. Nicolaes Tulp" (1632), Vermeer's meticulous "View of Delft" (ca. 1660), and his

The Royal Palace in The Hague

King Willem-Alexander's workplace is the majestic **Paleis Noordeinde** (www.koninklijkhuis.nl), on Noordeinde, just west of Lange Voorhout, which dates from 1553 but was only promoted to a palace in 1609 when it was bequeathed to Louise de Coligny, the fourth wife and widow of William of Orange. Dutch super-architect Jacob van Campen created much of what we see today in the 17th century, including the palace's H-shape form and serene neoclassical facades, but 200 years later, the palace was almost derelict. In 1815 restoration brought it back to a state suitable for a royal residence, and although it isn't open to visitors, you can view it from the street and from the surrounding landscaped gardens; combine a stroll in the Royal Park with a visit to the **Mauritshuis** (see below) and the **Dutch Parliament Buildings** (see above).

iconic "Girl with a Pearl Earring" (ca. 1660), the painting that sky-rocketed Scarlett Johansson's career.

Temporary exhibitions scheduled for 2015 include highlights from New York City's Frick Collection and an in-depth examination of the Dutch genre of self-portrait painting.

The **Galerij Prins Willem V** (Buitenhof 33; ✆ **070/302-3435;** Tues–Sun noon–5pm) is a separate annex to the Mauritshuis. There are few internationally known works, but look out for Jan Steen's shiver-inducing "The Toothpuller" (1651), and give thanks for modern dentistry techniques.

Korte Vijverberg 8. ✆ **070/302-3456.** www.mauritshuis.nl. Admission 14€ adults, 11€ students, 7€ seniors, free for children 18 and under. Admission 18€, including entrance to Galerij Prins Willem V. Daily 10am–6pm (Thurs till 8pm). Closed Jan 1 and Dec 25.

Panorama Mesdag ★ ART GALLERY   One of the strangest of The Hague's artworks (and the next best thing to visiting seaside Scheveningen) is secreted away on a quiet side street in the affluent Mesdagkwartier. The Panorama Mesdag is the prize exhibit at its eponymous museum, the largest painting in The Netherlands at more than 14m (45 ft.) high and 120m (400 ft.) in length, and the only Dutch "painting in the round" to be in its original location. The extraordinarily precise 360-degree "cyclorama" of the coastal resort of Scheveningen as it was in 1881, painted by Hague School artist Hendrik Willem Mesdag, is a masterly exercise in perspective. The townhouses, churches, lighthouses, coastline, sea, sand dunes, and fishing boats of 19th-century Scheveningen are all represented in minute, accurate detail. The painting is suffused with soft, clear light, and when the painting is viewed from the observation gallery in the center of the exhibition room, artificial dunes separate observers from the painting, creating an illusion that you could simply step right into the landscape.

Although Mesdag was a much-respected figure in the world of Dutch art, this is undoubtedly his marine masterpiece, produced with assistance from his wife Sientje and several other artists. As well as the Mesdag family collection of 19th-century landscapes and a few examples of Barbazon School works, temporary exhibitions are also held in the gallery—often retrospectives of contemporary Dutch artists.

Zeestraat 65. ✆ **070/310-6665.** www.panorama-mesdag.com. Admission 10€ adults, 8.50€ students, 5€ children 4–11. Mon–Sat 10am–5pm, Sun noon–5pm. Closed Jan 1, Apr 27, May 29, June 8–9, and Dec 25–Dec 26.

Vredespaleis (Peace Palace) ★ HISTORIC BUILDING   American philanthropist Andrew Carnegie donated over a million dollars towards the construction of this immense mock-Gothic palace, home to the International Court of Justice and the Permanent Court of Arbitration. The building was designed by French architect Louis Cordonnier and completed in 1913; today it can be visited only by guided tour with reservations made online ahead of time. You'll get to visit most of the ornate apartments and marvel at the grandiose gifts given by each of the participating countries: crystal chandeliers made with real rubies and emeralds and each weighing 1,750kg (3,900 lb.) from Delft; incredible mosaic floors from France; a huge Turkish carpet woven in 1926 in Izmir; and an immense 3,500kg (7,700 lb.) vase from Czar Nicholas of Russia. If the courts are not in session, your guide will take you inside the International Court of Justice, which handles all of the United Nations' judicial cases. The new visitor center to the left of the main gates highlights the history of the Peace Palace with an exhibition and short film.

Carnegieplein 2. ✆ **070/302-4242.** www.vredespaleis.nl. Tour tickets 8.50€ adults, free for children 10 and under. Visitor Center: Tues–Sun 10am–5pm (mid-Nov to mid-Mar 11am–4pm). Guided tours: Mon–Fri 10 and 11am, and 2, 3, and 4pm (4pm tour not always offered). Tours last 50 min. or 1½ hr.

Especially for Kids

Like Amsterdam, The Hague is a happily child-friendly city, with plenty of rolling parks and the nearby beaches of Scheveningen (p. 135). It's also got several attractions aimed at kids, kicking off with Holland's only **IMAX theater at Omniversum** (President Kennedylaan 5, at Stadhouderslaan; ✆ **0900/666-4837;** www.omniversum.nl). A different film is screened every hour from a roster of six or seven titles covering subjects as diverse as underwater exploration and space travel. The films themselves are in Dutch, but English translations are available via headphones.

Right outside Omniversum is an elongated 10-foot-tall statue of Nelson Mandela, a photo opportunity for parents and kids alike. Almost next door is **Museon** (Stadhouderslaan 37; ✆ **070/338-1338;** www.museon.nl), The Hague's hyper-interactive museum of science and nature. Aiming to be both educational and fun, it's a very hands-on affair, with plenty of buttons to press, smells to sniff, and movies. While not enormous, there's enough to distract curious youngsters for a couple of hours. Then for a change of pace, head to the top of **Hague Tower** for afternoon tea in The Penthouse and far-reaching views across the city (next to HS station at Rijkswijkseplein 786; ✆ **070/305-1000;** www.thehaguetower.com). The Hague's tallest skyscraper reaches

Herring Days

Scheveningen must be the place most obsessed with herring in this herring-obsessed land. On the first Saturday in June, in the Dutch equivalent of French restaurants racing to buy the first bottles of Beaujolais Nouveau, fishing boats compete to land the season's first *nieuwe haring* (new herring) during the annual, colorful Vlaggetjesdag (Flag Day) event (p. 36). The fresh-caught fish is considered a delicacy; it's eaten whole (minus the head and the tail) or chopped with minced onion. Year-round the fish are pickled as *maatjes*. Buy herring from sidewalk vendors, beachfront fish stands, and trailers towed onto the beach.

scheveningen

A chic beach resort with a tongue-twister name, Scheveningen is 5km (3 miles) northwest of The Hague center and is best reached by Tram no. 9, thanks to interminable traffic jams on weekends, and most every day during the summer. This glossy seaside enclave sports a cast of upscale restaurants, accommodations, designer boutiques, and abundant night-time entertainment. Until early in the 19th century, this was a sleepy fishing village set amid the dunes on the North Sea coast, but as its beaches began to attract vacation crowds, Scheveningen evolved into an internationally known spa with its own distinct identity; as time has gone on it has become a suburb—albeit a charismatic one—of The Hague. The fairytale 19th-century waterfront **Steigenberger Kurhaus Hotel** (p. 136) still draws celebrities from around the globe.

The beach zone is called **Scheveningen Bad**—but it's actually pretty good. A 3km (2-mile) promenade borders the wide, sandy beach and once had as its highlight the Scheveningen Pier; sadly this burnt down in 2013 but there's still realms of beach stuff to occupy your time, from sunbathing, splashing in the waves, surfing, sand yachting, fishing, cycling, and hiking along the North Sea dunes.

At **Sea Life Scheveningen ★**, Strandweg 13 (✆ **070/354-2100;** www.sealife.nl), you can observe denizens of the deep, including sharks as they swim above your head in a walk-through underwater tunnel. The aquarium is open daily 10am to 6pm (July–Aug until 8pm; closed Dec 12 and 25). When booked in advance online, admission is 12€ for adults (16€ in person) and 9€ for children 3 to 11 (13€ in person).

Museum Beelden aan Zee (Sculptures on the Seafront) ★★, Harteveltstraat 1 (✆ **070/358-5857;** www.beeldenaanzee.nl), is an off-beat museum built into the sand dunes steps from Scheveningen's busy boardwalk. Most of the sculptures take the human form and many are portraits, including an installation featuring the Dutch Royal Family. Terraces overlooking the sea are strewn with sculptures, and on the promenade outside the museum you'll find "Fairytale Sculptures by the Sea," a permanent installation that's free of charge, comprised of cartoonlike figures by New Yorker Tom Otterness. The museum is open Tuesday to Sunday 11am to 5pm. Admission is 12€ adults, 6€ children 13 to 18.

Scheveningen has three **tourist information** points: Boekhandel Scheveningen, Keizerstraat 50 (Mon–Sat 9am–6pm); in the NH Hotel Atlantic, Deltaplein 200 (daily 8am–11pm); and in Kantoorboekhandel De Vulpen, Frederik Henderiklaan 179 (Mon, Wed, Fri 9am–6pm; Tues 9am–7pm; Sat 9am–5pm; Sun 1–5pm).

an impressive 132m (433 ft.) and is regarded as the city's answer to New York City's Flatiron Building.

But The Hague's biggest attraction for youngsters lies a short ride on tram 9 away from the city center towards Scheveningen (see above). Here you'll find **Madurodam ★★** (George Maduroplein 1, at Koninginnegracht; ✆ **070/416-2400;** www.madurodam.nl), a well-conceived theme park showcasing The Netherlands in miniature. Dutch townscapes and famous landmarks—the Anne Frank Huis and Rijksmuseum in Amsterdam; the Binnenhof and Mauritshuis in The Hague; and Rotterdam's Euromast—act as a brilliant introduction to the wonders of The Netherlands and what kids can expect to see in other cities.

Where to Stay & Eat

The oh-so-refined **Hotel Des Indes** (Lange Voorhout 54–56; ℂ **070/361-2345;** www. hoteldesindesthehague.com) comes highly recommended if you have deep pockets or are traveling on an expense account. The **Steigenberger Kurhaus Hotel** (Gevers Deynootplein 30; ℂ **070/416-2636;** www.kurhaus.nl) in Scheveningen has wonderful North Sea views and every possible luxury, too. More moderately priced suggestions include the eco-friendly **Court Garden** (Laan van Meerdervort 96; ℂ **070/311-4000;** www.hotelcourtgarden.nl), an oasis of green principles a stone's throw away from the Peace Palace (see above). Another reasonable choice is the **Hotel Sebel** (Prins Hendrikplein 20; ℂ **070/345-9200;** www.hotelsebel.nl) with simple furnishings and a couple of ground-floor rooms that have access to a leafy garden.

Dining options abound along Prinsenwaal Straat and there's lots of **bar action** around the Grote Markt. **Restaurant Café UNO Den Haag** (Grote Markt 1; ℂ **070/220-1117;** www.unodenhaag.nl) in particular serves killer cocktails. In Chinatown, the **Kee Lun Palace** (Wagenstraat 95; ℂ **070/384-9988**) rustles up a decent chow mein and Singapore noodles.

ROTTERDAM ★★

58km (36 miles) SW of Amsterdam; 23km (14 miles) SE of The Hague

A mere hour from Amsterdam by train, Rotterdam is an utterly different city; in fact it is Holland's fastest growing city with a harbor front that's changing by the day. In Rotterdam there are no tangles of old streets, no canals, and no 17th-century town houses; instead, there's an abundance of sleek contemporary architecture, spacious shopping malls, and one of the world's busiest ocean harbors. This bustling metropolis has risen from the ashes of Nazi bombing in 1942, which reduced it to rubble overnight. Any surviving traces of Old Rotterdam are found in Delfshaven (Delft Harbor) and Oude Haven (Old Harbor).

At the war's end, Rotterdammers looked on their misfortune as an opportunity and approached their city as a clean slate. They relished the chance to create an efficient, workable modern city. The results, although not always elegant, have created a city looking forwards, full of innovative architecture springing up along the river that brings in so much of its wealth.

Essentials

GETTING THERE   Most people fly into Amsterdam's **Schiphol Airport** and take the 55-minute trip to Rotterdam on Netherlands Railways (23€ round-trip).

From Amsterdam, two to six **trains** depart each hour round the clock. On **NS Hispeed Fyra** trains, the ride takes 40 minutes; on ordinary InterCity trains, around 70 minutes. The round-trip fare from Amsterdam is 29€. For more details, visit **www.ns.nl**.

By **car** from Amsterdam, take A4/E19, and then A13/E19; expect delays during commuter times—or to be honest, most of the time.

VISITOR INFORMATION   There's a tourist information center at the railway station: **VVV Rotterdam Centraal,** Stationsplein 45 (no phone; www.rotterdam.info), open daily 9am to 5:30pm. A second tourist office is **ROTTERDAM.INFO** on Binnenwegplein at Coolsingel 195–197 (ℂ **010/790-0185;** www.rotterdam.info). The office is open daily 9:30am to 6pm.

Rotterdam

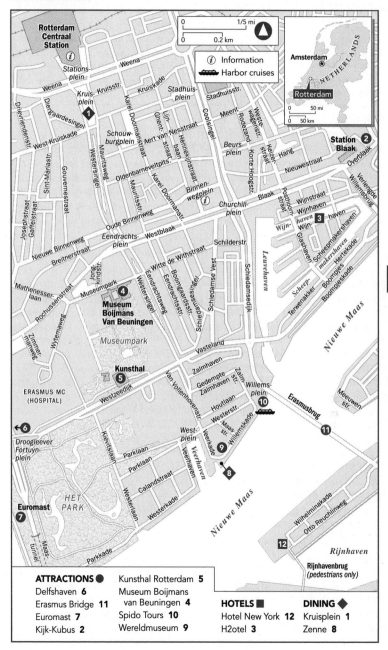

Rotterdam Centraal Station ⓘ

⓪ 1/5 mi
⓪ 0.2 km

ⓘ Information
🚢 Harbor cruises

Amsterdam ✦
NETHERLANDS
Rotterdam
0   50 mi
0   50 km

Stationsplein
Weena
Weena
Kruis-plein ❶
Kruisstr.
Kruiskade
Stadhuisplein
Stadhuisstr.
Meent
Coolsingel
Westewagenstr.
Rodezand
Keizerstraat
Hang
Nieuwestraat
Station Blaak ❷
Overblaak
Verlengde Willemsbrug

Karel Doormanstraat
Lijnbaan
Ghent.straat
Aert van Nesstraat
Hennekijnstraat
Beursplein
Korte Hoogstr.

Drievriendenstr.
Diergaardesingel
West-Kruiskade
Mauritsweg
Westersingel
Oldenbarneveltplts.
Karel Doormanstr.
Binnenwegplein ⓘ
Churchillplein
Blaak
Wijnstraat
Wijnhaven
Wijn-haven ❸ -haven
Wijn-
Wijnhaven
Scheepmakershaven
makershaven
Hertekade

Sint-Mariastr.
Gouvernestraat
Mauritsstr.
Oude Binnenweg
Westblaak
Eendrachtsplein
Schilderstr.
Glashaven
Boompjes
Boompjeskade

Josephstraat
Gaffelstraat
Gouvernestraat
Nieuwe Binnenweg
Breitnerstraat
Jong-kindstr.
Witte de Withstraat
Eendrachtsweg
Eendrachtsstr.
Boomgaardssingel
Boomgaardsstr.
Schiedamse Vest
Schiedamsedijk
Leuvehaven
Scheep-Terwenakker

Mathenesserlaan
Rochussenstraat
Museumpark ❹
Museum Boijmans Van Beuningen
Museumpark
Westersingel
Schiedamssingel
Nieuwe Maas

Zimmermanweg
Wytemaweg
Vasteland
Zalmhaven
Kunsthal ❺
Zalmhaven
Gedempte Zalmhaven
Zalm-str.
Willemsplein ❿ 🚢
Erasmusbrug
Meeuwenstr.

ERASMUS MC (HOSPITAL)
Westzeedijk
Kievitslaan
Van Vollenhovenstr.
Houtlaan
Westerstr.
Maas-str.
Willemskade
❶❶

←❻
Droogleever Fortuynplein
Westplein
Veerkade
Wereldmuseum ❾
Parklaan
Veerhaven
Parklaan
❽
Calandstraat
Westerlaan
Westerkade
Nieuwe Maas
Wilhelminakade
Otto Reuchlinweg

Euromast ❼
HET PARK
Maastunnel
Parkkade
❶❷
Rijnhaven
Rijnhavenbrug
(pedestrians only)

ATTRACTIONS ●
Delfshaven **6**
Erasmus Bridge **11**
Euromast **7**
Kijk-Kubus **2**
Kunsthal Rotterdam **5**
Museum Boijmans van Beuningen **4**
Spido Tours **10**
Wereldmuseum **9**

HOTELS ■
Hotel New York **12**
H2otel **3**

DINING ◆
Kruisplein **1**
Zenne **8**

GETTING AROUND Once in Rotterdam, you can use the trams and the Metro with the same **OV-chipkaart** public transportation card used in Amsterdam (p. 57) on the extensive **RET** (www.ret.nl) public transportation network of bus, tram, and Metro. Get a transport map from the tourist offices (see above).

Explore the Maas waterfront using waterbuses operated by **RET Fast Ferry** (see above) and **Watertaxi Rotterdam** (www.watertaxirotterdam.nl).

Taxi stands are sprinkled throughout the city. You can hail cabs on the street, or by calling **Rotterdamse Taxi Centrale** (*℃* **010/462-6333;** www.rtcnv.nl) or **Rotterdam Taxis** (*℃* **062/651-9697;** www.rotterdam-taxis.com).

Exploring Rotterdam

Euromast ★★ HISTORIC BUILDING   This slender, 185m-tall (607-ft.) tower is indisputably the best vantage point for an overall view of Rotterdam and its environs; on clear days, you can see about 30km (20 miles). You can have lunch or dinner in the **Euromast Brasserie,** 96m (315 ft.) above the harbor park, while enjoying spectacular views of the port. A rotating elevator departs from here for the **Euroscoop viewing platform** at the very top of the spire. From the Brasserie level, for an additional payment (53€), you can abseil or rope slide back to the ground—definitely not for the faint of heart.

Parkhaven 20. *℃* **010/436-4811.** www.euromast.nl. Admission 9€ adults, 6€ children 4–11. Apr–Sept daily 9:30am–11pm, Oct–Mar daily 10am–11pm.

Museum Boijmans van Beuningen ★★★ ART GALLERY   Rotterdam's leading art museum is one of Europe's best and showcases the story of Western art from medieval times to the present. The collection is the result of a happy conjoining of two bequests from rich Dutch art collectors; F.J.O. Boijmans donated his collection to the city in 1847 and D.G. van Beuningen followed suit in 1955. Running from Old Dutch Masters to contemporary glassware, the highlights of this wonderful collection of 140,000 works include Pieter Breughel's peerless Old Testament offering "The Tower of Babel" (ca. 1553), which warrants minute inspection for all its detailed activity; scores of delicate drawings by Renaissance artist Fra Bartolommeo; Rembrandt's winsome portrait of his son, entitled "Titus at his Desk"; and a collection of Gerrit Rietveld's distinctive colored wooden furniture. The artwork is housed in a sleek red brick edifice by Adrianus Van der Steur and has now extended into further airy glass galleries; it is the premier attraction on Rotterdam's Museumpark and is surrounded by tranquil sculpture parks, lawns, and fountains.

Museumpark 18–20. *℃* **010/441-9475.** www.boijmans.nl. Admission 13€ adults, 6€ students, free for children 18 and under. Tues–Sat 11am–5pm. Closed Jan 1, Apr 27, and Dec 25.

Wereldmuseum ★★★ MUSEUM   Reflecting the rich maritime heritage of The Netherlands, the World Art Museum has cobbled together thousands of historic artifacts from across the world, many picked up by Dutch sailors as they plundered the world during the 17th-century Golden Age. The result is a beautiful, vibrant, and unusual series of displays of tribal artwork not seen anywhere else, from Tibetan prayer flags to primitive Australian Aboriginal paintings and beautiful Indonesian hand-printed batiks, showcased alongside African carvings and a luscious collection of silk textiles embroidered in gold. The museum is housed in a lovely Art Nouveau building that contains a classy restaurant affording views out across Rotterdam harbor.

Willemskade 25. *℃* **010/270-7172.** www.wereldmuseum.nl. Admission 13€ adults, free for children 12 and under. Tues–Sun 10:30am–5:30pm. Closed Jan 1, Apr 27, and Dec 25.

The Port of Rotterdam handles more ships and more cargo every year than any other port in Europe, and it is the world's third-busiest port after Shanghai and Singapore. A dredged channel, the **Nieuwe Waterweg (New Waterway)** connects Rotterdam with the North Sea and forms a 40km-long (25-mile) deepwater harbor known as **Europoort.** The Netherlands owes a fair piece of its prosperity to the port, which employs 86,000 people. The port authority handles around 35,000 ships, 16 million containers, 160 million tons of crude oil, and 450-million metric tons of cargo annually. Container ships, cargo carriers, tankers, and careworn tramp ships are waited on 24 hours a day by a vast retinue of people and automated machines—trucks, trains, and barges all moving hither and thither in a blur of activity. A trip around the harbor may be one of the more unusual experiences to be had in The Netherlands, and the sheer scale of the operation will make your jaw drop.

Contemporary Architecture in Rotterdam

The first thing any visitor notices about Rotterdam is its architecture. Nicknamed "Manhattan on the Maas," it's a shiny, new city rising phoenixlike from the ashes of its destruction in one terrible night during World War II. With only wisps of the old gabled townhouses left around Delfshaven and Oude Haven, this is a skyline of innovative buildings, its iconic landmark the elegant lines of the **Erasmusbrug cable bridge,** nicknamed "the Swan" and floodlit at night.

Looking positively old-fashioned these day, a city landmark near Oude Haven is the geometric chaos of quirky, cube-shaped apartments balancing atop tall concrete stalks; the elevated, treehouselike and custard-yellow Kubuswoningen (Cube Houses) were designed by Dutch architect Piet Blom in the early 1970s. One of these lopsided little abodes, the **Kijk-Kubus (Show-Cube),** Overblaak 70 (✆ **010/414-2285;** www.kubus woning.nl), is open for visits daily 11am to 5pm. Admission is 2.50€ for adults, 2€ for seniors and students, 1.50€ for children 4 to 12.

Skyscrapers glitter in the burgeoning downtown area and around the banks of the River Maas, where abandoned wharves have all but disappeared under a slew of stylish new builds. As the city's heavy industry migrated northwest towards the North Sea, the **old port area** has been revamped with innovative skyscrapers including the Norman Foster-designed World Port Center, the Maastoren office block, and the New Orleans building, currently the tallest residential structure in The Netherlands at 43 stories; all can be seen on a **boat tour of the harbor** (see below).

Rem Koolhaas designed the Museumpark's Kunsthal Rotterdam in the 1990s, setting a precedent for stylish public buildings that has been followed by the red-brick New Luxor Theatre, the frothy bubbles of the Drijvend Paviljoen (Floating Pavilion) in the Rijnhaven, and the dynamic Red Apple apartment block. The sparkling carapace of the new Markethal (Market Hall) is still under construction and even the tourist office at Rotterdam Centraal (see above) is housed behind a sparkling new glass facade.

Delfshaven

But not all of Rotterdam is brand new. Take the Metro to the tiny harbor area known as **Delfshaven (Delft Harbor),** a neighborhood that the German bombers somehow missed when they bombed the city to smithereens in 1942. Historically this is one of

Kinderdijk (www.kinderdijk.nl), a tiny community between Rotterdam and Dordrecht, on the south bank of the Lek River, has 19 water-pumping windmills; that means 76 mill sails, each with a 13m (42-ft.) span. It's a spectacular sight, and one important enough for Kinderdijk to have been placed on UNESCO's World Heritage list.

By regulating the level of water, Kinderdijk's windmills guarded the fertile polders (reclaimed land) of the Alblasserwaard. The **Windmill Exposition Center** at Kinderdijk gives a detailed explanation of windmills' technical characteristics and the part they played in the intricate system of water

control. It also looks at the people and the culture that developed on the polders.

The mills operate on Saturday afternoons in July and August 2:30 to 5:30pm; the visitors' mill is open April to October Monday to Saturday 9:30am to 5:30pm. The most adrenaline-thumping way to get to Kinderdijk from Rotterdam is by RET high-speed catamaran (www.ret.nl), from the dock adjacent to the Erasmusbrug; this goes to the De Schans dock at Ridderkerk for the local ferry across to Kinderdijk. If you're driving, take N210 east to Krimpen aan de Lek, from where a small car ferry crosses over the Lek River to Kinderdijk.

5

Rotterdam

SIDE TRIPS FROM AMSTERDAM

the most important places in Europe for U.S. citizens, for it was from here that the Puritan Pilgrim Fathers embarked on the first leg of their trip to found Massachusetts in 1620. Wander into the 15th-century **Pelgrimvaderskerk (Pilgrim Fathers Church),** Aelbrechtskolk 20 (www.pilgrimfatherschurch.nl), in which the pilgrims prayed before departure, and where they are remembered in special services every Thanksgiving Day. The church is open irregularly, but at least admission is free. Then peek into antiques stores and galleries, and check on the progress of this historic area's housing renovations.

Organized Tours

An essential part of the Rotterdam experience is taking a **Spido Harbor Tour ★★** (© 010/275-9988; www.spido.nl) of **Europoort** on board a two-tier boat with indoor and outdoor seating and open decks. April to September, departures from the dock below Erasmus Bridge run daily every 30 to 45 minutes from 9:30am to 5pm; October to March, departures are limited to two to four times a day. The basic harbor tour is a 75-minute sail along the city's waterfront; between April and September an extended (2¼-hr.) trip also runs daily at 10am and 12:30pm. In July and August, you can make all-day excursions along Europoort's full length to the Delta Works sluices. Tours start at 11€ for adults, 7€ for children 4 to 11.

If you're traveling with kids, head straight for the bright-yellow **Pannenkoekenboot (Pancake Boat) ★,** Parkhaven (© 010/436-7295; www.pannenkoekenboot.nl), moored at the foot of the Euromast to get high on sugary treats. Departures on the family cruise are year-round on Saturday and Sunday at 1:30pm. The 2½-hour cruise is 24€ for adults, and 20€ per child.

For sheer novelty value, try cruising down the canals aboard the world's first **Hot-Tug** (© 010/412-5449; www.hottug.nl), a floating, wood-fired hot tub that keeps you warm and cozy whatever the weather is doing around you.

Where to Stay & Eat

Some of Amsterdam's best beds for the night can be found at the **Hotel New York** (Koninginnenhoofd 1; ✆ **010/439-0500;** www.hotelnewyork.com), perched on the Maas with views downriver; if you're a fan of seafood, get a table at their **oyster bar** for a platter of *fines de claires.* At the other end of the price (and luxury) spectrum, the floating **H2otel** (Wijnhaven 20A; ✆ **010/444-5690;** www.h2otel.nl) combines budget accommodation with a warm welcome and a brilliant location within walking distance of the shopping center, Spido boat dock (see below), and the oddball Kubuswoningen (see above). Eating options include the **cafes** around historic Oude Haven, a sunny spot for eating al fresco, or the restaurants of Rotterdam's Chinatown around Kruisplein—where you'll also find Surinamese, Middle Eastern, and Japanese cuisine. A handy pit stop for lunch after taking a Spido tour, **Zenne** (Willemskade 27; ✆ **010/404-9696;** www.zenne.nl) serves plentiful supplies of simple dishes (lamb burgers, kebabs, *bitterballen*) on a terrace overlooking the river and the cute marina at Veerhaven.

BRUSSELS

B russels was kicked into the world spotlight when it became the capital city of the European Union in 1992. This is an honor that has both brought great wealth to parts of the city and caused decades of aggravation as fine old neighborhoods were torn down to make way for the soulless contemporary architecture of the E.U. quarter as well as the building of sometimes unnecessary boulevards to improve commuting time through the city.

So the Bruxellois have mixed feelings about their city's transformation into an international power center. At first the waves of Eurocrats swelling the residential ranks brought a cosmopolitan air—and money—to somewhat provincial Brussels, but many people nowadays wonder whether the city has lost its soul. After all, this city doesn't only mean politics and business. This is the place that inspired Art Nouveau and Surrealism; it worships comic strips, and prides itself on its ancient skills with handmade lace. It has one of the most glorious art galleries in the world as well as countless other enticing museums. Brussels is a gourmet destination, famed the world over for its haute cuisine, fine confectionary, and craft beers.

But it's not an easy city to know. Unlike Amsterdam, which welcomes all and sundry with hugs and laughter, Brussels wrestles with its tourists. Service does not always come with a smile, social unease is evident even in the city center, and pockets of opulence are sharply contrasted by districts of degradation and dilapidation. Despite all this, the Bruxellois have preserved their individuality and the city's spirit lives in its traditional cafes and bistros, where you'll eventually find the convivial ambience that is peculiarly Belgian.

ESSENTIALS

Arriving

BY PLANE **Brussels Airport** (*℡* **0900/70000** for general and flight information, *℡* **322/753-7753** from outside Belgium; www.brusselsairport. be; airport code BRU) is 15km (9 miles) northwest of Brussels city center. This airport handles most of Belgium's international air traffic. There is one terminal that handles all flights, national and international. Moving walkways connect passengers with the Arrivals Hall and Passport Control, Baggage Reclaim, and Customs. Conveniences like free luggage carts, currency exchange, ATMs, restaurants, bars, shops, baby rooms, restrooms, and showers are all on tap. The Sheraton Brussels Airport Hotel is located directly outside the airport's main entrance.

For tourist information and to make hotel reservations, go to Brussels Airport **Information Desk** in the Arrivals Hall; it is open daily 6am to 9pm.

One of the best discounts is the **Brussels Card** (www.brusselscard.be), available from all Brussels tourist offices (see below). Valid for 1, 2, or 3 days, and costing 24€, 36€, and 43€, respectively, it allows free use of public transportation; free and discounted admission to about 30 of the city's museums and attractions; and discounts at some restaurants and other venues, and on some guided tours. It comes with an informative booklet about the sights and a map.

The **Brussels Airport Express train service** to Brussels's three main rail stations (Bruxelles-Nord, Bruxelles-Central, and Bruxelles-Midi) has up to four departures hourly daily between 5:30am and 11:30pm, for a one-way fare of 8.50€. The ride to Bruxelles-Central takes 17 minutes and trains leave from the basement level of the airport. Most airport trains have wide corridors and extra space for baggage.

Every half-hour from the airport's bus platform C outside Arrivals, **Airport Line** no. 12 (Mon–Fri 8am–8pm) and no. 21 (Mon–Fri 8–11pm and Sat–Sun 5am–11pm) depart to the European District in the city. The fare is 8€ for a round-trip ticket purchased from a ticket machine before boarding the bus and 12€ return for one purchased onboard. For more info: ℂ **32/70-232-000;** www.stib-mivb.be.

Taxis that display an orange sticker depicting a white airplane offer reduced fares (around 45€) from the airport to the center city.

Brussels-South-Charleroi-Airport (ℂ **0902/02490** for general and flight information, 322/7815-2722 from outside Belgium; www.charleroi-airport.com; airport code CRL) is 55km (35 miles) south of Brussels. It is the domain of European budget flights rather than transatlantic services; there are Brussels City Shuttle (www.brussels-city-shuttle.com) connections every 30 minutes between the airport and Brussels-Midi/Zuid rail station. Round-trip fare is 28€.

BY CAR Major expressways to Brussels are E19/A16 from Amsterdam (driving time: 2 hr. 20 min. on a good day) and the E19/E17 from Paris (driving time 3½ hr.). Take the E40/A10 from Bruges and Cologne. If possible, avoid driving on the hell on wheels that has become the R0 Brussels ring road; if you miss your turn off, expect to go all the way around again. Once you're installed in your hotel, leave the car at a parking garage. Brussels is choked with traffic even in the middle of the day, parking is scarce, and one-way systems baffling.

BY TRAIN The Brussels metropolitan area has three main rail stations: **Bruxelles-Central,** Carrefour de l'Europe; **Bruxelles-Midi,** rue de France (the Eurostar, Thalys, TGV, and ICE terminal); and **Bruxelles-Nord,** rue du Progrès. All three are served by Métro, tram, or bus lines, and have taxi stands outside. For train information and reservations, call ℂ **02/528-2828** or visit www.sncb.be.

From London, Brussels is served by **Eurostar** (ℂ **08432/186-186** in Britain; ℂ 44/1233-617-575 from outside the UK; www.eurostar.com); from Paris, Amsterdam, and Cologne by **Thalys** (ℂ **320/7079-7979;** www.thalys.com); from everywhere in France apart from Paris by **TGV** (ℂ **3635** in France; ℂ 33/892-353-535 from outside France; www.voyages-sncf.com); and from Frankfurt by **ICE** (ℂ **0900/9296;** 0.35€ per minute; www.nsinternational.nl).

Warning: Attracted by rich pickings from international travelers, bag snatchers roam the environs of Gare du Midi, and pickpockets work the interior. Do not travel to

Brussels's architectural heritage has taken a hit—by unscrupulous property developers, venal local officials, and the unstoppable steamroller of Euro-construction. The phenomenon has been dubbed "Brusselization"—the destruction of beautiful old buildings and their replacement by dreary office towers.

But Brussels has been tampered with before, when its wide boulevards were created and the River Senne was covered up in 1871, and with further development by King Léopold II, who tried to transform his city into a style befitting a colonial power, with great palaces and gardens.

or depart from the station on foot if you can avoid doing so; take a taxi or use public transportation. Inside, keep a close eye on your possessions. You'll be appreciative of the strong police presence.

BY BUS **Eurolines** (© 08717/818-178 in Britain or 32/02-274-1350; www.euro lines.com) buses from London, Paris, Amsterdam, and other cities arrive at the bus station below Bruxelles-Nord train station.

Visitor Information

The city tourist organization, **Visit Brussels** (© 02/513-8940; www.visitbrussels.be), has several offices around the city and their website is also excellent for forward planning. The most centrally located office is on the ground floor of the Hôtel de Ville, Grand-Place and is open daily 9am until 6pm. If you're up in place Royale, **Brussels Info Place (BIP)** is open Monday through Friday 9am to 6pm, weekends 10am until 6pm.

There are additional tourist information offices at the Information Desk in the Arrivals hall at Brussels Airport (daily 6am–9pm) and in the main hall at Gare du Midi rail station (daily 9am–6pm). The office at rue Wiertz 43 is for visitors to the European Parliament and is open daily 10am to 6pm. All offices are closed on January 1 and December 25.

For English-speaking visitors, a useful publication is the weekly **"Brussels Unlimited,"** containing information on cultural events, shopping, and more. Its sister publication, the monthly **"The Bulletin,"** covers local news and current affairs; it can be found online at www.xpats.com.

City Layout

Brussels is divided into **19** *communes* **(districts)**—"Brussels" being both the name of the central commune and of the city as a whole (which comprises Belgium's autonomous Brussels Capital Region, often called Urbizone). The city center was once ringed by fortified ramparts but is now encircled by the broad boulevards known collectively as the Petite Ceinture (Little Belt). Most of the city's premier sightseeing sights are in this zone. Around 14 percent of the zone's total area of 160 sq. km (63 sq. miles) is occupied by parks, woods, and forest, making Brussels one of Europe's greenest urban centers.

You'll hear both French and Dutch (well, Flemish) along with a babel of other tongues spoken on the streets of Brussels. The city is bilingual: Bruxelles in French and Brussel in Dutch/Flemish, and confusingly for many a map-reader, street names and places are in both languages. Grand-Place is Grote Markt in Dutch; Théâtre Royal de la Monnaie is Koninklijke Munttheater. *Note:* Rather than translate place names into three languages in this chapter, the French place names are utilized.

Brussels is flat in its center and western reaches, where the now-vanished River Senne once flowed (p. 162). To the east, a range of low hills rises to the upper city, which is crowned by the Royal Palace and has some of the city's most affluent residential and prestigious business and shopping districts. The **Grand-Place** stands at the heart of the city and is both a starting point and reference point for most visitors.

The Neighborhoods in Brief

The Lower Town The **Bas de la Ville,** the core area of the Old Center, has at its heart the **Grand-Place** (p. 158) and its environs. Two of the most traveled lanes nearby are restaurant-lined **rue des Bouchers** and **Petite rue des Bouchers,** part of an area known as the **Ilot Sacré (Sacred Isle).** A block from the Grand-Place is the classical, colonnaded **Bourse (Stock Exchange).** A few blocks north, on **place de la Monnaie,** is the Monnaie opera house and ballet theater (p. 177), named after the coin mint that once stood here. Brussels's busiest shopping street, pedestrianized **rue Neuve,** starts from place de la Monnaie and runs north for several blocks. Just north of the center lies **Gare du Nord** and nearby place Rogier. Central Brussels also includes the **Marché-aux-Poissons (Fish Market)** district.

The Upper Town The **Haut de la Ville** lies east of and uphill from the Grand-Place, along rue Royale and rue de la Régence and abutting the unpretentious, working-class **Marolles** district (p. 171). Lying between the Palais de Justice and Gare du Midi, the Marolles has cozy cafes, drinking-man's bars, and inexpensive restaurants; its denizens even speak their own dialect. The Upper Town is spread along an escarpment east of the center, where you find **place du Grand-Sablon** (p. 159) as well as the Royal Museums of Fine Arts (p. 166) and the museums of the place Royal. If you head southwest and cross the broad **boulevard de Waterloo,** where you find the most exclusive designer stores, you come to **place Louise.**

Avenue Louise Beyond the city center, things start to get hazier. From place Louise, Brussels's most fashionable thoroughfare, **Avenue Louise,** runs south all the way to a large wooded park called the **Bois de la Cambre.** On either side of **Avenue Louise** are the classy districts of **Ixelles** and **Uccle;** they're both good areas for casual, inexpensive restaurants, bars, cafes, and shopping, and both border the wide green spaces of the Bois de la Cambre and the Forêt de Soignes.

European District East of the city center lies a part of Brussels whose denizens are regarded by many Bruxellois with the same suspicion they might apply to extraterrestrials. This is, of course, the **European Union district** (p. 166) around place Schuman, where the European Commission, Parliament, and Council of Ministers buildings jostle for space in a warren of offices populated by civil servants, journalists, and lobbyists (the area also is home to a wealth of restaurants and cafes that cater to Euro appetites). A quaint old neighborhood was made to disappear to make way for these noble edifices. North of Ixelles, the modern European Union district surrounds **place Schuman.** The **Cinquantenaire,** a park crisscrossed with tree-lined avenues, extends from just east of the European District to the Porte de Tervuren and is bisected east to west by avenue John F. Kennedy. At the park's eastern end are the museums of the monumental Palais du Cinquantenaire (p. 167) and the Arc du Cinquantenaire.

Bruparck In the north of the city (and something of a leap of the imagination) is the **Bruparck.** Inside this recreation complex, you'll find the Mini-Europe theme park (p. 173); the Kinepolis multiplex movie theater; and the Océade water park. Beside this stands the Atomium (p. 172), Brussels Planetarium, Roi Baudoin Soccer Stadium, and the Parc des Expositions congress center.

Getting Around

ON FOOT   Brussels's center city is small enough that walking is a viable option and in fact there's no better way to explore the historical core, especially the myriad tiny streets around Grand-Place. It's also a pleasant stroll uptown through the pedestrianized Mont des Arts to place Royale. Outside these areas, city traffic is both heavy and frantic, creating a smelly, wearisome experience for walkers. To see the best of the city, divide your time into walking tours and utilize the excellent public transportation to get to your destination. For example, take the Métro out to Merode to explore the museums of Parc du Cinquantenaire (p. 167).

Be careful when crossing roads at black-and-white pedestrian crossings that do not have signals; pedestrians do not have legal priority over cars on these crossings. Likewise watch out for vehicles turning right or left at traffic lights, even when the green flashing lights indicates you are allowed to cross; this is quite legal and catches many a visitor off guard.

BY PUBLIC TRANSPORT   Brussels has an excellent, fully integrated transit network—Métro (subway), tram (streetcar), and bus—and the network operates daily 5am to midnight, after which a limited NOCTIS night-bus network takes over until 3am, heading out to the suburbs every 30 minutes. It is run by **STIB** (Rue Royale 76; ✆ **070/232-000;** www.stib-mivb.be).

Maps of the transport system are available free from the city tourist office on Grand-Place (p. 159), and transit maps are posted at all Métro stations as well as bus and tram stops. Timetables are also posted at all tram and bus stops.

Up to 4 children ages 5 and under can ride for free along with a fare-paying adult. Fares for a single-ride **JUMP ticket** on public transport are 2.10€ when purchased onboard and 2€ when purchased before boarding. Whatever ticket you need, you must purchase it before boarding Métro trains; you may purchase bus and tram tickets onboard. A JUMP booklet of 5 tickets costs 8€, or 14€ for 10 journeys. A 1-day JUMP ticket costs 7€, 2-day tickets are 13€, and 3-day tickets are 17€. These can be purchased from the GO vending machines in Métro stations. You can also buy transport tickets at KIOSK sales points, open Monday through Sunday 6:30am until 9:30 or 10:30pm in 14 major Métro stations including Gare Centrale, Gare du Midi, De Brouckère, Gare du Nord, Louise, and Schuman. Other sales outlets are the tourist office in Grand-Place (p. 159) and BIP, home of eB! (p. 169) in rue Royale, as well as numerous news agents.

Validate your ticket by inserting it into the orange electronic machines inside buses and trams and at the access to Métro platforms. Although the one-ride JUMP ticket

---

Personal Safety in Brussels

Brussels is generally safe around the tourist attractions, but there is a growing trend of pickpocketing, theft from cars, and muggings (p. 147) in places such as Métro station foot tunnels and streets just out the center of the city. Take sensible precautions with your belongings, particularly in obvious circumstances such as on crowded Métro trains. Be especially vigilant around Bruxelles-Midi and Gare du Nord stations and when withdrawing cash from ATMs at night on quiet streets.

must be revalidated on each leg of your journey, you're allowed multiple transfers within a 1-hour period of the initial validation.

If possible, plan your journey to avoid the crush at morning and evening rush hours. And again, watch out for pickpockets, especially at busy times, and avoid walking alone in deserted access tunnels, particularly after dark—the risk of being mugged is small but not entirely absent.

BY TRAM & BUS An extensive network of tram lines provides the ideal way to get around the city. Both trams and urban buses are painted in gray-and-brown colors. Their stops are marked with red-and-white signs and often have a shelter. You stop a tram or bus by extending your arm as it approaches so the driver can see it; if you don't signal, the bus or tram won't stop.

BY METRO The Métro is quick and efficient, and covers many important center-city locations, as well as the suburbs, the Bruparck recreation park (p. 145), and the Heysel congress center. Stations are identified by signs with a white M on a blue background. A trip underground takes you into an art center: Métro stations are decorated with specially commissioned paintings, installations, and other artworks by contemporary Belgian artists (p. 170).

BY TAXI Taxi fares start at 2.40€ between 6am and 10pm and at 4.40€ between 10pm and 6am, increasing by 1.80€ per kilometer inside the city (tariff 1) and 2.70€ per kilometer outside Brussels (tariff 2)—so make sure the meter is set to the correct tariff. Tip and taxes are included on the meter price, and you need not add an extra tip unless there has been extra service, such as help with heavy luggage (although drivers won't refuse tips). All taxis are metered. They cannot be hailed on the street, but there are taxi stands on many principal streets, particularly in the center city, and at rail stations. To request a cab by phone, call **Taxis Verts** (**(** **02/349-4949;** www.taxis verts.be).

BY CAR Driving in Brussels is akin to life during the Stone Age: nasty and brutish. Normally polite citizens of Brussels turn into red-eyed demons once they get behind the steering wheel. Driving is fast, except at rush hour, and always aggressive. At rush hour (which lasts about 2 hr. either side of 9am and 5pm), it is almost impossible to move on main roads inside the city and on the notorious R0 outer ring road (beltway). Sundays and very early mornings are slightly better, and with the exception of Friday night, evenings after about 7pm are not too bad.

Park your car either at your hotel or in one of the many public parking garages—your hotel can furnish the address of the nearest one—and do not set foot in it again until you're ready to leave the city. Parking charges are about 15€ per day; it's worth it. A stout pair of shoes, good public transportation, and an occasional taxi ride will get you anywhere you want inexpensively and hassle-free. If you must drive in Brussels, watch out for the notorious *priorité de droite* (priority from the right) traffic system.

[FastFACTS] BRUSSELS

ATMs The easiest and cheapest way to get cash overseas is through an ATM—the **Cirrus and Plus networks** span the globe. Although some debit and credit cards can be used overseas without incurring charges, most banks charge a fee for international withdrawals—check with your bank before you leave home, and find out your daily limit. There are ATMs all over Brussels, and most are open 24/7, although you'll want to be a bit cautious about withdrawing cash in quiet areas outside the main tourist areas after dark.

Business Hours Stores open Monday to Saturday from 9 or 10am to 6pm. On Friday evening, many center-city stores stay open until 8 or 9pm. Most stores close on Sunday, except the tourist-orientated ones around the Grand-Place. The majority of museums open Tuesday through Sunday from 10am until 5pm, and most close on Monday, which is the day to head out of town, perhaps to Bruges, Ghent, or Antwerp.

Doctors & Dentists For doctors, call **Médi Garde** ((✆ **02/479-1818**) or **SOS Médecins** ((✆ **02/513-0202**) and ask for an English-speaking doctor. For emergency dental care, call (✆ **02/426-1026.**

Embassies See p. 239 in chapter 9.

Emergencies Dial (✆ **112** for police, ambulance, paramedics, and the fire department. This is a nationwide toll-free call from landline, mobile, or pay phone. For routine police matters, go to **Brussels Central Police Station,** rue du Marché au Charbon 30 ((✆ **02/279-7711;** Métro: Bourse), just off the Grand-Place. Some Brussels police officers have a poorly developed sense of public service, and a surly and unconcerned attitude to visitors' problems is not uncommon, even at this office where tourists in difficulty often end up. Many officers do, however, speak at least some English.

Internet Access Most hotels in Brussels offer free internet access as part of the room price, although perversely some more expensive ones still charge extra. Some areas in central Brussels provide free access to Wi-Fi hotspots; the Urbizone network is available in train stations, stores, hotels, bars, and restaurants in the postal code 1000 district.

Pharmacies In Belgium, a pharmacy is called either an *apotheek* or a *pharmacie* and sells both prescription and nonprescription medicines. Regular hours are Monday to Saturday from around 9am to 6pm. A centrally located pharmacy is **Grande Pharmacie De Brouckère,** Passage du Nord 10 ((✆ **02/218-0575**). Pharmacies post details of nearby **all-night and Sunday pharmacies** on their doors, or you can call (✆ **09/001-0500** to find out the nearest 24-hour pharmacy. Alternatively, go to the website www.servicede-garde.be and type in your area code to find the nearest 24-hour pharmacy; the site is in French and Dutch but it is very easy to navigate.

Post Office The national mail company is known as **bpost** ((✆ **02/201-2345;** www.depost laposte.be); most post offices are open Monday to Friday 9am to 5pm. The office at Bruxelles de Brouckère, boulevard Anspach 1, is open Monday to Friday 8:30am to 6pm and Saturday 10am to 6pm. The office at the Gare du Midi, avenue Fonsny 48a, is open 24 hours a day.

WHERE TO STAY

The most popular Brussels districts in which to stay are in the extended zone around the **Grand-Place;** in the upper town district around place Stéphanie and boulevard de Waterloo; and along upmarket **avenue Louise.** The most noticeable lodgings in these areas are large, glittering three- and four-star establishments, yet there are numbers of decent medium-priced and even budget hotels to be uncovered in the streets around the Grand-Place and in the Ixelles district to the south of avenue Louise. The **European District** presents something of a special case: Its hotels are convenient for visiting Eurocrats, politicians, lobbyists, and media people, but that doesn't make them a good choice for tourists.

Hotels in the upper price range, including deluxe hotels of just about every international chain that wants to be represented in the "capital of Europe," have a wealth of facilities and efficient, although often impersonal, service. At every level, hotels fill up during the week with E.U.-related business travelers and empty out on weekends as well as during July and August. In these off-peak periods, rates can drop as much as 50 percent, making Brussels the perfect destination for weekend breaks.

Obviously the best way of securing rooms in your hotel of choice is to book online well in advance but if you find yourself stuck, staff at **Brussels tourist offices** (p. 144) can make reservations for the same day if you go to their offices in person and pay a small fee, which is deducted by the hotel from its room rate.

Self-Catering in Brussels

If you would prefer to have a space to call your own in the city, there are plenty of self-catering options in Brussels. **Aparthotels** (p. 152) have five buildings in the city center; check out www.b-aparthotels.com. **Adagio Aparthotel** (www.adagio-city.com) offers luxurious studios and apartments in two addresses, one near the European Union district and one in the Anspach shopping mall. For recommended accommodation agencies or couch surfing opportunities, see p. 60.

Lower Town
VERY EXPENSIVE

Hotel Amigo ★★★   In a prime position just off the Grand-Place, the five-star Amigo is an elegant destination hotel with a surprisingly warm, welcoming ambience for such an upmarket outfit. Owned by the Forté family, its chic but understated style shows the sure hand of designer and British TV star Olga Polizzi, who had the good sense to retain the historic flagstone lobby from the building's previous incarnation as a prison. All the public spaces are kitted out with a wealth antiques, sculptures, and wall tapestries, and the vast bedrooms are decorated in tasteful shades of gray and black; each one is adorned with Magritte or Tintin prints. The equally huge bathrooms all have separate showers and baths and the suites get Jacuzzis too. Ask for a room with a view of the Town Hall's fantastic Gothic spire, so close you can almost reach out and touch it. Breakfast is a wonderful experience, with waitress service, as befits the price; by night the breakfast room transforms into the expensive Bocconi Italian restaurant, overseen by Fulvio Perangelini, and the bar brings in well-heeled Brussels couples to enjoy a cocktail or two.

Rue de l'Amigo 1–3, 1000 Brussels. ✆ **02/547-4747.** www.hotelamigo.com. 173 units. 265€–467€ doubles, 1,272€–4,500€ suites. Valet parking 35€/day. Restaurant, bar, concierge, health club, Wi-Fi 20€/day.

Métropole ★★   Even if you're not staying here, the hotel is worth a visit on its own account, as it is the very epitome of Belle Epoque magnificence, just a few blocks away from the Grand-Place and still owned by the brewing family who bought it in 1895. An ornate, marble-and-gilt interior complete with soaring ceilings and lavishly ornamented public rooms distinguishes this late-19th-century glamour puss from the herd of impersonal five-star hotels in Brussels. The sumptuous guest rooms are all

HOTELS ■

Apart-Hotel **6**
Auberge de Jeunesse
  Jacques Brel **5**
Espérance **1**
The Hotel **12**
Hotel Amigo **8**
Made in Louise **16**
Métropole **2**

RESTAURANTS ◆

Belga Queen **4**
Coin de Mer **7**
Comme Chez Soi **9**
Fanny Thai **3**
La Quincaillerie **15**
Le Wine Bar Sablon
  des Marolles **14**
Lola **11**
Pistolet Original **10**
Restaurant Bon-Bon **13**

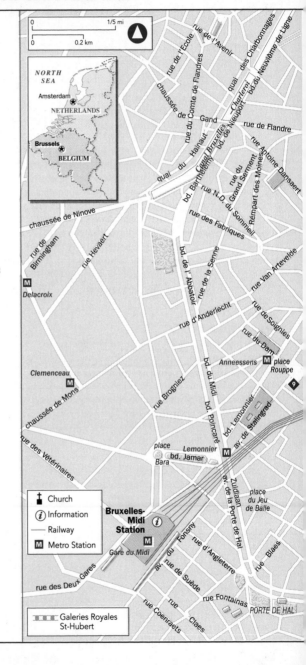

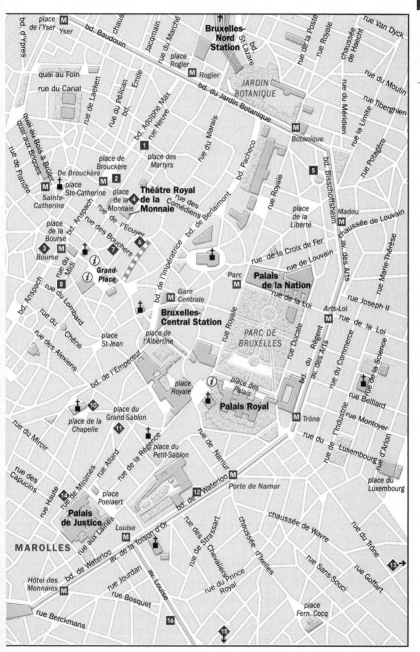

place de l'Yser [M] Yser
bd. d'Ypres
bd. Baudouin
chaus
Jacqmain
rue du Marché
Bruxelles-Nord Station
bd. St-Lazare
rue de la Poste
rue Royale
chaussée de Haecht
rue Van Dyck
quai au Foin
rue du Canal
rue de Laeken
rue du Pélican
bd. Emile
place Rogier
[M] Rogier
bd. du Jardin Botanique
JARDIN BOTANIQUE
rue du Moulin
rue Tiberghien
quai au Bois-à-Brûler
quai aux Briques
rue de Flandre
bd. Adolphe Max
rue Neuve
rue du Marais
bd. Pacheco
[M] Botanique
rue du Méridien
rue de la Limite
rue Potagère
[1]
place des Martyrs
place de Brouckère
[5]
bd. Bisschoffsheim
De Brouckère [M] [2]
place Ste-Catherine
[M] Sainte-Catherine
place de la Monnaie [4]
Théâtre Royal de la Monnaie
rue des Comédiens
bd. de Berlaimont
rue Royale
place de la Liberté
[M] Madou
chaussée de Louvain
rue Marie-Thérèse
place de la Bourse
[M] Bourse [3]
rue du Midi
rue de l'Écuyer
rue des Bouchers [7]
[6]
bd. de l'Impératrice
rue de la Croix de Fer
rue de Louvain
av. des Arts
rue Joseph II
[8]
(i) (i) Grand-Place
rue du Lombard
Gare Centrale
Parc [M]
Palais de la Nation
rue de la Loi
Arts-Loi [M]
rue de la Loi
rue du Chêne
rue des Alexiens
place St-Jean
place de l'Albertine
Bruxelles-Central Station
PARC DE BRUXELLES
rue Ducale
rue du Régent
av. des Arts
av. de l'Industrie
rue du Commerce
rue de la Science
rue Belliard
bd. de l'Empereur
place Royale (i)
place des Palais
Palais Royal
[M] Trône
rue Montoyer
[10]
place du Grand-Sablon
place de la Chapelle
[11]
rue de la Régence
place du Petit-Sablon
rue de Namur
rue du Luxembourg
rue d'Arlon
rue du Miroir
rue des Capucins
rue Haute
[14] rue des Minimes
rue aux Laines
place Poelaert
bd. de Waterloo [M]
Porte de Namur
[12]
chaussée de Wavre
place du Luxembourg
rue du Trône
Palais de Justice
MAROLLES
Louise [M]
av. de la Toison d'Or
rue des Strassart
chaussée d'Ixelles
rue Goffart
[13] →
Hôtel des Monnaies [M]
bd. de Waterloo
rue Jourdan
rue Bosquet
av. Louise
rue du Prince Royal
rue des Chevaliers
rue Sans-Souci
place Fern. Cocq
rue Berckmans
[16]
[15]

Brussels is a green city with a great expanse of parklands and gardens; it is in fact one of the greenest cities in Europe. Once a hunting preserve of the dukes of Brabant, the **Parc de Bruxelles (Brussels Park)** on rue Royale near the Palais Royal (p. 164), was laid out in the 18th century as a landscaped garden. In 1830, Belgian patriots fought Dutch regular troops there during the War of Independence. Later it became a fashionable place to stroll and to meet friends. Although not very big, the park manages to contain everything from carefully trimmed borders to rough patches of trees and bushes, and it has fine views along its main paths, which together with the fountain form the outline of Masonic symbols. Diseased chestnut trees have been cut down and lime trees replaced with sturdier specimens; statues have been restored and cleaned; and the 1840s bandstand by Jean-Pierre Cluysenaer has been refurbished and now hosts summer concerts. The cleanup also diminished the unwholesome nighttime activities in the park, making it safer for all, although a lone nighttime wander around is still probably not the thing to do.

individually decorated with classic furnishings and some rather startling color schemes; the suites are positively OTT with luxurious soft furnishings and antique desks. There's so much available in the hotel it hardly seems worth leaving the building; the sophisticated French restaurant, **L'Alban Chambon;** the Belle Epoque **19ième Bar;** and the sidewalk **Cafe Métropole;** as well as a boutique flogging expensive fripperies. Check out this place online; you can snap up some amazing bargain room rates.

Place de Brouckère 31, 1000 Brussels. ⓒ **02/217-2300.** www.metropolehotel.com. 305 units. 88€–215€ doubles, 325€–675€ suites. Some room rates include buffet breakfast. Valet parking 25€/day. Restaurant, lounge, cafe, business center, boutique, concierge, health club, spa, free Wi-Fi.

MODERATE

Apart-Hotel ★ With 5 blocks of self-catering apartments scattered through central Brussels, Apart-Hotels offer top-level accommodations with all conveniences from well-equipped kitchens to comfy beds with quality linen bedding, DVDs, and a daily cleaning service. Just be careful which address you go for; the apartments in rue des Dominicains have a brilliant location on a pretty alleyway just steps away from the Grand-Place and all the restaurants around rue des Bouchers, but the noise level ratchets up to an unbearable level come weekend nights. And while these rooms were obviously once decked out with sleek, quality furnishings, time has taken its toll and they are now looking more than a little beaten up. The glossy alternatives at boulevard du Regent 58 make better, quieter options and they are a brief Métro ride away from the action in the Grand-Place.

Rue des Dominicains 25, 1000 Brussels. ⓒ **02/743-5111.** www.b-aparthotels.com. 200 units. 107€–179€. Parking 25€/day. Wi-Fi 10€/day.

Espérance ★ In a small alleyway off the boulevard Anspach, this former *maison de passé,* where rooms were rented out by the hour to women of the night, is now a small hotel with compact rooms decorated in primary colors; their bathrooms are pristine but also on the tiny side. One bedroom preserves the architecture and raffish feeling of the original Art Deco incarnation, and not surprisingly, it's the most expensive. The freestanding bath poses proudly in the middle of the room, with a wooden screen to push into place should you feel modest. The **Taverne bar** downstairs remains a perfect Art Deco specimen with stained-glass windows and aged wooden furniture; it doubles as the breakfast room (included with some rates), as well as a restaurant serving up simple dishes like pasta along with those drinks. It's simple and delightful, although the side street can be a little daunting at night. If you are thinking of staying here, bear in mind that there's no elevator and the staircase is steep.

Rue du Finistère 1–3, 1000 Brussels. © **02/219-1028.** www.hotel-esperance.be. 13 units. 89€–160€ doubles. Breakfast included in some room rates. Public parking 15€/day. Free Wi-Fi.

INEXPENSIVE

Auberge de Jeunesse Jacques Brel ★★ This amiable, rather ramshackle hostel has the reputation of being the best in Brussels. It's on a small road leading up to the delightful place des Barricades. Because the hostel has been shoehorned into an old house, rooms are of odd shapes and sizes, so you take potluck. The total bed capacity is 170, spread over 40 rooms, which hold from two to eight beds and can be sold either on a bed basis or as entire private rooms. The decor is basic; you're here for the value and the company of like-minded youthful travelers. The bar, open from 7pm to 1am, gets packed most evenings. Simple suppers of pasta and pizza are on offer for around 8€, and there's an exceptional, almost purely organic buffet breakfast.

Rue de la Sablonnière 28, 1000 Brussels. © **02/219-5676.** www.lesaubergesdejeunesse.be. 40 units. 30€ shared room–97€ private room. Breakfast included in room rate. No parking. Free Wi-Fi.

Upper Town
EXPENSIVE

Made in Louise ★ When Made in Louise burst on to the Brussels scene in 2012, this chic family-run boutique hotel quickly became a force to be reckoned with. Located in a residential neighborhood, the former town house is an historic, protected building; its owners have cleverly used what could have been a major restriction to enhance the feel of a private family home. On the ground floor there's a smart black-and-white bar, a generously sized pool room, and a cafe/breakfast room. The vast central staircase leads to spacious landings filled with artworks and to the elegantly furnished guest rooms, each of which has a unique style. A room with striped wallpaper feels masculine and bold; another, with vivid, blue-flowered wallpaper, is much more feminine; a room with a rough wooden headboard and pale colors has a rustic vibe. All rooms have bathrooms that are of a generous size, with custom-made vanity units designed to look original to the house. The separate cottage has 10 rooms overlooking the internal courtyard; these are good for stays of a week or longer, as they come with well-equipped kitchenettes.

Rue Veydt 40, 1050 Brussels. © **02/537-4030.** www.madeinlouise.com. 48 units. 79€–325€ doubles. Rates include buffet breakfast. Parking 15€/day. Bar, free Wi-Fi.

The Hotel You can't miss The Hotel. It's the 24-story white building on the boulevard de Waterloo, which is the location of Gucci, Armani, and similar posh boutiques, and the main high-end shopping street of Brussels (p. 173). Once a Hilton, The Hotel is now owned by the Swedish group Pandox AB and was completely renovated at the end of 2013. Its swish rooms are both well designed and practical, with plenty of lighting and mirrors that swivel so you get a back as well as front view. The decor is classy, with lots of blacks, deep browns, white, and beige. Every room has a massive bed, a built-in desk, a large sofa in front of the window with a circular table, and throws on the bed. Bathrooms are concealed behind sliding glass panels, so from the washbasin you can brush your teeth and admire the view at the same time. Unless you suffer from vertigo, book one of the rooms on the top floors and go for a corner room with panoramic views on two sides.

Boulevard de Waterloo 38, 1000 Brussels. ✆ **02/504-3335.** www.thehotel-brussels.be. 421 units. 110€–210€ doubles, 360€ suites. Rates include buffet breakfast. Parking 35€/day. Spa, fitness room, free Wi-Fi.

WHERE TO EAT

Food is a passion in Brussels, which boasts more Michelin-star restaurants per head than Paris. People here regard dining as a fine art and their favorite chef as a grand master. It's just about impossible to eat badly, no matter what your price range. The city has no fewer than 1,500 restaurants and even if you're on a tight budget, you should try to set aside the money for at least one big splurge in a fine restaurant—nourishment for both the soul and the stomach.

The Brussels restaurant scene covers the entire city, but there are a couple of culinary pockets you should know about. It has been said that you haven't truly visited this city unless you've dined at least once along **rue des Bouchers** and its offshoot, **Petite rue des Bouchers,** both of which are near the Grand-Place. Both streets are lined with an extraordinary array of ethnic eateries, most with a proudly proclaimed specialty, and all with modest prices. Reservations are not usually necessary in these colorful and crowded restaurants; if you cannot be seated at one, you simply stroll on to the next one. Be prepared for barking waiters eager for business as you wander down the streets, but it's all very good natured.

There's also the cluster of fine restaurants at the **Marché aux Poissons (Fish Market),** a short walk from the Grand-Place around place Ste-Catherine. This is where fishermen once unloaded their daily catches from a now-covered canal. Seafood, as you'd expect, is the specialty. A well-spent afternoon's occupation is to stroll through the area to examine the bills of fare exhibited in windows and make your reservation for the evening meal. Don't fret if the service is slow: People take their time dining out in Brussels.

Lower Town
VERY EXPENSIVE

Comme Chez Soi ★★★ FRENCH   This fine restaurant has two Michelin stars and offers classic French cuisine at its most refined. Dinner is served in an opulent Art Nouveau dining room resplendent with swirling woodwork and delicate garlands of wrought iron, and under the influence of chef Lionel Rigolet, service is attentive but delightfully unstuffy. With menus changing seasonally, most of the ingredients are organic and all are prepared with loving care and attention to the most minute of details; menus might encompass cod with Mechelen asparagus or quail stuffed with sweet pepper and artichoke. The wine list is stellar, as you would expect from such an august establishment, which may well be the gastronomic blowout of your trip to Brussels. Book for dinner as far ahead as possible; getting a table at short notice is more likely at lunchtime. You can also choose to eat in the kitchen to spy on the chefs at work.

Place Rouppe 23. ✆ **02/512-2921.** www.commechezsoi.be. Reservations required. Lunch 55€, dinner main courses 43€–173€, fixed-price menus 94€–199€. Tues–Sat noon–1:30pm and 7–9:30pm.

quick bites IN BRUSSELS

In business since 1873, the snack bar **Au Suisse,** boulevard Anspach 73–75 (© **02/512-9589;** www.ausuisse.be), serves great sandwiches with fresh ingredients and homemade sauces. This is the place to try a raw-herring sandwich (the seafood in general is ace), and you can sip an iced *frappé* on the sidewalk terrace at lunchtime.

For a tasty breakfast, lunch, or snack, head for the convivial **Roi des Belges** ★, rue Jules Van Praet 34 (© **02/513-5116**), on the corner of trendy place St-Géry. The soup of the day or a decent salad won't set you back more than a few euros, or you can just nurse a coffee while reading the newspaper or chatting with your neighboring diners.

Another seductive invitation is the aroma of **fresh Brussels waffles,** sold from street stands around the city. Generally thicker than American waffles, they cost about 3€ and are smothered in sugar icing. The stands are all pretty decent and there's not much reason to try one over another. Should you want to sample an impressive range of toppings and accompaniments, head to the specialist **Aux Gaufres de Bruxelles,** rue du Marché aux Herbes 113 (© **02/514-0171;** www.belgiumwaffle.com).

You could also do a lot worse than try any of the little **Greek, Turkish, Middle Eastern,** and **Israeli** places around the Grand-Place, where you can fill up on moussaka, kebabs, salad, and falafel for as little as 5€. And if you're after basic fare to fill up on while knocking back the *trippel* beer, **A La Mort Subite** (p. 178) has a menu of very simple cheese and salami-type snacks that certainly don't break the bank.

And don't forget those *frites* (fries). Belgians usually eat their favorite snack with mayonnaise rather than ketchup. Prices run from around 2.50€ to 4€ for a *cornet* (cone); toppings, such as peanut, tartare, samurai (hot!), or curry, cost extra. Brussels is dotted with dozens of fast-food stands serving *frites* in paper cones. One of the best, **Maison Antoine** ★, place Jourdan 1 (© **02/230-5456;** www. maisonantoine.be), in the European District, has been in situ since the 1940s. You'll have to join the line at peak times, but the wait for its fries, made from fresh-peeled potatoes, is worthwhile.

EXPENSIVE

Belga Queen ★ CONTEMPORARY BELGIAN   Light and space are the signature design themes of this most spectacular of brasseries; it's blessed with a long dining room swathed in a decorative stained glass ceiling and marble pillars and is set in a Belle Epoque building that was formerly a bank. Dishes include buckets full of mussels, foie gras, salmon, and duck, and can be slightly hit or miss in content. Nevertheless, it is a beautiful place in which to eat alongside stylish young locals, and you'll be served by a wait staff fully committed of the gravity of their calling. In addition to the restaurant, the Belga Queen offers an oyster bar and a beer bar, as well as what must be the last cigar lounge in Belgium, hidden down in the basement. There's an offshoot in Ghent.

Rue du Fossée aux Loups 32. © **02/217-2187.** www.belgaqueen.be. Reservations recommended on weekends. Lunch 18€, dinner main courses 23€–47€. Daily noon–2:30pm and 7pm–midnight.

MODERATE

Coin de Mer ★ BELGIAN   One of scores of seafood restaurants tucked away around the Grand-Place, Coin de Mer has a buzzing atmosphere in bright-white,

Most restaurants serve lunch between noon and 2pm, and reopen for dinner from 7 to 10pm, with brasseries staying open all day. Almost every eatery in Brussels offers a *menu du jour* at lunchtime, consisting of a fixed menu with a couple of two- or three-course options—often with a glass of table wine thrown in—that are often markedly good value in this expensive city. If you are yearning to try one of the fancier restaurants but can't face the bill, try them out for lunch and save your money for sampling the beer.

simple surroundings, and a fast turnover of people grabbing at the chance to sample their vast seafood platters. These great piles of delectability come with crab, lobster, oysters, cockles, and razor clams all fresher than fresh. Other great choices here include the classic *moule-frîtes* combo and dishes of delicious Spanish paella. Service is surprisingly cordial and relaxed, which is why this place stands out from its neighbors.

Rue de la Fourche 31–35. ℂ **02/503-0703.** Main courses lunch 14€, dinner 18€–28€. Mon–Fri noon–3pm and 6–11:30pm, Sat–Sun noon–midnight.

Fanny Thai ★★ THAI   In spite of the unfortunate name, this is simply the best Thai in Brussels, run by young, enthusiastic wait staff with a vibe so casual it's virtually a cafe. The dining area has one bare brick wall adorned with a giant face of Buddha, who solemnly overlooks proceedings as the waiters scoot daintily around the cramped tables. Go beyond the usual green shrimp curry and try the fish cooked in herbs and wrapped in banana leaves, or chicken sautéed with basil—all delicious and not too heavy handed with the chili. Fanny Thai gets so busy you might have to wait for a table but there are plenty of drinking dens scattered along the street in this trendy part of town near the Bourse.

Rue Jules Van Praet 36. ℂ **02/502-6422.** Main courses 14€–28€. Mon–Fri noon–3pm and 6–11:30pm, Sat–Sun noon–11:30pm.

Upper Town
EXPENSIVE

Lola ★★ BRASSERIE   Genteel elderly couples and smart young things, tourists as well as suits clearly working for the E.U.—all are cheerfully welcomed in this smart and savvy contemporary brasserie. The long, narrow canteen-style room is decked in cheery colors and industrial-style piping. The pan-European menu includes Scottish smoked salmon with horseradish cream as well as good Belgian shrimp croquettes. For main courses, the duck breast with caramelized apples and cider and mashed potatoes, and the roast scallops both hit the spot. The wine list is moderately priced, and the older waiters are some of the most professional—and friendliest—in town. Lola deserves her success.

Place du Grand Sablon 33. ℂ **02/514-2460.** www.restolola.be. Mains 12€–34€. Daily noon–3pm and 6:30–11:30pm, Sat–Sun noon–11:30pm.

MODERATE

Le Wine Bar Sablon des Marolles ★★ TRADITIONAL BELGIAN   A glass of wine from the short but good list, and a selection of plates from the menu, is just the thing after a morning spent shopping at the famous *brocante* market in the place du Jeu de Balle (p. 176) or in the antiques shops of the Marolles (p. 171). The surrounding area is scruffy and working class and proud of it, and this wine bar is located in a 17th-century house with wooden floors, chairs, and tables; the simple surroundings are elevated by the vast paintings and prints on the walls. The short menu is cleverly put together, with plates that are ideal for sharing from 8€ to 10€. Try the chicken liver pâté, geese rillettes, or sardines with olive oil. More substantial dishes could include smoked sausage with Puy lentils or beef braised in red wine. There's also a fish dish that changes daily, and a good selection of cheese for dessert as well as a well-priced wine list, which includes champagne by the glass.

Rue Haute 198. ℂ **02/496-0105.** www.winebarsablon.be. Main courses 10€–20€. Wed–Sat 6–11pm, Sat–Sun noon–3pm.

INEXPENSIVE

Pistolet Original ★ BELGIAN   A *pistolet* is a filled, crusty bread roll—something that every Belgian child grows up on—so Valérie Lepla struck a rich, nostalgic vein when she named her deli-cafe in the smart Sablon district. It's invariably packed with just about every level of Brussels society, either eating pistolets in the cheerful cafe or lining up at the deli counter to take them home. Pistolet Original makes a perfect spot for lunch after rummaging around the weekend antiques markets. A few of the available fillings: Ardenne ham, shrimp, sharp-tasting pickles, rollmops (pickled herring filets), roast beef, celery root, braised chicory, blood pudding, *potjesvlees* (Flemish terrine), and butter or chocolate. You could come here on a daily basis and still not go through all the possibilities. Wash things down with beer or wine, coffee or tea. If it's good enough for Lionel Rigolet, the former chef at the three-Michelin-star Comme Chez Soi (p. 154), it's certainly good enough for the rest of us.

Rue Joseph Steven 24–26. ℂ **02/880-8098.** www.pistolet-original.be. Main courses 4€–8€. Daily 8am–6pm.

Suburbs

VERY EXPENSIVE

Restaurant Bon-Bon ★ HAUTE CUISINE   Chef Christophe Hardiquest is one of Belgium's top young chefs, a name to watch as he collects Michelin stars (he's up to two). He opened the first Bon-Bon in Uccle in 2001 before moving in 2011 to an Art Nouveau house in Woluwe-Satin-Pierre, the city's posh diplomatic quarter. The move made the restaurant a hit: You must now book dinner months in advance. Billed as a *salon d'artisan cuisinier* (the salon of an artisan chef), this is a serious monument to dining. Chef believes strongly in the connection between the region and the taste of a product—only ingredients that have the location-specific *appellation d'origine contrôlée* designation are used here. The set menus may include the likes of Axuria milk-fed lamb from the Pyrenees, which is coated in a black-bread crust. The wine list is as

Be on Your Guard in the Ilot Sacré

A few restaurants in this colorful restaurant district just off the Grand-Place take advantage of tourists. If you decide to dine at a restaurant not reviewed here—and you don't want to get fleeced—be sure to double check the price of everything *before* you order it. Most visitors leave the Ilot Sacré with no more serious complaint than an expanded waistline, but a little caution is in order.

serious as the service is impeccable; you can also sit at the bar and watch the chefs toil away in the open kitchen.

Avenue de Tervueren 453. $\mathcal{C}$ **02/346-6615.** www.bon-bon.be. Reservations required. Fixed-price menus 80€–175€. Tues–Fri noon–1:30pm, Mon–Fri 7:30–9pm. Closed Sat–Sun.

EXPENSIVE

La Quincaillerie ★★★ BELGIAN/FRENCH Open since 1988, this gorgeous restaurant set the benchmark for the others that followed it into the Châtelain district. Inside a former ironmonger shop built in 1903, La Quincaillerie has a beautiful Art Nouveau exterior and an interior of wrought-iron balconies, polished brass, and a huge clock. It's always buzzing as waiters deliver dishes with style to a chic clientele. The restaurant takes the environmental route with ingredients, using sustainable fish sources; lamb from its own farm in Bresse, France; locally procured vegetables; and organic and biodynamic wines. This is combined with an interesting menu, which may include grilled bone marrow, pig's trotters, and toasted sourdough bread for a starter; and Challans duck with leeks and dauphinoise potatoes as a main. There's also a formidable range of fish and seafood available.

Rue de Page 45. $\mathcal{C}$ **02/533-9833.** www.quincaillerie.be. Reservations recommended. Lunch menu 14€, fixed-price menu 29€, dinner main courses 19€–34€. Tues–Sat noon–2:30pm, 7pm–midnight.

EXPLORING BRUSSELS

Brussels offers so much to the visitor that the city can feel overwhelming; there are more than 75 museums alone as well as the glorious architecture of King Léopold I's purpose-built city, and one of the best fine-art galleries in the world. Most of the sights are clustered around the Grand-Place in the lower town, and the rue Royale in the upper town; these areas are within easy walking distance of each other, connected by the landscaped Mont des Arts, which leads up to Place Royale from Place de l'Albertine. If you head out into the suburbs, there's a comprehensive public transport system that will get you around easily, but do be aware that this city has its share of social problems and a nighttime walk around areas such as Anderlecht is not a wise idea.

The City's Principal Squares

GRAND-PLACE ★★★

Ornamental gables, medieval banners, gilded facades, sunlight flashing off gold-filigreed rooftop sculptures, and a general impression of harmony and timelessness—there's a lot to take in all at once when you first enter the **Grand-Place.** Once the pride of the Habsburg Empire, it has always been the heart of Brussels.

Arriving in the Grand-Place for the first time is sheer breathtaking magic: a UNESCO World Heritage–listed expanse of elaborate guild houses smothered with gilt and statuary. The buildings you see today are mostly 18th- and 19th-century replicas of the original buildings, which were reduced to rubble by invading French troops in 1695. Louis XIV's army lined up its artillery on the heights of Anderlecht and blasted away at the medieval Grand-Place, using the Hôtel de Ville (Town Hall) spire as a target. The French destroyed the square, but ironically the Town Hall spire escaped undamaged. The timber-fronted buildings of the city's trading and mercantile guilds were not so fortunate. But the Bruxellois weren't about to let a mere French king do away with their centuries-old corporate headquarters; the guildsmen had the place up and running again within 4 years, on the same grand scale as before but in the baroque style known as the Flemish Renaissance. The Town Hall, however, although badly damaged by Louis's guns, is the real thing and dates from the early 1400s. It still dominates the Grand-Place, sitting on its southwestern flank with a facade smothered in statues of biblical figures; the highly ornate central tower is still a useful local landmark, although now more often used by lost tourists than invading armies. The City Hall is open for tours of its sumptuous Neo-Gothic public apartments (p. 163) and magnificent marble staircase; it also now houses a branch of the **Brussels tourist office** (p. 144).

Opposite the Town Hall is the ornate facade of the 19th-century neo-Gothic Maison du Roi, location of the **Museum of the City of Brussels** (see below), where displays include the wardrobe of outfits donated to the **Manneken-Pis** (see below). Spanning the eastern side of the Grand-Place is the Maison de Ducs de Brabent, a series of seven ornate town houses that formerly belonged to powerful guilds such as the tanners, stonemasons, and sculptors. In the northwestern corner of the square is the Maison de Roi d'Espagne (House of the Spanish King), which was the base of the bakers' guild.

Every day a flower market fills the Grand-Place with fragrance and hardly a week passes without some concert or performance here. The biggest festival is Brussels's famous **Florialentime flower festival,** which takes place over a weekend in mid-August and sees the square filled with a carpet of flowers. There are lots of expensive cafes within the opulent wood-beamed interiors of old guild houses; their upper-floor windows overlooking the Grand-Place offer some of the best views in Europe and their terraces are suntraps for an evening beer.

PLACE DU GRAND SABLON ★★

Although the traffic passing through it diminishes the experience, **place du Grand Sablon** is filled with sidewalk cafes and lined with gabled mansions; upmarket locals consider it a classier destination than the Grand-Place. The Grand Sablon and its environs are antiques territory; many of its mansions have been turned into antiques stores or art galleries with pricey merchandise on display; other high-end names pitching up here include Christian Louboutin and Marcolini Chocolate, plus a sprinkling of posh cafes. On Saturday and Sunday mornings an excellent antiques market sets up its stalls in front of **Notre-Dame du Sablon** (p. 165). This flamboyantly Gothic church has five naves and glorious, slender stained-glass windows; it was built with money donated by the city's wealthy Guild of Crossbowmen in the 15th century.

PLACE DU PETIT SABLON ★

Just across busy rue de la Régence is the Grand Sablon's little sister, the **place du Petit Sablon.** This contains an ornamental garden with a fountain and pool, and it's a tranquil little retreat from the city bustle. The 48 bronze statuettes adorning the wrought-iron fence surrounding the garden symbolize Brussels's medieval guilds. The two statues at the head of the pond commemorate the Catholic counts of Egmont and

---

Free Stuff

Some Brussels museums, like the Cinquantenaire (p. 167), Magritte (p. 165), the Museum des Sciences Naturelles (Museum of Natural Sciences; rue Vautier 29; ✆ 02/627-4238; www. naturalsciences.be) and the Royal Museums of Fine Arts of Belgium (p. 166), offer free admission the first Wednesday afternoon of every month. Others like BELvue and Coudenberg (p. 164) have free admission on the first Sunday of the month.

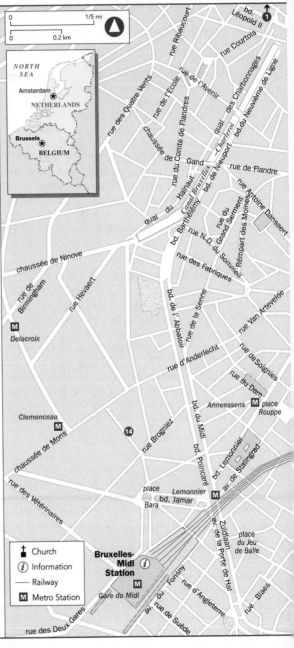

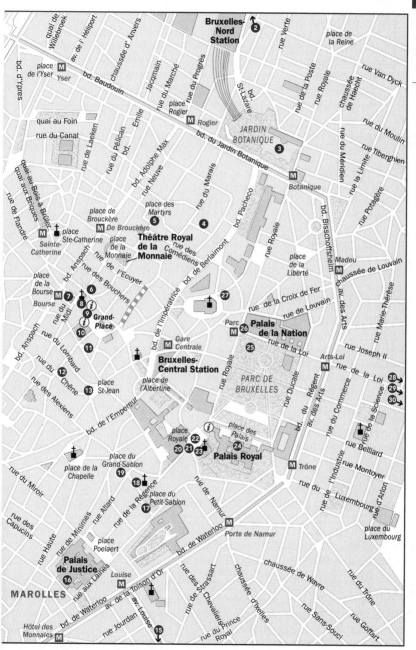

Brussels is constructed on a river called the Senne (Zenne in Dutch). In the late 19th century, the City Fathers had it covered up for health reasons (it stank and carried many diseases), and it continues to flow underground. Glimpses of the missing river can still be seen in a tiny courtyard off place St-Géry in the Lower Town, which was once the biggest island in the river. Today the river is reasonably clean and fish have once more been sighted swimming in it.

Hornes, who were beheaded in 1568 for rebelling against Spain's Holy Inquisition in the Low Countries.

PLACE ROYALE ★

Brussels's royal square is at the meeting point of rue de la Régence and rue Royale, the two thoroughfares that hold many of the city's premier sights, including the Musée Magritte (see below) and BOZAR (p. 177). The Musées Royaux des Beaux-Arts de Belgiques (see below) are at the west end of place Royale. This 18th-century square was laid out in neoclassical style and is graced by a heroic **equestrian statue** of the leader of the First Crusade, Duke Godefroid de Bouillon. On the north face of the square is the **Eglise St-Jacques-sur-Coudenberg.** Archaeologists have excavated the foundations of the Royal Palace of Emperor Charles V on the square, and the site has been covered over again to form the Coudenberg museum (see below).

PLACE DES MARTYRS ★

Some years back, the once-elegant 18th-century **place des Martyrs,** in the Lower Town near the Théâtre Royal de la Monnaie, was in a sorry state and crumbling to the ground. It entombs the "500 Martyrs" of Belgium's 1830 War of Independence. The square has been extensively restored, and although it lost some of its former ragged charm in the process, it is once again an attractive public place.

The Lower Town

Cathédrale des Sts-Michel-et-Gudule ★ CHURCH   Rising above the hectic chaos of the Lower Town on Treurenberg in a no-man's land between the Lower and Upper Towns, this magnificent twin-towered Roman Catholic church is the "purest flowering of the Gothic style"; its choir is Belgium's earliest Brabantine Gothic work. Begun in 1226, it was officially consecrated as a cathedral as recently as 1961. The 16th-century Habsburg Emperor Charles V donated the superb stained-glass windows in the Chapelle du St-Sacrément. Apart from these, the spare interior decoration focuses attention on the soaring columns and arches as well as the extravagantly carved wooden pulpit, which depicts Adam and Eve being expelled from Eden, and the statues of the Apostles lined up along the columns supporting the central aisle. It's the official wedding and funeral church of the Belgian Royal Family and contains the glossy black tombs of heroic Brabantine dukes.

In the **crypt** lie the foundations of the earlier Romanesque church dating from the 11th century. The **Trésor (Treasury)** is also worth visiting for its glowing ecclesiastical vessels in gold, silver, and precious stones.

Parvis Ste-Gudule. ⓒ **02/217-8345.** www.cathedralestmichel.be. Admission: cathedral free, crypt and archaeological zone 2.50€, treasury 1€. Mon–Fri 7am–6pm, Sat 8am–3:30pm, Sun 2–6pm.

Centre Belge de la Bande-Dessinée (Belgian Center for Comic-Strip Art) ★★ MUSEUM Grown-ups will love this place as much as kids do. The center is dedicated to comic strips and takes a lofty view of what it calls "the Ninth Art," comparing the Bayeaux Tapestry, Hogarth, and Hokusai with comic-strip creators. As icing on the cake, it's in a restored Art Nouveau department store from 1903, the Magasins Waucquez (designed by Victor Horta; see above). Hergé's Tintin and Snowy greet visitors at the top of the elegant staircase—Hergé himself had a hand in the design of the center—and beyond this is a comic-character wonderland, relating the story of cartoons from vague idea to published comic strip. All the big names appear in drawings and models, a library of 30,000 books, and in permanent and special exhibits, including Tintin, Asterix, Lucky Luke, the Smurfs, Charlie Brown, Andy Capp, Superman, and Batman.

Rue des Sables 20. © **02/219-1980.** www.comicscenter.net. Admission 8€ adults; 6€ seniors, students, children 12–18; 3€ children 11 and under. Tues–Sun 10am–6pm. Closed Jan 1 and Dec 25.

Fondation Jacques Brel ★ MUSEUM Dedicated to Belgium's most famous singer and actor, Jacques Brel, this museum offers an overview of his life and work from his birth in 1929 to his death in 1978. Born into an affluent family, Brel composed songs on the piano as a child and made his first record in 1953; he then hotfooted it to Paris, touring almost incessantly for the next 15 years. Along the way he became one of Europe's foremost singer-songwriters, famously morose and sentimental by turn. In 1966, he held his final concert at the Olympia Theatre in Brussels and moved to America, subsequently having a hit on Broadway with the musical "Man of La Mancha." He died in Tahiti and is buried close to artist Paul Gauguin. Set up by his daughter, this place offers a smattering of Brel memorabilia, tracks from his albums, snippets from his movies, and an in-depth examination of his life. Hardened fans of the Belgian crooner and contemporary of Edith Piaf might also consider the 3-hour Brel-themed walking tour around central Brussels.

Place de Vieille Halle aux Blés 11. © **02/511-1020.** www.jacquesbrel.be. Admission 5€ adults, 3.50€ seniors and students. Sept–June Tues–Sun noon–6pm, July–Aug daily noon–6pm. Closed Jan 1, May 1, Nov 1, Nov 11, and Dec 25.

Hôtel de Ville (Town Hall) ★★ HISTORIC BUILDING Easily the most extravagant in a square full of extravagant buildings, the dazzling Town Hall dates from 1402 and is a masterpiece of Gothic design, with a lacy facade ornamented with dozens of arched windows and sculptures displaying drunken monks, a sleeping Moor and his harem, and St. Michael slaying a female devil. The enormous (almost) central tower rears 66m (215 ft.) high and is visible for miles around.

The interior is a mélange of the best and most lavish styles from Gothic to Louis XIV and can be toured only by appointment. The mirrored Gothic Hall is a spectacular highlight of the visit to this ultimate monument to urban power, as are the 16th- to 18th-century Flemish tapestries depicting the trades of the guildsmen who commissioned them to hang in the series of embellished council chambers.

Grand-Place. © **02/548-0447.** www.brussels.be. Admission (guided tours only) 5€ adults; 3€ seniors, students, and children 6–12; free for children 5 and under. Tickets sold at tourist office in Grand-Place (p. 159). Guided tours in English, French, or Dutch Apr–Sept Tues 10am–5pm, Wed 10am–noon, Thurs 2–5pm. Closed Jan 1, May 1, Nov 1, Nov 11, and Dec 25.

Musée du Costume et de la Dentelle (Costume and Lace Museum) ★★ MUSEUM Set up in 1977 to celebrate the long tradition of making textiles and lace in Flanders, this collection is surprisingly engaging. As well as ecclesiastical vestments and fine samples of delicate handmade lace from Bruges and Mechelen, you'll find cabinets full of panama hats (a bit of an obsession in Brussels; scores of stores sell them), Barbie dolls with their many costume changes, and plenty of carefully conserved and elaborately embroidered gowns from the 18th and 19th centuries. Best of all are the cheery displays of 1960s fashion, including tiny miniskirts and bright-red raincoats.

Rue de la Violette 12. © 02/213-4450. www.costumeandlacemuseum.be. Admission 4€ adults, 3€ seniors and students, 2€ children 5 to 18, free for children 4 and under; free first Sun each month, free for children 17 and under Sat–Sun. Tues–Sun 10am–5pm. Closed Jan 1, May 1, Nov 1 and 11, and Dec 25.

Musée de la Ville de Bruxelles (Museum of the City of Brussels) ★ MUSEUM   Found in the opulent neo-Gothic Maison du Roi (King's House; see above), which—despite its name—never housed any kings, the museum documents the history of Brussels. Founded in 1860, showpieces among this broad collection include original Gothic statuary that once adorned the Town Hall, fine tapestries from Brussels's textile workshops, and plans showing how the city developed. But most people visit out of curiosity (or disbelief) to see the nigh-on 800 costumes acquired by the diminutive Manneken-Pis statue around the corner (see above); it seems that every time an overseas VIP visits Brussels (which is quite often these days, it being the E.U. HQ), they bring yet another outfit for the little statue.

Grand-Place. © 02/279-4350. www.brussels.be. Admission 4€ adults, 3€ seniors and students, 2€ children 6–15, free for children 5 and under. Tues–Sun 10am–5pm. Closed Jan 1, May 1, Nov 1, Nov 11, and Dec 25.

The Upper Town

BELvue Museum & Coudenberg ★ MUSEUM   Housed in the former Coudenberg Palace, these two museums are uneasy bedfellows, both very interesting in their own right but not working together to form a cohesive picture of Brussels history. The BELvue occupies the first floor of the palace, with views out across the Parc de Bruxelles, and relates the story of Belgium through the struggles for independence

---

A New Art

A new design style appeared toward the end of the 19th century and flourished for a few decades across Europe. It was called Art Nouveau and its prime materials were glass and iron, which were worked with decorative curved lines and floral and geometric motifs. Belgium produced one of its greatest exponents in **Victor Horta** (1861–1947); his work can be seen all over Brussels and especially at the **Tassel House** (1893; rue Paul Emile Janson 6) and the **Hôtel Solvay** (1895; avenue Louise 224). His own house is open to the public: the **Musée Horta (Horta Museum;** see p. 170) in St-Gilles, a southern suburb of Brussels.

Fans of the city's superb legacy of Art Nouveau architecture should check out the works of **Gustave Strauven** (1878–1919), the Brussels-born student of Horta. Strauven's signature is his use of blue and yellow bricks. He designed around 100 private houses in Brussels, including the slender **Maison Saint-Cyr** (1903) at square Ambiorix 11. This flamboyant, almost sensuous Gaudíesque masterpiece of curling wrought-iron, curved windows, and swirling brick was built for the artist Georges Léonard de Saint-Cyr by Strauven when he was a 22-year-old student.

Dressing the Manneken-Pis

The celebrated **Manneken-Pis** statue features a tiny, chubby boy peeing into a fountain. For some reason, it has been adopted as a symbol of Brussels. Located on the corner of rue du Chêne and rue de l'Etuve, 2 blocks from the Grand-Place, the minute bronze statue is only 60cm high, which is a shock to most people who seek him out expecting something on a grander scale. Most of the time the Manneken-Pis goes about his business stark naked, although always surrounded by an over-excited bunch of trippers snapping pictures. On high days and holidays he is dressed in a range of outfits dedicated to the city over the centuries. Louis XV of France began the tradition of presenting colorful costumes to the statue to make amends for the French abduction of the statue in 1747.

His 800 or so outfits can be seen in the Musée de la Ville on the Grand-Place (see below). *Note:* This is not the original statue, which was prone to theft and anatomical maltreatment; the original was removed for safekeeping.

It's known that the miniscule effigy has graced the city since at least the time of Philip the Good, who was Count of Flanders in 1419. Among the speculation about the boy's origins are that he was the son of a Brussels nobleman who got lost and was found while answering nature's call; another is that he was a patriotic Belgian kid who sprinkled a hated Spanish sentry passing beneath his window. Perhaps the best theory is that he saved the Town Hall from a sputtering bomb by extinguishing it—like Gulliver—with the first thing handy.

from The Netherlands and the final breakaway in 1830 to its present (almost) unified political state. Displays include black-and-white film, heaps of old weapons, and some graphic images of Flanders trenches in World War I. The Coudenberg dives down underneath the palace to explore the vast maze of tunnels that were at street level in the 17th century; the tentacles of the museum spread right under the Place Royale, taking in former kitchens, chapels, a few Roman remains, and whole streets that were covered over when King Léopold I started construction of his palatial new city in the 1860s. Don't go down there without a map!

Place des Palais 7. © **070/220-492.** www.belvue.be. Admission 5€ adults, 4€ seniors, 3€ students 18–25, free for children 17 and under. Mon–Fri 10am–5pm, Sat–Sun 10am–6pm.

Eglise Notre-Dame du Sablon (Church of Our Lady of the Sablon) ★ CHURCH   This flamboyant late-Gothic church, dating from around 1400 to 1594, was paid for by the city's powerful Guild of Crossbowmen. It is noted for its four-fold gallery with brightly colored stained-glass windows, illuminated from the inside at night, in striking contrast with the gray-white arches and walls. Worth seeing are the two baroque chapels decorated with funeral symbols in white marble. The church is the burial place of several members of the aristocratic German Thorn und Taxis dynasty, servants of the Habsburg empire, who lived in place du Petit Sablon (see above).

Rue Bodenbroek 6. © **02/511-5741.** http://up.catho-bruxelles.be/bxlcentre. Free admission. Mon–Fri 9am–6:30pm, Sat–Sun 10am–6:30pm.

Musée Magritte ★★ MUSEUM   Do not confuse this spectacular collection with the museum in artist René Magritte's Brussels home (p. 170). The Magritte Museum opened in 2009 and is now under the umbrella of the Musées Royaux des Beaux-Arts

THE european DISTRICT

Home to the European Commission, European Parliament, Council of Ministers, and related institutions, Brussels has no less than 1.2 million sq. m (12.7 million sq. ft.) of office space packed with 25,000-plus Eurocrats to back up its "Capital of Europe" tag. Entire neighborhoods full of character were swept away to make room for them, causing resentment among local residents.

To tour the heartland of European Union governance, take the Métro to Schuman station. If you wish to view that exotic species, the European civil servant, in its native habitat, take the tour Monday to Friday as the district is dead on the weekend.

Your first sight is the X-shaped Palais de Berlaymont, the commission's former headquarters at Rond-Point Schuman. Across rue de la Loi, the Council of Ministers headquarters, the Consilium, is instantly recognizable

for its facade's lavish complement of rose-colored granite blocks. On its far side, take a soothing stroll through Parc Léopold, an island of green tranquility at the heart of the Euro District. This little park is laid out above an ornamental lake and was originally conceived as a zoo and science park. The zoo didn't fly for long, but a cluster of scientific institutes dating from the late 19th and early 20th centuries still occupies part of the terrain. Among these is the **Museum des Sciences Naturelles (Museum of Natural Sciences).**

A walk through Parc Léopold brings you to the postmodern European Parliament and International Conference Center, an architectural odyssey in white marble and tinted glass. Take the passageway through the building's middle to place Luxembourg, an old square that looks lost and forlorn in comparison to its powerful new neighbors.

de Belgique. Located in the Hôtel Altenloh, a neoclassical mansion dating from 1779, the gallery is connected by underground passageway to the main building of the Musées Royaux next door. The collection holds more than 150 works of Magritte's eccentric, surreal works and covers all periods of his oeuvre, exhibiting musical scores and photos of his private life as well as signature works such as his series "The Dominion of Light" and "The Domain of Arnheim."

Place Royale. 📞 **02/508-3211.** www.musee-magritte-museum.be. Admission 8€ adults, 6€ seniors and students, 2€ ages 6–26; combination ticket with all four museums 13€ adults, 9€ seniors and students, 3€ ages 6–26; free all ages 1st Wed afternoon each month.

Musées Royaux des Beaux-Arts de Belgique (Royal Fine Arts Museums of Belgium) ★★★ MUSEUM This humungous behemoth dedicated to art is undergoing drastic changes (slated to be completed by mid-2015), so be prepared for long waits, confusing signage, and short-tempered staff. Now comprising six different collections, the Royal Fine Arts Museums have four galleries under one roof here in the place Royale. These consist of the **Musée Old Masters, Musée Modern,** and **Musée Fin-de-Siècle,** which are connected by underground passageway to the **Musée Magritte.** The other two are **Musée Meunier,** celebrating the work of sculptor Constantin Meunier (rue de l'Abbaye 59) and the **Musée Wiertz,** displaying the works of Belgium's foremost Romantic artists (rue Vatier 62).

There is more than enough in place Royale to keep art lovers happy, probably for days. The beautiful, spacious galleries show off Belgian works from the 14th-century

Flemish Primitives to 20th-century Surrealists. In the Old Masters section are Hans Memling portraits from the late 15th century; works by Hieronymus Bosch; Lucas Cranach's sublime "Adam and Eve," and Pieter Brueghel the Elder's bizarre works, including "Adoration of the Magi" and "Fall of Icarus," in Room 68.

Next door, in a circular building leading off the main entrance, the modern art section is being re-organized at press time, so a tiny percentage of the collection's treasures are on revolving display: You may see Van Gogh, Delvaux, Matisse, or Dalí.

In the same complex, but with a different entrance, the **Musée Fin-de-Siècle** highlights the works of late 19th-century Belgian favorite James Ensor, along with six rooms full of beautiful Art Nouveau furniture. (For the **Musée Magritte,** see above.)

In fast-track mode, you could see the Brueghel, Rubens, and Magritte collections in just about an hour. However, to do this fantastic, comprehensive art museum any kind of justice at all, you'll need to set aside between 3 and 4 hours, although most serious art lovers won't be dragged out before a full day has passed.

Place Royale 1–3. ℂ **02/508-3211.** www.fine-arts-museum.be. Admission per museum 8€ adults, 6€ seniors and students, 2€ ages 6–26; combination ticket with all four museums 13€ adults, 9€ seniors and students, 3€ ages 6–26; free all ages 1st Wed afternoon each month. Tues–Sun 10am–5pm. Closed Jan 1, May 1, Nov 1, Nov 11, and Dec 25.

Parc du Cinquantenaire

Designed to celebrate the half-centenary of Belgium's 1830 independence, the **Cinquantenaire (Golden Jubilee) Park** was a work in progress from the 1870s until well into the 20th century. Extensive gardens surround the triumphal Arc du Cinquantenaire, topped by a bronze chariot representing "Brabant Raising the National Flag" and flanked by colonnaded pavilions housing three fine museums; plan to spend the day here to really do all three justice. Autoworld and the Royal Museum of the Armed Forces and Military History face each other across the gardens; the Musée du Cinquantenaire is tucked away around the back of Autoworld.

Autoworld ★★ MUSEUM   Even if you're not a petrol head, this display of over 500 historic cars is fascinating, as it so clearly defines the development of the combustion engine and its importance in modern-day culture. The chronological collection starts with motorized tricycles from 1899 and moves on through the first petrol-engine car designed by Carl Benz in 1886, to bright-yellow racing Bugattis from 1911 and majestic 1922 Bentleys. Performance cars on display from recent years include Ferraris and Fernando Alonso's F1 Renault. The new permanent exhibition "Belgium in Autoworld" looks at the relationship of Belgium with the car—who knew that this little country was one of the world's leading car manufacturers in the years leading up to World War I?

Parc du Cinquantenaire 11. ℂ **02/736-4165.** www.autoworld.be. Admission 9€ adults, 7€ seniors and students, 3€ children 6–12, free for children 5 and under. Apr–Sept daily 10am–6pm; Oct–Mar Tues–Fri 10am–5pm, Sat–Sun 10am–6pm. Closed Jan 1 and Dec 25.

Musée du Cinquantenaire ★★★ MUSEUM   Somewhat Tardis-like, the Cinquantenaire appears quite manageable when viewed from its neo-classical exterior but once inside, the task of getting around in under 4 hours seems quite impossible. This place is vast, with a collection of millions of decorative arts finds from across the world and all periods. The exhibits are divided into four themes (Antiquity, Archaeology, European, non-European) and romp comprehensively through prehistory and ancient civilizations in Egypt, Greece, Rome, Asia Minor, and the Far East. Fascinating, colorful ornamental *objets d'arts* are elegantly displayed in glass cabinets. In fact,

Scores of comic-strip murals have been scattered around Brussels since the city began to celebrate Belgium's passionate love affair with *bande-dessinée* (comic-strip art) in 1993. Among the cartoon characters honored on the sides of houses and stores are **Tintin** (rue de l'Etuve 37), running down a fire escape together with Captain Haddock and Snowy; **Lucky Luke** (rue de la Buanderie 21), as always drawing his Colt faster than his shadow; and just along the street, **Asterix and Obelix** (rue de la Buanderie 33), leading a charge of the gallant Gauls against the rotten Romans.

For a general overview of the history of Belgian comic books, the **Centre**

Belge de la Bande Dessinée (see above) is a good starting point. If you want to see as many of these street murals as possible, then be warned that a lot of them are in off-the-beaten-track districts. Getting there will give you an idea of what Brussels looks like away from its tourist heartlands—not greatly inspiring, it must be said—at the cost of a great deal of Métro-, tram-, and bus-hopping, and considerable shoe leather. The Brussels tourist office has come up with several **self-guided tours** that avoid the gloomier of city backstreets; visit www.visitbelgium.com/?page= comic-strip-walk-in-brussels.

you'll find anything and everything here, from mummies to Easter Island statues to Art Nouveau glassware.

If you have limited time, head for the fascinating Indonesian collection to admire ivory Balinese shadow puppets and wooden models of traditional houses on stilts; the Chinese exhibit for hand-carved, wooden, red-and-gold day beds and delicate, hand-painted silk screens; and the Native American displays to discover feathered head-dresses and beaded leather jackets. At the time of writing, 7 galleries were closed for a much-needed renovation, but don't let that put you off a visit (renovations should be completed in 2015). There's still more than enough here to see in one shot.

Parc du Cinquantenaire 10. © **02/741-7211.** www.kmkg-mrah.be. Admission 5€ adults, 4€ seniors and students, 1.50€ children 5–17, free for children 4 and under. Free admission first Wed afternoon each month. Tues–Fri 9:30am–5pm, Sat–Sun 10am–5pm. Closed Jan 1, May 1, Nov 1, Nov 11, and Dec 25.

Musée Royal de l'Armée et d'Histoire Militaire (Royal Museum of the Armed Forces and Military History) ★★ MUSEUM With more than enough to entertain for 3 or 4 hours, this vast museum is stuffed with a colorful, chaotic hoard of weaponry, uniforms, vehicles, and airplanes spanning a millennia of military history and while it's a joy to explore, it's very confusing to navigate. Attempts have been made to streamline the exhibitions and there are now several themed galleries examining aspects of wars from medieval times right down to World War II (several closed at press time). Still, the most impressive section of the museum is the massive, glass-walled hangar-style atrium containing more than 100 military planes and heli-copters from Spitfires, Hurricanes, and Junkers to Soviet MiGs and French Mirages. The European Forum of Contemporary Conflicts takes a salutary look at current wars being fought by European powers across the globe.

Parc du Cinquantenaire 3. © **02/737-7811.** www.klm-mra.be. Free admission. Tues–Sun 9am–5pm. Closed Jan 1, May 1, Nov 1, and Dec 25.

Suburbs

Musée Bruxellois de la Gueuze (Museum of Gueuze Brewing) ★★
BREWERY/MUSEUM The last lambic brewery still operating in Brussels is a family-run affair where organic lambic beers have been produced since 1900. This boutique brewery has built a thriving business in its quaintly old-fashioned premises, running self-guided tours of the traditional cooperage and brewing rooms, offering a bistro menu in the **Cantillon restaurant,** and selling T-shirts alongside its 10 brews.

Highly prized by beer buffs among these are Rosé de Gambrinus, flavored with raspberries, and the top-quality Grand Cru Bruocsella, which is matured for 3 years in oak casks. Despite the best attempts of one (now universally known) shockingly rude member of the staff, a visit here is both informative and entertaining. The location in Anderlecht is not great, however. Be prepared for some of the rougher elements of Brussels life to be on show.

Rue Gheude 56. ℰ **02/521-4928.** www.cantillon.be. Admission 7€. Mon–Fri 9am–5pm, Sat 10am–5pm. Closed Jan 1, May 1, Nov 11, and Dec 25.

Brews from Brussels

Brussels is known for its *lambic* beers, which use naturally occurring yeast for fermentation, are often flavored with fruit, and come in bottles with champagne-type corks. They're almost akin to sweet sparkling wine. Try raspberry-flavored *framboise* or cherry-flavored *kriek.* If you prefer something less sweet, order *Gueuze,* a blend of young and aged lambic beers.

Musée David et Alice van Buuren ★★ MUSEUM One of the most unusual museums in Brussels, the unsung Van Buuren is set in a stylish Art Deco house built in 1928 and surrounded by romantic gardens in the salubrious suburb of Uccle. It was the property of wealthy banker David Van Buuren, who designed and commissioned his compact residence as a monument to Art Deco style and filled it with Art Deco treasures. Angular wooden paneling covers the walls and staircase, complimented by jewel-colored light fittings, fine Aubusson carpets, and a preparatory sketch for "The Fall of Icarus" by Pieter Brueghel the Elder (p. 167). The piano in the sitting room once belonged to Eric Satie. Upstairs, Van Buuren's office contains a handsome desk inlaid with shark skin, and the cabinets were crammed with valuable sketches from the

Understanding Brussels Today

eB! ★★★ is the latest attraction to join the museums clustered together around the place Royale (see above). It concentrates on providing a lively and informative snapshot of the city today—warts and all—and gets its message across loud and clear about contentious issues such as multicultural tensions; the Flemish/Dutch/French language dichotomy; urban development; and the need for greater green measures to conserve the city's limited energy resources. If all this sounds dull, it's not. The exhibitions come alive through interactive media, big screens and film, impressive color photography, and plenty of personal accounts. For a précis of where Brussels is today, this exhibition is a great place to start. You'll find it at BIP, place Royale 2–4 (ℰ **02/563-6399;** www.biponline.be). It's open daily 10am to 6pm, and best of all, it's free.

Many of Brussels's Métro stations have been decorated with works of art—painting, sculpture, mosaic, or installation—by leading Belgian modern artists. Taken together, they form an underground museum that you can tour for the price of a Métro ticket. Among the more interesting Métro stations are **Bourse,** in the center city, which has a mural of old Brussels trams by the surrealist painter Paul Delvaux; **Stockel,** the eastern terminus of line 1B, where the walls are decorated with strips from the comic series "Tintin" by local hero Hergé; and **Horta,** south of Gare du Midi, which pays homage to Brussels's Art Nouveau architect Victor Horta with wrought iron and stained-glass windows from Horta's seminal Maison du Peuple, which was demolished in the 1960s. STIB, which runs Brussels's public-transport system, have put together a leaflet on the underground art galleries; download it at **www.stib-mivb.be**.

likes of Van Gogh and Ensor (a handful of these were stolen in 2013). The gardens were also laid out in Art Deco style by Jules Buyssens and are best seen in spring, when they blaze with color. Undulating lawns lined with trees form the perfect setting for changing sculpture exhibitions.

Avenue Léo Errera 41. ⓒ **02/343-4851.** www.museumvanbuuren.be. Admission to garden and museum 10€ adults, 8€ seniors, 5€ students, free for children 11 and under; garden only 5€ adults, 4€ seniors, 2.50€ students, free for children 11 and under. Wed–Mon 2–5:30pm. Closed Jan 1 and Dec 25.

Musée Horta (Horta Museum) ★ MUSEUM   Given its short opening hours and extreme popularity, arranging a visit to this museum in Saint-Gilles is virtually a military campaign. To minimize waiting time outside in the huge lines that always seem to be there, aim to be standing outside at least 30 minutes before the doors open. However, even if you have to wait a while to gain entrance, once you're inside it's all worth it. Brussels considers itself the capital of Art Nouveau, the medley of related art styles that exploded across the Western world at the end of the 19th century. Drawing on exotic sources, including Celtic, Viking, Asian, and Islamic art, to make fine, sinewy architectural shapes, Art Nouveau was a hit from Paris to Prague. If Brussels is its capital, then Victor Horta is certainly its king, and his home and adjoining studio are a monument to his inspired creative vision. Every door, every doorknob, every piece of stained glass, every piece of furniture is designed along curvy, flowing, sinuous lines that could not contrast more with the straight angles and corners of the later Art Deco movement. The wrought-iron central staircase is reminiscent of that other great Art Nouveau master, Gaudí, as it flows and undulates upwards

Rue Américaine 25. ⓒ **02/543-0490.** www.hortamuseum.be. Admission 8€ adults, 4€ seniors and students, 2.50€ children 5–18, free for children 4 and under. Tues–Sun 2–5:30pm. Closed Jan 1, Ascension Day, July 21, Aug 15, Nov 11, and Dec 25.

Musée René Magritte MUSEUM   The famous Belgian surrealist artist René Magritte lived and worked in a meager town house in suburban Jette in northwest Brussels between 1930 to 1954. Maintained in its original state as a private museum, the house provides a rather slight glimpse at Magritte's career. You have to knock to gain entrance, and of the 19 rooms on view, most are protected with glass screens so you can only peer myopically into the detritus of his life, although you do get to see the dining room-cum-studio where he painted many of his fantastical masterpieces. On the first and second floors are a few original sketches, Magritte's easel and his trademark bowler hat, some letters and photographs, and a very protective chatelaine of the museum, who will trail your every move. Definitely one only for the ardent lover of Surrealism; everybody else is better off at the Musée Magritte in place Royale (p. 165). If you insist on going, take Métro 6 to Belgica.

Rue Esseghem 135. (*C*) **02/428-2626.** www.magrittemuseum.be. Admission 7.50€ adults, 6€ ages 9–22, free for children 8 and under. Wed–Sun 10am–6pm. Closed Jan 1 and Dec 25.

Organized Tours

BUS TOURS   Guided bus tours of Brussels last 2½ hours, operate throughout the year, and are available from **Brussels City Tours** ((*C*) **02/513-7744;** www.brussels-city-tours. com). The tours start at 30€ for adults, 28€ for seniors, and 15€ for children 17 and under. Reservations can be made through most hotels, and hotel pickup is often available.

CitySightseeing Brussels (www.city-sightseeing.com) offers the now-ubiquitous hop-on, hop-off circular tour of the city; with 2 lines servicing 22 stops at all major attractions, including Cinquantenaire (p. 167), Palais Royal (p. 164), and Atomium (see below). Prices start at 24€; departures vary from every 45 minutes in winter to every 15 minutes in July and August.

COACH TOURS   Viator ((*C*) **888/651-9785** in the U.S.; www.viator.com) offers a selection of guided tours around Brussels and also to Bruges, Antwerp, Ghent, and the Flanders battlefields.

WALKING TOURS   Brussels Walking Tours ((*C*) **02/495-320-362;** www.bravo discovery.com) operates a series of 9 themed walking tours, from Art Nouveau spotting to beer or chocolate tasting, discovering Jewish Brussels, or exploring the Marolles. They last around 2 hours and prices start at 8€. Meeting points vary according to tour, so check online for further details.

Sports & Outdoor Activities

BOWLING   The top bowling alley (with a laser-games facility, Q-Zar) is **Bowling Crosly,** boulevard de l'Empereur 36 ((*C*) **02/512-0874;** www.crosly.be).

HORSEBACK RIDING   In the south of Brussels, both the Bois de la Cambre and the Forêt de Soignes are great places for riding. Contact **Centre Equestre de la Cambre,** chaussée de Waterloo 872 ((*C*) **02/375-3408**); and **Royal Etrier Belge,** champ du Vert Chasseur 19 ((*C*) **02/374-6344;** www.royaletrierbelge.be).

The Marolles on the Rise

The gritty, down-at-the-heels Marolles district, lying to the west of the Palace of Justice, is an intriguing place where the old Brussels dialect called *Brusseleir* can still be heard. The generally poor community is under constant threat of encroachment from neighboring, far wealthier areas—a process the Marolliens resent with a passion. Locals remain resolutely unimpressed by the burgeoning "Capital of Europe," despite evidence of gentrification along rues Blaes and Haute, where classy antiques and design stores have begun their style invasion, creeping in among the multiethnic **cafes**. A daily **flea market** is held between 7am and 2pm in place du Jeu de Balle, which is now well served with Ethiopian, Moroccon, Turkish, Spanish, French, and Belgian **bars**.

ICE-SKATING   There's ice-skating from September to May at **Poseidon,** avenue des Vaillants 4 (℃ **02/762-1633;** www.ijsbaanposeidon.be).

SOCCER   The top local soccer club is **RSC Anderlecht,** avenue Théo Verbeeck 2 (℃ **02/522-1539;** www.rsca.be). During Continental tournaments, crack European soccer squads can often be seen in action at the stadium in Anderlecht.

Especially for Kids

Brussels is fast-paced, traffic-fumed, and chaotic, and is not always conducive to making life easy for visiting families. However, it is the home of a peeing statue (p. 165) and also to Tintin and his little white dog, Snowy. Kids have great fun spotting the murals of the intrepid pair in the streets (p. 168) and will appreciate the cartoons and comic strips on display in the **Centre Belge de la Bande Dessinée** (p. 163). And let's not forget that Brussels is also the home of chocolate; most children will jump at the chance of a guided tour around the **Musée du Cacao et du Chocolat** (Rue de la Tête d'Or; ℃ **02/514-2048;** www.mucc.be) as much as they will adore gazing longingly through the windows of the classy confectioners (see below).

But to really give the kids a good time, head out to Bruparck, north of the city center, to visit the **Atomium ★**. There's nothing quite like this cluster of giant silvery orbs representing the atomic structure of an iron crystal enlarged 165 billion times, rising 102m (335 ft.) like a giant plaything of the gods that's fallen to earth. Constructed for the 1958 World's Fair, the Atomium is visible from pretty much all over Brussels and it's a fair bet that when you stand underneath this vast construction, you'll be suitably impressed. There may be something last-century about this paean of praise to the wonders of 1950s science and technology, but the panorama from the Atomium remains spectacular. An elevator shoots up the central column to the five spheres currently open to the public; three provide a permanent record of Expo 58 and the other two host temporary art and science exhibitions. The highest sphere has a glass roof, permitting 360-degree views towards Brussels, and on a clear day Antwerp's cathedral spire can be spotted on the horizon. The Atomium is located at Square de l'Atomium, Bruparck, Heysel (℃ **02/475-4775;** www.atomium.be). Admission is 11€ adults; 8€ seniors, students, and children 12 to 18; 6€ children 6 to 11; free for children 5 and under. Combined tickets with Mini-Europe are available at 24€ for adults, 21€ seniors, 16€ for children 11 and under, free children under 1.2m (4 ft.) when accompanied by parents. It's open daily 10am until 6pm.

An Adventure with Tintin

Head to Louvain-la-Neuve, 27km (17 miles) southeast of Brussels, to visit the **Musée Hergé ★**, rue du Labrador 26 (℃ **010/488-421;** www.museeherge. com), which opened in 2009 to celebrate the work of Tintin creator Georges Remi (1907–83), known to all as Hergé. The building itself is part of the attraction—a minimalist and boxlike gleaming, white affair with a massive image of Tintin emblazoned on one facade. It was designed by the French architect Christian de Portzamparc, and exhibits more than 800 original drawings of Tintin. The museum is open Tuesday to Friday 10:30am to 5:30pm, and weekends 10am to 6pm (closed Jan 1 and Dec 25). Admission is 9.50€ for adults, 7€ for students, 5€ for children ages 7 to 14, and free for children 6 and under.

Conveniently almost next door is **Mini-Europe** ★, which will intrigue kids and adults alike as they stroll around iconic landmarks from member states of the European Union, including London's Big Ben, Berlin's Brandenburg Gate, the Leaning Tower of Pisa, and Montmartre in Paris. As the E.U. expands, new models appear at Mini-Europe; the latest arrivals are St. Mark's Church from Croatia, and a diorama celebrating the succession of King Philippe to the Belgian throne on July 23, 2013. *Son et lumière* and firework spectaculars are held on Saturday evenings in July and August. Tickets can be combined with a visit to the Atomium (recommended) and the rather dilapidated, adjacent Océade theme park (not recommended). Mini-Europe is adjacent to the Atomium (*✆* **02/478-0550;** www.minieurope.com). Admission is 14€ adults, and seniors, 11€ children 11 and under, free for children under 1.2m (4 ft.) when accompanied by parents. See above for combined ticket prices with the Atomium. Opening hours are mid-March to June and September daily 9:30am to 6pm, July and August daily 9:30am to 8pm, October through mid-January daily 10am until 6pm, with an annual closure between mid-January and mid-March.

SHOPPING

Brussels is not a city where you'll find shopping bargains. It's expensive—certainly as expensive as Paris, and more so than Amsterdam. As a general rule, the upper city around avenue Louise and Porte de Namur is more expensive than the lower city around rue Neuve and the center-city shopping galleries around La Monnaie and place de Brouckère. But that's not hard and fast; rue Haute in the upper city is currently inexpensive, although as more and more design and antiques stores open, this will cease to be the case. The Galeries Royales St-Hubert, in the lower city, are wildly expensive.

Shopping Areas

Rue Neuve, which starts at place de la Monnaie and extends north to place Rogier in the lower city, is a busy and popular area that's home to many boutiques and department stores, including the City 2 shopping complex. **Boulevard Anspach,** which runs from the Stock Exchange up to place de Brouckère, offers mid-range fashion boutiques and electronic-appliance stores, plus the **Anspach Center** mall.

Avenue Louise and **boulevard de Waterloo** in the upper city attract those in search of world-renowned, high-quality goods from Cartier, Burberry's, Louis Vuitton, and Valentino. The **place du Grand Sablon** is natural home of snooty antiques shops and expensive galleries, while trendsters hit edgy **rue Antoine Dansaert** for small, independent boutiques and contemporary designers.

Antiques & Art

Ma Maison de Papier ★   Owner Marie-Laurence Bernard is an enthusiast of vintage posters and sells only genuine pieces, all coming with a guarantee of authenticity. Her stock ranges from cutesy 1950s posters of cartoon animals and colorful travel posters used to advertise obscure destinations to more expensive 19th-century lithographs and even sheet music. Galerie de la Rue de Ruysbroeck 6. *✆* **02/512-2249.** www.mamaisondepapier.be.

Yves Macaux ★★   A specialist in Art Nouveau in the city that spawned the style, Yves Macaux's showrooms offer the finest in *objets d'art* from across Europe. Famed as a discerning dealer, his stock is always changing but the quality remains impeccable,

The Bruxellois know a thing or two about **chocolate.** So addictive are their confections that they should be sold with a government health warning. Just ask anyone who has ever bitten into one of those devilish little handmade pralines made by **Wittamer** (see below). You'll find some of the finest confections at **Mary** (see below); **Nihoul,** chaussée de Vleurgat 111 ($ 02/648-3796; www.nihoul.be); **Neuhaus** (see below); **Léonidas,** place du Grand Sablon 41 ($ 02/513-1466; www. leonidas.com); and . . . well, it's a long list. Many branches of the city's best chocolatiers are congregated at place du Grand Sablon and the Galeries Royales de St-Hubert.

Lace is another favorite that's widely available in the city, particularly around the Grand-Place. Purchase from **Maison Antoine** (Grand-Place 26; $ 02/512-4859) or **Manufacture Belge de Dentelle** (p. 177).

For local beers such as *gueuze, kriek,* and *faro*—among the 450 or so different Belgian beers—head for the **Musée Bruxellois de la Gueuze** (p. 169) or **Beer Mania** (see below). Both can ship beer overseas. Also check out the aisles in local supermarkets, where you'll find a great choice of beers at decent prices, too.

from pairs of hanging lamps by Koloman Moser to silver trays by master craftsman Henry van de Velde. Even if you can't afford to buy here, go visit the gallery for a peerless introduction to the delights of Art Nouveau. Rue des Champs Elysées 19. $ 02/502-3116. www.secessions.com.

Antiques Market

Place du Grand Sablon ★★★ The real deal, with stalls displaying high-end antiques from across northern Europe and an equally smart clientele who come to rifle through the oil paintings, sculptures, silverware, ceramics, and quality jewelry for the find of a lifetime. This is definitely not the place to show off your bargaining skills, as prices are generally deemed to be fair. The market opens Saturday 9am to 6pm, and again Sunday 9am to 2pm. Place du Grand Sablon.

Beer

Beer Mania ★★ With more than 400 beers on sale, from *kriek* to *trippel* brewed in the smallest micro-breweries to the big names like the Trappist beer Chimay, this place is heaven for beef buffs. And what's even better is that you can taste before you buy, so push the boat out and try something new, like Bush Ambrée, made at the Dubuisson Brewery in Hainaut—and at 12 percent, reputedly the strongest beer in Europe. Chaussée de Wavre 174. $ 02/512-1788. www.beermania.be.

Books & Multimedia

FNAC ★ This massive and reasonably priced French chain has spread through the main cities of Europe like a rash and carries English-language travel books, novels, DVDs, phone and camera accessories, computer games, and tablets. The branch in the giant **City2** multistory mall on Brussels's main shopping drag is always rammed with ex-pat folks looking for bargains. Concert tickets are also sold here. Rue Neuve. $ 02/275-1111. www.fnac.com.

Chocolate

Mary ★★   Established in 1919 by one of the very few female chocolatiers in Belgium, Mary Delluc, this traditional purveyor of pralines started life as a tea room. It has a delightfully old-fashioned air reflected in the sublime taste of its gourmet chocolates and in its pretty packaging, which has remained largely unchanged since the 1920s. From its small beginnings in rue Royal, the Mary empire has now spread as far afield as South Africa and Kazakhstan. Rue Royal 73. ℂ **02/217-4500.** www.marychoc.com.

Neuhaus ★★   Arguably the best of the Belgian chocolatier chains, Neuhaus is now a world-renowned name for its dangerously delicious handmade chocolates. There are now an extraordinary 20 stores in Brussels but this is the most central; make your selection from the range of cream-filled goodies and have them packed up to surprise the folks back home. Galerie de la Reine 25–27. ℂ **02/512-6359.** www.neuhaus.be.

Wittamer ★★★   Wittamer makes some of the best handmade pralines in the world, and even supplies them to the Belgian Royal Family. Its rolls, breads, pastries, and cakes have been winning fans since this store opened in 1910, and its hot pink wrapping paper is as well known in Belgium as the duck-egg-blue of Tiffany. Treats on offer include a huge variety of marzipan flavors in all different shapes, macaroons in rainbow colors, *marron glacés,* and homemade ice cream. Place du Grand Sablon 12. ℂ **02/512-3742.** www.wittamer.com.

Fashion

Annemie Verbeke ★★   A young designer from Ypres taking Brussels by storm, Annemie produces simple statement dresses, loose-fitting coats, and neatly fitted short jackets in a bright color palette of acidy yellows and oranges. As well as her flagship store in cool rue Antoine Dansaert, she has an outpost in Antwerp. Rue Antoine Dansaert 64. ℂ **02/511-2171.** www.annemieverbeke.be.

Delvaux ★★   Founded in 1829, Delvaux is justifiably regarded as one of the finest leather-and-accessory companies in Europe; demand for its high-brand luxury means that the Galeries Royales St-Hubert outpost of this Belgian design company do a roaring trade in some of the priciest handbags in the city. Designs are simple and boxy and will take fashionistas happily from work to weekend. Galerie de la Reine 31. ℂ **02/512-7198.** www.delvaux.com.

Idiz Bogam ★★★   For Brussels's most sought-after vintage fashions, hotfoot it down to the city's trendiest street. The sleek interior of Idiz Bogam is an artwork in itself, a far cry from the usual scrimmage of second-hand thrift stores. Expect a huge array of pre-loved clothes and accessories, all laid out in swathes of complimentary colors. Prices are not as cheap as they were. Rue Antoine Dansaert 76. ℂ **02/412-1032.**

Hatshoe ★★   This too-cool-for-school boutique sells luxurious shoes and boots to stylish women, all made by big-name designers such as Flemish designers Dries van Noten and Ellen Verbeek as well as international names such as Chloé, Jil Sander, and the

> ### Brussels Shop Opening Hours
>
> Stores normally open from 9 or 10am to 6pm Monday to Saturday. On Friday evening, many center-city stores stay open until 8 or 9pm. Most stores close on Sunday, except the tourist-orientated ones around the Grand-Place, and out of the center even the supermarkets operate limited Sunday opening hours.

Spanish great Balenciaga. There's also a small selection of menswear. Rue Antoine Dansaert 89. 🕿 **02/512-4152.** www.hatshoe.be.

Flea Market

Vieux Marché ★★★ The daily market on a large piazza in once-sleazy Marolles is a joy to rummage around; it has an eccentric bunch of stallholders selling an equally eccentric range of items from vintage clothes to knock-off watches. Those in the know go on Thursday, when there may be a sprinkling of antiques to be unearthed. Bargaining is sometimes acceptable, but play it by ear before diving in with insulting offers. The market's open daily 7am until 2pm (till 3pm weekends). Place du Jeu de Balle.

Flowers

Daniël Ost ★ The most exquisite flower shop in Brussels has as its backdrop an equally beautiful Art Nouveau location. Daniël Ost's wildly creative designs are heavily influenced by Japanese flower-arranging principles and are the perfect gift for the hostess if you are invited to supper in Brussels. Rue Royale 13. 🕿 **02/217-2917.** www.danielost.be.

Food & Wine

Maison Dandoy ★★ Founded in 1829, Dandoy is still *the* place for sweet-toothed treats after nearly 2 centuries. Sample the traditional Belgian house specialties: spicy cinnamon and brown-sugar *speculoos* cookies, still baked traditionally in wooden molds, or blow off the diet and choose organic ice cream in an array of flavors, crispy waffles coated with jam and cream, or gingerbread made to an ancient recipe with honey. Rue au Beurre 31. 🕿 **02/511-0326.** www.biscuiteriedandoy.be.

La Septième Tasse ★★ Everybody's first port of call for teas in all guises, this cluttered little Bruxellois institution has a lengthy menu to sample. Play safe with Earl Grey or Lapsang Souchong, or have your own brew blended from hundreds of aromatic choices. The shop also has committed, knowledgeable tea masters who are happy to share their knowledge of teas and make recommendations to customers—no mean feat in Brussels stores when service can verge on the brusque. Rue du Bailli 37. 🕿 **02/647-1971.** www.7etasse.com.

Gifts

Eurotempo ★ There's something a little cynical about selling E.U.-related souvenirs in the home of the European Community, but boy, they sell like hot cakes. Considering the current beleaguered state of political affairs in Europe, it is perhaps surprising that Eurotempo is still thriving; it's one of the most surprising marketing phenomena of recent years and its popularity is based solely on its ability to flog the European Union's logo—that famous blue flag with a circle of 12 stars—superimposed on umbrellas, T-shirts, aprons, golf balls, scarves, hats, knives, towels—you name it. But do you really want it? Rue du Marché aux Herbes 84. 🕿 **02/502-3747.** www.eurotempo.com.

Kids

The Grasshopper ★★ Despite its touristy location steps away from the Grand-Place, this is a lovely warren of a shop behind an elaborate Art Nouveau facade. With several floors, Grasshopper sells toys for kids of all ages, from building bricks for babies to cuddly stuffed animals and traditional wooden train sets to board games. There's a small section upstairs where you'll find English-language books for children too. Rue Marché aux Herbes 39-43. 🕿 **02/511-9622.** www.thegrasshoppertoys.be.

One of Europe's oldest shopping malls consists of the three interconnected, glass-roofed arcades of the **Galeries Royales St-Hubert** (www.galeries-saint-hubert.com). Constructed in Italian neo-Renaissance style and opened in 1847, architect Pierre Cluysenaer's elegant galleries are light and airy, hosting top-end boutiques Delvaux (see above), Oriande, Manufacture Belge des Dentelles (see below), Longchamp, numerous chocolate shops (Godiva, Neuhaus, Léonidas), sidewalk cafes, and street musicians playing classical music. The Galerie du Roi, Galerie de la Reine, and Galerie des Princes were the forerunners of city malls like Burlington Arcade in London, and lie just north of the Grand-Place, between rue du Marché aux Herbes and rue d'Arenberg.

Lace

F Rubbrecht ★   The best of several lace-selling stores in pole position to attract the hordes of tourists flocking through the Grand-Place, this high-end store has operated since 1957 and sells, along with the usual fare of ornate handmade bread baskets, bookmarks, and table napkins, a line of wedding veils and even garters for the bride. Christening gowns, bonnets, and minute lace shoes really have the cuteness factor. Grand-Place 23. ✆ **02/512-0218.** www.enjoylace.com.

Manufacture Belge de Dentelle ★   This oh-so-traditional store is based in the Galeries Royal St-Hubert and has been there since it opened in 1847; it is famous for only selling the very finest of handcrafted Belgian lace. Be prepared to dig deep into your pockets for the most delicate of tablecloths, net curtains, handkerchiefs, and intricate women's shirts. One of the sales assistants is usually busily showing off her lace making skills. Galerie de la Reine 6–8. ✆ **02/511-4477.** www.mbd.be.

ENTERTAINMENT & NIGHTLIFE

The Performing Arts

OPERA & BALLET   An opera house in flamboyant baroque style, the **Théâtre Royal de la Monnaie ★★**, place de la Monnaie (✆ **02/229-1211;** www.lamonnaie.be), is home to drama performances and chamber-music concerts as well as the **Opéra Royal de la Monnaie**—regarded as the best in the French-speaking world—and the **Orchestre Symphonique de la Monnaie.** The resident modern dance company, renowned Belgian choreographer Anne Teresa de Keersmaeker's group **Rosas ★★** (www.rosas.be), is noted for its innovative performances. The box office is at rue Léopold 4 and is open Tuesday to Friday noon to 6pm, Saturday 10am until 6pm. Ticket prices vary from 20€ to 350€ according to the event.

CLASSICAL MUSIC   BOZAR ★, rue Ravenstein 23 (✆ **02/507-8200;** www.bozar.be), aka the Palais des Beaux-Arts, is a lovely building designed by Victor Horta and now home to a mixed bag of cultural offerings from classical concerts by **Belgium's National Orchestra** to jazz and world music, movies, and a full program of plays. The box office is open Tuesday to Friday 11am to 7pm, with tickets running from 15€ to 100€, depending on the event.

In comparison with the "out-there" vibe of the Amsterdam gay world, the Brussels LGBT scene appears quite subdued, but there are several gay and lesbian bars along rue des Riches-Claires and rue du Marché au Charbon. **Macho Sauna,** rue du Marché au Charbon 106 (⌀ **02/513-5667;** www.machosauna.be), houses a gay sauna, pool, steam room, and cafe. It's open daily from noon to midnight.

Brussels Gay Pride takes place in May each year, a vibrant street party taking over the center of the city. For details of dates and schedules, click onto http://web.thepride.be.

For the inside slant on gay life in Brussels, stop by the gay and lesbian community center, **Tels Quels,** rue du Marché au Charbon 81 (⌀ **02/512-4587;** www.telsquels.be), open Monday to Friday 8:30am to 12:30pm and 2 to 7pm. On the same street there is a gay meeting room and cafe at **Rainbow House,** rue du Marché au Charbon 42 (⌀ **02/503-5990;** www.rainbowhouse. be). Both venues are run by volunteers.

THEATERS Brussels offers more than 30 theaters presenting performances in French, Dutch, and (occasionally) English. Foremost among these is the **Théâtre Royal du Parc ★★**, rue de la Loi 3 (⌀ **02/505-3040;** www.theatreduparc.be), a magnificent edifice occupying a corner of the Parc de Bruxelles, where classic and contemporary drama and comedies are performed. The **Théâtre National de la Communauté Française,** boulevard Emile Jacqmain 111–115 (⌀ **02/203-4145;** www.theatre national.be), offers avant-garde drama; and the **Théâtre Royal des Galeries,** Galerie du Roi 32 (⌀ **02/512-0407;** www.trg.be), is known for comedy and musicals. Bringing theater to the city in Flemish is the **Koninklijke Vlaamse Schouwburg,** quai aux Pierres de Taille 9 (⌀ **02/210-1112;** www.kvs.be), in a restored neo-Renaissance-style building dating from 1887.

Bars & Pubs

Now you're talking. Bars are where Brussels lives. It's hard to be disappointed, whether you pop into a neighborhood watering hole where a *chope* or *pintje* (a glass of beer) will set you back a mere 2.50€, or fork out several times as much in sleek, designer bars. In fact, even the expensive bars around Grand-Place are worth a visit for the scenery and grandeur of both architecture and service. Of the hundreds of bars in Brussels, the following all have their own distinct style and ambience.

A la Mort Subite ★★★ A Brussels institution, this place is always heaving with locals and tourists alike. Its strange name translates as "Sudden Death," which comes from a dice game the regulars used to play in days gone by. The decor is rudimentary, consisting of scruffy old wooden tables and chairs, stained-glass mirrors, and old photos. The real entertainment is watching the wait staff calmly going about their business in the great long drinking hall that's always packed to the rafters. Of the hundreds of bottled and tap beers sold here, the specialties are traditional Brussels brews: *gueuze, lambic, faro,* and *kriek,* and Trappist brews like Chimay. Rue Montagne aux Herbes Potagères 7. ⌀ **02/513-1318.** www.alamortsubite.com.

La Chaloupe d'Or ★ The grandest grand cafe in all Brussels occupies the majestic gilded facade of the former tailors' guild on the Grand-Place; don't waste your money eating here (you pay way over the norm for the location) but grab a table on the suntrap terrace in the early evening and watch the world go by. Service is hurried and prices are steeps but the views, the fizz by the glass, and the dozens of beer options all contribute to making this bustling bar a uniquely Belgian experience. Grand-Place 24–25. ⒸOZ/511-4161.

La Fleur en Papier Doré ★★   Located in a 16th-century town house and going strong since 1846, this pub always drew in poets, writers, and artists such as Magritte and the CoBrA guys (p. 99) like bees to a honey pot and it continues to do so with occasional poetry readings. This is a wonderfully atmospheric, cluttered old place, where customers gather round the entertaining *patron* for lively conversation and where all comers are welcome (yes, even tourists) as long as they show an interest in the *gueuze* and boutique beers on offer. Rue des Alexiens 55. Ⓒ **02/511-1659.** www.lafleur enpapierdore.be.

Le Cirio ★★   Just across the road from the Bourse (Stock Exchange), Le Cirio is often full of important-seeming gents who look like they've spent the day making millions. Inside it is a glorious whirl of Art Nouveau mirrors, brass bars, splendid chandeliers, and dark carved wood dating from 1886, where cheery waiters serve a curious concoction of half-wine, half-champagne in the same glass as well as a swathe of well-curated local beers. Rue de la Bourse 18. Ⓒ **02/512-1395.**

BRUGES

7

Graceful Bruges has drifted down the stream of time with all the self-possession of the swans that cruise its canals. To step into the old town is to be transported back to the Middle Ages, when Bruges (Brugge in Dutch) was among the wealthiest powerbases in Europe. Despite the city's turbulent past and two world wars fought around it, Bruges and its glorious monumental buildings have remained untouched by the passage of time; it's so picture-book perfect that in 2000, UNESCO awarded the entire city center World Cultural Heritage status.

Bruges is the capital town of West-Vlaanderen (West Flanders) province, and is the pride and joy of all Flanders. Medieval Gothic architecture is the real deal here, along with a layer of Romanesque; a touch of Renaissance, baroque, and rococo; a dab of neoclassical and neo-Gothic; and a smidgeon of Art Nouveau and Art Deco. But Gothic is what Bruges does best, in quantities that come near to numbing the senses—and likely would do so if it wasn't for the distraction of the city's contemporary animation. To what does it owe its Gothic glamor? In the 15th century, Bruges was a center for Hanseatic League trading, and with the growth of its wealth it acquired the rich heritage of civic buildings that you see today: guildhalls, exchanges, warehouses, and the residences of wealthy merchants.

ESSENTIALS

Arriving

BY PLANE

There are numerous daily flights to **Brussels Airport** (www.brussels airport.be) from 200 destinations across the world. Bruges is 107km (67 miles) from the airport, easily accessible by train, with one change at Brussels-Midi/Zuid. **Brussels-South-Charleroi Airport** (www.charleroi airport.com) is the domain of European budget flights; there are regular connections between the airport and Brussels-Midi/Zuid rail station for trains on to Bruges. See p. 232 for more details.

BY TRAIN

Two trains arrive in Bruges every hour from Brussels, four or five from Ghent, two from Antwerp, and up to three every hour from the ferry ports of Zeebrugge and Ostend (Oostende). The travel time is around 1 hour from Brussels, 25 minutes from Ghent, 1 hour and 20 minutes from Antwerp, and 15 minutes from both Ostend and Zeebrugge. Train information is available from **SNCB** (**Belgian Railways;** ✆ **02/528-28-28;** www. belgianrail.be).

From London, passengers can ride the **Eurostar high-speed trains** (www.eurostar.com) through the Eurotunnel and transfer for Bruges either at Lille in northern France or in Brussels. From Paris, **Thalys high-speed trains** (✆ **32-070/667-788,** 0.17€ per minute; www.thalys.com) go via Brussels to Bruges; on the slower and cheaper international trains, you transfer in Brussels. From Amsterdam, go via Brussels-Midi on the Thalys service.

Although the city is called Bruges in both English and French, look out for its Flemish name, BRUGGE, written on the station name boards. The station is on Stationsplein, 1.5km (1 mile) south of the center of town, a 20-minute walk or a short taxi or bus ride—choose any bus labeled CENTRUM and get out at the Markt to be in the center of the action.

BY BUS

Buses are less useful than trains for getting to Bruges, although there is frequent service from Zeebrugge and Ostend, and other Belgian seacoast resorts. The Bruges bus station adjoins the rail station. Schedule and fare information is available from **De Lijn** (✆ **070/220-200;** www.delijn.be/en).

Eurolines (www.eurolines.co.uk) operates a cheap daily bus service to Bruges from London, Amsterdam, Paris, Cologne, and other cities around Europe.

BY CAR

Bruges is 96km (60 miles) northwest of Brussels on the E40/A10; 50km (30 miles) northwest of Ghent on the E40/A10; 107km (66 miles) west of Antwerp on either the E17/A14 and E40/A10, or the E34, which bypasses Ghent; 18km (11 miles) south of the ferry port of Zeebrugge on E403 and N371; and 30km (19 miles) southeast of Ostend on E40/A10. From the Eurotunnel and Calais in France take E40/A16 east to Bruges.

Visitor Information

TOURIST OFFICES   There are three tourist offices in Bruges; the most central is the biggest and it's at the Historium in Markt. Opening hours are daily 10am to 5pm and it's always crowded. A second branch is at the Concertgebouw, 't Zand 34, inside the city's Concert Hall, about midway between the train station and the heart of town; it is open Monday through Saturday 10 to 5pm; Sunday and public holidays 10am to 2pm. The third information center is at the station itself and is open Monday to Friday 10am to 5pm, Saturday and Sunday 10am to 2pm. Call ✆ **050/444-646** or visit www.brugge.be.

Brugge City Card

For the avid museum-goer, the money-saving Brugge City Card is available from all the tourist offices, with the most convenient being at the Historium in Markt (see above). You get free entry to 27 museums, plus discounted entrance to several others; a free canal trip (p. 199); a trip up the Belfort (p. 192); discounts on theater tickets (p. 201) and bike hire (p. 183); and the chance to buy 3 days of transport on DeLijn buses (see above) for 6€. All this is priced at 40€ for a 48-hour pass, and 45€ for 72 hours. You can also order the Brugge City Card ahead of time at **www.bruggecitycard.be.**

events IN BRUGES

One of the most popular and colorful folklore events in Belgium is Bruges's **Heilig-Bloedprocessie (Procession of the Holy Blood)** ★, which dates back to at least 1291 and takes place every year on Ascension Day (fifth Thurs after Easter). During the procession, the bishop of Bruges proceeds through the city streets carrying the golden shrine containing the Relic of the Holy Blood (p. 39). Residents wearing Burgundian-era and biblical costumes follow the relic, acting out biblical and historical scenes along the way. The procession will take place on Thursday, May 15, 2015, and Thursday, May 5, 2016.

Every 5 years, the canals of Bruges are the subject and location of the **Reiefeest (Canal Festival)** ★★. This multi-day evening event takes place on 6 nonconsecutive days in August and is a combination of historical tableaux, dancing, open-air concerts, and lots of eating and drinking. The next Reiefeest is in 2018. (© **050/444-646;** www.brugge.be).

The **Praalstoet van de Gouden Boom (Pageant of the Golden Tree)** ★★★ celebrates the 1468 marriage of Charles the Bold, Duke of Burgundy, to Margaret of York with street processions in medieval costume, jousts, and a ceremonial recreation of the entry of Margaret into Bruges. It takes place every 5 years in the second half of August; the next one will be in 2017. (www.goudenboomstoet.be).

City Layout

Bruges is a circular tangle of medieval streets surrounded by canals and moats; the monumental squares of the Markt and the Burg lie fairly centrally, adjoined by a labyrinth of alleyways and dramatic, imposing buildings. The city's major attractions fan out from there, with many lying to the southwest and another pocket to the northwest.

Outside the canals are the suburban residential neighborhoods—they were formerly separate *gemeenten* (districts) with their own local government and not part of Bruges at all—where most residents have their homes, although of the 120,000 people who live in the city, around 20,000 actually live and work in the ancient center.

Getting Around

The gorgeous center of Bruges is compact and filled with cobbled pedestrians-only streets, which makes walking the best way to get around. Just don't go out for a day's sightseeing wearing kitten heels; those charming cobblestones can be really hard on your feet.

By Bus

Most city and regional buses are operated by **De Lijn** (© **070/22-02-00;** www.delijn.be/en) and depart from the bus station next to the train station on Stationsplein, or from a secondary station at 't Zand near the Concertgebouw (p. 201), and many buses stop at the Markt in the Old Town. Purchase your ticket from a De Lijn sales point or automatic ticket machine before boarding and you'll pay less than buying tickets on the bus. An *enkele rit* (one-way) ticket costs 1.30€ in advance, or 2€ on the bus for two zones, and 2€/3€ for three or more zones. A *dagkaart* (day pass), valid for the entire city network, costs 5€/7€ for 1 day; 10€/12€ for 3 days; and 15€/18€ for 5 days. A 1-day pass for children 6 to 11 is 3€/4.50€ and children 5 and under ride free.

By Bicycle

Cycling is a terrific way to get around Bruges. Unlike most Belgian cities, it has made cyclists privileged road users so they can travel in both directions on some—but not all—of the narrow, one-way streets in the center city. Others are one-way only and you'll be fined if you're caught riding against the traffic flow so keep a close eye on the street signs. Ride with caution, because the streets are filled with throngs of tourists likely to step out in front of you at any minute, but apart from that, the streets are gloriously traffic free and safe for families with older children to navigate by bicycle.

There are eight bike-rental points in the city, from **Fietspunt Station** on Stationsplein (✆ **050/396-826**) to **B-Bike Concertgebouw** (✆ **0479/971-280**) near the tourist office (p. 181) on 't Zand. Prices start at around 4€ per hour, or 12€ for a full day. There's a discount with the Brugge City Card at some rental outfits. If you don't fancy pedaling, hire an electric bike from **Electric Scooters** (Gentpoortstraat 62, ✆ **050/000-000;** www.electric-scooters.be; see p. 199) costing 30€ for 8 hours.

By Car

Don't drive. There's no point. Leave your car in your hotel parking garage; one of six **underground parking garages** in the center (expect to pay 9€ per day); one of four cheap **park-and-ride lots** next to the train station, which charge around 3.50€ per day; or a **free parking zone** outside the city center. It's a short walk into the heart of the Old Town from any of the parking lots. Parking rules are firmly enforced, and unlawfully parked cars will be ticketed, booted, or towed.

By Taxi

There are taxi stands at the Markt (✆ **050/334-444**) and outside the rail station on Stationsplein (✆ **050/384-660**).

[FastFACTS] BRUGES

ATMs The easiest and cheapest way to get cash overseas is through an ATM—the **CIRRUS** and **PLUS** networks span the globe. Although some debit and credit cards can be used overseas without incurring charges, most banks charge a fee for international withdrawals—check with your bank before you leave home, and find out your daily limit. There are ATMs all over Bruges.

Business Hours Stores usually open from 10am to 6 or 6:30pm Monday through Saturday. Some open Sunday afternoon, and those in the center of the city will open all day on Sunday in summer. Most museums close on Monday, but not the Stadhuis, Belfort, or churches. Everywhere is closed January 1, Ascension Day in the afternoon, and December 25.

Consulates Consulates and embassies are all in Brussels (p. 239).

Emergencies For any emergency (fire, police, ambulance), the number is ✆ **112** from any land line or cellphone. For 24-hour urgent but nonemergency medical services, call ✆ **078/151-590;** for dental services, call ✆ **0903/39969.** To report a theft, call ✆ **050/448-844.** Residents of E.U. countries must have a European Health Insurance Card (EHIC) to receive full health-care benefits in Belgium.

Internet Access Most hotels in Bruges offer Wi-Fi access for free. There's free, blanket broadband coverage of the city center and most cafes and restaurants also provide Wi-Fi hotspots.

Pharmacies Pharmacies are called *apotheek* in Flanders. Regular hours are Monday to Saturday 9am to 6pm (some close earlier Sat). Try **Steve Baert,** Wollestraat 7 (℃ **050/336-474**), just south of the Markt. All chemists have details of the nearby all-night and Sunday drug-dispensing pharmacies posted on the door. **Post Office** The main post office, BPost Markt, is at Markt 5 (℃ **050/331-411**); it is open Monday to Friday 9am to 6pm and Saturday 9am to 3pm.

WHERE TO STAY

If you love the idea of small, atmospheric accommodations, perhaps on the banks of a picturesque canal, then Bruges is the place for you. Don't even consider arriving without a room reservation because four million other visitors have had the same idea as you and they're all heading for Bruges. The city is Belgium's premier tourist destination and even though many visitors are day-trippers from Brussels, it's essential to make your hotel reservations at least 2 weeks in advance, especially at the height of summer. Having said that, if you do come into town without a place to stay, go straight to the tourist office in Markt (see above), which has a last-minute reservation service.

Parking in Bruges's tangle of narrow streets is difficult; if your hotel doesn't have a private garage, the city center holds six large public parking garages, all clearly marked on access roads and where charges will not exceed 9€ per 24 hours (see above). One of these will be within easy walking distance of your hotel, because everything is close by in tiny Bruges.

Expensive

Bonifacius ★★ An exclusive guesthouse tucked away behind the gabled facade of a glorious 16th-century mansion in the backstreets a step away from the Groeningemuseum (p. 196); staying at this little piece of heaven is like stepping back in time and into a world brightened with classy antiques and stylish decoration. With just a handful of rooms, all are beautifully appointed with top-quality, lavish furnishings and with spotless bathrooms with granite sinks and power showers. A decent breakfast is served in a suitably Gothic, tiled room overlooking the canal, and there's a suntrap roof terrace to bask on with a beer in the early evening. Need another reason to stay? The Michelin-starred **De Gouden Harynck** (www.goudenharynck.be) is just across the lane.

Groeninge 4, 8000 Bruges. ℃ **050/490-049.** www.bonifacius.be. 3 units. 300€–380€ double. Limited private parking 15€/day. Breakfast included in room rate. Breakfast room, concierge service, free Wi-Fi.

The Pand Hotel ★★★ On a cobbled side street just off Bruges's handsome central canal and within a stone's throw of the sightseeing action, the Pand is so tranquil and so genteel that tourists arrive and sink into a puffy cloud of comfort. It's housed in a higgledy-piggledy, elegantly restored 18th-century carriage house, with two refined lounges with leather sofas, dripping chandeliers, and a tiny bar in the luscious home-away-from-home public spaces. At press time, the suites were being done over in opulent Ralph Lauren designs; while all have Jacuzzi baths, some also have four-poster beds. Any day at the Pand gets off to a zippy start thanks to sterling cooked breakfasts—served in the leafy courtyard garden on summer mornings—produced from an old-fashioned range and a complementary glass of fizz that peps everybody up for a day's sightseeing. Although there is no restaurant, the eateries of Bruges are practically at the doorstep. This is just the place for a romantic weekend mini break. Bridget Jones would love it.

Pandreitje 16, 8000 Bruges. ☏ **050/340-666.** www.pandhotel.com. 26 units. 199€–265€ double, 249€–390€ suite. Parking 24€. Breakfast not included in room rate (22€). Bar, breakfast room, concierge, room service, free Wi-Fi.

Moderate

Hotel Jan Britto ★★   A fine example of the type of classy hotel that Bruges does so well, the Jan Britto has elegant period accommodations tucked behind an historic facade; in this case a listed 16th-century town house on a backwater side street. The elegant public rooms are decorated in period style, with vast stone fireplace and burgundy walls; they take on the atmosphere of a private club when full with chattering guests in the evening. Many rooms have vaulted ceilings and all are individually kitted out, perhaps with four-poster beds or gilded walls in heraldic style. While the suites are humongous—even by U.S. standards—this is also a good family-friendly option as several duplex rooms can accommodate up to four, and if you're traveling with a small wallet but you like your hotels big on charm, the Jan Britto has several budget rooms on offer, shoehorned into the old maids' quarters. Secreted away at the back of the hotel is a delightfully ornate Renaissance knot garden; it's just a charming spot to catch your breath after a day attacking the sights of Bruges.

Freren Fonteinstraat 1, 8000 Bruges. ☏ **050/330-601.** www.janbrito.com. 20 units. 99€–220€ double, 199€–380€ suite. Parking 10€/day. Breakfast included in room rate. Bar, breakfast room, concierge, free Wi-Fi.

Inexpensive

Hotel Egmond ★   The Egmond is located in a rambling mansion next to the romantic Minnewater (p. 198) and has just eight rooms, but the lucky few who stay here will find ample space, plenty of family-run attention to detail, and—best of all in this dynamic, crowded little city—peace and tranquility. Despite its quiet location, the Egmond is just a 5-minute walk from the Groeningemuseum (p. 196) and 10 minutes from Bruges's twin central squares of Burg and Markt. Looking like something that has just stepped out of a Vermeer painting, the interiors are all tiled floors, stone fireplaces, and wooden ceilings, and all of the simply furnished, traditional rooms feature views of the garden and the lake where swans float serenely about. There's an honesty bar where you help yourself to a drink and leave payment in the evening. Some rooms have air-conditioning but that's never a deal breaker in temperate northern Europe. Check in is before 6pm and if you're later than that, call the hotel for the entrance code.

Minnewater 15, 8000 Bruges. ☏ **050/341-445.** www.egmond.be. 8 units. 90€–140€ double. Rates include buffet breakfast. Parking 10€ (free when reservations are made online). Free Wi-Fi.

WHERE TO EAT & DRINK

The foodie choices in Bruges range from Michelin-starred to mobile stands in the Markt selling fries in paper cones, with just about everything between. There's no need to be snobbish by eschewing the "tourist" restaurants in the central squares; service is (almost) universally slick and charming, prices can be reasonable if you follow the "menu du jour," and all menus feature local specialties, which are, after all, what you certainly came to sample.

Before you commit to sitting down in a restaurant, check the prices on the menus that must—by law—be displayed outside. This will put a stop to any nasty surprises over the cost of the dishes on offer, but drinks are often a bone of contention in Bruges

Bruges Hotels & Restaurants

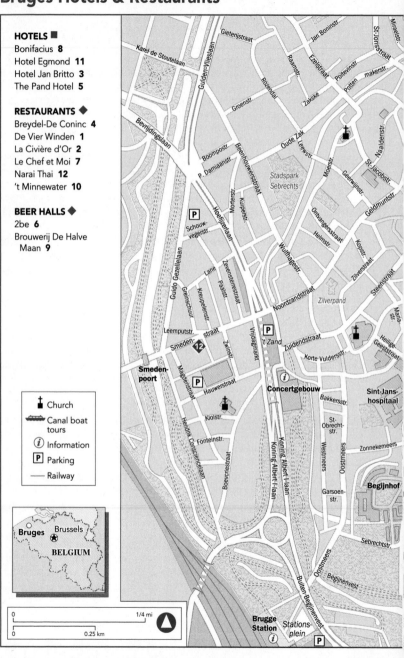

HOTELS ■
Bonifacius **8**
Hotel Egmond **11**
Hotel Jan Britto **3**
The Pand Hotel **5**

RESTAURANTS ◆
Breydel-De Coninc **4**
De Vier Winden **1**
La Cività d'Or **2**
Le Chef et Moi **7**
Narai Thai **12**
't Minnewater **10**

BEER HALLS ◆
2be **6**
Brouwerij De Halve
 Maan **9**

✝ Church
🚢 Canal boat
  tours
ⓘ Information
P Parking
— Railway

Bruges Brussels
★
BELGIUM

0   1/4 mi
0   0.25 km

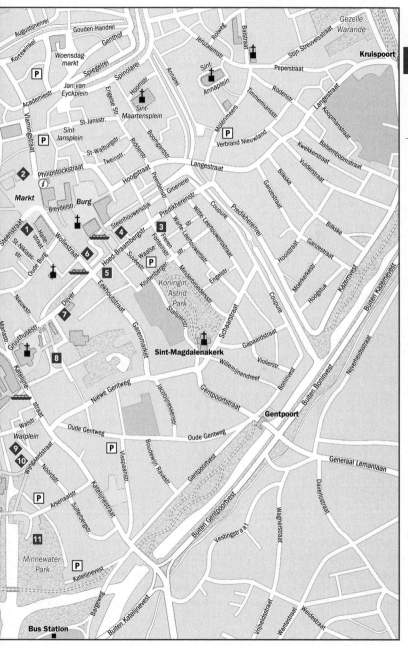

Kruispoort

Markt

Burg

Sint-Magdalenakerk

Gentpoort

Koningin Astrid Park

Minnewater Park

Bus Station

too; the prices often appear ramped up but unfortunately it's simply an expensive city. Beer and wine are better options than fizzy drinks, and remember, never, ever ask for tap water in a Flanders restaurant, unless it's for your dog. It's bottled water or bust.

Expensive

Breydel De Coninc ★★ SEAFOOD   With a reputation as one of the best seafood restaurants in Bruges, De Coninc is just off the Markt, with a surprisingly pared-down interior, simple wooden tables, and stripped pine floors. Luckily punters don't come for the ambience but instead for the platters of shellfish, eels, and lobsters prepared in countless different ways. Try a pail full of plain mussels or another favorite Flemish dish, *waterzooï* stew with fish and vegetables in a thick, creamy sauce. Non-fish eaters can choose from steak or steak, so this is perhaps not the number-one dining spot for vegetarians.

Breidelstraat 24. ℭ **050/339-746.** www.restaurant-breydel.be. Main courses 24€–46€. Thurs–Tues noon–3pm and 6–9:30pm.

Le Chef et Moi ★★ BELGIAN   This classic little gem is creeping up the foodie destination charts in Bruges and is definitely one for booking ahead of time, partly due to the high quality of the cuisine and partly due to the fact that it's tiny. Oil paintings cover the walls, chandeliers drip crystal, and the intimate dining room is lit by candlelight at night. Every sitting runs like clockwork, thanks to the hospitality and skills of owner-chef Stefaan Cardinael (one to watch in the future) and maître d' Caroline Saeys. Menu choice is limited to what is available seasonally and what Cardinael feels like cooking, but the results are always sublime; dishes might include scallops, skate wing, or milk-fed roast lamb. A fine wine list adds to the pleasurable experience.

Dijver 13. ℭ **050/396-011.** www.lechefetmoi.be. Fixed-price lunch 22€, dinner 35€. Tues–Sat noon–2pm and 6:30–10pm.

Moderate

Narai Thai ★ THAI   Always busy with tourists escaping the ubiquitous mussels and Flemish stew in favor of fragrant plates of crab cakes and grilled prawns with chili, this decent Thai is a little way out of the city center, just west of 'Zand and the Concertgebouw (p. 201). Proceedings kick off with a sharp, coriander-and-lemongrass-infused tom yam soup, followed by choices such as piles of beef fried in chili and basil or traditional Thai green chicken curry, both served with an abundance of noodles or rice. Set menus for sharing are good value and offer a variety of dishes from sea bass to fried beef with oyster sauce. For cowardly European palates, levels of spiciness are marked by each dish on the menu, happily even the hottest (awarded two chilis) are tasty and well short of volcanic.

Smedenstraat 43. ℭ **050/680-256.** www.naraithai.be. Main courses 14€–23€. Business lunch 23€. Sharing menu 40€ per couple. Daily noon–2:30pm and 6pm–midnight.

Inexpensive

De Vier Winden FLEMISH   It's not haute cuisine but this place has amazingly cheap meal deals considering its location right at the foot of the Belfort (p. 192) on the Markt. Order a liter of rosé wine, tuck into the brasserie staples such as *coq au vin,* mussels, seafood platters, and pasta, and finish off your feast with a crème brûlée. You'll have plenty of time to admire the sheer chutzpah of the waiters, who have obviously all been doing their job since time began, and manage to mix humor with a firm hand when directing skittish tourists around the menu.

Markt 9. ℭ **050/331-933.** Main courses 7€–18€, fixed-price menu 20€. Daily 10am–10:30pm.

La Civière d'Or ★★ BELGIAN   A triumvirate of restaurants all under a family-owned banner right opposite the handsome Belfort (p. 192), this is three venues rolled into one, offering brasserie, cafe, and fine-dining menus. It's one of the best options in the (sometimes) hit-or-miss row of restaurants on the Markt, in terms of price, ambience, and level of waiting-staff charm. Grab a table outside, order a bucket full of mussels, a plate of frites, a Belgian beer, and sit back to watch the action on the dramatic stage that is the Markt. After all, this place just celebrated its 67th anniversary so it must be doing something right. It's exactly what Bruges is all about.

Markt 33. ℭ **050/343-036.** www.lacivieredor.be. Main courses 10€–18€, fixed-price lunch 18€. Daily 10am–midnight.

't Minnewater ★ CREPERIE   The perfect family respite from the surging crowds in Bruges's swarming museum district, this is an easygoing crêperie that won't break the bank. Bribe fractious youngsters with a chocolate-smothered pancake or tuck into mussels and tasty carbonnade on the exceptionally reasonable fixed-price menu. In winter there's a welcoming log fire inside, and in summer there are lakeside views from the al fresco terrace out front. It's also a decent pit stop for afternoon tea if you hit a museum-fueled energy low in the middle of the afternoon.

Wijngaardstraat 28. ℭ **050/341-300.** Main courses 5€–15€, fixed-price lunch menu 15€. Daily 4:30pm–12:30am.

Bruges Beer Halls

2be ★★★   Part store selling the city's most comprehensive selection of beer and part pub overlooking Bruges's best viewing point on the canal corner at Rozenhoed-kaai, 2be is rammed all day every day with Belgian beer fans anxious to sample as many brews as possible. There are usually seven draft beers on offer that change with the seasons, but might include Brugse Zot from the Half Moon Brewery (see below) fruit beers, *trippels,* and white beer. Service is perfectly polite and the wait staff are well informed on the pedigree of their beers, but it can be somewhat brusque, mostly owing to the constant crowds that surge in to sample the wares. However, the beer is fresh and the views over the canal from the little terrace just gorgeous. There's little in the way of nourishment to soak up the alcohol so things can get a little boisterous on weekend evenings.

Wollestraat 53. ℭ **050/611-222.** www.2-be.biz. Daily 9:30am–7:30pm.

Brouwerij De Halve Maan (Half Moon Brewery) ★   While I award this place one star not for its nonsensical brewery tour (p. 194) but for the chance to taste the beer afterwards, the pub at the Half Moon is actually pretty good. There's a swanky modern bistro and covered terrace where pickings from the menu include burgers, mussels, and summer BBQs on the food front, but most people wash up here to savor the beers, including the fruity *Brugse Zot* (Bruges Fools) and fearsomely strong "quadruppel" Straffe Hendrik ales.

Walplein 26. ℭ **050/444-222.** www.halvemaan.be. Daily 10am–6pm.

EXPLORING BRUGES

A hot-favorite contender for the title of Europe's tiniest, most romantic city, Bruges is really one big magical attraction—a fairy-tale confection of gabled houses, meandering canals, magnificent squares, and narrow cobblestone streets. What is most astonishing is the consistently warm welcome its residents provide to the swarms of visitors

Bruges Attractions

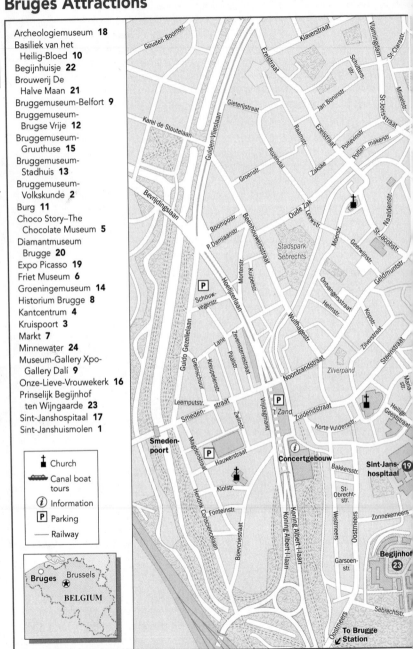

✝ Church
🚣 Canal boat
  tours
ⓘ Information
P Parking
— Railway

Bruges ★ Brussels
BELGIUM

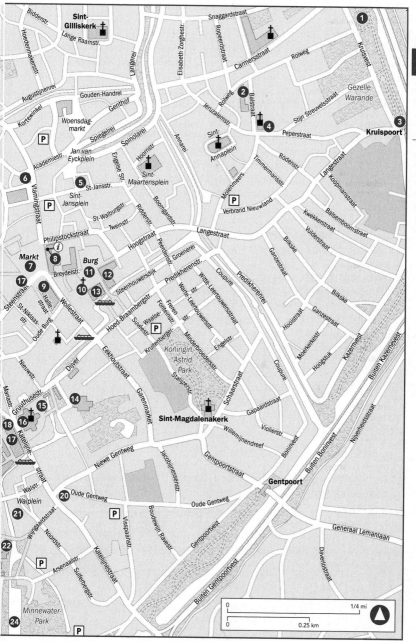

Bidderstr.

Sint-
Gilliskerk †

Lange Raamstr.

Hoedenmakersstr.

Augustijnenrei

Kortewinkel

Gouden-Handrei

Woensdag-
markt

Genthof

Spiegelrei

Langerei

Elisabeth Zorghestr.

Snaggardstraat

Ropeerdstraat

Rolweg

Carmersstraat

Rolweg

Gezelle
Warande

Kruisvest

①

②

Balstraat

③ Kruispoort

Jeruzalemstr.

Rolweg

Stijn Streuvelsstraat

④

Peperstraat

Academiestr.

Spinolarei

Jan van
Eyckplein

P

Sint-
Maartensplein

Hoornstr.

Engelse Str.

Sint
Annaplein

Molenmeers

Rodenstr.

Timmermansstr.

Langestraat

Koopmanstraat

Vlamingstraat

⑥

⑤ St-Jansstr.

Sint-
Jansplein

P

St-Walburgstr.

Riddentr.

Tweinstr.

Boomgardstr.

Verbrand Nieuwland

P

Kwekerstraat

Balsemboomstraat

Vuldestraat

Philipstockstraat

Hoogstraat

Langestraat

Bilske

Ganzestraat

Bilske

Markt
⑦ ⑧ i

Breydelstr.

Burg
⑪ ⑫

⑩ ⑬

Peerdstraat

Groenerei

Predikherenstr.

Witte-Leertouwersstraat

Coupure

Predikherenrei

Ganzestraat

Hoolstraat

⑰ ⑨

St-Niklaas str.

Steenstraat

Halle-straat

Wollestraat

Oude Burg

†

Hoed-Braambergstr.

Steenhouwersdijk

Walse-str.

Freren Fonteinstr.

Minderbroedersstr.

Warte-Leertouwersstr.

Engelstr.

P

Hoogstuk

Moerkerkestr.

Ganzestraat

Kazernvest

Buiten Kazernvest

Nieuwstr.

Dijver

Eekhoutstraat

Kruitenberger.

Koningin
Astrid
Park

Stalijzerstr.

Coupure

Buiten Boninvest

Mariastr.

Gruuthusestr.

⑭

⑮

⑱ ⑯

⑰ Kateline-

straat

Garenmarkt

Schaarstraat

Sint-Magdalenakerk †

Gapaardstraat

Violierstr.

Willemijnendreef

Boninvest

Nijverheidsstraat

Walstr.

Walplein

⑳ Oude Gentweg

Niewe Gentweg

Jacobijnessenstr.

Gentpoortstraat

Gentpoort

⑳

⑳

P

Visspaanstr.

Boudewijn Ravestr.

Oude Gentweg

Gentpoortvest

Generaal Lemanlaan

P

Wijgaardstraat

Noordstr.

P

Arsenaalstr.

Katelijnestraat

Sulferbergstr.

Buiten Gentpoortvest

Davenstraat

Minnewater-
Park

⑳

P

0   1/4 mi

0   0.25 km

who swallow the place up every summer. The basis for this goes way beyond mere economics—the good burghers of Bruges have a deep love for their show-stopping city and are only too delighted that others share their enthusiasm.

The Markt

The gigantic open space of Markt is lined with venerable facades swathed in heraldic banners; together with the adjacent Burg (p. 193), these two great squares formed the commercial and administrative heart of Bruges and are today the focal point of its sightseeing adventure. Most of what you'll want to see is less than 10 minutes' walk away from these two squares.

Bruggemuseum-Belfort (Belfry) ★★ HISTORIC BUILDING The Belfort was, and still very much is, the symbol of Bruges's civic pride. What poet Henry Wadsworth Longfellow in 1856 called "the beautiful, wild chimes" of its magnificent 47-bell carillon peal out over the city every quarter-hour, and several times a day in longer concerts during the summer. The ornate tower is the biggest in Belgium and stands 83m (272 ft.) high; its lower section dates from around 1240, the corner turrets were added in the 14th century, and the upper, octagonal section in the 15th century. Climb an exhausting 366 steep steps to the tower's summit for panoramic views of Bruges and the surrounding countryside all the way to the sea. Pause for breath at the second-floor Treasury, where the town seal and charters were kept behind multiple wrought-iron grilles.

From the 13th to the 16th century, much of the city's commerce was conducted in the Hallen (Market Halls), below the Belfort. Now they are the location of the **Museum-Gallery Xpo-Gallery Dalí,** which allows a fun-filled glimpse into the surreal world of Salvador Dalí, Spain's strangest artist. A vibrant collection of his sculptures, paintings, sketches, and glassware are presented in a suitably bizarre but beautifully curated display incorporating mirrors, sparkly blue lighting, and splashes of gold against a backdrop of bright blues and crimsons. Pride of place goes to Dalí's joyfully wacky bronzes, which include his famous spindly elephants and a cast of "Man on Dolphin," as well as a series of sketches taken from "Alice in Wonderland." Half the charm of this exhibition is its unexpected contrast to the medieval beauty of the building housing it.

Markt 7. © **050/448-711.** https://bezoekers.brugge.be/musea-2. Admission 8€ adults, 6€ seniors, 4€ children 6–25, free for children 5 and under. Daily 9:30am–5pm. Closed Ascension Day afternoon and Dec 25.

Historium Brugge ★★ MUSEUM Housed in an intricate balcony-and-tower–adorned Gothic Revivalist building next to the Provinciaal Hof (Provincial Palace; see p. 193), the Historium is located above the tourist information office (p. 181) and aims to explain all the twists and turns of the city's turbulent history in an approachable and entertaining manner. The exhibit leads you on a romp through 15th-century Bruges with a series of interactive experiences using film, music, holograms, sounds, and smells with the aid of multilingual headphones. Afterwards catch your breath with a complementary tasting at the **Duvelorium Grand Beer Café**—which has incomparable views over Markt—in the same building.

Markt 1. © **050/270-311.** www.historium.be. Admission 11€ adults, 9€ students, 5.50€ children 2–14, 30€ families. Daily 10am–6pm. Closed Jan 1 and Dec 25.

The **sculpture group** in the center of the Markt depicts a pair of Flemish heroes, butcher Jan Breydel and weaver Pieter de Coninck. The two led an uprising in 1302 against the wealthy merchants and nobles who dominated the guilds, and went on to win an against-the-odds victory over French knights later that same year in the Battle of the Golden Spurs (p. 28). The small, castle-like building called the **Craenenburg** (it's now a restaurant) at the corner of Sint-Amandsstraat was used by a rebellious citizenry to imprison the Habsburg Crown Prince and future Emperor Maximilian of Austria in 1488 over a small matter of increased taxes. In revenge for that humiliation, Maximilian later wounded Bruges's pride by transferring his capital to Ghent and hit the city's pocketbook by transferring its trading rights to Antwerp. The large neo-Gothic **Provinciaal Hof (Provincial Palace)** dates from the 1800s and houses the government of the province of West Flanders.

The Burg

The Burg is the second of Bruges's vast piazzas, just steps away from the Markt. It parades a similar array of beautiful medieval buildings, which together add up to a time-traveler's trip through the history of European architecture. On this site, Baldwin Iron Arm, Count of Flanders, built a fortified castle (or *burg*) in the late 9th century, around which a village developed into Bruges. The rest, as they say, is history.

Basiliek van het Heilig-Bloed (Basilica of the Holy Blood) ★★★ CHURCH   The Basilica of the Holy Blood is a double-decker church housing a 12th-century Romanesque chapel and a Gothic upper floor; it is well worth a visit for the mind-boggling richness of its decor and the ecclesiastical treasures found in the accompanying museum. The lower Chapel of St. Basil is the repository of one of the most venerated relics of Christ in Europe—a fragment of cloth reputedly stained with the blood of Christ, wiped from his body after the crucifixion by Joseph of Arimathea. Legend has it that the relic was brought back to Bruges from Jerusalem after the second Crusade by the Count of Flanders, Diederik van de Elzas, who donated it to the church in 1150.

The relic is embedded in a rock-crystal vial, which itself is held inside a small glass cylinder adorned at each end with a golden crown. It is kept in a magnificent tabernacle on a side altar in the chapel and is brought out daily (btwn. 11:30am and noon, and 2 and 4pm) so the faithful can pray to it, parade in front of it, and maybe even kiss it. But remember that if you go up to inspect the vial, you will be expected to donate to the upkeep of the church, a fact that is made all too clear by the attendant clergy.

In the Basilica Museum, the magnificent reliquary created by Bruges goldsmith Jan Crabbe has a gem-encrusted case styled as a medieval castle and topped with a golden statue of the Virgin. This houses the relic on its annual pilgrimage around the streets of Bruges in the colorful **Procession of the Holy Blood** (p. 182) on Ascension Day.

Burg 13. ℰ **050/336-792.** www.holyblood.com. Basilica free admission; museum 2€. Nov–Mar 24 Thurs–Tues 9:30am–noon and 2–5pm; Mar 25–Oct daily 9:30am–noon and 2–5pm. Mass Fri–Wed 11am. Museum closed Jan 1, Nov 1, and Dec 25.

Bruggemuseum-Brugse Vrije (Liberty of Bruges) ★ HISTORIC BUILD-ING   The center of the city's judiciary until 1984, the Landhuis (Palace) of the Liberty of Bruges also served as the administrative HQ of the region of Flanders around Bruges from the Middle Ages onward. Much of it was rebuilt between 1722 and 1727 and the palace now houses the city archives. It's chiefly visited for the exceptional **Renaissancezaal (Renaissance Chamber)** ★★, which has been restored to its original 16th-century condition, and a monumental black marble fireplace decorated with a carved alabaster frieze and topped by an oak chimneypiece carved with statues of Emperor Charles V, who visited Bruges in 1515, and his grandparents: Emperor Maximilian of Austria, Duchess Mary of Burgundy, King Ferdinand II of Aragon, and Queen Isabella I of Castile. That's quite memorable in itself for the size of some of the wooden codpieces. The gloomy oil painting by Gillis van Tilborgh was executed in 1659 and clearly shows the Charles V fireplace on its right-hand side, behind all the aldermen dressed in black robes.

Burg 11a. ℂ **050/448-711.** https://bezoekers.brugge.be/musea-2. Courtyard free admission; Renaissance Hall 4€. Daily 9:30am–12:30pm and 1:30–5pm. Closed Ascension Day afternoon and Dec 25.

Bruggemuseum-Stadhuis (Town Hall) ★ HISTORIC BUILDING   This lacy Gothic structure was built in 1376, making it one of the oldest town halls in Belgium. The statues in the niches of the facade are 1980s replacements of the originals by Jan van Eyck, which were destroyed by pro-French rebels in the 1790s. Go in to check out the glowing, ostentatious beauty of the **Gotische Zaal (Gothic Room)** ★★ upstairs; it is adorned with 19th-century wall murals depicting highlights from Bruges's history amid intricate gilded patterning all topped by a spectacular, vaulted and gilded oak ceiling.

Burg 12. ℂ **050/448-711.** https://bezoekers.brugge.be/en/stadhuis-city-hall. Admission 4€. Daily 9:30am–5pm. Closed Ascension Day afternoon and Dec 25.

Other Sights in Bruges

Brouwerij De Halve Maan (Half Moon Brewery) ★ BREWERY   The Half Moon is one of Bruges's last family-owned working breweries and has operated on its present site near the Begijnhof since 1856. Today, it produces the famous Brugse Zot (Bruges Fools) and Straffe Hendrik, which averages around 14 percent alcohol; all can be sampled in the brewery's own brasserie. Unless you're an enthusiastic beer buff, don't waste your time taking the brewery tour, because there isn't really very much to see. Instead, just get down to sampling some of the potent brews in the smart brasserie or on the pretty courtyard terrace.

Walplein 26. ℂ **050/444-222.** www.halvemaan.be. Tours 7.50€. Guided tours last 45 minutes on the hour: Apr–Oct Sun–Fri 11am–4pm, Sat 11am–5pm; Nov–Mar Sun–Fri 11am–3pm, Sat 11am–4pm. Closed Dec 25–26 and Jan 1.

Bruggemuseum-Gruuthuse ★★ MUSEUM   The Flemish nobleman Lodewijk van Gruuthuse, who was a counselor to the dukes of Burgundy in the 1400s, lived in some considerable style in this ornate Gothic, brick-built mansion. The vast courtyard and equine statue above the intricate entrance rather sets the standard of opulence for the interior, which is crammed with extravagantly carved stone fireplaces, oak balconies, and gilded wooden ceilings. From his first-floor landing, Van Gruuthuse even enjoyed his own private pew overlooking the Onze-Lieve-Vrouwekerk (Church of Our Lady; see below) next door. Among all this luxurious detailing is a superb collection of silverware, ceramics, glassware, tapestries, and ecclesiastical robes, all representing the very best of 15th-century Flemish crafts and skills.

Dijver 17. © **050/448-711.** https://bezoekers.brugge.be/en/gruuthusemuseum. Admission 8€. Tues–Sun 9:30am–5pm. Closed Ascension Day afternoon and Dec 25.

Bruggemuseum-Volkskunde (Folklore Museum) ★ MUSEUM

Housed in a row of 8 whitewashed houses formerly belonging to the Shoemakers Guild, the Folklore Museum recreates a slice of Bruges from the turn of the 20th century. Displays include a school classroom, a milliner's workshop, a pharmacy, and a candy store, where sweets are made on the first and third Thursday afternoon of the month. There's a collection of clay pipes, puppet shows, and a pretty selection of handmade lace as well as the chance to sample a traditional Flemish beer in the **De Zwarte Kat** (the Black Cat) inn.

Balstraat 43. © **050/448-711.** https://bezoekers.brugge.be/en/volkskundemuseum-folklore-museum. Admission 4€. Tues–Sun 9:30am–5pm. Closed Ascension Day afternoon and Dec 25.

Choco-Story–The Chocolate Museum ★ MUSEUM

This privately owned museum takes advantage of Bruges's reputation as a center of chocolaty excellence and strolls through the coca bean's backstory from its origins among the Aztecs to the chocolate drink taking Europe's royal courts by storm in the 1500s. There are a few Aztec artifacts, display of delicate Limoges china, and a couple of interesting facts along the way. For example, did you know that saucers were developed to stop fine Parisian ladies from dripping hot chocolate down their embonpoint? Still, it's fun for kids and there's a chocolate-making demonstration at the end, where you get to taste the products. Courses in the delicate art of chocolate making can be booked ahead of time online.

Wijnzakstraat 2. © **050/612-237.** www.choco-story.be. Admission 7€ adults, 6€ seniors and students, 4€ children 6–12, free for children 5 and under. Daily 10am–5pm. Closed Jan 1, 2nd and 3rd week of Jan, Dec 24–25, and Dec 31.

Expo Picasso ★★ ART GALLERY

More former wards of the Sint-Janshospitaal (p. 197) have been requisitioned for this unsung modern-art museum situated around a tranquil central garden. Along the gentle meander from Impressionism to Picasso, the 200 plus artworks kick off in 1874 with paintings and drawings by Monet, Renoir, Degas, and Rodin. Along with drawings by Magritte, Chagall, Matisse, and Cocteau, Miró has a corridor full of fluid lithographs to himself, but the standout pieces belong to Picasso. His line drawing "Colombe Bleue" from 1961 charms in its simplicity,

---

The Old Walls of Bruges

Medieval Bruges was heavily fortified, totally encircled by its circular walls and further protected by a moat and defense towers. The walls were largely knocked down in the 19th century and today only the moat and four of the nine 14th-century, powerfully fortified gates have survived. Of these, the **Kruispoort** is the most monumental, looking like a mini-castle complete with drawbridge and defending the city's eastern approach routes. The others are (clockwise from the railway station in the southwest) the imposing **Smedenpoort; Ezelpoort,** which is known for the many swans that grace the moat beside it; **Kruispoort;** and **Gentpoort.**

while the subject matter of his emotive and dynamic bullfighting prints, executed for Federico García Lorca, may not appeal, there is no denying their beauty and elegance. Chances are you'll probably have this little treasure to yourself so make the most of it.

Mariastraat 38. ℭ **050/476-100.** www.expo-brugge.be. Admission 8€ adults, 6.50€ seniors and children 7–18, free 6 and under. Daily 9am–5pm. Closed Jan.

Friet Museum (Fries Museum) ★ MUSEUM
Owned by the same crew as Choco-Story, the fries museum throws up (not literally) facts and figures about the rise of the humble potato to its current position as one of Belgium's best-loved dishes. Highlights, such as they are, include a dissertation on the Irish potato famine and an entertaining film about the progress of the spud from ground to frozen fry. One star is accorded for this being the only fries museum in the world.

Vlamingstraat 33. ℭ **050/340-150.** www.frietmuseum.be. Admission 7€ adults, 6€ seniors and students, 4€ children 6–12, free for children 5 and under. Daily 10am–5pm. Closed Jan 1, 2nd and 3rd week of Jan, Dec 24–25, and Dec 31.

Groeningemuseum ★★★ MUSEUM
Housed in a gallery purpose built in the late 1920s near a cluster of other Bruges museums, the Groeninge ranks among Belgium's leading art galleries with a collection that covers Flemish painting from the 15th to the 20th centuries.

It is most famous, however, for its stellar hoard of masterpieces by the Flemish Primitives, with around 30 works by master artists such as Jan van Eyck (who worked in Bruges from 1430 until his death in 1441), Rogier van der Weyden, Hieronymus Bosch, and Hans Memling, all hung in light-flooded galleries. Standout pieces among all this glory include Bosch's almost-surreal triptych "The Last Judgment" (ca. 1486) with its scattering of sticklike suffering sinners; Gerard David's horrific "Judgment of Cambyses" (1498), which depicts an errant judge being sentenced and flayed alive; Van Eyck's glowing portrait of his wife Margareta (1439); and Hans Memling's paintings with long, lugubrious faces.

As the museum progresses through the Flemish repertoire, more secular themes start to appear, including portraits by Pieter Porbus and Anthony van Dyck, as well as the slightly sinister "Lord Byron on his Deathbed" by Joseph Denis Odevaere (ca. 1826). Later works encompass paintings by James Ensor and the Belgian surrealists René Magritte and Paul Delvaux.

Entrance to the Groeningemuseum also includes access to the adjacent **Arenthuis,** which shows temporary exhibitions and a permanent collection of lithographs and sketches by Anglo-Welsh artist Sir Frank Brangwyn. Don't dismiss this—if time permits be sure at least to see his vibrant "Slave Market," which looks for all the world like a Gustav Klimt painting, plus the "British Empire Panel" (1925–30), one of a series commissioned for the House of Lords in London, UK.

Dijver 12. ℭ **050/448-711.** https://bezoekers.brugge.be/en/groeningemuseum-groeninge-museum. Admission (combined ticket with neighboring Arentshuis) 8€. Tues–Sun 9:30am–5pm. Closed Ascension Day afternoon and Dec 25.

Kantcentrum (Lace Center) ★ MUSEUM/SHOP
At one time there were more than 2,000 lace makers in Bruges, and today this combination of workshop, museum, and shameless retail opportunity is where the ancient art of lace creation is passed on to the next generation. There are lace-making demonstrations each afternoon between 2 and 5pm and the store also sells everything you need to make lace, from bobbins to thread. Courses are available if booked online in advance.

Bruges's Windmills

Where once 25 windmills graced the outskirts of Bruges, now only four survive. They are found in the park that abuts the old city walls on their eastern flank between Kruispoort and Dampoort; of these, two are open to the public in summer and both are grain mills coming under the banner of Musea Brugge, which also runs the city's main museums. The **Koeleweimolen** was built in 1765 and was moved to its present spot from the Dampoort in 1996, while the **Sint-Janshuismolen** has been in situ since 1770. Both windmills are found along Kruisvest and share the same opening times and admission: May to August Tuesday through Sunday 9:30am to 12:30pm and 1:30 to 5pm; admission 3€ adults, 2€ seniors and ages 6 to 25, free for children 5 and under.

Balstraat 16. ℂ **050/330-072.** www.kantcentrum.eu. Admission 3€ adults; 2€ seniors, students, and children 7–12; free for children 6 and under. Mon–Sat 10am–5pm. Closed Jan 1, Ascension Day afternoon, and Dec 25.

Onze-Lieve-Vrouwekerk (Church of Our Lady) ★★ CHURCH

It took 2 centuries (13th–15th) to build this landmark church, whose soaring 122m (400-ft.) spire can be seen for miles around Bruges. Among the many art treasures here is a beautiful Carrera marble sculpture of the "Madonna and Child" produced by Michelangelo in 1504. It was bought by a wealthy Bruges merchant called Jan van Mouskroen and donated to the church in 1506. Other impressive artworks include a "Crucifixion" by Anthony van Dyck and the imposing bronze tombs of Charles the Bold, Duke of Burgundy, and his daughter Mary. The church is currently under long-term restoration until early 2016 and although it is still open, the tombs are not accessible and there is little to see.

Onze-Lieve-Vrouwekerkhof Zuid. ℂ **050/448-711.** https://bezoekers.brugge.be/en/onze-lieve-vrouwekerk-church-of-our-lady. Admission 2€ until 2016, then 6€. Mon–Sat 9am–5pm, Sun 1:30–5pm.

Sint-Janshospitaal (St. John's Hospital) ★★ MUSEUM

The oldest wards in the former Sint-Janshospitaal date from the 13th century; it had an 800-year tradition of caring for travelers who fell ill on the road, only closing in 1976. The 17th-century apothecary in the cloisters near the hospital entrance is still furnished traditionally with rows of glass bottles containing mysterious lotions and potions. The medieval hospital wards are filled with antique beds, sedan chairs, and rather macabre surgical instruments that will probably titillate the kids. However, the main reason for a visit is the magnificent collection of paintings by the German-born artist Hans Memling (ca. 1440–94), who moved to Bruges in 1465 and became one of the city's most famous residents. Commissioned in 1479 to produce six paintings for the hospital, his delightful, radiant works are now found among a hodgepodge of church silver and mediocre religious paintings in the barnlike, timber-roofed chapel. Here you'll find Memling's exquisite *tondos*, the surprisingly small golden Ursula Shrine, and the sublime three-paneled altarpiece of St. John the Baptist and St. John the Evangelist.

Mariastraat 38. ℂ **050/448-711.** https://bezoekers.brugge.be/en/sint-janshospitaal-saint-johns-hospital. Admission 8€. Tues–Sun 9:30am–5pm. Closed Ascension Day afternoon and Dec 25.

A Quiet Corner of Bruges

Since it was founded in 1245 by the Countess Margaret of Constantinople, the **Prinselijk Begijnhof ten Wijngaarde (Princely Beguinage of the Vineyard) ★**, Wijngaardstraat (℃ **050/330-011;** www.monasteria.org), at the Minnewater (Lake of Love), has been one of the most tranquil spots in Bruges, and so it remains today. *Begijns* were religious women, similar to nuns, who accepted vows of chastity and obedience but drew the line at poverty, preferring to earn a living by looking after the sick and making lace.

The *begijns* may be no more but the Begijnhof has been occupied by Benedictine nuns since 1928, and they strive to keep the old traditions alive. This beautiful little cluster of 17th-century whitewashed houses surrounds a lawn shaded by poplar trees and makes a marvelous escape from the din of the outside world. One of the houses, the **Begijnhuisje (Beguine's House),** is now a museum. The Begijnhof courtyard is always open and admission is free. The Beguine's House is open Monday to Saturday 10am to 5pm, Sunday 2:30 to 5pm. Admission is 2€ for adults, 1.50€ for seniors, 1€ for students and children 8 to 11.

Especially for Kids

When children vacation in cities, the result is not always great, but in spite of its concentration of museums, churches, and lace shops, Bruges is absolute heaven for kids. They can explore the city by **canal boat** or **pony-and-trap,** and also navigate the pedestrianized streets safely by **bike** (see below for all). In fact, the city itself is the attraction for some children, who love the notion that around every corner there's a 1,000-year-old building or some hidden courtyard.

And nowhere else will you find museums with such child-appeal factor as the **Fries Museum** (p. 196), which tells the story of the humble potato, or **Choco-Story** (p. 195) where they can learn about the process of making the world's favorite sweet treat and take a master class in the art. The **Historium** (p. 192) offers the city's most child-appropriate introduction to Bruges, with a dynamic and entertaining walk-through exhibition encompassing film, multi-media, and interactive exhibits. The **Archeologiemuseum (Archaeological Museum)** at Mariastraat 36a (℃ **050/448-711;** https://bezoekers.brugge.be/en/archeologiemuseum-archeological-museum) is also designed with kids in mind, with lots of interactive displays, the occasional skeleton, and medieval costumes to dress up in.

The cuisine of Belgium, with its waffles, fries, omelets, and toasted sandwiches, lends itself to junior appetites—try the *frietkoten* **(fries stands)** in the Markt—as do the numerous yummy **chocolate stores** (see below). And winter visits to Bruges turn up Christmas fairs and an ice rink in the Markt plus wacky installations on Stationesplein during the **Snow & Ice Sculpture Festival,** which lasts from mid-November to early January (p. 40).

Organized Tours & Excursions

It's practically law that every visitor to Bruges should take a **boat cruise ★★** around the city canals. There are five landing stages, the most convenient for tourists being the two along Dijver, but all are marked with an anchor icon on maps available at the tourist office (p. 181). These open-top canal boats can be scorching in hot weather and bracing in cold, but they only last 30 minutes, they are free with the **Brugge City Card** (p. 181), the commentary is multi-lingual, *and* they reveal a uniquely satisfying view of the city. They operate March to November daily 10am to 6pm, with weather-dependent departures between December and February. A half-hour cruise is 7.60€ for adults, and 3.40€ for children 4 to 11 when accompanied by an adult.

Wherever you are in Bruges, you'll hear the clip-clop of horses' hooves, so if you fancy a tour of the city by **horse-drawn carriage** (*caleche* in Flemish), the departure point is on the Markt between March and November, carriages are stationed on the Markt (in the Burg on Wed mornings) between 9am and 6pm. The 35-minute ride is 39€ per carriage for up to five people; there's a jumping off point for you and a resting point for the horses at the Beguinage (see above); see if you can spot the fountain nearby that's adorned with two horses' heads.

If you'd appreciate a little help uncovering the secrets of Bruges, hire a **local guide.** The tourist office (p. 181) runs walking tours from April through September costing 9€ (free for kids 11 and under) for a 2½-hour schlep through the pretty streets to all the main sights. Tours depart at 2:30pm daily from the Concertgebouw (see below), with Sunday kick off at 10:30pm in July and August. During October the tours only run on the weekend, leaving at 2:30pm.

For more information on all the tours mentioned above, check out the tourist office website **visitbruges.be**.

Tuesday through Saturday between March and September, eco-friendly scooters can be hired from **Electric Scooters** (Gentpoortstraat 62; ✆ **050/000-000;** www.electric scooters.be) for a potter around the streets of the city or out to Damme (see below). Prices start at 35€ for 2 hours, with a reduction of 25 percent for holders of the Brugge City Card (p. 181).

International tour companies such as **Viator** (✆ **888/651-9785** in the U.S.; www. viator.com) offer comprehensive guided day tours of Bruges from Ghent (p. 212), Brussels, and Amsterdam as well as out to the battlefields of Flanders (p. 227).

SHOPPING

Bruges is too tiny to keep pace with Brussels or Antwerp when it comes to shopping, but it certainly has its moments. This little city is a monument to the skills of lace-makers, chocolatiers, and brewers. You'll find souvenir shops selling machine-made lace concentrated around Mark and Burg, but the best, and way more expensive, hand-made types of lace are bobbin, ribbon, princess, or needlepoint. If you're after a hand-crafted chemise or tablecloth, check out **Rococo** at Wollestraat 18 and **Point de Rose** on the same street at Wollestraat 27. Souvenirs of a more perishable nature include Oud-Brugge cheese from **Diksmuids Boterhuis** at Geldmuntstraat 23, and marzipan from **Brown Sugar** at Mariastraat 1, but best of all chocolate, which Bruges is simply mad for. Pick up delicious arrays of calorie-laden confectionary from **Mary** at Kateli-jnestraat 21, or the four branches of **ChocOHolic** on Katelijnestraat and Wollestraat.

Local **beers** such as Straffe Hendrik, Brugs Tarwebier, and Brugge Tripel can be tracked down at **2be** on Wollestraat 53 (p. 189), or **Bacchus Cornelius** at Academies-traat 17 (www.bacchuscornelius.com), where you'll also find a selection of stone-bottled, ginlike liqueur *jenever* (p. 72).

If you're looking for unusual gifts for back home, try the slice of Christmas that is **De Witter Pelikaan** at Vlamingstraat 23 for festive baubles and handmade wooden toys.

A day IN DAMME ★

Photogenic Damme is just a 7km (4½ miles) hop from Bruges and was once the city's outer harbor where trading ships plied their cargoes, but the inlet of the River Zwin silted up in 1520 and the city lost much of its strategic importance. The marriage of Charles the Bold, Duke of Burgundy, to Margaret of York took place here celebrated with great pomp and ceremony.

Today, it's a place to spend a happy day pottering around, enjoying the red-brick Gothic architecture and the polder landscape cut through with canals. Start off in the **Markt** by admiring the Gothic (Stadhuis) Town Hall and the statues of Charles and Margaret on the facade. In the middle of the market square stands a statue of 13th-century Flemish poet Jacob van Maerlant (1230–96) and opposite the Stadhuis, at Jacob van Maerlantstraat 13, is the 15th-century **Saint-Jean d'Angély Huis ★**, where Charles and Margaret made their dynastic marriage in 1468.

Damme's **Visitor Centre** (Jacob van Maerlantstraat 3; ✆ **050/288-610;** www. toerismedamme.be) is found in the stately 15th-century Huyse de Groote Sterre, which also shares space with the strange **Uilenspiegelmuseum (Tijl Uilenspiegel Museum).** Uilenspiegel was a 14th-century Flemish troubadour who was adopted as a lucky mascot by the village of Damme; his eponymous museum relates his story and there are several statues dedicated to him around the village. Admission is 2.50€ for adults,

5€ for a family. Opening hours for both tourist office and museum are April to September Monday through Friday 9am to 6pm, Saturday and Sunday 10am–noon, 2 to 6pm; October to March Monday through Friday 10am to noon, 2 to 6pm, Saturday and Sunday 2 to 5pm.

Running south from the Markt at Kerkstraat 33 is the Gothic **Sint-Janshospitaal (St. John's Hospital),** which opened its doors in 1249. The former hospital now houses a small museum of liturgical bits and bobs that's open Tuesday to Thursday plus Saturday and Sunday 11am to noon and 2 to 6pm, and Monday and Friday 2 to 6pm. Admission is 1.50€.

You can easily get to Damme by road from Bruges (drive, cycle, or catch the De Lijn [p. 182] **bus no. 43** that departs seven times daily from Bruges train station and the Markt) but the most memorable way to arrive is by boat; the small sternwheeler **Lamme Goedzaak ★** departs from Noorweegse Kaai 31 in the north of Bruges, five times daily from April to mid-October. The half-hour cruise along the poplar-lined canal passes through a landscape straight out of an old Flemish painting. Round-trip tickets are 7.50€ single (11€ round-trip) for adults, 7€ (9.50€) for seniors, 6€ (8.50€) for children 3 to 11, and free for younger children. Schedules and other details are available from **Rederij Doornzele** (✆ **09/233-8469;** www.boot damme-brugge.be).

Most stores are open Monday to Saturday 9am to 6pm, with hours extended to 9pm on Friday. Many open on Sunday as well, especially in summer.

If you're after a piece of silverware or pre-loved diamond rings, the weekend **Antiques and Flea Market** on Dijver puts on a fine show alongside the canal from March to October, Saturday and Sunday from noon to 5pm.

BRUGES AFTER DARK

For information on what to do in the evening, pick up the free monthly newsletter **"events@brugge"** from the tourist office, hotels, and performance venues or check online at www.brugge.be for details of what's on where.

The Performing Arts

The ultramodern **Concertgebouw** ★★ ('t Zand 34; ✆ **070/223-302;** www.concert gebouw.be), the home base of the **Symfonieorkest van Vlaanderen (Flanders Symphony Orchestra;** ✆ **050/840-587;** www.symfonieorkest.be), is the city's main venue for opera, classical music, theater, and dance. This has left the former principal venue for these events in Bruges, the circa-1869 **Stadsschouwburg (City Theater;** Vlamingstraat 29; ✆ **050/443-060;** www.ccbrugge.be), to back up the mother ship by mounting smaller-scale performances. Theater at both venues is likely to be in Dutch or French, and rarely, if ever, in English.

Contemporary dance, drama by rising artists, rock and pop concerts, festivals, and lots of children's activities are held in the futuristic **Magdalena Concert Hall (MaZ** for short; Magdalenastraat 27; ✆ **050/443-060;** www.ccbrugge.be).

One for **jazz fans:** Between October and May there are free jam sessions in the foyer of **Kunstencentrum (Arts Center) De Werf** (Werfstraat 108; ✆ **050/330-529;** www.dewerf.be) every second Monday of the month at 8pm. Also on the agenda here are productions for children, contemporary drama, and dance.

The summer months between April and October see high drama of a different sort each Friday and Saturday night with fire-eating, falconry, juggling, and feasting at a **mock medieval banquet** to celebrate the wedding of Charles the Bold, Duke of Burgundy, to Margaret of York in the hallowed setting of the neo-Gothic former **Heilige-Hartkerk (Sacred Heart Church).** Tickets for this historical extravaganza range from 45€ to 74€ (half price for children 11–14; children 10 and under not permitted) from Celebrations Entertainment (Vlamingstraat 86; ✆ **050/347-572;** www.celebrations entertainment.be). Shows start at 7:30pm.

SIDE TRIPS
FROM BRUSSELS
& BRUGES

8

Brussels and Bruges may be Belgium's Big Two visitor destinations, but to ignore the delights of other cities would be doing both yourself and this cultured country a huge disservice. Although not many places can match Bruges for sheer medieval good looks, **Ghent** and **Antwerp** make a jolly good attempt, and many Belgians consider them the true heartland of Flemish culture; certainly when it comes to contemporary dynamism, they are hands-down winners.

Historic **Mons** is the capital of French-speaking Hainaut, the green and pleasant, lake-speckled land that stretches along most of Belgium's border with France. 2015 sees the city take on the mantle of European City of Culture for the year, so this polished little city has been all spruced up. Geared up as a partner city in this City of Culture honor is handkerchief-size **Mechelen** in Flanders—your chance to discover a hitherto little-known Flemish treasure house. And given that the years 2014 through 2018 see the centenary of World War I, now's an appropriate time to attend the emotional Last Post service in **Ypres** to commemorate those who died in the trenches of Flanders Fields.

All the side trips suggested in this chapter are achievable as day trips from Brussels or Bruges, but the gritty resurgence of Ghent and the sleek sophistication of Antwerp really merit an overnight visit, so a couple of dining and sleeping suggestions are included for both cities. And while it's perfectly possible to visit the battlefields of Flanders in a (long) day from Brussels, the journey west from Bruges to Ypres and Passendale is considerably shorter, a distinct plus point, especially if you're traveling with kids.

ANTWERP ★★

48km (30 miles) N of Brussels

Until a few years ago, Antwerp was one of western Europe's secret places, known only to a lucky few, but now it's been discovered big time. Owing its historical wealth to its location on the Schelde (Scheldt) River, the city's reputation as a thriving port and diamond-trade center is well deserved, but that's far from all there is to say about this booming, high-brow, and—in some small parts—seedy city. The capital town of the province of Antwerpen boasts monuments from its wealthy medieval, Renaissance, and

Belgium

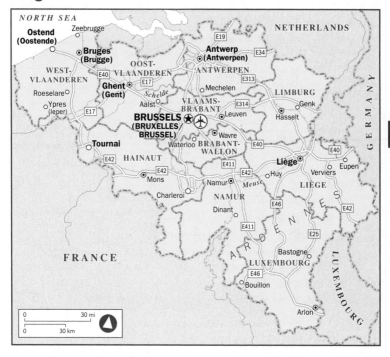

baroque periods; a magnificent cathedral; a fine-arts museum full of Old Flemish masterpieces (closed until 2017); a maze of medieval streets; and a thriving nightlife and cool cultural scene. Given all this, it's no surprise that international visitors to Belgium have been remedying their former neglect of the city. Yep, Antwerp is on the up.

Essentials

GETTING THERE

BY PLANE   **Brussels Airport** is the main international airport for Antwerp (p. 232). A few budget flights (including Flybe from London Southend) arrive at **Antwerp Airport** (✆ **03/285-6500;** www.antwerp-airport.be; airport code ANR) in Deurne 7km (4½ miles) east of the city. De Lijn buses no. 51, 52, and 53 take 15 minutes between the airport and Rooseveltplein, close to Antwerp Centraal Station. The taxi fare to downtown is around 20€.

BY TRAIN   **SNCB trains** run in approximately 50 minutes between Brussels-Midi and Antwerp Centraal Station, which is 1.5km (1 mile) east of the Grote Markt. Trains leave every 15 minutes and fares are 15€ round-trip. For more details, go to www.belgianrail.be.

BY CAR   Two main arteries connect Antwerp and Brussels: the A1/E19 via Mechelen (p. 229) and the A12. Journey time is 1 hour and 15 minutes.

Antwerp

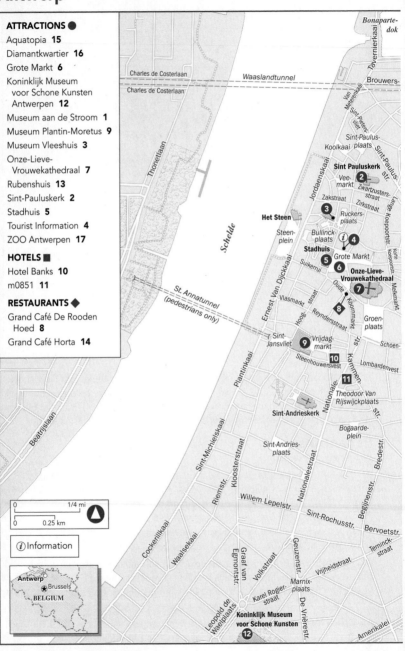

ATTRACTIONS ●

Aquatopia **15**

Diamantkwartier **16**

Grote Markt **6**

Koninklijk Museum
voor Schone Kunsten
Antwerpen **12**

Museum aan de Stroom **1**

Museum Plantin-Moretus **9**

Museum Vleeshuis **3**

Onze-Lieve-
Vrouwekathedraal **7**

Rubenshuis **13**

Sint-Pauluskerk **2**

Stadhuis **5**

Tourist Information **4**

ZOO Antwerpen **17**

HOTELS ■

Hotel Banks **10**

m0851 **11**

RESTAURANTS ◆

Grand Café De Rooden
Hoed **8**

Grand Café Horta **14**

ⓘ Information

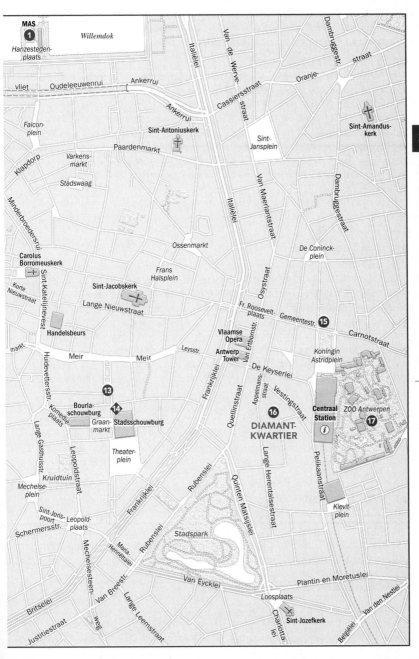

MAS ❶

Willemdok

Hanzesteden-
plaats

vliet   Oudeleeuwenrui   Ankerrui

Van de Werve straat

Italiëlei

Oranje-

Dambruggestr.

straat

Falcon-
plein

Klapdorp

Ankerrui

Cassiersstraat

Sint-
Jansplein

Sint-Amandus-
kerk

Sint-Antoniuskerk

Paardenmarkt

Varkens-
markt

Stadswaag

Italiëlei

Van Maerlantstraat

Dambruggestraat

Minderbroedersrui

Ossenmarkt

De Coninck-
plein

Carolus
Borromeuskerk

Frans
Halsplein

Korte
Nieuwstraat

Sint-Jacobskerk

Osystraat

Sint-Katelijnevest

Lange Nieuwstraat

Fr. Roosevelt-
plaats

Gemeentestr. ❶❺

Carnotstraat

Handelsbeurs

markt

Huidevettersstr.

Meir   Meir

Leysstr.

Vlaamse
Opera

Antwerp
Tower

Van Ertbornstr.

De Keyserlei

Koningin
Astridplein

Frankrijklei

Appelmans-
straat

Vestingstraat

Komedie-
plaats

❶❸

Bourla-
schouwburg

❶❹

Graan-
markt

Stadsschouwburg

Quellinstraat

❶❻

DIAMANT-
KWARTIER

Centraal
Station
ⓘ

ZOO Antwerpen

❶❼

Lange Gasthuisstr.

Leopoldstraat

Theater-
plein

Pelikaanstraat

Kievit-
plein

Kruidtuin

Mechelse-
plein

Sint-Joris-
poort

Leopold-
plaats

Schermersstr.

Frankrijklei

Rubenslei

Quinten Matsijslei

Lange Herentalsestraat

Mechelsesteen-
weg

Van Breestr.

Maria-
Henriëttalei

Rubenslei

Stadspark

Britselei

Van Eycklei

Plantin en Moretuslei

Belgiëlei

Van den Nestlei

Justitiestraat

Lange Leemstraat

Loosplaats

Charlotta-
lei

Sint-Jozefkerk

VISITOR INFORMATION

Antwerp Tourism & Convention is at Grote Markt 13 (☎ **03/232-0103;** www.visit antwerpen.be) and opens Monday to Saturday 9am to 5:45pm, Sunday and holidays 9am to 4:45pm (closed Jan 1 and Dec 25). The **Information Desk** at Centraal Station is open the same hours as the main tourist office.

GETTING AROUND

The integrated public-transportation system of **bus, tram,** and **Premetro trams** in Antwerp is run by **De Lijn** (☎ **070/22-0200;** www.delijn.be). Other than pounding the pavement of this pocket-size metropolis, tram is the best way to get around. The most useful services for tourists are lines 2, 3, 5, and 15, which run between Centraal Station and Groenplaats near the cathedral; and lines 10 and 11, which run past the Grote Markt. Purchase your ticket from the De Lijn sales point in the station and tourist office before boarding and you'll pay 20 percent less. The most useful ticket for sightseers is the *dagkaart* (**day card**), valid for the entire network; it costs 5€ in advance, 7€ once on the tram.

Regulated **taxis** wait outside Centraal Station and in Groenplaats; otherwise call **Antwerp Tax** (☎ **03/238-3838;** www.antwerp-tax.be). After 10pm, an extra 10€ is added to the fare.

ANTWERP'S PORT

When you come down to it, if there were no River Schelde, there would be no Antwerp. The city's location close to the point where the river meets the tidal Westerchelde estuary made it a strategic port as far back as the 2nd century B.C. Antwerp was a trading station within the powerful medieval Hanseatic League but, unlike Bruges, did not have the status of a full-fledged *Kontor,* with its own separate district and mercantile installations. In the early days, ships moored along the city's wharves, where the Steen (see below) now stands; nowadays the port has moved 13km (8 miles) downstream to docks that jam up against the Dutch border. After Rotterdam, Antwerp is Europe's second biggest port for goods handled, and the third biggest (after Rotterdam and Hamburg) for containers.

On the waterfront in the center of town, Antwerp's oldest building, **De Steen (The Castle),** Steenplein 1, is a glowering stone-built 13th-century fortress on the banks of the river that once overlooked Antwerp's port. It is currently closed to the public with no plans to reopen, but it's worth a glance for its mighty proportions and the bizarre statue of what appears to be a giant peeing on two small boys at the foot of the left-hand steps.

Exploring Antwerp

Most visitors to Antwerp head straight for the warren of winding streets in the medieval Old Town, which fan out from the Grote Markt. South of there, the old shipping warehouses along Vlaamsekaai and Waalsekaai have burst back into life as edgy bars, restaurants, and art galleries. The area around Centraal Station, east of De Keyserlei and Koningin Astridplein, is more than a little seedy and has problems with drug dealing and prostitution; best leave that area well alone at night.

Grote Markt ★★ HISTORIC SQUARE A lovely 16th-century square lined with buzzing sidewalk cafes and restaurants filled with Antwerp's sleek residents, the Grote Markt is the city's social and cultural epicenter. Dominated by the neoclassical Brabo Fountain, it is surrounded by majestic buildings like the many-gabled **Huis den**

Save your feet on all those cobbled streets and take a **circular tour** of Antwerp's attractions in a **mini electric tram;** you'll start off in the Groenplaats, trundle around the cobbled lanes of the Old Town, pass the Gothic facades in Grote Markt, venture through the main shopping thoroughfares, and potter along the Schelde riverfront to MAS (see below). There are seven departures a day during summer, on the hour from 11am until 5pm; tickets cost 6€ for adults, 4€ for children ages 4 to 12. See **www.touristram.be** for details.

Spieghel at Grote Markt 9. This was a meeting place for great Renaissance thinkers such as Erasmus and Sir Thomas More, who was in Antwerp when he began to write "Utopia" in 1515.

The Renaissance **Stadhius (City Hall)** takes up the entire west side of the Grote Markt and was designed by Cornelius Floris de Vriendt; it is an outstanding example of the Flemish mannerism that replaced Antwerp's early Gothic architectural style in the 16th century; it has a splendid central tower and a pleasing, symmetrical frontage. The hall was burned during the city's sack by invading troops in the "Spanish Fury" of 1576 and rebuilt in 1579. If you are lucky enough to get inside, look out for the frescoes by Hendrik Leys, a 19th-century Antwerp painter; otherwise content yourself with admiring the building's orderly proportions and gilded coats of arms as well as counting the flags of the ever-growing European Union that flutter constantly from the facade.

Grote Markt. 🕐 **03/221-1333.** Guided tours Mon–Wed and Fri–Sat 2 and 3pm (council business permitting). Tickets 1€.

Koninklijk Museum voor Schone Kunsten Antwerpen (Antwerp Royal Museum of Fine Arts) ★★★ MUSEUM   Hidden behind this massive neoclassical edifice is the world's biggest and best collection of paintings and frescoes by Peter Paul Rubens. Other artists displayed here include the Flemish Primitives Jan van Eyck, Rogier van der Weyden, Hans Memling, and Pieter Brueghel, as well as more recent Belgian favorites James Ensor and Paul Delvaux. Alas this glorious gallery, normally stuffed with the loot of 500 years of great painting, is closed for restoration until 2017 so if peerless Flemish art is your addiction, you'll have to get your fix at the Groeningemuseum in Bruges (p. 196), although a few works from KMSKA are on display in the **Golden Cabinet at Museum Rockoxhuis** (Keizerstraat 10-12; 🕐 **03/201-9250;** www.rockoxhuis.be).

Leopold de Waelplaats 2. 🕐 **03/238-7809.** www.kmska.be. Closed until 2017.

Museum aan de Stroom (MAS) ★★★ MUSEUM   Located in Antwerp's blooming Willemdok harbor area, sandwiched between the traditional city center and the brutal sprawl of the port, MAS is a multi-floored homage to Antwerp, its people, and its culture today. Sitting on a dock commissioned by Napoleon, the museum was designed by Dutch architects Neutelings and Riedijk and looks like a pile of untidy Lego bricks clamped loosely together with teeth of glass. It opened in May 2011; the five themed floors of interactive and entertaining artworks, photos, newspaper cuttings, video, newsreel, and nearly half a million other artifacts offer an insightful explanation of how much the city owes to its riverside position on the River Schelde, to its immigrants, and to its diamond industry (p. 209). Temporary exhibitions are found in the small galleries on the walkway outside the main building, there's a panorama across the city from the 9th-floor roof, and a couple of decent watering holes too; in fact **Restaurant 'Zilte** is so decent it has garnered two Michelin stars. Altogether this is a carefully conceived museum showcasing a thoroughly modern city and its multi-racial occupants.

Hanzestedenplaats 1. ✆ **03/338-4400.** www.mas.be. Admission 5€ adults, 3€ seniors and ages 12–25, free for children 11 and under; temporary exhibition prices vary. Tues–Fri 10am–5pm, Sat–Sun 10am–6pm. Closed Jan 1, May 1, Nov 1, and Dec 25.

Museum Plantin-Moretus ★★ MUSEUM   The patrician 16th-century residence of Christoffel Plantin, inventor of one of the world's most popular printing fonts, has been awarded UNESCO World Heritage status for its period rooms, gardens, and collection of original printing presses dating as far back as the 16th century. In 1555, Plantin established a workshop in his stately mansion, and its output contributed greatly to Antwerp's reputation as a center of printing excellence in the Low Countries; today it is laid out as if the compositors and printers had just put down their tools for the day. Rubens, that local boy made good, illustrated many of the books published by the Plantin-Moretus workshop and painted some of the family portraits displayed in the museum; a further incitement to visit is the rare chance to see a Gutenberg Bible dating from 1455.

Vrijdagmarkt 22–23. ✆ **03/221-1450.** www.museumplantinmoretus.be. Admission 8€ adults, 6€ seniors and students ages 19–26, 1€ free for children 18 and under. Tues–Sun 10am–5pm. Closed Jan 1–2, May 1, Nov 1, and Dec 25.

Museum Vleeshuis (Butcher's Hall Museum) ★ MUSEUM   Scattered around the Grote Markt and nearby streets are several fine examples of 16th-century guild houses. Just north of the square stands the former Butcher Hall, a handsome gabled, Gothic structure with a tower at each corner and worthy of a star for its construction from stripes of alternating white and red brick. The interior now functions as a "museum" of pretty much anything a bit old that has to do with music; the so-called "Sounds of the City" exhibition only warrants a mention here for the fine harpsichords and Delftware mandolins on display in the middle of a few period costumes and a couple of historical paintings. It's unbearably hot inside the vaulted interior and the museum staff seemed as bored as I was. Actually, give the museum a miss altogether and just admire the funky Gothic architecture on the outside.

Vleeshouwersstraat 38–40. ✆ **03/292-6100.** www.museumvleeshuis.be. Admission 5€ adults, 3€ ages 12–26, free for children 11 and under. Thurs–Sun 10am–5pm. Closed Jan 1–2, May 1, Ascension Day, Nov 1–2, and Dec 25–26.

Antwerp City Card

Save much money as you see the sights with the Antwerp City Card, which is valid in three chunks of time, costing 19€ for 24 hours, 25€ for 48 hours, and 29€ for 72 hours. This permits free entrance to 17 museums and three churches as well as free use of the public transport system, a city map, and discounts at ZOO Antwerpen (see below) as well as on various stores and restaurants. The card is also available as an app; check **www.visitantwerpen.be** for more details.

diamonds ARE ANTWERP'S BEST FRIENDS

Antwerp remains the world's leading market for cut diamonds and second only to London as an outlet for raw and industrial diamonds, despite intense competition from India, Dubai, and Israel. The raw facts are sparkling enough: 84 percent of all the world's diamonds pass through Antwerp at some point on their journey from rough stone to polished, set gem. There are four diamond-trading houses in Antwerp and together they comprise an industry that turns over 147 million euros for the city each year. The trade, with its diamond cutters and polishers, workshops, brokers, and merchants, is centered on the few heavily guarded streets that form the city's **Diamantkwartier (Diamond Quarter)**, a surprisingly down-at-the-heels area steps away from Centraal Station. It is regulated by the Antwerp World Diamond Center (www.awdc.be) and mostly run by members of the city's Hasidic Jewish community, who found a niche market when they arrived in Antwerp in the 15th century.

To buy diamonds or watch them being cut, visit the glittering jewelry stores in the Diamond Quarter. **Diamondland,** Appelmansstraat 33a (✆ **03/229-2990;** www.diamondland.be), is the city's biggest diamond salesroom and offers guided tours of its workshops as well as trustworthy, personalized, and knowledgeable service for serious buyers (all tax-free for non-E.U. visitors).

In addition to perusing the stores and nosing around the Diamond Quarter, the **Antwerp Diamond Bus** hop-on, hop-off tour stops at all the areas associated with the diamond industry (www.antwerp-city-tours.be) and there's a small permanent exhibition in the Diamond Pavilion outside the MAS (see above). Admission 5€ adults, 3€ seniors and ages 12 to 25, free for children 11 and under.

Onze-Lieve-Vrouwekathedraal (Cathedral of Our Lady) ★★
CHURCH Antwerp's iconic landmark is a masterpiece of Brabantine Gothic architecture—and in fact the largest Gothic structure in Belgium. And the cathedral breaks more records too—it also boasts the tallest church spire in the country, an ornate affair looming 123m (404 ft.) over the city's ancient heart. Looking from the main entrance to the cathedral, you'll see that a second tower, intended to be of similar size, was never completed, giving the facade an oddly lopsided aspect. Begun in 1352 to a design by Jean Appelmans, whose statue stands outside, the cathedral was finally completed in 1521; its backstory includes a destructive fire in 1533, devastation by Protestant rebels during the religious wars of the 16th century, de-consecration by anticlerical French revolutionaries in 1794, and a slow rebirth after Napoleon's final defeat in 1815.

Its interior is a gleaming, white affair with seven aisles supported by 125 pillars, its embellishment a heady mix of baroque and neoclassical stained-glass windows, carved wood pulpits and lecterns, and tombs of the Bourbon royal family, but pole position goes to the four exquisite Rubens altarpieces: The two standout pieces are his "The Raising of the Cross" (1610) and "The Descent from the Cross" (1614). During July and August, the cathedral bells peal out in a 49-bell carillon concert on Sunday from 3 to 4pm and on Monday from 8 to 9pm.

Groenplaats 21. ✆ **03/213-9951.** www.dekathedraal.be. Admission 6€. Mon–Fri 10am–5pm, Sat 10am–3pm, Sun 1–4pm. Closed to tourist visits during services.

Rubenshuis (Rubens House) ★★★ HISTORIC SITE   Touch Antwerp's cultural heart at the house where the city's most illustrious son lived and worked. Far from being the stereotypical starving artist in a garret, the artist Peter Paul Rubens (1577–1640) amassed a tidy fortune from his light-kissed paintings, which allowed him to build an impressive mansion in 1610 when he was just 33. Today you have to beat off the tourist hordes to file through one gloriously OTT period apartment after another, all richly decorated with fine furniture, marble Roman sculptures, and examples of Rubens's exquisite portraiture, including one of Anthony van Dyck, who was his pupil. When you've fought your way through the house, take a breather in the Renaissance courtyard garden (which could do with a good weeding, quite frankly) and reflect on the sumptuous lifestyle of patrician Flemish gentleman in the 17th century.

Wapper 9–11. (€) **03/201-1555.** www.rubenshuis.be. Admission 8€ adults, 6€ seniors and students ages 12–25, free for children 11 and under. Tues–Sun 10am–5pm. Closed Jan 1–2, May 1, Ascension Day, Nov 1, and Dec 25–26.

Sint-Pauluskerk (St. Paul's Church) ★★ CHURCH   Although there was a monastery on this site as early as 1256, the present St. Paul's Church dates from the late 17th century and exhibits a cheerful clash of spindly Gothic exterior and a calm, white interior with hints of gilded baroque flourish. It is chiefly notable for the unsung collection of paintings by Rubens and his pupil Anthony van Dyck that line the outer aisles. The works of Rubens are "The Flagellation" (painting number 7 of the "Stations of the Cross" sequence in the left-hand aisle) and "The Adoration of the Shepherds" just in front of the choir on the same side. Van Dyck's contribution was "The Bearing of the Cross" (number 9 in the "Stations of the Cross"). If you get lucky, the choir may perform a 13th-century plainsong during Mass on Sunday morning.

Veemarkt 14. (€) **03/221-3321.** www.sint-paulusparochie.be. Free admission. Apr–Oct daily 2–5pm. Mass Sun 10:30am.

Especially for Kids

Antwerp is too high maintenance to be the best of destinations for kids, but it offers enough to keep them happy for a couple of days. Try **harbor cruises** with Rederij Flandria ((€) **03/231-3100;** www.flandria.nu), rides in the **electric tram** (p. 207), and dazzling them with diamonds (see above). If that fails, then abandon all ideas of discovering the secrets of the **Rubenshuis** and the **MAS** (see above for both) and head straight for **ZOO Antwerpen** ★★ (Koningin Astridplein 20–26; (€) **03/224-8910;** www.zooantwerpen.be), which has an enviable reputation for animal conservation and success in breeding rare animals. The 10-hectare (25-acre) zoo is housed in something of an Art Nouveau masterpiece, although whether the 5,000 animals appreciate this is doubtful. The 950 species include endangered okapi and red pandas, rare Siberian tigers and Arabian oryx, aviaries, polar bears, gorillas, panthers, and cuddly koalas, along with a reptile house and a petting zoo for toddlers. Right across the road is **Aquatopia** (Koningin Astridplein 7; (€) **03/205-0750;** www.aquatopia.be), with 40 aquaria filled with marine creatures from sea horses to sharks; kids can explore underneath the sea by submarine.

Where to Stay & Eat

Antwerp has carved a niche for itself in the sleek, contemporary hotels market; it abounds with small, privately owned places that reflect its status as a world capital of cool. One such bastion of hip is **m0851 guestrooms** (Nationalestraat 19; (€) **0496/213-264;** www.m0851.be), which manages to excel despite only having two guestrooms. Every modern comfort is laid out above a store of the same name selling ravishing leather accessories. It's in the heart of the fashion streets and within a quick leap of the bars and restaurants of the Grote Markt. Another young hotel is **Hotel Banks** (Steenhouwersvest 55; ✆ 03/232-4002; www.hotelbanks.be), which has fine mood-setting practices (free *prosecco* on arrival, complementary tapas in the evening, a great "breakfast on a plate" concept), but miniscule rooms.

To experience Flemish hospitality at its best, head for **Grand Café De Rooden Hoed** (Oude Koornmarkt 25; ✆ 03/289-0909; www.deroodenhoed.be), a smart, traditional brasserie serving up pails of mussels Antwerp-style with leeks, garlic, and cream, plus a wait staff that funnier than most comedy routines. For slick service in Art Nouveau surroundings after visiting the Rubenshuis, grab a table on the terrace at **Grand Café Horta** (Hopland 2; ✆ 03/203-5660; www.grandcafehorta.be) for scrumptious Thai beef salads and multi-decker club sandwiches.

> ### Room for Misunderstanding
>
> A word of warning to budget travelers: The phrase "tourist room," which in other cities means an accommodations bargain in a private home, means something rather different in Antwerp—it's a discreet way of advertising very personal services that have nothing to do with a room for the night and everything to do with a room for an hour.

Shopping

With its worldwide reputation as a city of designer flair and fashion to uphold, Antwerp just pips Brussels to the post as a shopping destination, largely thanks to world-renowned graduates of the city's Fine Art Academy like Anne Demeulemeester, Dries van Noten, and Dirk Bikkembergs.

The long shopping street of Meir has mid-range international chains and department stores, while the upmarket stores and boutiques have colonized the area south of the Grote Markt between Steenhouwersvest and Komedieplaats; here you'll find Diane von Furstenberg, Gucci, Ralph Lauren, Petite Filou, and many others. For lace, scour the streets surrounding the cathedral and for diamonds, head for Appelmansstraat and nearby streets around Centraal Station.

Antwerp After Dark

Antwerp is as dynamic after dark as it is busy during the day. The main entertainment zones for visitors are Grote Markt and Groenplaats, which are both packed with **bars, cafes, and theaters;** High Town (Hoogstraat, Pelgrimstraat, Pieter Potstraat, and vicinity) for **jazz clubs and bistros;** Stadswaag for **jazz and punk;** and the Centraal Station area for **discos, nightclubs, and gay bars.** The red-light district here, concentrated in Riverside Quarter, is much rougher than the one in Amsterdam and is definitely not a tourist attraction.

THE PERFORMING ARTS

Antwerp takes pride in being a citadel of Flemish culture. Two of the region's stellar performance companies are based here: the **Vlaamse Opera (Flanders Opera;** Frankrijklei 1; ✆ 070/22-0202; www.vlaamseopera.be), run in conjunction with the opera house in Ghent (p. 220), and the **Koninklijk Ballet Vlaanderen (Royal Flanders Ballet;** Kattendijkdok-Westkaai 16; ✆ 03/234-3438; www.koninklijkballet vanvlaanderen.be).

Contemporary music, hard-hitting drama, and dance is the province of performances at the multi-staged **deSingel,** Desguinlei 25 (✆ **03/248-2828;** www.desingel. be), and big-name concerts (Pharrell Williams, Miley Cyrus, and Jack White played here in 2014) are held at the **Sportpaleis Antwerp** (Schijnpoortweg 119; ✆ **03/400-4040;** www.sportpaleis.be).

GHENT ★★

48km (30 miles) NW of Brussels

In the past, Ghent was considered the poor relation of Bruges, but the comparison doesn't hold up these days. Ghent's monuments and townscapes might not be so picture perfect as those of Gothic Bruges, but then few places are. Instead of sitting on its (considerable) laurels, Ghent is a city with attitude, forward thinking and cosmopolitan but with a rough edge to it that makes the place thrum with possibilities. Life moves fast in the capital town of Oost-Vlaanderen (East Flanders) province; it's got a pretty face, yes, but currently it's a bit careworn, not all powdered and puffed like Bruges. Tourists are welcomed here with open arms but they don't make the city tick as they do in Bruges, as Ghent is also an important university city, an inland port, and an industrial center. Largely thanks to its 60,000-strong student population, Ghent compensates for its less precious appearance with a vigorous, gritty social and cultural scene, with bars, restaurants, and clubbing options aplenty.

Essentials

GETTING THERE

BY PLANE Brussels Airport is the main international airport in Belgium (p. 232) but a coach service runs nine times a day between **Brussels-South-Charleroi Airport** (p. 232) and Bruges via Ghent, making this small airport easier to access. Tickets are 5€ one-way and schedule details are available at www.flibco.com.

BY TRAIN Ghent is a 35-minute train ride from Brussels, and there are at least five direct trains every hour between the two, with a round-trip fare of 18€. The main station of **Gent-Sint-Pieters** is on Koningin Maria-Hendrikaplein, 2km (1½ miles) south of the center city. Tram No. 1 runs into the Korenmarkt.

BY CAR Take A10/E40 from Brussels; the journey takes 45 minutes when the traffic is clear.

VISITOR INFORMATION

The **Visit Ghent tourist office** is a fabulously modern affair with a James Bond–esque computer table offering multilingual information. It's in the former Fishmarket (Sint-Veerleplein 5; ✆ **09/266-5660;** www.visitgent.be) and is open daily 9:30am to 6:30pm.

GETTING AROUND

Ghent has an excellent, integrated **tram and bus network** plus a single **electric trolley-bus** line, all operated by **De Lijn** (✆ **070/220-200;** www.delijn.be). The four tramlines (1, 4, 21, and 22) stop at **Gent-Sint-Pieters station** and at multiple points throughout the city center. Purchase your travel ticket from the De Lijn sales point in the station before boarding and you'll pay 20 percent less. The most useful ticket for sightseers is the *dagkaart* **(day card)** valid for the entire network; it costs 5€ in advance, 7€ from the driver once on the tram.

Ghent

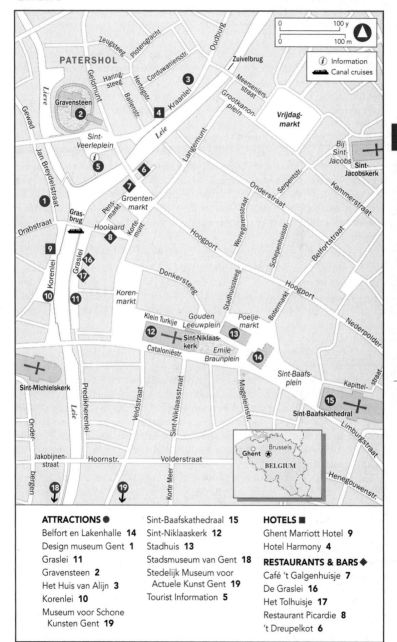

0 100 y
0 100 m

ⓘ Information
🚢 Canal cruises

PATERSHOL

Gravensteen ❷

Sint-Veerleplein

Vrijdag-markt

Bij Sint-Jacobs

Sint-Jacobskerk

Grasbrug

Groenten-markt

Hooiaard

Koren-markt

Sint-Michielskerk

Klein Turkije

Gouden Leeuwplein

Sint-Niklaas-kerk

Poelje-markt

Emile Braunplein

Sint-Baafs-plein

Sint-Baafskathedral

Jakobijnen-straat

Hoornstr.

Volderstraat

Brussels
Ghent ✪
BELGIUM

ATTRACTIONS ●

Belfort en Lakenhalle **14**
Design museum Gent **1**
Graslei **11**
Gravensteen **2**
Het Huis van Alijn **3**
Korenlei **10**
Museum voor Schone Kunsten Gent **19**

Sint-Baafskathedraal **15**
Sint-Niklaaskerk **12**
Stadhuis **13**
Stadsmuseum van Gent **18**
Stedelijk Museum voor Actuele Kunst Gent **19**
Tourist Information **5**

HOTELS ■

Ghent Marriott Hotel **9**
Hotel Harmony **4**

RESTAURANTS & BARS ◆

Café 't Galgenhuisje **7**
De Graslei **16**
Het Tolhuisje **17**
Restaurant Picardie **8**
't Dreupelkot **6**

There are plenty of regulated **taxis** with ranks in the streets; you'll find them outside **Gent-Sint-Pieters** and **Ghent Dampoort stations** as well as on Korenmarkt. Otherwise call **Vtax** (𝒞 **09/222-2222;** www.v-tax.be).

Exploring Ghent

This is a city best seen by walking its streets, gazing at its gabled guild houses and private mansions, and stopping on its bridges to take in the waterside views. Ghent's historical monuments have not all been prettified; some of them look downright gray and forbidding, which, oddly enough, gives them a more authentic feel. The city's heart surrounds the funnel-shaped piazza of **Korenmarkt,** and this is where local big wheels had their residences in times past. Most of the city's major sights—including the **Stadhuis** (p. 218), **St. Bavo's Cathedral** (p. 217), and the **Belfort** (p. 214)—are close by. To the north lies the foreboding **Gravensteen Castle,** and beyond that is the revamped medieval enclave of **Patershol,** today something of a hot drinking and dining spot. The River Leie winds through the city center on its way to join the River Schelde and a network of canals leading to the port. Citadelpark, location of the **Museum voor Schone Kunsten Gent** (p. 216) is in the south of the city near Gent-Sint-Pieters station, and is one to avoid at night thanks to recent drug dealings and muggings.

Belfort en Lakenhalle (Belfry and Cloth Hall) ★ HISTORIC SITE   The glorious medieval ensemble of the Belfry tower and Cloth Hall stand across the sweeping square of Botermarkt from Sint-Baafskathedraal (St. Bavo's Cathedral, see below) and form a glorious medieval ensemble. The 14th-century **Belfry** holds the great bells that have rung out Ghent's civic pride down the centuries; the most beloved was a giant bell known as Roland (1315), which was used as the city's alarm bell. It was destroyed by Emperor Charles V in 1540 as punishment for Ghent's insubordination against the Spanish. No fewer than 28 of the 54 bells that now make up the tower's huge carillon were cast from Roland's broken pieces. The massive Triomfanten bell, cast in 1660, now rests in a small park at the foot of the Belfry, still bearing the crack it sustained when it broke in 1914. Take the elevator to the Belfry's upper gallery, 66m (217 ft.) to see the bells and take in fantastic **panoramic views of the city;** it's a great way to get your bearings as well as enjoy the medieval splendor beneath you. A great iron chest was kept in the Belfry's *Secreet* (strongroom) to hold the all-important charters that spelled out privileges the guilds and the burghers of medieval Ghent wrested from the counts of Flanders.

The **Cloth Hall** at the foot of the Belfry dates from 1425 and was the gathering place of wool and cloth merchants. A baroque extension from 1741 on Goudenleeuwplein was used until 1902 as a prison, dubbed De Mammelokker (the Suckler). The name comes from a relief above the doorway that depicts the Roman legend of Cimon,

---

Your Sightseeing Passport to Ghent

Save money as you sightsee with the **CityCard Gent,** available from **Visit Gent** (see above) in time allotments of 48 hours for 30€ or 72 hours costing a bargain 35€. The pass includes free use of the city's public transportation and admission to key museums and monuments, a city map, and a 50-minute boat trip from either **Rederij De Gentenaer** or **Gent Watertoerist** (p. 220 for both).

Ghent's main square is **Vrijdagmarkt**—huge, tree shaded, ever bustling, and surrounded by old guild houses hosting stores selling Ghent noses (a syrupy confection like an overgrown jelly baby in fruity flavors) and restaurants that sprout across sidewalks when the sun shines. There are markets here most weekends but historically this square has been the scene of much turbulence, a fact marked by the central bronze statue of 14th-century rebel leader Jacob van Artevelde, who fought the English ban on Flemish wool exports in the 14th century. The statue was erected in 1863 to commemorate Van Artevelde's assassination in 1345.

Few traditional sights clutter the small yet beguiling **Patershol** neighborhood along the west bank of the Leie River and north of the Lieve Canal, but it provides a charming taste of Old Ghent. The nest of narrow, pedestrianized streets and tightly packed brick cottages were built in the 17th century for the city's weavers, craftsmen, and tradesmen; about 100 of these buildings are protected monuments and have been delightfully revamped. Restaurants and bars have now flooded in to the area, making it a popular late-night drinking and clubbing spot.

starving to death in prison, being suckled by his daughter Pero. Appropriately, this newer section is now the office for the city's *ombudsvrouw* (ombudswoman).

Sint-Baafsplein. ⓒ **09/233-3954.** www.belfortgent.be. Admission 6€ adults, 4.50€ seniors, 2€ students 19–26, free for ages 18 and under. Daily 10am–6pm. Closed Dec 25–26 and Dec 31–Jan 1.

Gravensteen (Castle of the Counts) ★ HISTORIC SITE   "Menacing" is the word that springs to mind for this circular, gray fortress crouching like a great stone lion over the split in the River Leie. Gravensteen was clearly designed by the ruling counts of Flanders to keep the populace in line by sending out a harsh message to a rebellion-inclined citizenry. Although a wooden castle had existed for several centuries in this location, the turreted fortress we see today was built in 1180 by Philip of Alsace, the Count of Flanders. He had just returned from the Crusades and clearly intended to recreate the stern, foreboding crusader castles that are strewn on rocky crags across the eastern Mediterranean. If its 2m/6-foot–thick walls, battlements, and turrets failed to intimidate attackers, a well-equipped torture chamber awaited inside. Relics of the chamber—a guillotine, spiked iron collars, branding irons, thumb screws—are displayed in a small museum. Climb up to the battlements for great views of Ghent's rooftops and canals.

Sint-Veerleplein 11. ⓒ **09/225-9306.** www.gravensteengent.be. Admission 10€ adults, 7.50€ seniors, 6€ ages 19–25, free for children 18 and under. Apr–Oct daily 10am–6pm, Nov–Mar daily 9am–5pm. Closed Dec 25–26 and Dec 31–Jan 1.

Design museum Gent ★★ MUSEUM   Located in the Hotel de Coninck (ca. 1755), a baroque mansion with a lovely courtyard garden dominated by a huge ceramic urn and a modern extension grafted on to the rear, this decorative arts museum showcases the very best in world design. In the old wing, the exhibits range through period salons decked out with swagged curtains, frescoed ceilings, elaborate chandeliers, fine French furniture, and Chinese porcelain in typically aristocratic 18th- and 19th-century Flemish style. Oddly out of context here is a "book table" by contemporary Dutch designer Richard Hutten, entirely comprised of hardbacks and lacquered to give it a shiny, hard finish. In marked contrast to all that heavy, ornate, period luxury, the bright, light-filled new wing sings to a contemporary tune and features sublime examples of Art Nouveau furniture by Henry van de Velde and Paul Hankar, and even the Belgian master of the genre, Victor Horta. Seminal work from the 20th and early 21st centuries feature Alessi silverware, stools in recycled plastic by Bar und Knell Design, and chairs by Richard Gehry. Temporary exhibitions take on controversial subjects such as the use of plastic and pollution.

Jan Breydelstraat 5. ℭ **09/267-9999.** www.design.museum.gent.be. Admission 8€ adults, 6.50€ seniors, 2€ ages 19–26, free for children 18 and under. Tues–Sun 10am–6pm. Closed Dec 25–26 and Dec 31–Jan 1. Tram: 1 or 4 to Korenmarkt.

Het Huis van Alijn (House of Alijn) ★★ MUSEUM   Ghent's intriguing folklore museum may take visitors on a journey through 20th-century life but it's located in the only medieval *godshuis* (almshouse) still standing in the city. The House of Alijn dates back to the 12th century, stands around a neat courtyard garden, and over its long lifetime has functioned as a children's home and a hospital. Inside the clutch of whitewashed, gabled, and restored cottages are replicas of Ghent weaving and metalwork workshops as well as shop interiors of a sweet shops and a bakers, but the most fascinating rooms are those dating from the 1950s and 1980s—and oh, how dated the '80s decor looks. One long corridor features flickering home movies, mundane in subject but rich in vicarious detail from this story of every-day Belgian folk going about their lives. You might want to end your day's sightseeing here over a beer in the traditional tavern, **'t Cafeetse,** beside the River Leie.

Kraanlei 65. ℭ **09/269-2350.** www.huisvanalijn.be. Admission 6€ adults, 4.50€ seniors, 2€ ages 19–26, free for children 18 and under. Museum and tavern Tues–Sat 11am–5:30pm, Sun 10am–5:30pm. Closed Jan 1 and Dec 25.

Museum voor Schone Kunsten Gent (Ghent Fine Arts Museum) ★★ MUSEUM   Tucked behind a pillared, neoclassical facade on the edge of Citadelpark, the fine arts museum traces the story of Belgian art from the glowing, almost Byzantine religious art of the Middle Ages to modern day. Although it has its fair share of work by the Flemish Primitives—including the dark, gaunt "Bearing of the Cross" (ca. 1500) by Bosch, plus Rubens and Van Dyck—where this museum really excels is in its later offerings. The late 19th century was a period of great artistic flowering in Ghent, and this is reflected in the works by *fin de siècle* artists such as James Ensor and Theo van Rysselberghe, whose work bears an uncanny resemblance to the paintings of his American contemporary John Singer Sargent. The MSK has been beautifully renovated and now all artwork hangs evocatively highlighted against dark walls

---

Party Time in Ghent

If you hit town in July, you've crashed in on party heaven in Ghent. For 10 days around July 21, Belgium's greatest extended street party, the **Gentse Feesten (Ghent Festivities;** ℭ 09/210-1010; www.gentsefeesten.be) swirl through the city with concerts, from classical to indie and dance, street theater, performance art, puppet shows, a street fair, special museum exhibits, and riotous fun and games. See p. 39 for more information.

The Naked Truth

Prudish 18th-century Austrian Emperor Joseph II ordered the naked figures of Adam and Eve in **"The Adoration of the Mystic Lamb"** to be replaced by others with fig leafs covering their genitals. Today, the original Adam and Eve are back in their birthday-suit glory, and you can view the ridiculous replacement panels attached to columns near the cathedral's entrance.

embellished with bright-white neoclassical friezes. If contemporary artwork is your thing, there's an offshoot of MSK close by in Citadelpark at **SMAK** (see below).

Fernand Scribedreef 1, Citadelpark. ☏ **09/240-0700.** www.mskgent.be. Admission 8€ adults, 6€ seniors, 2€ ages 19–26, free for children18 and under. Tues–Sun 10am–6pm. Closed Dec 25–26 and Dec 31–Jan 1.

Sint-Baafskathedraal (St. Bavo's Cathedral) ★★★ CHURCH   Even if you see nothing else in Ghent, don't miss this massive cathedral. Don't be put off by its rather unimpressive exterior, a muddle of Romanesque, Gothic, and baroque architecture that was under scaffolding at the time of writing. Constructed in stages from the 13th century onwards, it is dedicated to Bavo, the patron saint of the city, and the interior is filled with sweet-smelling lilies as well as paintings, sculptures, memorials, and carved marble tombs. Art treasures in this glorious cathedral include Rubens's "The Conversion of St. Bavo" (1623) in the Rubens Chapel behind the elaborate high altar and the ornate rococo oak pulpit entwined with white marble statuary, but St. Bavo's showpiece, indeed the major artistic masterpiece of Ghent, is the 24-panel altarpiece **"The Adoration of the Mystic Lamb"** ★★ in the Villa Chapel, commissioned by a wealthy city alderman and completed by Flemish Primitive artist Jan van Eyck and his brother Hubert in 1432. The luminous use of oils and naturalistic portrayal of nature and people represented a giant step away from the rigid style of Gothic religious art. But besides its importance in the history of art, the "Mystic Lamb" is simply spellbinding. It is currently being restored, but at least two-thirds of the panels are present at any one time for viewing; the others are replaced by black and white images. Work will finish in 2017.

Sint-Baafsplein. ☏ **09/269-2045.** www.sintbaafskathedraal.be. Admission: cathedral free; "Mystic Lamb" chapel 4€ adults (includes audio guide in English), 1.50€ school children. Cathedral: Apr–Oct Mon–Sat 8:30am–6pm, Sun 9:30am–6pm; Nov–Mar Mon–Sat 8:30am–5pm, Sun 1–5pm; "Mystic Lamb" chapel: Apr–Oct daily 9:30am–5pm, Sun 1–5pm; Nov–Mar Mon–Sat 10:30am–4pm, Sun 1–4pm.

Sint-Niklaaskerk (St. Nicholas's Church) CHURCH   The first to be constructed of the triumvirate of church spires that dominate central Ghent, St. Nicholas displays a mixture of Romanesque elements and the Flemish Schelde Gothic architectural style. An impressive 13th- to 15th-century church, it is a veritable mountain of Tournai bluestone and was paid for by Ghent's wealthy medieval merchants as an ostentatious signal of their wealth to other Flemish cities. A baroque high altar and other rich decorations embellish the interior; these date from after the Protestant *Beeldenstorm* (Iconoclastic Fury) of 1566, during which Catholic churches across the Low Countries were ransacked. An extensive restoration is ongoing so currently the best way to appreciate the Gothic detailing of St. Nicholas's flying buttresses and slender stained-glass windows is from the viewing platform of the Belfort (see above).

Korenmarkt. ☏ **09/234-2869.** Free admission. Tues–Sun 10–5pm, Mon 2–5pm.

The Two-Faced Town Hall

Ghent's Stadhuis (Town Hall) hovers in the northeast corner of the Botermarkt, showing a rather plain Renaissance profile to the world. However, walk round the corner to Hoogpoort and you'll come face to face with a garishly ornamented Gothic face to the building. This came about because construction began in 1518, was interrupted, began again at the end of the century, halted once more in the early 1600s, and wasn't completed until the 18th century. The changing public tastes of those years are reflected in the building's conflicting styles. Tours of the Town Hall can be made Monday through Thursday at 2:30pm, costing 5€. Contact the Visit Ghent tourist office (p. 212).

Stadsmuseum van Gent (Ghent City Museum) ★★★ MUSEUM This museum, known as STAM, offers the perfect introduction to Ghent, as it details the development of the city from its medieval beginnings to the cultured city we meet today. It's housed in an eccentric space that flows from the 14th-century Bijloke Abbey through its neat knot of gardens and into a contemporary block of airy exhibition space with exterior walls made of glass, mirroring the historical progress of the city as it moves from medieval to modern. A chronological trail meanders through multimedia exhibits, images, archeological finds, artwork, and "listening benches" to bring Ghent's rich history to life in a museum that's stylishly curated and educational, yet also succeeds in being entertaining.

Godshuizenlaan 2. ✆ **09/267-1400.** www.stamgent.be. Admission 8€ adults, 6€ seniors, 2€ ages 19–26, free for ages 18 and under. Tues–Sun 10am–6pm. Closed Dec 25–26 and Dec 31–Jan 1.

Stedelijk Museum voor Actuele Kunst Gent (Museum of Contemporary Art) ★★ MUSEUM Better known by yet another acronym, SMAK is Ghent's primary attraction for contemporary art fiends, located in a 1930s building in Citadelpark near the Fine Arts Museum (see above). The permanent collection contains great works by Karel Appel of CoBrA fame and big international names like Andy Warhol and Christo, but they're not always on show. You're more likely to find wacky, weird, and sometimes wonderful temporary exhibitions (such as the rainbow-hued paintings and installations of American colorist Richard Jackson) showcase the work of Europe's leading contemporary artists; standards can be hit or miss so check what's on before a visit.

Citadelpark. ✆ **09/240-7601.** www.smak.be. Admission 8€ adults, 6€ seniors, 2€ ages 19–26, free for children 18 and under. Tues–Sun 10am–6pm. Closed Dec 25–26 and Dec 31–Jan 1.

The Medieval Harbor ★★★

Undoubtedly the most beautiful parts of Ghent are the medieval quays of **Graslei** and **Korenlei** just west of Korenmarkt. Facing each other across the Leie waterway, they were the site of Tusschen Brugghen, the city's medieval harbor. Both embankments are lined with rows of intricately gabled former guild houses, warehouses, and elegant town houses built in a variety of architectural styles between the 1200s and 1600s. It is fair to say that if all Ghent was as lovely as these two streets, it would give Bruges a run for its money. Although a considerable amount of restorative nip and tuck has been performed over the centuries, none of these majestic buildings have lost their medieval allure. To see them all lit up at night under the **Ghent Light Plan** (see below) is a genuinely breathtaking experience. By day, both quays are lined with tour-boat docks (see below).

GRASLEI

Graslei today is one of the city's most picturesque meeting points, awash with **bars and restaurants** backlit by graceful gabled gild houses. At no. 8, the Brabantine Gothic **Gildehuis van de Metselaars (Stonemasons' Guild House)** has graceful pinnacles and is decorated with a medallion of an angel and reliefs of the "Quatuor Coronati," four Roman martyrs who were the guild's patrons. It dates from 1527 but what you see is actually a 1912 reconstruction of a 16th-century guild house originally located on Cataloniëstraat.

No. 9, dating from 1435, was the first **Korenmetershuis (House of the Grain Measurers),** where officials weighed imported grain before it was transported to the Korenmarkt. Next door, at no. 10, is the solidly constructed **Het Spijker (Stockpile House),** dating from around 1200, where corn was stored. The front of its forward-leaning Romanesque facade reaches up to the world's oldest step gable. Inside is the chic restaurant and club **Belga Queen** (www.belgaqueen.be).

The tiny building squashed in at no. 11 is the **Tolhuisje (Little Customs House),** which was constructed in 1682 in the Flemish Renaissance style as the office of the city's corn revenue agent. It now houses a great little cafe, **Het Tolhuisje** (see below). Next door, nos. 12–13 were an annex to the **Korenmetershuis (House of the Grain Measurers)** and date from 1540; the patterned red-and-white brickwork was added in 1698.

No. 14, with a facade dating from 1531 covering the 14th-century building underneath, was the ornate Brabantine Gothic **Gildehuis van de Vrije Schippers (Guild House of the Free Boatmen)** ★. This is one of the finest sights on Graslei, decorated with symbols of sailing ships and sailors on its sandstone facade.

KORENLEI

Across the water from Graslei by the Sint-Michielsbrug (St. Michael's Bridge), Koren lei is a fine vantage point from which to appreciate the architectural wonders on the opposite bank. However, this street has many treasures of its own, most built later than the historic facades along Graslei.

The step-gabled 16th-century house constructed of red brick at no. 23 on the corner by the bridge was the **Brewers' Guild House.** The ultramodern **Ghent Marriott Hotel** (see below) has installed itself in a bunch of restored guild houses, with the main entrance at Korenlei no. 10. Next door, the redbrick, step-gabled building called **De Swaene (the Swans),** at no. 9, dates from 1609; it has a pair of gilded swan medallions on the facade, and in its time has been a brewery and a bordello.

Ghent Light Plan

In 2010, Ghent city fathers hatched a plan to light the city after dark. This had dual purposes: to increase safety at night and to show off the city's phenomenal architecture to its best advantage. Now you can follow the route through the streets on a 2-hour circular walk from Kouter in the south to Vrijdag-markt in the north, but by far the most spectacular sights are the medieval guild houses in Korenlei and Graslei. But don't get too sidetracked in Ghent's enticing bars as the illuminations, like Cinderella, disappear at midnight. You can download the walk for free from www.visitgent.be/en/node/9407.

At no. 7 is the pink-and-white-shaded **Gildehuis van de Onvrije Schippers (Guild House of the Tied Boatmen)** ★. Dating from 1739 and dubbed Den Ancker (the Anchor), it is a masterpiece of Flemish baroque architecture, with a graceful bell gable and carved dolphins and lions on the facade; that's all topped with a gilded weathervane of a sailing ship at full mast on the roof.

Cruising Ghent

A 50-minute **cruise** ★ on the canals with either **Rederij De Gentenaer** (℡ 09/269-0869; www.rederijdegentenaer.be) or **Gent Watertoerist** (℡ 09/269-0869; www.gent-watertoerist.be) is included in the **CityCard Ghent** package (p. 214) and is well worth it to see the historic buildings lining the medieval waterways. Tour boats sail from Graslei and Korenlei, and opening hours and costs are the same for both cruise companies: April to mid-October daily 10am to 5pm, mid-October through March daily 11am to 4pm. Without the card, cruises cost 6.50€ for adults; 6€ for seniors, students, and ages 13 to 25; 3€ for children 3 to 11.

Especially for Kids

As well as canal tours to explore the **medieval canals** (see above) and views from the top of the **Belfort** (p. 214), several of Ghent's major museums, including the **House of Alijn** (p. 216), **Design museum Gent** (p. 215), and **Ghent City Museum** (p. 218), have tours specially designed to appeal to kids. The torture chamber at **Gravensteen Castle** (p. 215), is guaranteed to enthrall gloomy, emo-inclined teenagers. As much of the city center is pedestrianized, it's safe to explore by bike; rent from **Max Mobiel vzw** (www.max-mobiel.be); prices start at 7€ per day. If all else fails, bribe the kids with must-have treats including fruity, pyramid-shaped *neuzekes* (Ghent noses) from the shops around the Vrijdagmarkt or Temmerman (Kraanlei 79).

Where to Stay, Eat & Drink

Many of Ghent's hotels are sandwiched into ancient buildings but hide interiors that are the very latest in contemporary design and comfort. Travelers with cash to spare need look no further than the immaculate temple to modern design and comfort that is the **Ghent Marriott Hotel** (℡ 09/233-9393; www.marriottghent.be), located in medieval mansions at Korenlei 10. The **Hotel Harmony** (Kraanlei 37; ℡ 09/324-2680; www.hotel-harmony.be) is another such gem, overlooking the Leie on the fringes of Patershol. The stylish rooms of this family-run establishment are so vast you can loose whole families in them and there's a tiny plunge pool squeezed in the garden at the back.

A night out in Ghent is never going to be a problem, with a proliferation of dining and drinking options from traditional grand cafes to gin-tasting houses. For lovely nighttime views over gracious guild houses, choose **De Graslei** (Graslei 7; 09/225-5147; www.restaurantdegraslei.be); the place buzzes in many languages and offers a typically Flemish menu of teeming seafood platters or *waterzooi* served with piles of fries. An on-trend lunchtime spot with a sunny terrace bang in the middle of Ghent's tourist heartland, **Restaurant Picardie** (Hooiaard 7; ℡ 09/233-8444) overflows with bonhomie and a menu of well-priced bistro staples.

Ghent After Dark

Although Ghent is up for a good night out on the town any time of year, its cultural calendar really hits the heights from October to mid-June, when international opera is performed in the 19th-century **De Vlaamse Opera,** Schouwburgstraat 9

(© **09/268-1011;** www.vlaamseopera.be), run in conjunction with the opera house in Antwerp (p. 211). This is regarded as one of the most spectacular and plushest concert halls in Europe, built in the 1840s and with an auditorium encrusted with gilding, red velvet, and frescoed ceilings.

Ghent's favorite after-dark entertainment is found among hundreds of atmospheric bars and taverns. Groentenmarkt, Korelei, and Graslei make the best trawling ground for a pub crawl in an easily navigable (and safe) area. The oldest drinking haunt in the city is **Café 't Galgenhuisje** (Groentenmarkt 5; © **09/233-4251**), normally rammed with students spilling out onto the square. A vast choice of Belgian beers are on offer at the miniscule tavern of **Het Tolhuisje** (Graslei 11; © **09/224-3090**), which is cleverly inserted into the smallest building on floodlit Graslei. But if there is one place that encapsulates the party vibe of Ghent, it's **'t Dreupelkot** (Groentenmarkt 12; © **09/224-2120;** www.dreupelkot.be), where you can spend an addictive hour or two sampling some 100 or so varieties of the ginlike liqueur *jenever* (p. 72); horrifically, it's even available flavored with chocolate.

MONS ★

51km (32 miles) SW of Brussels

Hainaut's provincial capital—and the *cultural* capital of French-speaking Wallonia— sits in the southwest of Belgium abutting the French border. Mons started life as a fortified camp constructed by Julius Caesar's Roman legions high in a landscape of rolling hills, and today, it's home to SHAPE (Supreme Headquarters Allied Powers Europe). Between those two military bookends, it has enjoyed a rich and eventful history. The Roman encampment morphed into a town when St. Waltrude, the daughter of a local nobleman, founded a convent here in the 600s.

Occupied repeatedly by opposing French and Austrian forces down the centuries, Mons eventually found its forte and grew wealthy through industrialization. The mining that brought in the money to help Mons expand has long since dried up and this pretty little place is oft wrongly overlooked on the tourist trail. However, there's plenty to please here, as Mons is blessed with one of the most handsome townscapes in Belgium. Start your exploration in the harmonious central Grand-Place, which is a masterpiece of civic and religious buildings dating from the 11th century onward. The year 2015 sees exciting times for Mons as it becomes European Capital of Culture, partnered with (among others) Namur (see below) in French-speaking Belgium and Mechelen (p. 229) in Flemish-speaking Flanders; art exhibitions, festivals, and street parties are planned. By the way, if you want to travel to Mons from a Flemish-speaking destination, it's called Bergen.

Essentials

GETTING THERE Mons is an easy day trip from Brussels, with trains departing between the two twice hourly; the ride takes about 50 minutes and the round-trip fare is 16€. The station is on place Léopold, a short walk west from the center of town. For more details, go to www.belgianrail.be. To get to Mons by **car** from Brussels, take E19; the journey takes around an hour.

VISITOR INFORMATION The **Maison du Tourisme du Pays du Mons** is at Grand-Place 22 (© **065/335-580;** www.visitmons.be). The office is open Monday to Saturday 9am to 6pm and Sunday 11am to 6pm.

GETTING AROUND Walking is the best way to get around in the Old Town, but free **Mons Intra Muros** mini-buses run on four routes between the station and the Grand-Place every 6 minutes Monday through Saturday 7am to 9pm.

Exploring Mons

BAM ★ MUSEUM The Beaux-Arts Mons (Museum of Fine Arts) occupies a purpose-built gallery on a side street off Mons' fine Grand-Place. As well as hosting concerts, the museum has a permanent collection of 19th- and 20th-century paintings and sculpture drawn from around Hainaut. Much more interesting to most tourists are the temporary exhibitions, which have focused on big names like Warhol and Surrealism.

Rue Neuve 8. (℃ **065/405-330.** www.bam.mons.be. Admission: permanent exhibitions 4€ adults, 2€ children 17 and under; temporary exhibitions 9€ adults, 6€ children 17 and under. Free first Sun each month. Tues–Sun 10am–6pm.

Beffroi ★★ HISTORIC SITE The first thing anyone notices about Mons is the baroque Beffroi (Belfry), a landmark UNESCO World Heritage Site that stands 87m (270 ft.) above the highest point of town on the square du Château; with typical Gallic bureaucracy it's only open by writing in advance to the tourist office (see above). Opposite the Belfry is the Chapelle St-Calixte, the oldest structure in town, dating from 1051. The chapel has a very meager **Musée du Château des Comtes (Museum of the Castle of the Counts)** containing a few ancient bits of crumbling statuary.

Square du Château. (℃ **065/335-580.** Admission 2.50€ adults, 1.25€ seniors and students 12 to 18, free for children 11 and under. Free first Sun each month. Tues–Sun noon–6pm.

Collégiale Ste-Waudru (Collegiate Church of St. Waltrude) ★★ CHURCH Dating from 1450, this remarkably lovely church in Brabantine Gothic style stands just below the Belfry. Inside its vast vaulted space is crammed with 16th-century sculptures and wooden wall carvings by Mons artist Jacques Du Brœucq (1505–84), while around the choir 16th-century stained-glass windows depict biblical scenes and banners hang in the slender Gothic window recesses. The church's treasury contains richly ornamented religious objects in gold—chalices, monstrances, and reliquaries—many of them dedicated in honor of St. Waltrude, along with sculptures, paintings, and vestments. At the entrance to the church, the ceremonial **Car d'Or (Golden Coach)** anticipates its annual spring outing, when it is paraded around town in a religious festival called **Ducasse de Mons** on Trinity Sunday.

Place du Chapitre. (℃ **065/335-580.** www.waudru.be. Free admission. Church: Mon–Sat 9am–6pm, Sun 9:30am–6pm; treasury: Tues–Sun noon–6pm.

Grand-Place ★★ HISTORIC SITE Almost everything you'll want to see in Mons is on or around the fountain-filled Grand-Place, a lovely spot to take half an hour out over coffee or a beer in the terrace cafes. The piazza is lined by a noble mix of splendid town houses and surrounded by steep, cobbled streets, and its centerpiece is the 15th-century Gothic **Hôtel de Ville (Town Hall),** topped with an unusual bronze bell tower. Inside the Town Hall are antique tapestries and paintings; access to the stately apartments is by free, guided tour arranged through the Visit Ghent tourist office (p. 212). At the rear of the Hôtel de Ville you'll find the tranquil **Jardin du Mayeur (Mayor's Garden),** filled with calming shrubs, flowers, and fountains. As you go through the arched doorway towards the gardens, it's customary to stop and rub the head of the monkey of the "Grand-Garde," an iron statue that's been granting good luck since the 15th century. Needless to say, he has a very shiny pate.

Town Hall: Grand-Place 22. Guided tours July–Aug Tues–Sat 2:30pm.

Musée des Arts Décoratifs (Museum of Decorative Arts) François Duesberg ★★ MUSEUM Arguably the most prepossessing museum in Mons, this privately owned decorative-arts collection is housed in a former bank opposite the Collegiate Church of St. Waltrude and has squirreled together a fine collection of neoclassical French and Belgian *objets d'art*. Standout pieces include fine sets of Meissen porcelain, silverware from rich guilds, and hundreds of gilt-embellished 18th-century timepieces—Michelin have awarded this clock collection with four stars—they are all beautifully displayed in glass cabinets reminiscent of the "curiosity cabinets" so popular with 18th- and 19th-century collectors.

Sq. Franklin Roosevelt 12. ℰ **065/363-164.** www.duesberg.mons.be. Admission 5€ adults, free for children 12 and under. Tues, Thurs, Sat–Sun 2–7pm.

Around Mons

Château de Beloeil (Beloeil Castle) ★★ CASTLE The "Versailles of Belgium" is the magnificent ancestral home of the aristocratic de Ligne family, a great moated palace sitting amid formal baroque-style gardens overlooking an ornamental lake. The Princes of de Ligne have called this magnificent castle their home since the 14th century but there was a fortified residence for at least 300 years before that. In summer the family open their sumptuous home to the public to show off the considerable style in which they live; each vast apartment is furnished in glamorous 18th-century French style, swathed with elaborately frescoed and gilded ornamentation and filled with priceless antiques, fine-spun carpets and tapestries, Old Master paintings, a lock of hapless Queen Marie Antoinette's hair, and more than 20,000 books.

Rue du Château 11, Beloeil (22km/14 miles northwest of Mons). ℰ **069/689-426.** www.chateaude beloeil.com. Admission: château and park 9€ adults, 8€ seniors, 4€ children 6–12; park only 4€ adults, 2€ seniors and children 6–12. Apr–June and Sept Sat–Sun 10am–6pm, July–Aug daily 10am–6pm.

Grand-Hornu ★ HISTORIC SITE As the Industrial Revolution hit the area around Mons, many families grew rich on the backs of their workers. One entrepreneur with a social conscience was mine-owner Henri de Gorge (1774–1832), who constructed Grand-Hornu between 1810 and 1830 in neoclassical style and attached to it 450 houses for his workers. Following the collapse of industry in the region, Gorge's utopian dream fell into dereliction before being restored in the 1970s. It's a fascinating, unlikely mixture of antiquarian sensibility and gritty industrial reality that showcases the Victorian entrepreneurial tradition at its best. A part of the site has been given over to the **Musée des Arts Contemporains** of Belgium's Francophone community and its exhibits of contemporary art.

Rue Ste-Louise 82, Hornu (13km/8 miles southwest of Mons). ℰ **065/652-121.** www.grand-hornu. be. Admission 8€ adults, 4€ seniors, 2€ children 6–18, free for children 5 and under. Tues–Sun 10am–6pm. Closed Jan 1 and Dec 25.

Maison Van Gogh (Van Gogh House) ★ MUSEUM During his days as a none-too-successful church missionary (ca. 1879–80), the tortured Dutch artist Vincent van Gogh lived in a bleak miner's cottage called the Maison du Marais (the "March House") in the Borinage coal-mining district. From this squat, brick-built house he preached the gospel to poverty-stricken mining families while honing his talent painting and drawing in the bleak, boggy countryside. His house has been restored as a monument to his skills, with an audiovisual presentation but sadly only one original Van Gogh sketch, "The Diggers" (1880). Unless you're a fervent devotee of Van Gogh, this place is not worth the detour, although 2015's European Year of Culture will see a Van Gogh exhibition installed here. Pop in if you're passing.

Rue du Pavillon 3, Cuesmes (3km/2 miles south of Mons). ℂ **065/355-611.** Admission 2.50€ adults, 1.50€ children 12–17, free for children 11 and under. Tues–Sun noon–6pm. Closed Jan 1 and Dec 25.

NAMUR ★★

56km (35 miles) SE of Brussels

The handsome old riverside town of Namur is the administrative capital of French-speaking Wallonia in southern Belgium. Sitting at the confluence of the Meuse and Sambre rivers, the town makes the perfect jumping off point for exploring the rolling hills and gastronomic delights of the Ardennes as well as the lavish chateaux of the Meuse Valley. But before you rush on, stop awhile in Namur, presided over by its massive citadel with all its family-friendly attractions, and offering some fine attractions of its own—museums and churches, and an abundance of cafes and restaurants in the narrow, atmospheric alleyways of Le Corbeil, the attractive old quarter of 17th-century brick houses strewn along the Sambre waterfront. If you visit when the weather is fine, take a *namourette* boat ride across the rivers; there are docks along the waterside.

Essentials

GETTING THERE　There are two **trains** every hour from Brussels to the Gare de Namur, square Léopold, an easy walk from the center of town; the journey takes 60 minutes and round-trip fares are 16€. For more details, go to **www.belgianrail.be**. The **bus station** is out front (www.infotec.be). By **car** from Brussels, take the A4/E411 southeast; you'll be there in under an hour.

VISITOR INFORMATION　The **Maison du Tourisme du Pays de Namur** is at square Léopold (ℂ **081/246-449;** www.mtpn.be), close to the rail station. The office is open daily 9:30am to 6pm.

GETTING AROUND　Namur is easily accessible on foot.

What to See & Do

Cathédrale St-Aubain (St. Aubain's Cathedral) CHURCH　The domed cathedral was designed by Italian architect Pisoni between 1751 and 1767 in a light, ethereal, late baroque style with an ebullience of columns, pilasters, cornices, and balustrades. It was constructed on the site of an earlier Romanesque church and its ancient belfry is incorporated into the present structure. The **Musée Diocésain et Trésor (Diocesan Museum and Treasury),** place du Chapitre 1 (ℂ **081/444-285**), just outside the cathedral, holds a small but impressive collection of ecclesiastical relics, gold plates, and jewel-encrusted diadems but in true Walloon style is only open by advance reservation by telephone.

Place St-Aubain. ℂ **081/220-320.** www.cana.be. Admission: church free; Diocesan Museum 3€ adults, 1€ children 6–12, free for children 5 and under. Museum Tues–Sat 11am–6pm (book ahead).

Citadelle (Citadel) ★★ HISTORIC SITE　A fortification has stood atop Namur's bluff crag since pre-Roman times, and the Citadel in various guises has seen much military action down the years. Today, however, its function is purely peaceful, for the fortified castle has become a rural entertainments complex with plenty of amusements to offer families. Kick off a visit by taking the **cable car** that runs up to the Citadel

THE grand châteaux OF THE MEUSE VALLEY

The banks of the River Meuse are liberally sprinkled with grand historic châteaux, often with moats and towers. Among the finest that you can visit are:

○ **Château d'Annevoie ★★★**, rue des Jardins 37, Annevoie (② 082/679-797; www.annevoie.be), is east of the Meuse on the N92 in between Namur and Dinant and offers charming formal water gardens in Italian, French, and English styles.

○ **Château de Freÿr ★**, Freÿr 12, Hastière (② 082/222-200; www.freyr.be), on the left bank of the Meuse, along N96 between Hastière-Lavaux and Dinant. The 17th-century summer retreat of the dukes of Beaufort-Spontin has a scenic riverside location and magnificent ornamental gardens.

○ **Château de Jehay ★★**, rue du Parc 1, Amay (② 085/824-400; www.chateaujehay.be), 18km (11 miles) southwest of Liège, off N614. Its lawns and gardens are beautified with sculptures and ramparts

fountains. Inside, rooms are filled with paintings, tapestries, lace, silver and gold pieces, jewels, porcelain and glass, antique furniture, and family heirlooms.

○ **Château de Modave ★★**, rue du Parc 4, Modave (② 085/411-369; www.modave-castle.be), 12km (7½ miles) south of Huy, off N641. Once the property of Liègeois prince-bishops and then cardinals of the Catholic church, this fine example of the Louis XIVth French style has a delightfully flamboyant interior and neatly planted terraced gardens.

○ **Château de Vêves,** rue du Furfooz 2, Celles-Houyet (② 082/666-395; www.chateau-de-veves.be), 8km (5 miles) east of the Meuse, off N94. An 18th-century folly styled as a medieval castle, Vêves looks almost more romantic than the real thing and offers plenty of medieval-themed entertainment that will enthrall kids.

and jump on the **electric train** that chugs around the castle; five themed **walking tours** detail the history of the citadel and there are two medieval-styled scented **gardens** to explore as well as **underground caverns** where Napoleon's troops once hid. A traditional **perfumery** and a small **amusement park** for young children are also found within the fortified walls, and in June 2015 a high-tech visitor center is set to open in the former barracks. Although the Citadel is open to roam all year around, its attractions only open with the tourist season from April until October.

Rte. Merveilleuse. ② 081/654-500. www.citadelle.namur.be. Admission: Citadel free; museums, guided visits, and excursion train 9€ adults; 6€ seniors, students, and children 4–17; free for children 3 and under. Citadel daily 8am–6pm; park Apr–Oct daily 10am–5pm. Closed Dec 20–Jan 4.

Musée Archéologique (Archaeological Museum) ★★ MUSEUM

Namur's archaeological museum is located in the town's late-16th-century former meat hall on the banks of the Sambre. Its displays include a scale model of Namur as it appeared back in 1750 and a surprisingly impressive haul of Roman treasure excavated from the tombs of soldiers buried here in the 4th and 5th centuries AD.

Rue du Pont 21. ② 081/231-631. Admission 3€ adults; 1.50€ seniors, students, and children 6–12; free children 11 and under. Tues–Fri 10am–5pm, Sat–Sun 10:45am–5pm. Closed Dec 25–Jan 2.

Musée Félicien Rops (Félicien Rops Museum) ★ MUSEUM Namur's best-known son was a 19th-century painter and engraver of the bizarre and the erotic. Félicien Rops led a disparate life, mostly among the fleshpots of Paris and Brussels but despite his flirtation with drugs and absinthe he was extraordinarily skillful and prolific, a fact attested to by the 3,000-odd drawings, aquatints, lithographs, and prints exhibited in his museum, which is safely tucked away from sensitive eyes on a narrow side street near his birthplace in the old quarter of town. Rops was indisputably one of the most outstanding engravers of the late 19th century and also a vastly underrated painter; the works hung in the museum include some of his pornographic images as well as his delicate, almost wistful, landscapes. Temporary exhibitions often compare his works with other greats of his time, such as Auguste Rodin.

Rue Fumal 12. ⓒ **081/776-755.** www.museerops.be. Admission 3€ adults (5€ for temporary exhibitions); 1.50€ seniors, students, and children 12–18 (2.50€ for temporary exhibitions); free for children 11 and under. July–Aug daily 10am–6pm, Sept–June Tues–Sun 10am–6pm. Closed Dec 24–25 and Dec 31–Jan1.

YPRES ★★

110km (68 miles) W of Brussels; 45km (28 miles) SW of Bruges

Set among the low, gentle slopes of the West Flanders Heuvelland (Hill Country), Flemish-speaking Ypres (Ieper in Dutch, and often pronounced "Wipers" in English) owed its early prosperity to the Flemish textile industry that peaked in the 13th century. Over the centuries, the handsome town was wholeheartedly trashed in one war after another, but by far the most devastating was World War I (1914–18); hardly a brick was left standing after 4 years of violent bombardment as Ypres became one of the slaughterhouses of the Western Front. In the few square miles of the Ypres Salient (see below), 250,000 soldiers from the British Empire, France, and Belgium were killed, along with an equal number of Germans. The tally of wounded on all sides reached 1.2 million.

Most visitors come to Ypres—today perfectly restored brick by brick to its former considerable grandeur—to remember those who fell on the surrounding battlefields and who rest eternally on the green breast of the Heuvelland. In the rolling countryside around the town, there are no fewer than 185 serene World War I military cemeteries, the last resting place of soldiers from across the globe. Pay homage to the brave of this most horrendous of wars in the deeply emotional, daily "Last Post" ceremony, which takes place at 8pm, come rain, shine, plague, or pestilence, under the hallowed arches of the town's neoclassical Menin Gate (see below).

Essentials

GETTING THERE   Many visitors combine a visit to Ypres with a stay in Bruges although it is perfectly possible to get there and back from Brussels in a (long) day for a round-trip train fare of 18€. **Trains** depart hourly from Bruges for the hour's trip to Ypres and round-trip fares are 16€; some services require a change at Kortrijk. Visit **www.belgianrail.be** for full details of schedules. From Brussels, take the A17/E40 to Ghent, then the A14 and the A19 west; the drive takes around 90 minutes. For the 50-minute **drive** from Bruges, take A17/E403 south to the Kortrijk interchange, and then A19 west; from the coast at De Panne, take N8 south.

VISITOR INFORMATION   **Toerisme Ieper** is in the Lakenhalle, Grote Markt 34 (ⓒ **057/239-220;** www.toerismeieper.be), in the center of town. The office is open

April to November 14 Monday to Friday 9am to 6pm, and weekends 10am to 6pm; November 15 through March, hours are Monday to Friday 9am to 5pm and weekends 10am to 6pm.

GETTING AROUND   Sights in town are easily reached on foot, though if you're arriving by train, you'll save time by taking almost any **De Lijn** bus (© **070/220-200;** www.delijn.be) from the bus station next to the train station for the 5-minute ride to the Grote Markt. Regulated taxis are available outside the train station.

SPECIAL EVENTS   Every 3 years on the second Sunday in May, Ypres celebrates a colorful pageant, the **Kattenstoet (Festival of the Cats;** see p. 38), during which the town jester throws cats from the Belfry to the people below. The custom originated centuries ago when cats were considered a "familiar" of witches, and evolved into the tradition of today's lively carnival, procession, and street partying. Thankfully these days the flying felines are fluffy toys. The next Kattenstoet is on May 10, 2015.

Exploring Ypres

Most of the gabled guild houses and mansions around the gorgeous Grote Markt are occupied now by restaurants, cafes, and hotels. At the western end of this central square, Ypres's medieval wealth is reflected in its extravagant Gothic **Lakenhalle (Cloth Hall)** ★★. The original was constructed between 1250 and 1304 along the Ieperlee River (long since banished underground) but was blown to pieces between 1914 and 1918 and reconstructed with painstaking care, although the work wasn't finished until 1967. Gilded statues once more adorn the roof, and a statue of Our Lady of Thuyne, the patron of Ypres, stands over the main entrance. Inside, you'll find the tourist office, and the upper floor houses the **In Flanders Fields Museum,** which is one of the most thought-provoking and visually stunning war museums in Flanders (see below).

The Cloth Hall's central **Belfort (Belfry)** is the oldest part of the building, dating from 1201, and has four corner turrets and a spire that rears up to 70m (230 ft.). You get fine views over the town from here, provided you're willing and able to climb the 264 steps to the upper gallery. Concerts chime out across the square from Belfort's 49-bell carillon between June and September on Saturday from 11am and Sunday from 3:30pm.

The arcaded Nieuwerck is an extension of the Cloth Hall dating from 1619 and houses Ypres's **Stadhuis (Town Hall).** You can visit the council chamber and view its fine stained-glass window for free Monday to Friday whenever the town hall is open.

The spire of the 13th-century Gothic **Sint-Martenskathedraal (St. Martin's Cathedral),** on Sint-Maartensplein, is another town landmark. Inside is the tomb of Cornelius Jansen (1585–1638), a bishop of Ypres who was condemned for heresy in 1642 as well as a much-revered statue of Our Lady of Thuyne. Britain's armed forces donated the stained-glass rose window in honor of Belgium's World War I soldier king, Albert I. The cathedral is open to visitors daily 8am to noon, and 2 until 8pm except during services. Admission is free.

Behind the cathedral, the **Munster Memorial** is in the shape of the Celtic Cross and honors Irish soldiers killed in World War I. Across the way, British and Commonwealth veterans made the **St. George's Memorial Church** (1929) in Elverdingsestraat a shrine to their fallen comrades. Wall-mounted banners and pew kneelers decorated with colorful corps and regimental badges add an almost festive air to what might otherwise be a somber scene. The church is open daily between April and September 9:30am to 8pm, October to March 9:30am until 4:30pm, and admission is free.

In addition to companies based in Ypres, many Brussels and Bruges tour operators (p. 171 and 199) run day trips to Flanders Fields. **Flanders Battlefield Tours** (www.ypres-fbt.be) and **Salient Tours** (www.salienttours.com) both run bus tours of the battlefields and memorials around Ypres, ranging from 2 hours to a full day. Prices begin at 30€ for a 2-hour tour. The Ypres tourist office (see above) offers details for the **In Flanders Fields Route,** a self-guided tour of 80km (50 miles) on signposted roads that cover all the main sights.

For a less ambitious, 1- to 2-hour self-guided tour by car, head out of town through the Menin Gate and take the N8 and turn off to Canadalaan, close to **Bellewaerde Park** (see below). Near the end of the lane, near **Sanctuary Wood Cemetery,** is a preserved stretch of trenches peppered with shell holes and shattered trees. Amazingly, almost no other sign remains of the vast network of muddy, waterlogged trenches—nature has reclaimed the once-tortured landscape. Nearby stands the **Canadian Monument** on Hill 62.

Return to the N8 and turn right. Take the N303 through Zonnebeke in the direction of Passendale (Passchendaele in French), and stop off at the **Tyne Cot Commonwealth Military Cemetery,** with its 12,000 graves surmounted by a Cross of Remembrance in white Portland stone. In 1917, Passendale was dubbed "Passionndale" by British and Commonwealth troops, who took the village at a cost of 140,000 lives. Head northwest from Zonnebeke towards Langemark, and on the crossroads with the N313, you'll find the Canadian St. Julien Memorial. On the north side of Langemark is the site of 44,000 graves at the **Deutscher Soldatenfriedhof (German Military Cemetery).** Return to the N313 and turn right to head back to Ypres.

The town's great offering to the war dead is the **Meensepoort (Menin Gate)** ★★★, the immense marble memorial arch at the east entrance to the Grote Markt. Inscribed on its walls are the names of the 54,896 British troops killed around Ypres between 1914 and 1917 that have no known grave. Every evening at 8pm, traffic through the gate is stopped while war veterans in dress uniform sound the plaintive notes of "The Last Post" on silver bugles, in a brief but moving ceremony that dates from 1928. Every evening this service attracts hundreds of spectators, who come to pay their respects to the fallen. Adjacent to the Menin Gate is the **Australian Memorial** in honor of more than 43,000 Aussies who lost their lives in the Ypres Salient (see below).

The impressive 17th-century **city ramparts** were designed by the French military engineer Vauban and are fronted by a moat that once surrounded the town; these are among the few structures not demolished during World War I. You reach them via stairs at the Menin Gate and walk around the battlements to the **Rijselsepoort (Lille Gate).**

In Flanders Fields Museum ★★★ MUSEUM   One of the world's most effective persuasions of the horrors of war, this award-wining museum presents a heart-rending interactive interpretation of the course of World War I brought alive by the judicious use of film, personal accounts, images of decimated and desolate Flanders battlefields, and sickening facts and figures that lay heavy on the heart. Most moving among a series of exhibits is the faltering account of the Christmas Truce, in which Allied and German troops laid down their weapons and played soccer in No-Man's Land. Thankfully, the tragic tales of senseless bloodshed carry an optimistic note for positivity and reconciliation in its final call for lasting world peace. This important museum won the 2000 Museum Award of the Council of Europe for its innovative presentation.

Cloth Hall, Grote Markt 34. © **057/239-220.** www.inflandersfields.be. Admission 9€ adults, 4€ children 7–18, free for children 6 and under. Apr to mid-Nov daily 10am–6pm, mid-Nov to Mar Tues–Sun 10am–5pm. Closed first 3 weeks of Jan and Dec 25.

Museum Godshuis Belle ★★ MUSEUM Ypres's treasured painting of the "Blessed" by an anonymous Master of 1420 is the star exhibit in this little museum housed in the reconstructed chapel of a 13th-century almshouse. There's also a surprisingly strong collection of religious paintings from the 16th to the 19th centuries, ancient furniture, tapestries, and silverware.

Rijselsestraat 38 © **057/239-220.** Admission 2.50€ adults, 0.50€ children 7–17, free for children 6 and under. Tues–Sun 10am–12:30pm and 2–6pm.

Stedelijk Museum (Municipal Museum) ★ MUSEUM Located in the Sint-Jansgodshuis, a 15th-century almshouse and one of the few buildings to have escaped obliteration in World War I, Ypres's civic collection offers a decent-enough romp through the pre-war years. Exhibits include ancient maps and a fine collection of masterly oil paintings plus works by Flemish artist Louise De Hem.

Ieperleestraat 31. © **057/239-220.** Admission 2.50€ adults, 0.50€ children 7–17, free for children 6 and under. Apr–Oct Tues–Sun 10am–12:30pm and 2–6pm, Nov–Mar Tues–Sun 10am–12:30pm and 2–5pm.

ESPECIALLY FOR KIDS

Bellewaerde Park, Meenseweg 497 (© **057/468-686;** www.bellewaerde.be), offers kids the chance to have a blowout after the solemnity of the war museums and cemeteries. This theme park combines white-knuckle rides with a wildlife reserve occupying various recreated natural environments, and plenty of gentle rides for the tiniest tots, plus audiovisual specials like the 4D film "Turtle Vision." Bellewaerde is set in what was once the wasteland of the World War I front lines. The park is open April to June daily 10am to 5pm (6pm weekends), July daily 10am to 6pm (7pm weekends), August daily 10am to 7pm (10pm Sat), and September to mid-October weekends 10am to 6pm. Admission is 25€ per family.

MECHELEN ★

34km (20 miles) E of Brussels

This unsung mini-city in Flanders is a stone's throw away from Brussels but light years away in attitude and ambience; once the capital of the Low Countries, its wealth came from the cloth trade in the 13th and 14th centuries, which were Mechelen's glory days. Once the political capital of Belgium headed to Brussels, Mechelen slowly slipped back into charming obscurity.

Thanks to its illustrious history, Mechelen has a gaggle of remarkable Gothic and baroque buildings at its heart, with its most important landmarks being the architecturally schizophrenic **Stadhuis (Town Hall)** and **St. Rumbold's Cathedral** on the gargantuan **Grote Markt.** Today much of the local action is centered around the

Vismarkt, a cobbled square that lies along the River Dijle and is bordered with canopied restaurants and bars; it connects to Grote Markt along the buzzy, busy parallel shopping streets of Begijnenstraat and IJzerenleen. The year 2015 sees Mechelen back in the headlines as it partners with Mons as European City of Culture; art exhibitions and festivals will mark the occasion.

Essentials

GETTING THERE   Mechelen is a short hop from Brussels, with **trains** departing between twice hourly; the journey takes under half an hour and the round-trip fare is 9€. Check www.belgianrail.be for schedules. You can get to Mechelen from Brussels by **car** in under half an hour if the traffic is not choked; jump on the A1/E19.

VISITOR INFORMATION   **Tourism Mechelen** is at Hallestraat 2-4-6 (*©* **070/220-008;** www.toerisme.mechelen.be), just off the Grote Markt. The office is open April through October Monday to Friday 10am–5pm, Saturday 10am–4pm, Sunday 12:30–4pm; November to March Monday to Saturday 10am–4pm, Sunday 12:30–4pm.

GETTING AROUND   Walking is much the easiest and most pleasant way to get around in Mechelen.

Exploring Mechelen

Standing out among the cluster of gabled and gaily painted town houses around Grote Markt, the spire of Mechelen's UNESCO-listed **Sint-Romboutskathedraal (St. Rumbold's Cathedral)** is the town's much-loved icon. From Thursday to Tuesday between 1 and 6pm, it's possible to clamber up all 514 steps to the panoramic Skywalk for views over the rooftops and the surrounding, pancake-flat countryside. Admission is 7€ adults, 5€ seniors, 2.50€ ages 3 to 16. Dating from 1452, the cathedral also has a famous 98-bell carillon that rings out every 15 minutes.

Opposite St. Rumbold's stands the UNESCO-listed 14th-century **Belfort (Belfry)** of the Stadhuis (Town Hall), which stood roofless for almost 200 years after the cloth trade in Mechelen died out. It was only finally deemed completed in 1911, but well before that it had the pinnacled, lacy facade of the Brabantine Gothic Palace of the Great Council adhered to its flank. To peek inside the Stadhuis, join the regular 2-hour **guided walk** of Mechelen (5€ for adults, 2.50€ for kids) that runs on weekends at 2pm from April until October (daily during summer school vacation) from the tourist office (see above).

Of the town's 18 museums and art galleries, the 2 worth hitting on a day trip are the **Kazerne Dossin Holocaust Centre** at Goswin de Stassartstraat 153 (*©* **015/290-660;** www.kazernedossin.eu) and the **Toy Museum** (p. 231), worlds apart in subject matter though they might be. The Kazerne Dossin is housed in a squat, white purpose-built museum on the site of the former Dossin barracks, where Mechelen's Jews and gypsies were held before deportation to the concentration camps of Poland during World War II. Combining its role as hard-hitting presenter of unpalatable facts—using interactive exhibits, gruesome images, and deeply moving personal accounts of the Nazi atrocities—with its mission as a peace center. The museum is open Thursday to Tuesday 10am to 5pm (closed Wed, Jan 1, Dec 25, and Jewish holidays). Entrance costs 10€ for adults, 4€ for ages 10 to 21, and free for younger kids. Kazerne Dossin won European Museum of the Year in 2014 for its heart-rending ruminations on war.

Altogether more upbeat in its subject matter, the **Speelgoedmuseum Mechelen (Toy Museum Mechelen;** Nekkerspoelstraat 21; ✆ **015/557-050;** www.speelgoedmuseum. be) is a charming place that will appeal to all ages. It boasts Europe's biggest collection of toys, ranging from model Napoleonic soldiers to Victoriana dolls and on through Matchbox cars from the 1950s to plastic Barbies and Kens; it will surely provide a warm blast of nostalgia for anyone over the age of 40. Open Tuesday through Sunday 10am to 5pm, admission is 8.50€ for adults and 6€ for children between 6 and 13.

PLANNING YOUR TRIP

Granted, Amsterdam, Brussels, and Bruges are not hard cities to come to grips with; they are containable in size, they have excellent public transportation systems, and most people speak English. Nevertheless, all trips overseas benefit from some advance planning, whether it is organizing accommodations or making a sightseeing itinerary. This chapter is designed to help you on your way, but don't forget, if you get stuck, the local tourist organizations in all three cities pride themselves on being able to solve any conceivable travel conundrum.

The information in this chapter is intended to cover trips to all three cities so it's valuable reading whether you are visiting one, two, or all three of them. Yet, close together though they are, each city has its own unique traits. For additional help in planning your trip—when to go, what the weather's like—and for more specific on-the-ground resources in Amsterdam, Brussels, and Bruges, see the "Essentials" and "Fast Facts" sections in chapters 4, 6, and 7.

GETTING THERE

By Plane
TO AMSTERDAM
Amsterdam Airport Schiphol (✆ **0900/0141** for general and flight information, ✆ 31-20/794-0800 from outside Holland; www.schiphol.nl; airport code AMS), 14km (9 miles) southwest of Amsterdam, is pronounced *Skhip*-ol and is universally regarded as one of the best airports in the world for its ease of use, its massive duty-free shopping center, and its outpost of the Rijksmuseum (p. 92). Located southwest of the city center, it is the main airport in The Netherlands, handling most of the country's international arrivals and departures.

TO BRUSSELS & BRUGES
Brussels Airport (✆ **0900/70000** for general and flight information, ✆ 32-2/753-7753 from outside Belgium; www.brusselsairport.be; airport code BRU), is 15km (9 miles) northwest of Brussels city center and 107km (67 miles) from Bruges. This airport handles most of Belgium's international air traffic. Bruges is easily accessible by train, with one change at Brussels-Midi/Zuid. **Brussels-South-Charleroi-Airport** (✆ **0902/ 02490** for general and flight information, 32-2/7815-2722 from outside Belgium; www.charleroi-airport.com, airport code CRL) is 55km (35 miles) south of Brussels and 150km (95 miles) from Bruges. It is the

domain of European budget flights rather than transatlantic services, and there are regular connections between the airport and Brussels-Midi/Zuid rail station for trains on to Bruges.

By Car

TO AMSTERDAM

A network of major international highways crisscrosses The Netherlands. European expressways E19, E35, and E231 converge on Amsterdam from France and Belgium to the south and from Germany to the north and east. These roads also have Dutch designations; as you approach the city they are, respectively: A4, A2, and A1. Amsterdam's ring road is A10. Distances between destinations are relatively short. Traffic is invariably heavy and delays are frequent but road conditions are otherwise pretty good, service stations are plentiful, and highways are plainly signposted.

TO BRUSSELS

Major expressways to Brussels are E19/A16 from Amsterdam (driving time: 2 hr. 20 min. on a good day) and the E19/E17 from Paris (driving time 3½ hr.). Take the E40/A10 from Bruges and Cologne. If possible, avoid driving on the hell on wheels that has become the R0 Brussels ring road; if you miss your turn, expect to go all the way around again! Once you're settled at a hotel, do yourself a favor and leave the car safe and sound in a parking garage.

TO BRUGES

Bruges is 96km (60 miles) northwest of Brussels on the E40/A10; 50km (30 miles) northwest of Ghent on the E40/A10; 107km (67 miles) west of Antwerp on either the E17/A14 and E40/A10, or the E34, which bypasses Ghent; 18km (11 miles) south of the ferry port of Zeebrugge on E403 and N371; and 30km (19 miles) southeast of Ostend on E40/A10. From the Eurotunnel and Calais in France take E40/A16 east to Bruges.

By Train

TO AMSTERDAM

Rail services to Amsterdam from cities in The Netherlands and across Europe are frequent and fast. International trains arrive at Centraal Station. **Nederlandse Spoorwegen (Netherlands Railways)** trains arrive in Amsterdam from destinations all over The Netherlands. Schedule and fare information on travel by train is available by calling ℂ **0900/9292** (0.70€ per minute) for national service, and ℂ **0900/9296** for high-speed international services (0.35€ per minute); or by visiting www.ns.nl.

The **Thalys high-speed train** connects Paris, Brussels, Amsterdam, and (via Brussels) Cologne. Travel time from Paris to Amsterdam is 3 hours, 20 minutes, and from Brussels 1 hour, 50 minutes. For Thalys information and reservations, call ℂ **320/7079-7979** or visit www.thalys.com.

On **Eurostar high-speed trains,** the travel time between London's St. Pancras Station and Brussels's Bruxelles-Midi Station (the closest connecting point for Amsterdam) is around 2 hours. For Eurostar reservations, call ℂ **08432/186-186** in Britain; ℂ 44/1233-617-575 from outside the UK; www.eurostar.com.

TO BRUSSELS

Brussels is served by **Eurostar** (see above) services from London; **Thalys** (see above) from Paris, Amsterdam, and Cologne; and **TGV** (ℂ **3635** within France or **33/892-353-535** outside France; www.voyages-sncf.com) and **ICE** (ℂ **0900/9296;** 0.35€ per minute; www.nsinternational.nl) from Frankfurt. The Brussels metropolitan area has three main rail stations: Bruxelles-Central, Carrefour de l'Europe; Bruxelles-Midi, rue de France (the Eurostar, Thalys, TGV, and ICE terminal); and Bruxelles-Nord, rue du Progrès. All three are served by Métro, tram, or bus lines, and have taxi stands outside. For train information and reservations, call ⓒ **02/528-2828** or visit www.sncb.be.

Warning: Attracted by rich pickings from international travelers, bag snatchers roam the environs of Bruxelles-Midi, and pickpockets work the interior. Although police presence is obvious, do not travel to or depart from the Bruxelles-Central station on foot if you can avoid doing so; take a taxi or use public transportation. Inside, keep a close eye on your possessions.

TO BRUGES

Two trains arrive in Bruges every hour from Brussels, four or five from Ghent, two from Antwerp. The travel time is around 1 hour from Brussels, 25 minutes from Ghent, 1 hour and 20 minutes from Antwerp. Train information is available from **SNCB (Belgian Railways)** at ⓒ **02/528-2828** or www.belgianrail.be.

From London, **Eurostar** passengers can transfer for Bruges either at Lille in northern France or in Brussels. From Paris, **Thalys high-speed trains** (ⓒ **320/7079-7979;** www.thalys.com) go via Brussels to Bruges. From Amsterdam, travel via Antwerp or Brussels either on Thalys or InterCity (IC) trains.

By Bus
TO AMSTERDAM

International coaches arrive at the bus terminal opposite Amstel rail station (Metro: Amstel) in the south of the city. **Eurolines** operates coach services between London Victoria Bus Station and Amstel Station (via ferry), with up to five departures daily in the summer. Travel time is just over 12 hours. For reservations, contact Eurolines (ⓒ **08717/818-178** in Britain or 31/88-076-1700 in Holland; www.eurolines.com).

TO BRUSSELS

Eurolines (ⓒ **08717/818-178** in Britain or 32/02-274-1350; www.eurolines.com) buses from London, Paris, Amsterdam, and other cities arrive at the bus station below Bruxelles-Nord train station.

TO BRUGES

Buses are less useful than trains for getting to Bruges, although there is frequent service from Zeebrugge and Ostend. The **Bruges bus station** adjoins the rail station. Schedule and fare information is available from **De Lijn** (ⓒ **070/22-02-00;** www.delijn.be/en).

Eurolines (see above) operates a cheap daily bus service to Bruges from London, Amsterdam, Paris, or Cologne.

GETTING AROUND
By Car

When it comes to getting around Amsterdam, Brussels, and Bruges, the best advice is to park your car and forget about it for the rest of your stay. The historic centers of all three cities are easily—and most enjoyably—explored on foot, and if you get tired, trams and buses take the strain off walking. Bruges and Amsterdam are flat and lend themselves to cycling—although don't chance it in the chaotic traffic of central Amsterdam or in hilly Brussels—details on how to hire bike are in the relevant destination chapters.

However, if you want to travel from city to city to see the sights as recommended in this book, a car is useful; the main expressways are well maintained and comprehensively signposted, but they're getting increasingly crowded. And Belgian drivers are known to be erratic, so public transport is very much an option, with intercity bus and train links short and frequent.

RENTING A CAR

All the international car-hire firms, including **Avis** (www.avis.com), **Budget** (www.budget.com), **Europcar** (www.europcar.com), and **Hertz** (www.hertz.com) have offices in the airports, in the city centers, and in the Chanel ports. Rates are typically cheaper if booked online.

To hire a car in Belgium and The Netherlands, you need a credit or debit card (for the deposit), a passport, and a driver's license. The car registration papers must be kept in the vehicle. The minimum age for drivers is 18, and on expressways, speed limits are 70kmph (43 mph) minimum, 120kmph (74 mph) maximum; in all cities and urban areas, the maximum speed limit is 50kmph (31 mph). Lower limits might be posted. Seat belts must be worn in both the front seats and in the back. In the car, you need to have a fire extinguisher, a basic medical kit, a red reflective warning triangle, and a reflective jacket. If you are driving a car from the U.K. or Ireland with the wheel on the right side, change the angle of your headlight beams with adaptor kits.

By Bus

Although other travel tickets can be bought, you have the option of using an electronic card called the **OV-chipkaart** on all Dutch public transportation (p. 57). Bus services in Amsterdam itself play second fiddle to the trams, thanks to the congested streets and

---

Public Holidays in Brussels & Bruges

January 1 New Year's Day
March/April/May Easter Sunday and Monday
April 27 King's Day
May 4 National Remembrance Day
May 5 Liberation Day (every 5 years, celebrated in 2015)
May/June Ascension Day
May/June Pentecost
July 11 Flemish-speaking community holiday

July 21 Independence Day
August 15 Assumption Day
September 27 French community holiday
November 1 All Saints' Day
November 11 Armistice Day
November 15 German-speaking community holiday
December 25 Christmas Day
December 26 Boxing Day

responsible TOURISM

The Dutch live in a tiny country that's so heavily populated they need to recover land from the sea, and they take protection of their environment very seriously. More than 60 percent of household waste is sorted, collected, and recycled. As a visitor, you are expected to play your part in this process and not toss stuff without checking if it's recyclable or reusable.

Generating power from the wind—an age-old Dutch skill—is growing apace. In 2012 Holland had 2,000 wind turbines on land and 96 offshore, producing 6 percent of its electricity from this renewable resource, a figure that's due to rise to 14 percent by 2020.

Obviously air travel has a profound effect on our environment, and for this reason the Dutch airline KLM is seeking new ways to cut emissions, such as offering ways for its passengers to fly CO_2-neutral. The initiative is called **CO2ZERO,** and money made is reinvested by KLM straight into selected sustainability projects. See **www.klm.com/travel/gb_en/about/co2/together/index.htm** for more details.

Cities in Belgium and The Netherlands all have excellent integrated public transportation systems; using them helps reduce greenhouse-gas emissions. Even if you rent a car for getting around, most main car-rental firms (see above) now offer green options, from renting a low-emissions car to making a payment to a CO_2-offset program.

All those bicycles you see in Amsterdam take cars off the street. Anyone who's not riding a bike is likely to be walking or getting around by tram, and visitors are encouraged to do likewise. There are many places where you can rent bikes, and public transportation is easy to use and efficient.

Belgium's Dutch-speaking Flanders region, including Bruges, comes close to sharing the Dutch commitment to getting around by bike, but in hilly, traffic-choked Brussels, the bike is a less-enticing mode of transportation. There's no need to drive, though, as the tram and Métro systems work well.

Many Dutch and Belgian hotels have signed up for becoming more energy efficient in all areas of operation, conserving water, decreasing the amount of unsorted waste, and more. Visit eco-friendly champions **Green Key (www.green-key.org)** to see what you can do to help, and check hotel reviews throughout this book for details on specific sustainable properties, in particular the Conscious Hotel Vondelpark and Court Garden Den Haag (p. 68 and 136), who both are ahead of the pack in leading the way into the future of green tourism.

tedious one-way systems. Outside the city there is a comprehensive service with many stops on every journey. Traveling by train is faster, but most regional bus companies have express lines between major destinations such as Rotterdam and Amsterdam. Regional and intercity bus services in The Netherlands are operated by **Connexxion** (www.connexxion.nl), **Arriva** (www.arriva.nl), **Veolia** (www.veolia-transport.nl), and **Qbuzz** (www.qbuzz.nl).

Brussels, Bruges, Ghent, and Antwerp all have excellent bus services within the cities themselves, but traveling between them will lead to headaches over complicated timetabling and route planning; the results are a slow journey with several intermediate stops. Fares and schedules are available from **STIB** (www.stib.be) for Brussels, and **De Lijn** (www.delijn.be) for Bruges and Flanders.

By Tram

Although other travel tickets can be bought, you have the option of using the electronic **OV-chipkaart** on all Dutch trams (p. 57). Amsterdam has blue-and-gray trams (p. 57) that are run by GVB (www.gvb.nl); they roll through most major streets and traverse the city way faster than the buses.

In Brussels, an **extensive network of tramlines** (p. 146) provides the ideal way to get around the city; in fact Brussels's trams carried 124 million passengers in 2013. The trams are run by **STIB** (www.stib.be) and painted in smart gray-and-gold; the stops marked with red-and-white signs. Stop a tram or bus by extending your arm as it approaches so the driver can see it; if you don't signal, it may not stop. There are no trams in Bruges.

By Metro

Brussels and Amsterdam both have modern metro systems. Although other travel tickets can be bought, you have the option of using the same electronic **OV-chipkaart** on all Dutch public transportation (see above), but you can't buy the OV-chipkaart in metro stations. Amsterdam's system is run by **GVB (www.gvb.nl)** and is still being expanded; it currently has four lines covering the inner city and commuter routes such as Amstelveen. The Métro in Brussels is run by **STIB (www.stib.be)** and is quick and efficient, and covers many important center-city locations, as well as the suburbs, the Bruparck recreation zone, and the Heysel congress center. There is no metro in Bruges.

ENTRY REQUIREMENTS

Visas

Citizens of the United States, Canada, the United Kingdom, Ireland, Australia, and New Zealand do not need a Visa for a visit to either Belgium or The Netherlands of less than 3 months. If you're a citizen of another country, check the regulations before you plan your trip. You can get these in English from the Ministry of Foreign Affairs: **www.diplomatie.be** for Belgium; **www.minbuza.nl** for The Netherlands.

Passports

Citizens of the United States, Canada, the United Kingdom, Ireland, Australia, and New Zealand need a valid passport to visit Belgium and The Netherlands.

It is advisable to have one or two consecutive blank pages in your passport to allow space for entrance and exit visas and stamps. You must have at least 3 months left on your passport *after* your trip has ended for customs in Belgium or The Netherlands to allow you in to the E.U.

Public Holidays in Amsterdam

January 1 New Year's Day
March/April/May Easter Sunday and Monday
April 27 King's Day
May 4 National Remembrance Day
May 5 Liberation Day (every 5 years, celebrated in 2015)

May/June Ascension Day
June Pentecost
December 25 Christmas Day
December 26 Boxing Day

Medical Requirements

No health and vaccination certificates are required for entry in to Belgium or The Netherlands, nor do you need any vaccinations before your trip.

Customs

WHAT YOU CAN BRING INTO AMSTERDAM, BRUSSELS & BRUGES

Arrivals from E.U. nationals: Duty-free shopping has been abolished in all European Union countries, so standard allowances do not apply to goods purchased in one E.U. country and brought into another. In this case, there are no import limitations for most goods for personal use, but the following guideline limits apply and are enforced: 800 cigarettes, 400 cigarillos, 200 cigars, and 1 kilogram of tobacco; 10 liters of liquor, 20 liters of aperitifs (port and so on), 90 liters of wine (of which 60 liters may be sparkling wine), and 110 liters of beer.

Travelers 17 and older from outside the European Union **traveling by air or sea** can bring in, free of duty, ONE of the following: 200 cigarettes, 100 cigarillos, 50 cigars, or 250 grams of tobacco; ONE of the following: 1 liter of liquor or 2 liters of sparkling or fortified wine. In addition, you can bring in 4 liters of wine and 16 liters of beer, plus other goods worth up to 430€ without having to pay tax for visitors arriving by air and sea.

Travelers 17 and older from outside the European Union **traveling by land** can bring in, free of duty, ONE of the following: 40 cigarettes, 20 cigarillos, 10 cigars, or 50 grams of tobacco; ONE of the following: 1 liter of liquor or 2 liters of sparkling or fortified wine. In addition, you can bring in 4 liters of wine and 16 liters of beer, plus other goods worth up to 300€ without having to pay tax for visitors arriving by air and sea.

Forbidden products include firearms, counterfeit goods, banned narcotic substances, and protected animals and plants and products made from these.

For more information, contact **Belgian Customs (www.fiscus.fgov.be)** or **Dutch Customs (www.douane.nl).**

[FastFACTS] AMSTERDAM, BRUSSELS & BRUGES

Area Codes It's **20** for Amsterdam, **2** for Brussels, and **50** for Bruges.

ATMs As in most of the rest of the world, the easiest way to get cash is from an ATM. Be sure you know your personal identification number (PIN) and daily withdrawal limit before departure. International travelers should confirm their cards are valid for withdrawals overseas. Look for ATMs with the Cirrus (www.mastercard.com) or PLUS (www.visa.com) network symbols, as these accept foreign-issued cards.

Business Hours Stores in Amsterdam open 9:30am to 6pm Tuesday, Wednesday, Friday, and Saturday. Many are closed Monday morning, opening at 1pm, most close all day Sunday, and some stay open on Thursday until 8 or 9pm. Most museums close 1 day a week (often Mon). Banks open mostly Monday through Friday 9am until 5:30pm.

Stores in Brussels open Monday through Saturday 10am to 6pm and most close on Sunday. Many museums close on Monday. Banks open mostly Monday through Friday 9am until 4:30 or 5pm.

Stores in Bruges open Monday through Saturday 10am to 6 or 6:30pm. Some open Sunday afternoon, and those in the center of the city open all day on Sunday in summer. Most museums close on Monday. Banks open mostly Monday through Friday 9am to 5:30pm.

Disabled Travelers

Some hotels and restaurants in Holland and Belgium provide access for people with disabilities, but the old town house hotels in the cities are often short on facilities for people with mobility issues. Both Brussels Airport and Amsterdam's Schiphol Airport have services to help travelers with disabilities through the airport. There's also comprehensive assistance for travelers with disabilities throughout the railway systems surrounding all three cities.

Most, but not all, trams in Brussels, Antwerp, Amsterdam, The Hague, and Rotterdam are accessible for travelers in wheelchairs; all new trams being introduced into service have low central doors that are fully accessible. The Metro systems in Brussels, Amsterdam, and Rotterdam, and the Premetro in Antwerp, are fully accessible. Bruges is so easily explored on foot that you'll have no need for public transport.

There's assistance for travelers in Belgium on **SNCB** (𝄞 **02/528-2828;** www.b-rail.be) trains and in

stations, and in The Netherlands with **NS** (𝄞 **030/ 235-7822;** www.ns.nl).

Drinking Laws The minimum drinking age in the E.U. is 18; proof of age is often requested at bars, nightclubs, and restaurants, so it's a good idea to bring passport or driver's license when you go out.

Electricity Holland and Belgium both run on 230 volts and 50 Hz. Most mobile phones, cameras, MP3 players, and laptops will need adaptors for the two- or three-pin plugs.

Embassies Dutch embassies are all in The Hague, the administrative capital of The Netherlands: **Australia,** Carnegielaan 4 (𝄞 070/310-8200; www.netherlands.embassy.gov.au); **Canada,** Sophialaan 7 (𝄞 070/311-1600; www.netherlands.gc.ca); **Ireland,** Scheveningseweg 112 (𝄞 070/363-0993; www.irishembassy.nl); **New Zealand,** Eisenhowerlaan 77N (𝄞 070/346-9324; www.nzembassy.com/netherlands); **United Kingdom,** Lange Voorhout 10 (𝄞 070/427-0427; www.britain.nl); **United States,** Lange Voorhout 102 (𝄞 070/310-2209; http://thehague.usembassy.gov).

Belgian embassies are all located in the capital, Brussels: **Australia:** Level 7, av. des Arts (𝄞 **02/286-0500;** www.dfat.gov.au); **Canada:** av. de Tervueren 2 (𝄞 **02/741-0611;** www.canadainternational.gc.ca); **Ireland:** chaussée d'Etterbeek 180 (𝄞 **02/282-3400;**

http://web.dfa.ie); **New Zealand:** Level 7, av. des Nerviens 9–31 (𝄞 **02/512-1040;** www.nzembassy.com/belgium); **United Kingdom:** av. d'Auderghem 10 (𝄞 **02/ 287-6211;** www.gov.uk/government/world/belgium); **United States:** Regentlaan 27, bd. du Régent 27 (𝄞 **02/811-4000;** http://belgium.usembassy.gov).

Emergencies In The Netherlands and Belgium, dial 𝄞 **112** for police, ambulance, paramedics, and the fire department. This is a nationwide toll-free call from landline, mobile, or pay phone.

Insurance All travelers should invest in travel insurance when visiting Europe. A typical policy provides cover for the loss of baggage, tickets, and—up to a certain limit—cash, as well as cancellation or delay of your journey. Sickness and accident benefits are often extra. Note that some all-risk home-insurance policies may cover your possessions when overseas, and many private medical plans include coverage when abroad. Residents of E.U. countries must have a European Health Insurance Card (EHIC) to receive full health-care benefits in Belgium.

Internet Access Most hotels in Holland and Belgium offer Wi-Fi access for free, although some of the more expensive ones charge a daily fee. KPN hotspots are scattered throughout Amsterdam; cost starts at 1.50€ for 15 minutes (p. 59). Some areas in central Brussels permit free access to Wi-Fi hotspots (p. 148), while there's free, blanket Wi-Fi coverage in Bruges's city center (p. 183).

Legal Aid If you get into trouble with the law, your first point of contact is likely to be the police. Many Dutch and Belgian (but by no means all in Brussels) police officers are disposed to go easy on foreigners on minor matters, and many of them speak English. If the problem is serious and you are arrested, you have rights similar to those in any Western democracy. You are not required to say anything self-incriminatory, and you will be given access to a court-appointed lawyer or permitted to contact your embassy or consulate (p. 239).

LGBT Travelers There is no discrimination towards LGBT travelers in Europe. You shouldn't have trouble finding information about the gay scene as it's well publicized in Amsterdam. "Gay News" (www.gay-news.com) and "Gay&Night" (www.gay-night.nl) are competing monthly magazines in both Dutch and English, available free in gay establishments around the city. Amsterdam hosts one of the world's most flamboyant Gay Pride events (p. 37) in August. For further information in Amsterdam,

try COC Amsterdam, Rozenstraat 14 (✆ **020/626-3087;** www.cocamsterdam.nl). The Gay and Lesbian Switchboard (✆ **020/623-6565;** www.switchboard.nl) can also provide advice. Both websites are in Dutch only although English speakers staff the offices and answer the phones.

In Brussels, contact the gay and lesbian community centers Tels Quels, rue du Marché-au-Charbon 81 (✆ **02/512-4587;** www.tel-squels.be); and La Maison Arc-en-Ciel, rue du Marché-au-Charbon 42 (✆ **02/503-5990;** www.rainbowhouse.be). For the scene in Bruges, contact Jong & Holebi in Brugge, Ezelstraat 131 (www.j-h.be). Belgium's main Gay Pride event takes place in Brussels in May.

Mail & Postage Amsterdam doesn't have post offices anymore; instead, branches of newsagents, supermarkets, and grocery stores have postal points run by PostNL. In Brussels, BPost offices are open Monday to Friday 9am to 5pm. The main post office in Bruges is BPost at Markt 5 and is open Monday to Friday 9am to 6pm and Saturday 9am to 3pm.

Mobile Phones Triband devices and iPhones work across Europe. Call charges are high when making international calls and roaming charges, especially for data download, can be extortionate; even checking voicemail can result in an expensive

phone bill. If you have a GSM phone and use it a lot, buy a European SIM card to use during your stay.

U.K. mobiles work in Belgium and Holland; ensure that the international call bar has been switched off and check call charges. Remember that you are charged for calls you *receive* on a U.K. mobile used abroad.

To rent a GSM mobile phone in Belgium, go to **Rent2Connect** (✆ **02/652-1414;** www.rent2connect.com), in the Arrivals hall at Brussels Airport. In Holland, go to **Telecom Rentcenter** (✆ **020/653-0999;** www.rentcenter.nl), in the Arrivals hall at Schiphol Airport.

If you have web access, use **Skype (www.skype.com)** or **Vonage (www.vonage.com)** to make free international calls from your laptop or mobile.

Money & Credit Cards Credit cards are the most widely used form of payment in The Netherlands and Belgium, with the exception of local stores and small businesses, which may well only accept cash. The most common are Visa and MasterCard, although American Express and Diners Club are also accepted. **Note:** Credit cards in Europe now largely operate on personal identification numbers (PINs), so check that you have one before traveling because it may be required to make a purchase. You can withdraw cash advances from your credit cards at banks or ATMs, provided you know your PIN, although most banks will charge fees of up to $3 for the service.

It's highly recommended that you travel with at least one major credit card. You must have one to rent a car, and hotels and airlines usually require a credit card imprint as a deposit against expenses. The value of the euro varies against other currencies. For current exchange rates, check **www.xe.com**.

Pharmacies For information about pharmacies in Amsterdam see p. 59; for Brussels, see p. 148; for Bruges see p. 183.

Safety In Amsterdam, Rotterdam, and even The Hague, be wary of pickpockets on trams, buses, at the main railway stations (especially Centraal Station in Amsterdam, which is a hotbed of nefarious activity); on busy shopping streets and in busy stores.

Outside the capital, Belgium is generally safe; even the big cities are low-crime areas. However, Brussels has experienced a creeping spread of drug-related crimes committed by poorly integrated members of immigrant communities. The Métro is plagued by muggers, so there is a constant police presence and video surveillance.

Don't walk around Bruxelles-Midi station or along deserted Métro corridors after dark; when other people are around, it's generally safe.

Both Brussels (Gard du Nord, Boulevard Adolphe Max, and Avenue Louise) and Antwerp (Schippersstraat, Vingerlingstraat, and Verversrui) have red-light zones, in which caution is in order. Don't confuse these places with the Red Light District in Amsterdam, which is a tourist attraction in its own right and usually safe for casual visitors. Brussels's red-light zone around Gard du Nord in particular is a low-life place, and although Antwerp's is not quite so bad, it's not the place for sightseers after dark.

Senior Travel Belgium and Holland both offer discounts for seniors on public transportation—by far the easiest way to get around the cities covered in this book. For train travel, these discounts begin at age 65 in Belgium, and at 60 in The Netherlands. Bus companies have different starting ages for discounted tickets and passes. Many sightseeing attractions and tour companies offer senior discounts, but these might apply only to local residents when they produce ID. Be sure to ask when you buy your ticket.

Smoking There's a blanket ban on smoking in public places across Europe, although not in the streets. It's fine to smoke a reefer in the coffee shops of Amsterdam, but not a cigarette (p. 16).

Student Travel Most attractions in Amsterdam, Brussels, and Bruges offer student discounts on admission; these are noted throughout the destination chapters. Check out the **International Student Travel Confederation** (**ISTC;** www.aboutistc.org) for travel information and the **International Student Identity Card (ISIC;** www.isic.org), for a card that permits savings on rail passes, plane tickets, and entrance fees. It also provides basic health and life insurance and a 24-hour help line. The card is valid for a maximum of 18 months. Apply for the card online. If you're no longer a student but under 31, you can get an **International Youth Travel Card** from **STA Travel** (www.statravel.co.uk), which entitles you to some discounts.

Taxes A value-added tax (BTW in Holland, TVA in Brussels) runs at 21 per cent on most good bought in stores. Visitors residing outside the European Union can recover this upon departure. Stores that offer tax-free shopping advertise with a **Global Blue (www.globalblue.com)** tax-free shopping sign in the window and will furnish shoppers with the correct forms and information to recoup their refund. Refunds are available only when you spend more than 50€ in a participating store.

Tipping Tipping is not a big deal in Europe, as in many instances a 15 percent service charge is already added to a bill. Round up bills in cabs, small bars, and cafes to the nearest Euro, and leave between 10 and 15 percent in restaurants only if service has been exemplary. In French-speaking Wallonia and Brussels, tipping is more common than in Flanders, where it is not expected.

Time Amsterdam, Brussels, and Belgium operate on Greenwich Mean Time (GMT) + one: 1 hour ahead of the U.K., 6 hours ahead of Eastern Daylight Time, and 8 and 12 hours behind Australian Eastern Standard Time.

Toilets Public lavatories are few and far between in Belgium and Holland, and when you do find them, you'll often have to pay 0.50€ for the privilege of using them.

Water The water in your hotel and at public drinking fountains is safe to drink.

Index

Accommodations

Restaurants